An Introduction to International Human Rights Law

An Introduction to International Human Rights Law

Edited by

Azizur Rahman Chowdhury
Jahid Hossain Bhuiyan

MARTINUS NIJHOFF PUBLISHERS

LEIDEN • BOSTON
2012

Library of Congress Cataloging-in-Publication Data

An introduction to international human rights law / edited by Azizur Rahman Chowdhury, Jahid Hossain Bhuiyan.
p. cm.
Includes bibliographical references and index.
ISBN 978-90-04-17972-1 (hardback : alk. paper)
1. Human rights. I. Chowdhury, Azizur Rahman. II. Bhuiyan, Jahid Hossain.

K3240.I63 2010
341.4'8—dc22

2010013726

This paperback was originally published in hardback under ISBN 978 90 04 17972 1.

ISBN 978 90 04 22682 1

This book is printed on acid-free paper.

Contents

Preface

The overwhelming dimension of human rights in the present global concept demands an elaborate and thorough exposition of the subject. It is undeniably a fact that most of the publications on human rights law are confined to mere compilation or examination and elucidation of international conventions or resolutions. As such, a crystallized analysis of the evolutionary aspects and the issues of contemporary human rights remain more or less unexplained in the relevant global literature. Recently, the developments in the global concept of human rights, as well as in the domestic arena of each State, have become so pervasive and overwhelming that one can hardly deny the importance and necessity of human rights in social development and, especially, law and justice. The efforts of the United Nations to implement and enforce human rights as a *sine qua non* of its determination to cater for world peace have been prominently emphasized in all United Nations Organization programs. The fundamental principle of saving mankind from the scourge of war has been substantiated in recent times on equal footing with projecting the inalienable rights of mankind. The contribution of a number of luminaries and experts on human rights law have not only provided the foundation for the contents of the present book, but also hopefully opened a new vista of human rights law insight for the readers including students, teachers, lawyers, judges, scholars, human rights activists, social development planners, politicians, governmental official, and staff of international and non-governmental organizations. It is our hope that this book will prove a milestone towards development of human rights both for the present generation and the posterity.

Azizur Rahman Chowdhury
Md. Jahid Hossain Bhuiyan

List of Contributors

Azizur Rahman Chowdhury is Professor at the Department of Law, Dhaka University, Dhaka, Bangladesh. He spent 36 years of his teaching in the Dhaka University. He has participated in several national and international conferences, and made substantial contribution through his papers. He has contributed many research articles.

Elvira Domínguez-Redondo, Ph.D. (2004) in Law, Universidad Carlos III de Madrid, is Senior Lecturer in Law at Middlesex University, London (UK). She is the author of, inter alia, Minority Rights in Asia (Oxford : Oxford University Press, June 2006).

George E. Edwards (Juris Doctor, Harvard), is the Carl M. Gray Professor of Law, Director of the Program in International Human Rights Law, and Founding Faculty Director of the Master of Laws (LL.M.) Track in International Human Rights Law at Indiana University School of Law-Indianapolis. He is widely published in International human rights law, has lectured in many countries, and has extensive experience representing NGOs in United Nations and domestic human rights advocacy.

Heli Askola, Ph.D. (2005) in Law, European University Institute, is Senior Lecturer at the Faculty of Law, Monash University. She is the author of, inter alia, Legal Responses to Trafficking in Women for Sexual Exploitation in the European Union (Hart Publishing, 2007).

Joshua Castellino, Ph.D. (1998) in Law, University of Hull, is Professor and Head of the Law Department at Middlesex University, London. He has published books on international law and is actively engaged in human rights discussions at inter-governmental, governmental and non-governmental levels.

Md. Jahid Hossain Bhuiyan teaches law in the Department of Law, ASA University Bangladesh. During his studies in Belgium he gained experience in legal practice with the lawyers of European countries. He has to his credit articles published in reputed journal of Australia, Bangladesh and India.

Michelo Hansungule, Ph.D. (1990) University of Vienna, is Professor of Human Rights Law, University of Pretoria, South Africa. He was Associate Professor of Human Rights Law, RWI, University of Lund, Sweden. He has written many articles in peer reviewed journals.

Mmatsie Mooki is LL.D candidate at the Centre for Human Rights, Faculty of Law, University of Pretoria, South Africa. She is working on women's rights particularly on the rights of women to abort.

Paula Gerber, Ph.D. (2008), is a Senior Lecturer at Monash University Law School and Deputy Director of the Castan Centre for Human Rights Law. She is the author of From Convention to Classroom: The Long Road to Human Rights Education (2008).

Rita Ozoemana is LL.D candidate at the Centre for Human Rights, Faculty of Law, University of Pretoria, South Africa. She is working on the right to development vis-à-vis discrimination specifically in the Niger Delta in Nigeria.

V. Seshaiah Shasthri, Ph.D. National Law University, is Associate Professor and Assistant Dean (Academic Affairs), Faculty of Law, National Law University, Jodhpur, India. He has published 18 research papers. He has participated and presented papers in 33 national and international conferences.

Vinodh Jaichand, J.S.D. (1996), University of Notre Dame, is Deputy-Director at the Irish Centre for Human Rights at the National University of Ireland, Galway. He has written a book and co-edited two books.

Introduction

Progressive Nuances in International Human Rights Paradigm

Writing an introduction to authorial contributions on *An Introduction to International Human Rights Law* requires a broad examination of a subject as old as mankind itself, and throughout such time the national and international developments have been many indeed. Themes of the illustrious works included in this discussion comprise of writings on international human rights law relating to civil and political rights; and social, economic and cultural rights. Interestingly, these rights are reiterated time and again as 'first' and 'second' generation human rights. In order to understand their importance, one must also consider issues of specific focus and relevance. For example, the rights of women and human rights education. Further, no understanding of such an endeavor to examine and appreciate the dimensions and developments of international and national significance can be said to be complete unless one understands the implementation mechanisms at the international level as well as the municipal level. Least to be said but the most important facet of such an appreciation is the application of internationally acknowledged standards of human rights within the municipal domains of the nations and challenges involved. Hence, the present endeavor which takes into account focused issues of relevance aims at bridging the gap in terms of the academic resources available to the reader, keeping in mind the vast segment of beneficiaries in the civil society being associated at different levels of human rights education.

The present collection of writings comprises of ten specific chapters carefully chosen by authors of repute and eminence, and these chapters may be broadly classified into three segments from a reader's point of view: (i) The first segment of chapters provides an introductory effort to the canvass of international human rights law, starting from the philosophical and conceptual level to the practical and implementation frameworks; (ii) The second segment of chapters focuses specifically on issues of specific relevance in the contemporary scenario, namely women's rights; human rights education and globalization of human rights; (iii) Importantly, the third segment of this book concentrates on the challenges and priorities before the implementation mechanisms and enforcement instruments.

The first chapter, *The Historical Development of International Human Rights*, demonstrates a great degree of reliance on various authorial viewpoints as the beginning point in the fundamental enquiry on what constitutes international human rights law. Taking the argument that the origin of international human rights law is recent, the author, at the threshold stage, refers to the interventionary roles that were predominantly played during the early twentieth century in developing 'international legal order'. For a greater part, the author looks into and chronologically examines the international instrumental evolutionary developments, but at the same time raises questions and concerns on the philosophical and normative notions in the limited regional developments. Examining the universal nature of human rights and European perspectives, the author takes a reader through an intricate analysis of various philosophers being associated with the analysis of State and individual relationship. Importantly, the author poses a distinct debate on human rights as moral ideas in diverse societies, religions and cultures, and brings into discussion various cultural notions. Special to the reader's interest is the evaluation of evolution of human rights in Africa. The discussion is significant and noteworthy, not merely for its threefold temporal classification, but for bringing into debate the institutions and related value concerns in the context of understanding and appreciating the scope and nature of human rights. For the same reason, the discussion titled *Practices, Principles, Norms and Experiences Versus Human Rights* certainly requires the reader to re-examine their own fundamental notions of human rights appreciation. At times in brief and at times in elaboration, the author draws parallels with the practices of different countries, interfacing them with religious notions and doctrines of practical importance. Thus, the author demonstrates a rich blend of enquiries, drawing the attentive concern of the reader to find answers to their own imagination.

In the context of "human rights" appreciation, no effort can be complete unless one specifically understands the underlying philosophical notions and the interconnecting rationale. For this reason, the second chapter, *Civil and Political Rights*, revisits the international and instrumental developments of the early twentieth century. Starting from the Universal Declaration of Human Rights, the author traces out the role and contribution of the United Nations Commission on Human Rights, a sub-committee of Economic and Social Council of the General Assembly. The author begins the analysis by referring to what otherwise are the two constantly debated views, namely human rights as inherent part of a liberal State, and human rights as obligations to be delivered upon by an interventionist State. The author follows up the debate further with the dichotomy that dominated the West and East split in the perception towards the importance and implementation of what otherwise are the inherent dimensions of human rights heritage in itself. The objective of the author being to provide an informative base to the reader, greater concentration is cast upon the codification of the civil and political rights under the International Covenant on Civil and Political Rights; nature and importance of rights; scope of the freedoms and extents of obligations on States Parties thereto, in addition to the institutional mechanisms with adequate illustrations and relevant case laws provided there under. The author does not leave any stone unturned in the endeavor to discuss the scope and utility of Optional Protocol to the Covenant and the conditionalities that must be complied with, in order that an individual gets the benefit to seek the redress before the recognized institutional mechanisms and the complexities involved there under as well. Merit of the analysis on the part of the author is to link the rights with contemporary State practices. Advocating that the human rights movement has come far from the time of the adoption of the Covenants, the author allows the reader to ponder the challenges in collective actions of States to uphold group rights; the extent to which the scope of rights and freedoms may be compromised, if not neglected; and importantly, how to transform the obligations of monitoring into a meaningful and purposive endeavor on the part of the States.

The third chapter, *An Introduction to Economic, Social and Cultural Rights: Overcoming the Constraints of Categorization through Implementation*, addresses the challenges and dilemmas involved in the very categorization of human rights into various folds. At the threshold, the author poses an intricate question of enquiry as to whether the international developments have any bearing on the State perception on the importance of implementation of rights through the recognition of individual complaints processes. The appreciation is surrounded by a deep sense of caution. Beginning with an admission on the unlimited contours of the subject, the author demonstrates a conviction on the 'false notions of distinctions' of human rights. Through a chronological examination of the developments of historic times and transforming into 20th century developments, the author looks into and evaluates the institutional contribution for the development of human rights. Besides being vehement on the branding and fixation of human rights into 'generation-centered notions', the author seeks support and justification from the 1993 Vienna Declaration and Program of Action and the new Optional Protocol to rectify this very contrast. Drawing a great length of similarity in the terminology and nature of obligations of States all the while, the author implores the reader to enquire as to whether 'non-justiciability' is a basis at all. Stating that the degree of implementation of human rights at various levels poses challenges to the State and that it is the very essence of governance, the author poses a question on the role of dispute-resolution systems in the implementation process. Interestingly, for the reader the poser is whether the non-derogation applies more in the context of social, cultural and economic rights as against the much-argued and well-believed notions of civil and political rights. On the functional front, the author forces the reader to consider whether the committee mechanisms designated under the international instruments are for name sake and symbolic reflections of States' non co-operation than due implementation. Referring to a vast variety of case laws spread across a variety of domestic and international jurisdictions and institutional mechanisms, the author finally places for the reader's appreciation the food for thought in the form of distinction between justiciability and enforcement.

The fourth chapter, *Women's Rights in International Law*, deserves special mention in the context of the present thematic discourse, for the authors effort deal with the rights of a specific segment of civil society often dominated by patriarchal concerns. Taking an introductory recourse as to the beginning discussion of the theme, the authors examine the threshold instruments of the 20th century and their preliminary emphasis upon the protection of rights of women as a specific emphasis, but finds little support in the initial and general instruments. It is for this reason the authors take a distinct discourse and examine a variety of international human rights instruments that have laid stress and emphasis upon the rights of women from a multifarious perspective. Examining the four major instruments of the early 1960s, the authors find support in the Western Feminist movement as the genesis of the assertion of women's rights in their independent sense and institutional mechanisms to facilitate the internalization of the rights and standards, and protection mechanisms to monitor the State responses and State enforcement processes. It is for this reason the authors effort deserve a distinct note of attention. For, in the process of examining the contours of each of these rights and standards, the authors ensure that the standards envisaged are viewed in an independent arena, as well as in the holistic context of the human rights movement. Given the nature of the emphasis the International Convention on the Elimination of All Forms of Discrimination against Women lays upon variety of forms of discrimination, the authors undertake an extensive examination of the rights and their scope, and especially the definition of discrimination and its manifest forms. Noteworthy are the dimensions relating to rights in political and public life, and socio economic aspects. Being inter-woven with the General Assembly resolutions and recommendations, the authors present a holistic view of the essence and content of these rights and protections and at the same breadth provide to the reader a chance to understand the mammoth responsibility cast on the States Parties to implement the same municipal regimes. For this reason, the authors examine the scope and extent of the responsibility of the International Committee specifically established. The authors also provide the inherent limitations of such international monitoring mechanisms in order to appreciate their importance. For this reason, the authors do not spare the required extent of critique in demonstrating that for all challenges surrounding women, the Convention in itself is not the panacea. Yet, one must examine the developments relating to the protection of rights of women in the light of the subsequently development movements and conferences at Cairo. Very important in the context of the authors discourse is the inter-linkage the authors attempt to bring between forms of violence and discrimination. For there is substance in the argument that every form of violence in one way or the other leads to discrimination at different levels and thus affects the human rights parameters in the holistic context. The illustrative effort of the authors is to examine the developments in relation to forms of violence across the globe and the forms of health vulnerabilities women are being exposed to. Hence, the emphasis of the authors on the context of Africa deserves the reader's special attention.

The Fifth Chapter, *"Globalization and Human Rights"*, is noteworthy on the specific count that it not only traces the scope, nature and extent of globalization, but also aims to examine the impact and implications of globalization on human rights. The author advances a critical examination of the established and emerging global economic, social and political processes on human rights concerns, keeping in mind State Obligations to respect and ensure human rights. The author guides the reader through both challenges and opportunities created by globalization. Cautioning on the sprawling effects of economic globalization and deregulation, the author highlights the inescapable obligation of State Parties to protect and ensure human rights. States, while affected by economic globalization, need to weigh the consequences of e.g. trade liberalization against potential adverse effects to human rights and, at times, being more circumspect in order to guarantee human rights in a more globalized environment. The analysis of the author, which evaluates globalization in terms of economic as well as socio-political dimensions, brings to the forefront a series of novel issues amongst which is the challenge posed to politically unstable societies in dealing with pressures and tensions between different social groups. Finally, the author also leaves the reader to ponder the cultural and ecological dimensions of globalization and how these will affect State Obligations.

The sixth chapter, *"Role of the UN in the Promotion and Protection of Human Rights"*, traces the role of the United Nations in the promotion and protection of human rights and places fundamental emphasis upon the States and their sovereignty within domestic jurisdictions. Perhaps, for this reason, the author proposes to identify a 'Model of Co-operation', wherein equal onus is also placed on the International Commission, both at the levels of codification and establishment of monitoring agencies in terms of the States' compliance. Tracing the emphatic point of origin as the conclusion of the Charter of the United Nations, the author extensively surveys the supporting provisions under the Charter. The author takes a three-fold approach and examines various ideologies and political considerations that: (i) shaped the development of the UN human rights standards and processes; (ii) molded the normative development of the United Nations in protecting and safeguarding the human rights; and importantly, (iii) influenced the establishment of the Charter and Treaty mechanisms in the implementation of the human rights standards. The chief merit of the chapter is the examination of the developments from a temporal perspective and the identification of the monitoring bodies' establishment and evolving. If the 1960s is an active period for the United Nations Commission to come out of the dominance and bring out Charter-based review procedures, the 1970s through to the 90s is a lull phase in international peace and security which witnessed the proliferation of new armed conflicts, placing institutional restraints and limitations on the United Nations to act proactively. As the author concludes, during the 1980s the international committee started responding more positively through the labels of globalization, wherein the civil society as an important stakeholder made its positive role resulting in the conclusion of new human rights instruments and monitoring mechanisms to strengthen the United Nations system as a whole. Thus, the new international order which marked the beginning of the 1990s brought in a new phase in the constructive contribution of the United Nations in promoting and safeguarding human rights. Taking the line of argument further that the International Bill of Human Rights is an important breakthrough in the normative development of the United Nations' protection and monitoring systems, the author examines the feasibility in building the jurisprudential linkages between the efforts and outcomes of the International Court of Justice. An interesting and noteworthy dimension of the author's analysis centres around the key developments that occurred within the United Nations system, namely the adoption of new human rights instruments at the United Nations level; and adoption of the resolutions by the organs of the United Nations. Building further the linkages amongst the Charter-based organs and procedures, the author's endeavor provides the reader space to see and appreciate the appropriateness of the importance and contribution of the domestic mechanisms. Noteworthy for a special reference is the analysis relating to the universal periodic review, which brings in the feasibility of inter-relationship amongst the United Nations Commissioner on Human Rights, national human rights instruments and the relevant human rights non governmental organizations.

The eighth chapter, *"Do States have an obligation under International Law to provide Human Rights Education?"*, is an extremely thought-provoking approach to understanding the obligation to provide education about human rights. Tracing the history of human rights education as a part of the United Nations' mandate, the author argues that there is a link between the provision of human rights education and the development of a culture of human rights. She suggests that the provision of human rights education should be embraced as a proactive measure by the States, rather than seen as a reactive measure to deal with a problem after its occurrence. The author undertakes a scholarly analysis of the nature and extent of the human rights education mandate and a variety of UN instruments before moving to a contemporary examination of the General Assembly's Decade for Human Rights Education and the ongoing World Program for Human Rights Education. The author concludes that while there has been strong international effort to promote human rights education, the domestic implementation by States remains weak. Accepting that there are numerous obstacles and challenges to the full realization of human rights education, the author provides the reader with some realistic approaches designed to overcome the hurdles and increase the level of human rights education in schools.

The ninth chapter, *"Application of International Standards of Human Rights Law at Domestic Level"*, being a subject of intense debate over a long span of time, addresses to the issues from the contemporary perspectives and the challenges of States at the domestic level. Beginning with the basic argument that human rights as envisaged under the Universal Declaration of Human Rights are really universal in their spirit and content, the author develops the further argument that these propositions of universality required codification from an implementation point of view, which the international community has vigorously addressed in the post-United Nations phase. Referring to the development of international human rights standards codification as a "lag process", the author at the first phase reiterates the importance of States' role in the implementation through the establishment of domestic institutions and mechanisms. Interestingly, the author reiterates the importance of declarations as the first step in the crystallization of international aspirations, although adoption of international conventions with binding obligations is the major step in the codification of human rights standards with the agreements on the part of States Parties on the extents of standards versus State obligations. Delving further into the importance of signature and ratification as the important procedural follow-up steps, the author draws the reader's attention to the divergent State practices when the human rights standards envisaged under the international instruments get to be applicable in the domestic context. The author further analyzes the implications of an important State response relating to the automatic application of international standards versus application through the adoption of specific domestic legislation. Taking the assistance of illustrative analysis of States in the context of the chosen seven international human rights instruments, the author leaves little room for the reader to think of any other alternative examples, for the illustrations are far beyond any uncertainty. Debating on the traditional doctrine of 'State Sovereignty' and 'domestic implementation of international human rights standards', and terming the latter as the 'engine room' of universal instruments on human rights, the author probes the international human rights instruments to examine how affirmative action on the part of States Parties is more an internal aspect of their obligations than as the often-viewed approach of an external prerogative. Terming the internal aspect of State's Obligation as "obligation for positive discrimination", or the "elevator mechanism", the author examines the legitimacy of this State's Obligation through various examples and illustrations. Offering varieties of justifications for the State's responses to implement through domestic mechanisms, the author identifies what could be characterized as the essential contours of the normative transportation into the domestic domain. While illustrating through specific conventions and linking very often to the the State's practices, the author retains the natural flow of cohesiveness and highlights the importance of the State's consent in transforming soft law into the specific domestic legal regime. Thus, the light thrown by the author on the inescapable conclusion of the State's imperative realization towards the domestic application of human rights standards, both in the contexts of effective governance and accomplishment of larger social and political goals, cements one's conviction and belief that in the sphere of international human rights standards application the State's willing role is of crucial significance.

The tenth chapter, *"Role of Regional Human Rights Instruments in the Protection and Promotion of Human Rights"*, being of crucial significance in the effective realization of the State's obligations, begins with a poser to the reader as to how far the manifestations of any supra-national mechanism would go in concomitance to the recognized notions of state sovereignty. At the same time, the authors also try to help the reader realize the international obligations are far superior to the domestic justifications. Taking a three-fold approach in dealing with the subject, the authors outline at the threshold of the analysis, namely, the circumstances leading to the adoption; scope of rights and guarantees contemplated; and, the safeguarding procedures. Keeping the article informative to the reader, the authors with ease and continuing thought-flow highlight the key aspects of each of the regional human rights conventions. In the context of the European Convention on Human Rights and Fundamental Freedoms, 1950, noteworthy issues for the reader are: (i) the complaint-making procedure for an individual to the Commission. As the authors carefully acknowledge, it is more of a history, for the Commission no longer has any role to play. Enumerating the scope of the convention as well as all the protocols exhaustively, the authors provide a holistic view of the rights and characterize as to why the Convention and its protocols stand on a separate footing to any other regional endeavor. One of the interesting features of this article is the effort of the authors to examine the scope of the rights and freedoms guaranteed and powers of the State to impose limitations, wherein the authors provide well-examined case laws. Examining the American endeavor of 1969 at length, the authors trace out as to how, even prior to such an instrumental realization, the American Commission has significantly contributed for the realization of human rights in the American context. Drawing on parallel lines of thematic discussion to the European Convention, the authors provide a clear insight into the significant facets of rights safeguarded and the institutional characteristics. A noteworthy effort of the authors in this regard that deserves a specific mention is the detailed analysis on the role and functions of the Commission and procedure for individual complaint mechanisms. The graphic description relating to the role and contribution of the Organization of American States Special Rapporteur provides a deep and thought-provoking understanding to the reader as to how the institution over a period of its functioning not only gained credibility for its existence, but even legitimized its contribution. Examining at length the institutional characteristics of the Inter-American Court, the authors provide a holistic overview, prompting a reader further to examine each of the meritorious contributions. The third important component of this exhaustive analysis is the regional effort at the African level. The author raise the reader's understanding to a new level of examination by facilitating as to why the African Charter is being seen as the manifestation of the aspirations of peoples' rights unlike the two earlier instruments. Terming the recognition of individual and collective rights as an 'important breakthrough in the development of the regional human rights instruments', the authors provide another comparative perspective of the institutional similarities, leaving the reader to examine the intricacies in this regard. The authors effort to highlight the African endeavor as an advanced effort is noteworthy, for it not only highlights the characteristics of the African Commission, but also its inherent limitations. Terming the adoption of the African Charter as a "challenging and daunting task for the African Community", the authors outline the imminent realities before the African Community. Thus, as the authors succinctly sum up, while the regional human rights instruments have contributed to the effective realization of the regional relevance, the reader is left with more questions than answers.

The seventh chapter explores non-governmental organizations (NGOs) focused on human rights. Since the birth of the modern human rights era in the 1940s, human rights NGOs have significantly contributed to promoting and protecting international human rights globally. In this chapter, entitled *"Attributes of Successful Human Rights Non-Governmental Organizations (NGOs) – Sixty Years After the 1948 Universal Declaration of Human Rights"*, the author defines the terms "NGO" and "human rights NGO", places human rights NGOs into various conceptual categories, and then identifies and analyzes traits that tend to be possessed by successful, effective human rights NGOs. The author also identifies numerous codes of conduct and ethics that were created to help ensure human rights NGOs' transparency, accountability, credibility, and efficacy. These codes have been implemented in various countries, and subscribed to by a wide range of NGOs. The author argues that human rights defenders might benefit from adopting the mentioned attributes for successful human rights NGOs, which are invariably incorporated into the codes of conduct and ethics he highlights.

Azizur Rahman Chowdhury
Md. Jahid Hossain Bhuiyan

Chapter One

The Historical Development of International Human Rights

*Michelo Hansungule**

1. *Introduction*

What constitutes international human rights law? Patrick Macklem states that international human rights law refers to the overarching mission to protect universal features of the human being from the exercise of sovereign power.[1] He further states that human rights possess international legal significance 'because they monitor the distributive justice of the structure and operation of the international legal order itself'.

At least all legal scholars are agreed with Macklem and Jack Donnelly.[2] International human rights law emerged as a distinct field of international law only in the aftermath of the Second World War.

Therefore, an introduction to international human rights law affords one a rare opportunity to retrace the difficult steps concerning the development of a fast growing branch of law. International human rights law is fairly recent

---

* Michelo Hansungule is Professor of Law in the Centre for Human Rights, Faculty of Law, University of Pretoria, South Africa.

[1] Patrick Machlem, *What is International Human Rights Law? Three Applications of a Distributive Account* (Texas: Bernard and Andre Rapoport Center for Human Rights and Justice University of Texas School of Law, 19 November 2007).

[2] Jack Donnelly, *International Human Rights. Dilemmas in World Politics*, 2nd ed. (Colorado/ Oxford: Westview Press, 1998). Donnelly says 'before World War II, human rights were rarely discussed in international politics', p. 3. A short while ago, an American Visiting Professor to the Centre had to repeat himself to his largely student audience when he was contradicted by one of the LL.M students. The student had argued that it was not true as stated by the professor that international human rights is of recent origin. Of course the student had mixed human rights with international human rights. As a discipline, human rights as we shall show in this chapter has ancient upbringing, stretching as it does to the period of enlightenment. However, international human rights law emerged only with the establishment of the United Nations which spearheaded the current architecture of the UN Human Rights System. It also inspired the development of regional human rights systems around the world.

in origin. Until the Second World War, international human rights law was not a familiar theme in text books on international law. Learned authors on international law kept their vows when rolling out themes for their various works by strictly adhering only to the traditional subjects of international law. Hence, apart from the sources of international law as well as relations between municipal and international law, scholarly writers have concerned themselves such classical issues as territorial sovereignty, personality and recognition, recognition of states and government, incidence and continuity of statehood, territorial integrity, law of the sea including continental shelf and the governing regime on high seas.

Others include state jurisdiction and jurisdictional competence, privileges and immunities of foreign States, responsibilities of states and admissibility of state claims, international organizations, tribunals and the whole question of judicial settlement of international disputes, etc. Very little has been devoted to human rights let alone international human rights in such studies. For example, in his classic book, Principles of International Law, Ian Brownlie only devoted fifteen pages on international protection of human rights out of the seven hundred and forty-eighty pages. Malcom Shaw, on the other hand, tried to devote some attention to human rights in his work also on International Law but still far less than the attention he devoted to the traditional subjects of international law.[3] Human rights not being one of the classical subjects of so-called 'hard international law', no scholar would dare stray into. Even today, international human rights, when it ever makes it to classical textbooks on international law, usually do so rather grudgingly as an afterthought. Most major works on international law continue to ignore this growingly important subject largely because of traditional attitudes in which international law is limited to the classical terrain.

Similarly, the conduct of states with one another has in keeping with classical theory tended to stay clear of international human rights. Because of the attitude that international law has nothing to do with human rights which were treated as matters suitable for the domestic sphere, international relations stay quite clear of human rights. Rarely do human rights issues ever make it to the agendas of bilateral or multilateral discussions among states. Dictated by the principle of non-interference in internal affairs, relations between States quite often overlook human rights. It is quite often for states to continue to cooperate such as to conclude trade agreements or sign peace treaties with pariahs of human rights violation because of the principle that international law deals

[3] Ian Brownlie, *Principles of Public International Law*, 4th ed. (Oxford: Clarendon Press, 1990); Also see Malcolm N. Shaw, *International Law*, 4th ed. (Cambridge: Cambridge University Press, 1997).

only with subjects of international law and issues of human rights fall under the domain of domestic law. Therefore, except for the principles of diplomatic protection of the nationals of one state in another State's territory, protection of minorities and refugees, and a few others, international law has been interpreted and applied restrictively in international relations to the extent it often excludes human rights.

But this is now changing. Though historically limited solely to relations between States, international law has over the years been warming up to human rights.[4] It has of course taken years for international law to change course and begin to entertain human rights but it is changing. The outbreak of the Second World War and the atrocities that took place during the war was the main motive for the change of attitude. Millions of people were slaughtered during the war while the international community, save for the few Western powers, stood by. Based on the general principle that human rights did not have the status of international law, States treated the egregious violation of human rights of the victims of the Second World War as none of their business. Even the Western powers that intervened did so not necessarily in order to protect human rights but because the war was threatening the international legal order. Had the killings of the Jews and others been limited to Germany, it would be difficult to imagine Western countries rolling out their war machines to protect victims. But it was precisely due to the atrocities of the Second World War which acted as a 'wake-up call' to the world leaders to begin to think that the pre-war international legal order needed fundamental revision in order to hold international peace and security together. Therefore, the establishment of the United Nations (UN) in 1945 a major turning point in the development of international law from merely 'the laws of nations' to embracing such issues as human rights. Since the adoption of the UN Charter, and immediately thereafter the Universal Declaration of Human Rights (UDHR),[5] international law has come to deal with non-classical issues including human rights, environmental rights, trade and development issues, etc. The UDHR is the first authoritative international footprint on the path towards the collective affirmation by the international community to the supremacy of the human being over his man-made institutions.

But the 'cold war' in the post war era held up this change to some degree. Even though affirming the importance of the human being in international law through the UN Charter, post-war politics was dictated by fear particularly

---

4 See Henry J. Steiner and Philip Alston, *International Human Rights in Context. Law, Politics and Morals*, 2nd ed. (Oxford: Oxford University Press, 2000); Similarly, Donnelly, *International Human Rights.*

5 www.unhchr.org

among super-powers of each other. This led to the military build-ups including acquisition of nuclear and other armaments especially among super-powers which undermined the gains made in the aftermath of the war to establish the UN. Again, the principles of non-intervention and non-interference of one State by another or others defined international relations between nations as before the outbreak of the war. The fall of the Berlin Wall following perestroika[6] which swept across Europe in the late 1980s to early 1990s is what led to the present climate in which human rights are truly gaining international status.

This change has slowly been taking regional dimensions. In Africa, for example, States have come full-circle from extreme obsession with sovereignty in which human rights were strictly matters of domestic domain to the liberal systems and institutions that is now characteristic of the African Union (AU)[7] all in a historic space record of less than fifty years. The AU has established a Commission of Experts for the purposes of promoting human rights on the continent as well as a continental Court fully mandated with the power to judge human rights situations and entertain victims of violations of human rights in the same States that only a while ago, no organ of the continental body would dare question. This is the situation elsewhere in the world. For hundreds of years now, human rights were 'internal' and therefore have been subject of internal domestic systems, institutions and procedures which defined their content and dictated their application. But with the historical decision in December 1948 to adopt the Universal Declaration of Human Rights (UDHR), human rights took international dimension.

Only last year, the UDHR was celebrating its sixty-years since adoption of the Declaration on 10 December 1948. Adoption of the UDHR marks a major milestone in the historical development of the international human rights law. That presidents and prime ministers, queens and kings, foreign ministers and other senior officials from north and south, east and west joined hands together to express their collective approval to a document setting forth minimum values which cut across divergent cultures, traditions, religions and systems is the single most important sign of how far the world has gone towards building a solid foundation for a world based on respect for human rights. While the majority of countries particularly in the third world did not participate in deliberations leading to the adoption of the UDHR precisely because they were denied the very freedom the Declaration affirms, subsequent conduct illustrated in their acceptance of the historic document upon their attainment of statehood confirms the endorsement world-wide of the ideas embedded in this instrument.

---

[6] See Salvatore Peledda, *On being Human. Interpretations of Humanism from The Renaissance to the Present*, 1997.

[7] www.AU_org

However, it will take far more than half a decade for the principle of human rights in international law to become reality. To the majority of people around the world, the principle of international human rights is still wishful thinking. Many centuries ago, Thomas Hobbes mocked the idea of natural rights and others joined in the laughing. Hobbes and his colleagues suggested that belief in human rights is equal with belief in witchcraft. Millions of victims of human rights violations around the world today are likely to identify with Hobbes and others about human rights. Reality which cannot be ignored is that there has been more blood than human rights in this same period throughout the world. Internally and internationally displaced populations around the world have quadrupled since the idea to take human rights to the international domain. There are probably more hungry people and more malnourished children in the world today than when the UDHR was adopted. Everywhere in the world, human rights are still being openly challenged. Therefore, there is a lot that needs to be done to make human rights in the international sphere reality.

2. *Some Historical Perspectives on Human Rights*

It is noted here that concerns for human rights are as old as humanity. All societies, African peoples included, have grappled with human rights issues. Philosophers of every race and creed have for centuries been concerned with the nature of humanity, interpersonal relationships, and the position of individuals as members of groups.[8] The philosophy in Africa is respect for dignity and respect for human beings not for what they have but because they are human beings. The traditional concepts of African human rights can be traced to personal rights such as privacy, freedom of expression, right to participation, right to access land, the role of women and access to justice. It is argued that pre-colonial African human rights systems in their undiluted form got contaminated by slavery and colonialism. That slavery by its very nature denied the valued right to dignity while colonialism on the other hand cancelled all the indigenous rights which existed prior to colonization including freedom of expression, movement and participation to mention but a few. For fear of State, Africans that normally freely express themselves against their government and authority in their natural habitat began to check their tongues as to whom they are speaking to and what they are saying. Similarly, the colonized suddenly

[8] O. Oko. Elechi, "Human Rights and The African Indigenous Justice System," (A Paper for Presentation at the 18th International Conference of the International Society for the Reform of Criminal Law, 8–12 August 2004, Montreal, Quebec, Canada) (accessed 28 September 2008), 2.

found they had no rights to move freely in their country without the aid of a Pass Book, as in apartheid South Africa. Unless your employer signed the Book, you can move from A to B at your pain. Colonialism introduced a ruthless colonial state system which effectively dismantled the freedoms pre-colonial societies enjoyed.

Appreciating the African society in its entirety is not very simple. Often than not, in the human rights discourse there is a tendency to emphasis universal values and forget the challenge this approach poses to African values. It is recognized that pre-colonial Africa had coherent notions and concepts of human rights although it was philosophically different from those understood by Western philosophy. Although African human rights concepts were not written down, they were enumerated in the family, kinship and the community. The lack of reliability of the historical record as presented today is that our knowledge of pre-colonial Africa is derived almost exclusively from reports compiled in the late nineteenth and early twentieth centuries. In this regard revisionist historians have put forward a convincing case to show that the authors of these accounts did as much to create the world they were writing about as to describe it.[9] This discussion will analyze the concept of human rights as it obtained in traditional African society to show that pre-colonial Africa had built in notions of human rights although not written down or called by that name. The conclusion is that the debate that Africa didn't have human rights notions is a generalization and indicative of the negative prejudices against African values.

3. *Universal Rights*

Human rights are often held to be universal[10] in the sense that most societies and cultures have practiced them throughout most of their history.[11] All societies cross-culturally and historically manifest conceptions of human rights. This has generated a large body of literature on so-called non-western conceptions of human rights. While Arab literature makes serious attempts to trace human rights to Koranic texts, Hindu's describe their caste system as a traditional, multidimensional view of human rights. But interestingly, Dustan M Wai in his article "Human rights in sub-Saharan Africa" claimed, for instance, that it is

[9] T. W. Bennett, "Human Rights & the African Cultural Tradition," *Transformation Journal* no. 22 (1993): 35 (accessed 28 September 2008).

[10] Brownlie, *Public International Law*; Also See Shaw, *International Law*.

[11] Jack Donnelly, "The Relative Universality of Human Rights," *Human Rights Quarterly* 29, no. 2 (2007): 284.

not often remembered that traditional African societies supported and practiced human rights.[12]

Such claims to historical or anthropological universality confuse values such as justice, fairness, and humanity needs with practices that aim to realize those values. In other words, there is a big difference between being fair as a human attribute and being fair, but not kind, in the application of the law. To uphold human rights, police officers need not necessarily be kind to the suspect or accused person but must interpret and apply the law correctly. Correct interpretation and application of the law is being consistent with human rights. Rights – entitlements that ground claims with a special force – are a particular kind of social practice. Human rights – equal and inalienable entitlements of all individuals that may be exercised against the State and society – are a distinctive way to seek to realize social values such as justice and human flourishing. There may be considerable historical/anthropological universality of values across time and culture. No society, civilization or culture prior to the seventeenth century, however, had a widely endorsed practice, or even vision, of equal and inalienable individual human rights.[13]

For example, Dunstan Wai also argues that traditional African beliefs and institutions sustained the view that certain rights should be upheld against alleged necessities of State. This confuses human rights with limited government. Government has been limited on a variety of grounds other than human rights, including divine commandment, legal rights, and extralegal checks such as a balance of power or the threat of popular revolt.[14]

4. *The European View*

In Europe, human rights are considered as a body of principles and rules placed in the hands of the individual, as a weapon thus enabling him to defend himself against the group or entity representing it.[15] Jack Donnelly and Rosa Howard are proponents of the dominant discourse of human rights maintain that traditional African society does not have a concept of human rights because human rights are typically western innovations. They are connected to the civilization of Europe suggesting that Europe only had human rights during industrialization.[16] It was during this period that the "individual" emerged. When people

[12] Ibid.

[13] Ibid., 284–285.

[14] Ibid., 285.

[15] "Address delivered by Leopold Sedar Sengor, President of the Republic of Senegal" (1979).

[16] Michelo Hansugule, "Human Rights from an African Perspective," August 2008, paper presented to LLM in Human Rights and Democratisation class 2008 on 1st August 2008.

(Europeans) travelled out of their countries and found jobs in other parts of Europe, they needed recognition and protection far from home hence the emergence of the individual rights. This view further held that since Africa had not yet industrialized, it cannot have human rights emanating from within itself.

Underlying such foundational or core rights theory is the ever present compelling ethic of Immanuel Kant. Kant's ethic maintains that persons typically have different desires and ends, so any principle derived from them can only be contingent. However, the moral law needs a categorical foundation, not a contingent one. The basis of all moral law must be prior to all purposes and ends. The basis is the individual as a transcendental subject capable of an autonomous will. Rights then flow from the autonomy of the individual in choosing his or her ends, consistent with a similar freedom for all.

Philosophers like John Locke and Jean-Jacques Rousseau, spoke about the notion of natural rights in pre-industrial societies. Therefore they were speaking only for Europe and not for non-European societies. John Locke for instance spoke about the three rights of man in a state of nature-life, liberty and property. He did not state dignity may be he was saying that dignity is embedded in those three rights. But life, liberty and property were for "the European man" not even the woman. Property right in this context will also include slave ownership which was purely for Europeans. Therefore it can only make sense to suggest that he was speaking for the Europeans (slave owners) as having property rights not Africans who were the slaves and therefore the property of the slave masters.

Following John Locke's Treatise,[17] some western scholars formed the notion that human rights ideas first developed in the modern western society. This was largely influenced by the French and American Revolutions which were believed to be struggles for human rights in the form of Liberations.[18]

Contrary to the above belief, it has been held that human rights ideas and practices arose not from any deep western cultural roots but from the social, economic and political transformations of modernity. They thus have relevance wherever these transformations have occurred, irrespective of the pre-existing culture of the place. This argument in a sense includes Africa as part of the cultural milieu from which human rights could have developed.

Furthermore, there is nothing in classical or medieval culture that specially predisposed Europeans to develop human rights ideas. Even early modern Europe, when viewed without the benefit of hindsight, seemed a particularly unconducive cultural milieu for human rights.

---

[17] John Locke, *Two Treatise On Government* (London: Printed for R. Butler, W. Reid, W. Sharpe, and John Bumpus, 1821) (1689).

[18] Donnelly, "Universality of Human Rights," 287.

4.1. *The Idea of Human Rights in Contemporary Western Context*

Historically, human rights, in western society, were shaped particularly during the period of the renaissance. It is also during this period that human rights at the time natural rights were given definitive meaning. A central theme of human rights is the principle of equality which underpinned the latter revolutions in France, Britain, Russia and America. The conflict of interest in Europe between bourgeoisie and aristocrats gave birth to freedom and equality. According to Jorn Rusen:

> The declarations of human and civil rights in the late 18th century were preceded by long chain of events extending back into Classical and Medieval times. By conceiving of nature as meta-political authority of legitimation and critique, Classical Antiquity created the intellectual preconditions for reflecting on political rule in terms of human rights. Responsibility for appealing to this authority was delegated by the thinker of Antiquity to human reason, i.e. the capacity to engage in the methodologically structured conceptual argumentation informed by experience. Later, Christianity attributed to this meta-political legitimatory authority the quality of human subjectivity, for the Christian notion of God having become an individual human being placed the divine quality of the world order – which the Greeks had rationalized as the metaphysics of nature – in a fundamental relation not only to human nature but also to each individual specimen of human life. Thus it could be said that Christianity allowed the meta-political legitimatory authority of political domination to pass into human, thereby giving it a new social and human quality. And finally, the middle Ages generated a third necessary precondition for the regulation of political rule in terms of human rights, namely the linking of rule to a form of written concordat between ruler and subject. These so called sovereign contracts, the most famous example of which Magna Carta Libertatum, make rule contingent on a written code of principles agreed between ruler and subjects. The final decisive intellectual step towards a modern conception of human and civil rights was then taken by the enlightenment, which opened this concordat out to independent public use by subjecting it to human reason.

4.2. *Analysis of History*

The above summary is remarkable history which shows how Western world came to possess the idea of rights, but this concept was not absolute in a sense that it still had contradiction. These contradictions in the realization of the concept of right do not suggest that the Western had a developed concept which was superior to that of Non-western culture, at that period. In the Western world as already indicated not all the people were qualified as human; there was slave trade, women were not allowed to vote and those who did not own property were not full qualify as human, particularly in America.

Jorn Rusen observed: 'By conceiving of nature as meta-political authority of legitimation and critique, Classical Antiquity created the intellectual preconditions for reflecting on political rule in terms of human rights', one sees reasons not to totally agree and, it's important to show disagreement here because, those who argued that in non-western culture there was no concept of rights have used the imperfection witnessed in other-cultures' concept of rights to deny the existence of such concept. The understanding brought by Classical Antiquity was contrary to basic understanding of human rights such as equality, for it was capable of producing different result depending on a person's understanding of what it meant to be human. The double standard observed in relation slave trade, women raised a debate as to whether it was natural or unnatural law.

In the previous paragraph Jorn Rusen went on to acknowledge the contribution and influence of the Christianity in the meta-political authority of legitimatory authority of political domination and as result giving it a new social and human quality. However, the influence and contribution of Christianity was not as good as it was made to sound by him. The influence was not in harmony with the sense of reasoning and science. For instance, Galileo was asked by the Church to take back his words that the earth rotates on its axis beneath unmoving sun. Similarly, Christianity regarded native Brazilians as cannibals who eat dead human flesh and therefore were morally inferior to Europeans. This was in order to justify domination of the natives by the colonizer. So, Christianity cannot be said to have had the moral ground necessary for the legitimation of political authority. Instead, it was associated with domination and oppression. The irony is that the 17th century which was the beginning of advances towards freedom in Europe and Western countries was also an era in which the brutality of Slavery was defended by leading religious figures.

Also in the last portion of the paragraph, Jorn Rusen mentioned about sovereign contracts such as Magna Carta Libertatum and step taken by the Enlightenment to open up this agreement to the independent public use by putting it under the influence of the human reason. However, this was the period which demonstrates clearly that State and church were not for but against rights to equality and freedom of expression. And just like non-western parts of the world, there is no clear evidence to demonstrate that the right to equality preached during this period was sociologically realized by black men, women to the same level white men enjoyed it. The following two paragraphs support this view:

> This is the background of the 18th-centuary Enlightenment. Europeans were changing, but Europe's institutions were not keeping pace with that change. The church insisted that it was the only source of truth, that all lived outside its bounds were damned, while it was apparent to any reasonably sophisticated person that most human beings on earth were not and had never been Christians – yet they had built great and inspiring civilizations. Writers and speakers grew restive at the omnipresent censorship and sought whatever means they could to evade or even denounce it.

> Most importantly, the middle classes – the bourgeoisie – were painfully aware that they were paying taxes to support a fabulously expensive aristocracy which contributed nothing of value to society (beyond, perhaps, its patronage of the arts, which burghers of Holland had shown could be equally well be exercised by themselves), and that those useless aristocrats were unwilling to share power with those who actually managed and – to their way of thinking, – created the national wealth. They were to find ready allies in France among the impoverished masses who may have lived and thought much like their ancestor, but who were all too aware that with each passing year they were paying higher and higher taxes to support a few thousand at Versailles in idle dissipation.

5. *Human Rights as Moral Ideas in Diverse Societies, Religions, and Cultures*

Religion, faith, culture and sense of reasoning have had great influence in civilizing the human being or giving him moral sense of what is right and wrong, hence, there is great possibility of seeing human right idea in any civilization and not only western civilization. It is important to look at the practices and principles of the different ancient societies as they result into and are part of religion, faith, culture and political structure, in order to discover the concepts of the human rights. For instance, there was mutual exchange of loyalty and protection of rights between rulers and community members in many ancient societies. The codes of conduct in many religions and old societies highlighted love, benevolence and compassion to one another. Though not vesting a right, this code could give rise to a legally-binding right. In particular, the code of conduct underpins the essence of human dignity, a cornerstone of human rights.

5.1. *Jewish*

In the Jewish tradition, human rights are understood to be responsibilities obligatory on the Jewish individual by Divine Decree. These are seen in the positive and negative commandments known as *mitsvot.* The commandments are in two groups: one relates to the kingdom between God and human and another relates to the kingdom between human and human. In the following quotes, one sees the perspective of Jewish tradition in relation to the right to life and the right to dignity:

> Central principles in Jewish tradition are the sacredness of human life, the preservation and the protection of human dignity, for human beings were created in the image of God, 'Male and female he created them' (Genesis 1,27), and co-creator with the task to mend the world (*letaken olam*). The use of plural in the expression of the deed of creation 'Let us create the human' (*naase adam*) is to be understood as an indication that God could create the human only with his cooperation. 'You

> and I let us together create a mensch with free will' (Hassidic commentary). Man is thus not only in search of God but God is also in search of man.[19]
>
> Although the human should always remember that he or she has been created later than the lowest animal and should care for all living, he or she is according to the psalmodist little lower than the angels crowned with glory and might, ruling over the work of creation of God (Psalm 8). Thus one who destroy one human being is considered as if they have destroys the whole universe (Talmud Sanhedrin 37A). The overriding principle is *Pikuach nefesh*, the obligation to preserve life, also one is own, even when by doing so one is breaking the commandments. There are only three specified instance in which martyrdom is required: when one is ordered to murder, to rape or to worship idols publicly (Talmud Sanhedrin 74A). 'Once a man came to his teacher and informed him: "The ruler of my city told me to kill this one and if not that I would be killed." The teacher replied: "you should be killed and not kill. How do you know that his blood is redder than yours, maybe his blood is redder?" '(Talmud Psachim 28B)[20]

The latter paragraph shows that there is contradiction in the Jewish tradition when it comes to the right to life. For even though it says there is obligation to preserve life, also one's own, it takes different ways when specifying the situation in which one shall give up his own life. This makes one to wonder where is the sacredness of life, how does one's life become of less value than life of a person whom he or she is asked to murder, rape or when he or she is asked to worship idols publicly. The contradiction does not just end there; its way of viewing life as 'holy' surprisingly does allow keeping of slaves or female servants unless there is infliction of body harm to a slaves or female servant by the master, this standard is lower than standard of right to life that exist today, though one could argue that the world today still allows the imprisonment of human being. Moreover, it does provide for revenge. The following quote set out this:

> The life of the slaves should be protected. Thus when a master has hit his slave so that he loses his tooth or his female servant so that she loses her eye, he should let them go free (Exodus, 21, 21). The passage which states this follows the one which deals with a life, an eye for an eye, a tooth for a tooth. It is clear from the context that one is commanded to apply moderation – not taking more than a tooth.[21]

One could see the right to dignity, life and equality in the Jewish commandments, though these rights have not directly or openly been mentioned. The effect of some of these commandments amount to the same values the today

[19] Awraham Soetendorp "Jewish Tradition and Human Rights," in *The Essential of Human Rights*, ed. Rhona K. M. Smith and Christien van den Anker (New York: Oxford University Press, 2005), 211.

[20] Ibid., 212.

[21] Ibid., 213.

human rights represent. Looking at 'Thou shalt love thou neighbour as thyself, I am the ever being God' (Lev 19:18) and 'you should love the stranger, for strangers you have been in the land of Egypt' (Lev 19:34). While these are duties or responsibilities of one individual to another, the accomplishment of these duties by one individual gives another a chance to enjoy right to dignity, life and equality.

6. *Africa*

The evolution of human rights in Africa is viewed at three cascading levels i.e. pre-colonial, colonial and post-colonial phase. Below, we take a critical look at the pre-colonial or indigenous phase before Africa got into contact with the outside world. This (pre-colonial) is an important phase of development because it explains Africa in its original sense. The colonial phase of development as the term suggests is the period when Africa like various parts of Asia was under alien rule. This is the time Africa got into contact with the outside world and therefore with international law. Colonialism brought Africa onto the international stage even though only as colonies represented by European masters. An important feature of international law then is that it legalized both slavery and colonization itself. This is a period in which, under the 'watchful eye of Christianity', human rights of the local people were grossly violated. Local people were denied basic rights like participation and, therefore, the right to vote solely on the grounds of their skin-colour. Discrimination was rampant during colonization. Decolonization ushered in a new era in which former oppressed people assumed their destinies and became their own rulers. Former colonies became fully-fledged States with capacity in international law to enter into relations with other States including their former colonial powers. On independence, African States joined the United Nations and the then Organization of African Unity (OAU) now the African Union (AU) through which they subscribed to several international human rights instruments. This, however, did not immediately improve their human rights situations. Below is a brief exposition of the African society *vis-à-vis* human rights.

6.1. *Kinship and Human Rights*

Without the organizing potential of a central State, African societies were still largely dependent for their cohesion on the kinship system.[22] The typical

[22] Max Gluckman, *The Ideas in Barotse Jurisprudence* (Manchester: Manchester University Press, 1963), 4–5.

African family was extended thus a household would contain a man, his wives and their children, his unmarried brothers and sisters, possibly his parents, and any kinfolk or other people who chose to attach themselves to him. This unit provided for all the individual's material, social and emotional needs. Such kin-based societies are characterized by the overriding emphasis placed on loyalty to the family,[23] and the stress placed on duties rather than rights.[24] In Africa individualism would not be valued as it is in the west. Rather, a person would be expected to compromise his or her interests for the good of the larger unit; to stand on one's rights would be thought anti-social. It follows that whenever rights were in issue they would be the concern of the family as a group.

The foregoing point has special relevance for the welfare of children. In the African tradition, children's rights were not seen as burden but rather a welcome addition to any household, where it would be assured of food, shelter and support. There were no formal mechanisms to protect children, but then none would have been necessary. Abundant land, a subsistence economy, and the highly developed sense of generosity due to all family members, underwrote the support obligation.[25] African law had no concern with a child's right to a proper upbringing; its interest was in a family's right to claim the child as one of its members.[26]

6.2. *Gender in Traditional Africa*

A woman in pre-colonial Africa might lack all formal legal capacities but this did not constitute gender discrimination as women were respected members of the family and community, and they too were guaranteed lifelong support within the framework of the extended family.[27] The human rights of women epitomize questions about the relationship of the individual to the group.[28] According to Matua individual rights cannot make sense in a social and political vacuum, devoid of the duties assumed by individuals.[29]

---

[23] Meyer Fortes, *Kinship and the Social Order* (London: Routledge and Kegan Paul, 1969), 233–4.

[24] Gluckman, *Barotse Jurisprudence.*

[25] Thomas William Bennett, "Maintenance of minor children: a problem of adapting customary law to meet social change," *Acta Juridica* (1980): 115–25.

[26] W. J. Goode, *The Family* Englewood Cliffs, NJ: Prentice Hall 24.

[27] Bennett, "Maintenance of minor children," 33.

[28] Diana J. Fox, "Women's Human Rights in Africa: Beyond the Debate Over the Universality for or Relativity of Human Rights," *African Studies Quarterly* 2, issue 3 (1998), http://web.africa.ufl.edu/asq/v2/v2i3a2.htm

[29] Makau Wa Matua, "The Banjul Charter and the African Cultural Fingerprint: An Evaluation of the Language of Duties," *Virginia Journal of International Law* 35 (1995): 340.

6.3. *Practice, Principles, Norms and Experiences in Africa vis-à-vis Human Rights*

Looking at the practice, principles, norms and experience of the ancient African societies, one could expect to see the African idea of human rights, if there was any. Also there are African writers who have argued that the belief and idea of human rights existed in the ancient Africa and there are writers who deny this, but the honest truth is that it's difficult to come across sources on history of human rights in Africa prior to enlightenment period, because ancient Africans had no tendency to document their history due to oral devolve. Therefore, the focus here is going to be in pre-colonial African societies.

Although there are counter claims that there is confusion between human dignity and human rights against those who claim that there was existence of human rights in pre-colonial Africa, yet one is not doing anything wrong by looking at the claim of existence.

Just like western world, the African pre-colonial history was not peaceful and blissful, there was abuse of power, though not kind of omnipotent State exercising absolute control over its subject.

Focusing on the standard that guided social, legal and political framework in the two ancient societies, Akamba of East Africa and Akans of West Africa, one could see the idea of right which show justice and sustain of individualism:

> The Akambas of East Africa were symptomatic of the less rigidly organized societies, whereas the Akans of West Africa were characteristic of the more centralized state systems. In Akan thought, the individual had both descriptive and normative characteristics. Both endowed a person with individual rights as well as obligations. Similarly, the Akamba believed that "all members were born equal and were supposed to be treated as such beyond sex and age. The belief prevailed in both societies that, as an inherently valuable being, the individual was naturally endowed with certain basic rights.[30]

In Akan political framework, the heads of different lineages of kinship were, in turn, form the town council which was chaired by Chief of Akan. A Chief way of ruling was not by command for a council was to reach decision by way of agreement. And if constituents were not pleased by the decision of the council could criticize openly. According to Kwasi Wiredu, "there was no doubt about the right of the people, including the elders, to dismiss a chief who tried to be oppressive."[31]

An individual had to qualify in the Akamba society in order to be allowed to join the elder's council which meant that he or she had to be committed

---

[30] Makau Mutua, *Human Rights: A Political and Cultural Critique* (Philadelphia: University of Pennsylvania Press, 2002), 75.

[31] Ibid., 76.

to the community and responsible in his personal affairs. By personal affairs it meant an individual had to have stable family which include spouse and children. Like Akan, the Akamba council was open forum which made decision by agreement. The role of council was to make customs and norms which are followed by the community.

In the above explanation about the political structure of Akamba and Akon, one could see the intention to deliver justice by the authority and also right to freedom of expression being exercised, especially where the council decision could be criticized by the constituents. The participation of the community members in the council does also show respect to them and hence certain aspect of the right to dignity. However, something which make pre-colonial Africa little different from Western world, but similar to Jewish culture is duties which an individual is expected to perform to the community and family.

According to Makau Mutua is that much of the historical studies in relation to existence of individual human rights in pre-colonial Africa were done without giving attention to the judicial process which existed then. In the study done by Mutua:

> A preliminary examination of both the Akan and Akamba societies strongly indicates individual-conscious systems of justice. With respect to the Akamba, a party to a complaint appeared before the council of elders in the company of his jury, a selection of individuals who enjoyed the party's confidence. Unlike Western-style jurors, the Akamba jurors did not hand down a verdict, but advised the party on how to plead and what arguments to put forth to win the case. They had to be steeped in Kamba law, customs, and traditions. The threat of the administration of Kithitu, the Kamba oath, which was believed to bring harm to those who lied, encouraged truthfulness.[32]
>
> In Akan society, the presumption of innocence was deeply embedded in social consciousness. According to Wiredu, "it was an absolute principle of Akan justice that no human being could be punished without trial." The Akans, like the Akamba, also recognized a wide range of individual rights: murder, assault, and theft were punished as violations of the person.[33]

Moreover, similar discovery can be found in the Sotho Chiefdom of South Africa:

> None of Sotho Chiefdoms was a military kingdom in which authority was maintained by force: order was secured rather through negotiation and compromise, and early travellers noted that the freedom of criticism of authority (the chief) in public assembly was much greater than was then permitted in Europe.[34] Moshoe-

[32] Ibid.

[33] Ibid., 77.

[34] Monica Wilson and Leonard Thompson, eds., *The Oxford History of South Africa*, vol. I (Oxford: Clarendon Press, 1969), 158.

> shoe, as Paramount Chief, would in theory have had the power to make the ultimate decision in matters of law, and his court would have acted as ultimate court of appeal from all other courts. But in practice, unless he was in a particularly strong position to manipulate personal loyalty, patronage, and factional rivalries over some issue, he was unable to override the customs of the nation against the will of the people. Had he attempted to change a law or custom without consulting his counsellors and without allowing the change to be canvassed both publicly and thoroughly before it was adopted, he ran the risk that any disaffected portion of his people might withdraw its allegiance and transfer it to another chief. Among the Sotho it was normal before important changes were made to hold a *pitso,* where any proposed change would be freely discussed by commoners as well as chiefs.[35]

All the above quotes reveal that in the pre-colonial Africa there was justice awareness and system which has a lot in common with the modern justice system. The modern perception that man is innocent until found guilty in the court of law could be reflected in the Akamba's principle that no human being could be punished without trial. Also similar to the modern legislature, there was people's right to participate in the public assembly (*pitso*) or through their representative in the council. Therefore, there was kind of check and balance to limit the power of the rulers.

However, there were also cultures and practices which contradicted the idea of human rights and human dignity. And some of these practices were Akamba's way to obtain confession by subjecting a suspect of serious crime to water or fire ordeal, likewise, the Akans would take a life of a common citizen to accompany a chief who has just died, so that a dead chief could have assistance in his journey to the land of the dead. Opinion of the minors and women were not sought out in the decision making process. The division of labor based on gender had also unrealistic social norms, for example, men were not to be seen in a kitchen. Any of these practices contradicted one or two of the human rights; it could be right to life, right to dignity or right to equality.

6.4. *Political Participation*

Talk about African culture and social institutions presuppose a distinctive tradition; one located in the pre colonial time. Thus, we learn that in Africa people suffered no systematic discrimination or oppression:

> The notion of due process of law permeated indigenous law; deprivation of personal liberty or property was rare; security of the person was assured, and customary legal process was characterized not by unpredictable and harsh encroachments

---

[35] Sandra Burman, *Chiefdom Politics and Alien Law* (London and Basingstoke: The MacMillan Press, 1981), 27.

> upon the individual by the sovereign, but by meticulous, if cumbersome, procedures for decision-making. The African conception of human rights was an essential aspect of African humanism sustained by religious doctrine and the principle of accountability to the ancestral shades.[36]

It has been observed that traditional African societies were democratic and egalitarian, and allowed for the participation of all adults in the decision making process. Even in communities with Kings or Chiefs, decisions were reached only after full consultation with community members.[37] All participating adults were free to express their opinions on issues before decisions can be reached. Again, all decisions were reached through a consensus. No one is punished for holding opposing views on issues, and no attempt was made to suppress any voice. In some cases, decisions on issues are deferred until all the constituting members or groups of the community are represented. According to Sithole:

> Things are never settled until everyone has had something to say. African traditional council allows the free expression of all shades of opinions. Any man has full right to express his mind on public questions.[38]

The chief's authority was determined by a complex interplay of factors: the rules of succession, personal prestige, control of ritual and the number of followers he might have attracted. A despotic chief would face revolt or secession.[39] In other words, if people do not revolt against his misrule, they could leave him and either join other kingdom or establish new country. This ensured that no ruler could afford to rule autocratically. All governmental functions were confounded in one office, the chief-in-council. Although there was no separation of powers,[40] this did not result in oppressive rule. The African chief did not enjoy a continuing unquestioned right to command; his authority had to be continually recreated situationally, in specific contexts. This is expressed in the formula that chiefs could not rule on their own, but only in constant consulta-

---

[36] Asante, "Nation building and human rights in emergent African nations," *Cornell International Law Journal* (1969): 73–74.

[37] OO Elechi, "Women and (African) Indigenous Justice Systems," in *Pan- African Issues in Crime and Justice*, ed. Anita Kalunta-Crumpton and Biko Agozino (London: Ashgate Publishing Limited, 2004).

[38] Kwame Gyekye, *African Cultural Values: An Introduction* (Accra, Ghana: Sankofa Publishing Co., 1996), 153.

[39] Isaac Schapera, *Government and Politics in Tribal Societies* (London: C. A. Watts and Co, 1956), 211.

[40] Ian Hamnett, *Chieftainship and Legitimacy, an Anthropological Study of Executive Law in Lesotho* (London: Routledge and Kegan Paul, 1975), 67.

tion with their councillors and people.[41] Thus an old saying has it that 'chiefs ruled by grace of their people.'[42]

Although traditional African history is not written, orally transmitted literature and the scanty writings has at least shown how these ethical systems served the goal of human dignity quite as effectively as any western code of human rights could. Human rights are not an end in themselves; they are merely a means to achieve the goal of human dignity. Once ends and means are separated, it becomes apparent that human dignity may be realized in Africa, although through different social mechanisms.

6.5. *African Judicial System*

African notion of justice was substantive as opposed to Western notion which is procedural. Access to justice in traditional Africa as such was guaranteed as it was seen as an entitlement to everybody. As such, everybody was admitted to the proceedings and any one would come up to give evidence in the open gathering without fear or favor. The community of elders sat in markets or under big trees and heard cases as and when they were brought without the resource burden of the Western culture where the construction of courts and the general infrastructure constrains the ordinary man from accessing justice let alone the quality of justice administered. African justice lacked an appeal process on the basis that it was not based on procedure and so an appeal was considered unnecessary.

Consideration of the African judicial process reveals that in several respects it contained a better guarantee of procedural fairness than its western counterpart. The ideal sought by African courts was a reconciliation of the disputants approved by the community.[43] And, because reconciliation required a slow but thorough examination of any grievance, the parties had every opportunity to voice their complaints in a relatively sympathetic environment. By comparison, the highly professionalized, western mode of dispute processing seems designed to alienate and confuse the litigant. Punitive sentencing as is known today is Western notions as in traditional African society, the commission of an offence, breakdown of law and order was not blamed on the individual accused or groups accused but the whole community shared the blame for the commission of offences and the breakdown of law and order in the community. Unlike victims under African state based justice systems, victims under African indigenous

[41] W. D. Hammond-Tooke, *Command or Consensus: the Development of Transkeian Local Government* (Cape Town: David Philip, 1975), 65.

[42] Isaac Schapera, *A Handbook of Tswana Law and Custom*, 2nd ed. (Oxford: Oxford University Press, 1955), 84.

[43] J. F. Holleman, *Issues in African Law* (The Hague: Mouton, 1974), 16–47.

justice are accorded access to mechanisms of justice and to prompt redress. Remedies such as restitution, material and emotional support were provided.

Nsereko notes that African customary legal processes focused mainly on the victim rather than on the offender. The goal of justice was to vindicate the victim and protect his/her rights. The imposition of punishment on the offender was designed to bring about the healing of the victim rather than to punish the offender. In any conflict, rather than punish the offender for punishment sake, the offender was made to pay compensation to the victim. Compensation according to Nsereko goes beyond restitution. It also represents a form of apology and atonement by the offender to the victim and the community.[44]

African indigenous justice system allows for the active involvement and participation by victims, offenders, their families and friends, and the entire community in defining harm and in crafting a resolution acceptable to all concerned. The goal is to restore those who have been harmed. Victimization creates opportunities for victims, offenders and the community members to meet and discuss the crime and its aftermath. Strenuous efforts are afterwards made to restore the victim and offender back into the community as positive contributing members of the community. African indigenous justice is able to condemn behavior and yet retain respect and love for the wrong-doer. Africans believe human-beings are capable of change and therefore deserve a second or even a third chance.

The South African Truth and Reconciliation Commission process was based on the restorative principle, known as *ubuntu*[45] in the Zulu, South African language. Desmond Tutu, the chief architect of the Truth and Reconciliation Commission describes the *ubuntu* principle, as the greatest good is communal harmony.[46]

Slavery and colonialism, without question, are momentous historical forces with the greatest influence on African culture and development. Both slavery and colonialism degraded and exploited African peoples, and this left a lasting

---

[44] D. D. N. Nsereko, *Victims of Crime and their Rights. In Criminology in Africa*, ed. Tibamanya mwene Mushanga (Rome: United Nations Interregional Crime And Justice Research Institute (UNICRI), 1992).

[45] Justice Mokgoro of South Africa defines *Ubuntu* – a Zulu word as a lifestyle or unifying world-view of African societies based on respect and understanding between individuals. *Ubuntu* has been translated as humaneness, and is derived from the expression: *umuntu ngumuntu ngabantu* (a person is a person because of other people/ a person can only be a person through others.) It envelopes values of group solidarity, compassion, respect, human dignity, conformity to basic norms and collective unity.

[46] Desmond Tutu, "The Truth and Reconciliation Process – Restorative Justice," a Lecture Delivered by Archbishop Desmond Tutu to the Longford Lecture Series, Canada on 16 February 2004.

negative effect on the African peoples' psyche, economy and culture. Further, colonialism disturbed the natural process of state formation, created alien social structures and institutions, and introduced new relations of production. The African judicial adjudication process was diluted during colonialism when chiefs were appointed on salaried status to adjudicate and they in most cases combined traditional African justice notions with the Western notions.

6.6. *Egypt is Part of Europe*

It is easy to assume that the mindset which states that Egypt is part of Europe is the same mentality which is saying there did not exist the concept of human right in pre-colonial Africa. Either is Rhoda Howard, Jack Donnelly or somebody else, most often than not, have based their conclusion on the contradiction and imperfection seen in the pre-colonial concept of human rights. These contradictions and imperfections were not unique attribute of the pre-colonial Africa, but also common in other part of the world. Hence, anyone who says pre-colonial Africa had no concept of human rights based on these imperfections or contradiction is having mentality which does not want to associate Africa with any kind of civilization.

Those who deny the existence of human rights conception in the pre-colonial Africa, among them, Jack Donnelly stated that "African societies had concepts and practices of human dignity that simply did not involve human rights." In his specific words Jack Donnelly said, "Even where Africans had personal rights against their government, those rights were based not on one's humanity but on such criteria as age, sex, lineage, achievement or community membership." By this Donnelly meant that there is human right when one is entitle to a right simply as human being. Rhoda Howard states that Human rights are "in the sense that individual have the right to make claims on or against the state."

Having the arguments of the Jack Donnelly and Rhoda Howard in the mind and considering experiences and practices of the Akamba and Akan societies in the pre-colonial Africa, one is bound to disagree with both Jack Donnelly and Rhoda Howard. The disagreement comes as result of the fact that in the pre-colonial Akamba and Akan, an individual could not be punished without going through a trial and be found guilt. This indicates the presence and respect of the individual right which was given to him or her because he or she was human being. And as to the individual's right against a State, it has to be remembered that there were public assemblies in pre-colonial societies in which an individual could express opinion or disagreement against State. An individual with the persuasive argument could rally support against authority or State.

7. *Middle East (Islamic World)*

In the Islamic world there is close connection between religion and how to govern a State. This provide essential base for law and idea of kind of authority and consequently concept of right.

The political authority and legal expert could not explain the legal principles by going away from the Koran, because the Koran was and is still considered eternal and holy in the Islamic world. Therefore, to solve social and political problem in the early centuries, *Sharia* (set of laws) was developed with emphasize on the Koran. This *Sharia* was interpreted with the help of what prophet Mohammed did or said (*Hadith*), independent reasoning (*Ijtihad*) and with agreement of the jurists (*Ijma*).

The Sunni community agreed that all the Koran interpretations, those were to be done to give Koran its final shape, were completed in the ninth century. The Shia did not agree with this belief and to them independent reasoning remained important source of law, though it was restricted by the obligation not to go way from the examples set by Imam who was sinless and incapable of era. These two factors, after certain period, made Sharia to be firm and insensitive to reality.

Although Sunni said about Ijtihad being completed by ninth century, this has not always been realistic true, since history shows that there have been different ways to make the law suitable for different political and social needs. And this involved debate about doubtful points in relation to possible interpretation.

In Islamic world human rights are not attributed to an individual simply because is human being, but due to his Islamic faith. However, the Islamic perspective does provide the foundation for human right concept, because it stresses on equality of all believers and individual does have important place. And by believers, it means Muslim believers as distinctively from non-Muslim believers. However, the distinction which the religion draws between men and women contradict the concept of human rights.

The relationship between authority and society can be understood by looking at the importance of the duty in the Islamic religion, a place of an individual, the equality of the believers and the fact that the ruler is not above the law and is answerable for the implementation of law. In this manner the ruler also provides assurance of the spiritual welfare of people.

7.1. *Contradictions in the Islamic Laws*

The laws which were intended to guide the authority and assure the welfare of the community but not individual, did not provide for a way to remove a ruler who was not complying with the human rights. And what was even worse was the fact that the disagreement and struggle (*fitna*) in early centuries after the death of the Mohammed, gave excuse to the jurists to promote loyalty to any kind of government without regard to whether is dictatorship. Therefore, there were kind of absolute States.

Islamic Law also has other contradictions such as; direction to murder people who worship idols or who don't believe in Islam, Jews and Christian in the Islamic world are considered as second class citizens, men and women do not have equal rights, there was harsh corporal punishment (*Hadd*) such as cut off the hand. The following quotes elaborate:

> The position of Christian and Jewish minorities is different from that of 'unbelievers' due to theirs categorisation as 'People of the Book'. Within Muslim society they are ensured certain rights, such as security of person and property, freedom of worship and a degree of communal autonomy. But they are also restricted in many ways. They are subject to a poll-tax (*jizya*), they are not allowed to preach openly and proselytise and are forbidden from holding the highest political offices. Being a non-Muslim in an Islamic state entails the status of a second-class citizen. Minorities enjoy religious tolerance rather than religious freedom. Yet it must be noted that in the history of Islamic empire these minorities have enjoyed relative security during long periods.[47]
>
> The inequality between the sexes is flagrant in traditional Islamic law and doctrine. Certain women's rights are secured. The woman has a right to inheritance; to be a party to a contract in marriage and not an object for sale; to manage her own property; and some rights to divorce. But these, even though important, are only limited rights. A man is allowed to use physical violence against his wife; he can divorce her without explanation; he can be polygamous if he so chooses; he has exclusive rights of custody over the children in case of separation; and the testimony of one male witness is equal to that of two women. Attitude to women are shaped by the belief that their sexuality poses a threat to social order and must therefore be concealed and controlled.[48]

8. *Asia*

Asia is politically, historically, economically, cultural and diverse continent with different forms and levels of civilizations. In fact, the earliest signs of human rights can be traced to Asia. The Cyrus Cylinder written during the reign of King Cyrus of Persia in Iran which is thousands of years long before the UDHR has been said to contain the first expressions on human rights.[49] Similarly, documents like the Edicts of Ashoka issued by Ashoka the Great of

---

[47] Katerina Dalacoura, *Islam, Liberalism and Human Rights* (London: I. B. Tauros and Co, 2003), 46.

[48] Ibid.

[49] www.wikipeda.org/wiki/Human _rights

India between 272–231 BC carried several norms that too could be said to be the earliest references to human rights. The Constitution of Medina of 622 AD said to have been drafted by Prophet Muhammad and which constituted formal agreement between all significant tribes and families of Yathrib later known as Medina, including Muslims, Jews and Pagans, is probably the first constitution or treaty which entertained diverse human rights. Therefore, long before the English Magna Carta of 1215, the British Bill of Rights of 1689, and of course the American and French Declarations of 1776 and 1789 respectively, a lot of ground had already been covered in Asia towards what became known as human rights.

In India the concept of human rights is tracked down from within the concept of *Manusmriti*, *Vasudhaiva kutumbakam* and Kautilya's *Arthasastra*, but yet is admitted that western experience through French, English and American revolutions made India aware of human rights. The Indian history shows that through war and treaties rights were decided.

The ancient Indian concept of human rights and humanitarian laws based on wars and regulated humanitarian laws to be adopted before, during and after war. The yardstick to measure human rights during ancient period was mostly conducted in the field of battle. The ancient writings contained rules of warfare that were laid down in the legal texts such as *Manusmriti* or the code of *Manu* (200 BC to AD 100), the *Mahabharat* (1000 BC), Kautilya's *Arthastra* (300 BC) and Sukranitisar of *Sukracharya*.[50]

Manudharma and other ancient writings enumerated military targets and what should not be attacked, such as all places of religious worship, houses of individuals who were not participating in warfare, or property that was not in the hands of the armed forces as such, which could not be attacked or destroyed by fire or by any other means. According to Manu the following individuals must not be slain: 'one who is sleeping; who is without his armour; one who is naked; who is deprived of his weapons; one who is looking on and not fighting, as one who is engaged in fighting with another person.[51]

The Indian history has also very close relationship with Hindu religion which is oldest in Asia and gave birth to other religions such as Buddha, Sikh, etc. In this history one finds social custom of what's morally right called *Dharma*. In explaining *Dharma*, Mamta Rajawat stated that, 'these are identified and recognized in Indian civilisation from time immemorial as the basic conditions for peaceful and progressive life.'[52] Moreover, *Moksha* (salvation), *Artha* (Economic Prosperity) and *Kama* (Pleasure of sensuous activities) were part of big picture

---

[50] Chiranjivi J. Nirmal, *Human Rights in India* (New Delhi: Oxford University Press, 2000), 2.

[51] Ibid., 2.

[52] Mamta Rajawat, *Burning Issues of Human rights* (Delhi: Kalpaz Publications, 2001), 125.

shaping spiritual and ethical values of the Hindu societies. All these principles are contained in the *Vedas*, *Smirits* and *Puranas*. The following quotes elaborate these values:

> The material attainment through Artha and Kama-two most important worldly pursuits were an integral part of Dharma and the purpose of all these achievements was the realisation of the ultimate end of life-Moksha. Individual was considered basic unit of the society and he has to be given all the facilities and conditions for attainment of excellence in all these directions.[53]
>
> These facilities and conditions are the basic human rights. These are regarded as the instruments for achieving objectives of Dharma, Artha, Kama and Moksha. These four cardinal values (chaturbarg) constituted the ancient cultural heritage-of India. Although there were some contradictions and contentions to the basic values, these principles ultimately pre-dominated the spiritual life of Indians.[54]

In Hindu spiritual and ethical values, just like in the Jewish Culture, there were rights and responsibilities. *Dharma, Moksha, Artha* and *Kama* were to guarantee and advance a bunch of human rights such as right to equality, right to happiness, right to religion, right to social security, right to protection, right to human treatment, right to justice and right to education, etc. These human rights went with the mutual duties.

8.1. *Right to Equality*

The right to equality also known as *Samanata* or *Samya* is considered as important basis of Indian culture through which happiness is possible. While *Vedas* talk about *Dharma*, the integral part of *Dharma* such as *Rig Veda* and *Atharva Veda* put together Charter of equality. It's in the *Rig Veda* where is stated "no one is superior or inferior. All are brothers and all should strive for the interest of all and progress collectively".[55] And in the same way *Atharva Veda* stated, "All have equal rights in article of food and water".[56] Both of these principles are similar to today right to equality.

8.2. *Right to Religion*

As mentioned before, Hindu religion is one of the oldest religions, but also has different sects which necessitate freedom of religion. These different sects found different ways of living in harmony as Mamta Rajawat put it:

---

[53] Ibid., 126.

[54] Ibid.

[55] Ibid., 130.

[56] Ibid.

> We differ in the modes of worshipping God and we address God in various names whether it is Ishwar or Allaha. Therefore, eminent sages and saints and sadhaks of India have been emphasising on the religious equality and harmony and the Right to religion has been recognised as an integral part of harmony. The above rule of Dharma is very unique to Indian Culture and civilisation. It required the State to give equal protection not only to believers of God but also to disbeliever of God.[57]

8.3. *China*

The real life and ethical thought of the Chinese people since ancient times relate to Confucianism (as tradition), but today even politics relate to it. Confucianism started around 2500 years ago, but the track down of idea could lead to the teaching of Confucius around 551 BC – 479 BC. Confucius came up with a way to interpret traditions (Confucianism) and new meaning to such traditions. A lot of Confucian thinkers were influenced by his new way of interpretation and new meaning. The following is the elaborate meaning of Confucianism:

> The Confucian ethical tradition is a system of human relationships based on virtue of *ren*. The moral ideal for each individual is the attainment of *ren* – the highest and most perfect virtue. *Ren* is a human quality, an expression of humanity, which can be manifested in a wide range of dispositions from personal reflection and critical examination of one's life to respect, concern and care for others. In dealing with oneself, *ren* requires us to 'overcome the self through observing the rites' (*The Analects*, Book XII: 1). In dealing with others, *rens* asks us to practise the art of *shu* – 'do not impose on others what we ourselves do not desire' (*The Analects*, Book XII: 2), an ethics of sympathy and reciprocity similar to the Golden Rule in other traditional religions and Kantian tradition.[58]

8.4. *Contradiction*

It has been said that Confucianism avers that human beings are totally social and cultural beings. Therefore, Confucianism is contrary to the concept of human rights, because in the concept of human rights an individual deserves human rights simply because he is a human being. However, the above quote shows that Confucianism is about achieving *ren* which is human quality, an expression of humanity which shows itself through a wide range of natural tendency of personal reflection. Therefore, in the Confucianism there is respect for human being simply because is human being, and this respect means nothing else than not persecute human quality and expression of it, not to suppress

---

[57] Ibid., 134.

[58] J. Chan, "Confucianism and Human Rights," in Rhona K. M. Smith, and Christien van den Anker (eds.), *The Essential of Human Rights* (London: Hodder Arnold, 2005), 56.

right to dignity, right to life and right to equality through which one sees an expression of humanity.

It is my opinion that Confucianism provides not only foundation but is also compatible with the concept of human rights, unless you look at it with the prejudice. Although Confucianism extends to the social relationship, it does stress the individual achievement of human quality, an expression of humanity. The critical examination of one's life to respect, concern and care for others does not mean that moral duties or rights arise only from social relationship, it just an emphasize to stop selfishness for when oneness disappear thereby remain wholeness which is total harmony of individuals.

9. *Post-War Developments*

Based on the UDHR, several declarations, conventions and covenants have been developed to spearhead international human rights. Of particular importance as indicated already is the two Covenants adopted simultaneously in 1966: covenants on economic, social and cultural rights, and civil and political rights. The two Covenants, the UDHR as well as the first Optional Protocol to the Civil and Political Rights Covenant constitute the International Bill of Rights. The International Bill of Rights was followed by the 1979 Convention on the Elimination of all forms of Discrimination against Women (CEDAW). In 1984, the international community, through the United Nations, returned to the drawing board and adopted the historic Convention against Torture, Inhuman and Degrading Punishment or Treatment. With the exception of two States, the 1989 Convention on the Rights of the Child has been ratified by all States. New conventions include the Convention on migrants, Convention on Persons with Disabilities, etc.

Besides 'hard' conventions or treaties, the international community has adopted several declarations which constitute important landmarks towards a more refined system of international human rights architecture. Among these include the Rio Declaration (1991), the Vienna Declaration and Programme of Action (1993), Durban Declaration (2001), Johannesburg Declaration (2002), etc. It is also important to mention the 1949 Geneva Conventions and now the 1998 Statute of the International Criminal Court (ICC) as well as the 1951 Refugee Convention among these landmarks. The upsurge of violence, conflict and war across the world in post-UDHR era left hundreds of thousands of people including women and children dead while millions more displaced and seeking refugee abroad. In the process, it became necessary to develop a system of accountability for serious breaches of international law while providing for the protection of refugees and the displaced. Besides *AD-HOC* Tribunals for the former Yugoslavia, Rwanda, etc., the international community established the International Criminal Court (ICC) which is a permanent judicial arm to try serious breaches of international law. In a show of collective resolve against impunity, the international community dragged incumbent and past presidents and prime ministers before the *ad-hoc* tribunals and lately the ICC to account for their misdeeds. Also initially begun as temporary, the UN High Commissioner for Refugees (UNHCR) has since become permanent arm of the United Nations. The UNHCR affords much-needed protection to the refugees. Outside the formal human rights system, the International Committee of the Red Cross (ICRC) has been doing a lot of important work responding to humanitarian needs across the world. Therefore, in terms of normative standards, the international human rights system has in the sixty years of its existence come full-circle. Including now the Human Rights Council, an elaborate system of monitoring of the implementation of these standards by a host of treaty-bodies such as convention-based thematic committees, working groups, experts, has been instituted under the supervision of the UN High Commissioner for Human Rights. Various chapters in this book engage the normative standards, institutions and challenges.

10. *Conclusion*

Human rights, therefore, is not purely a Western invention. It cannot be. Neither did the concept of human rights originate from any particular part of the world. Arguably, all peoples of the world do not assent to the same basic values and beliefs, but what is certain is that every society has been concerned with the notion of social justice, the relationship between the individual and his/her political authorities. As Roberts and Merrills point out, the struggle for human rights is as old as world history itself, because it concerns the need to protect the individual against the abuse of power by the monarch, the tyrant, or the State.[59] In concurring with Herskovitz the notion that human rights are Western phenomenon is seriously flawed. The mockery and hypocrisy exhibited by the West in colonizing two-thirds of the world, while supporting the claim for human rights. It should not be forgotten that while colonial regimes drafted and signed the Universal Declaration of Human Rights, they simultaneously committed atrocities in the name of the civilizing mission.

As Oloka argues, we need not restate the fact that the colonial epoch in Africa represented the negation of all categories of human rights in pre-colonial Africa; from the basic right of self-determination to the freedoms of expression

[59] Paul Gordon Lauren, *The Evolution of International Human Rights: Visions Seen* (Philadelphia: University of Pennsylvania Press, 1998), 11–12.

and association.[60] Welch puts the matter in proper perspective when he says: freedom of expression was subjected to significant restraints when Africa was divided among various colonial powers. The limits imposed in the colonial period were in many respects enhanced following independence, rather than relaxed or abolished.[61]

As Mutua argues, in the West the language of rights primarily developed along the trajectory of claims against the State, entitlements which imply the rights to seek an individual remedy for a wrong. The African language of duty, however, offers a different meaning for individual/State-society relations; while people had rights, they also bore duties. Our minds should not be preoccupied and with questions as to whether in traditional Africa the notion of human rights existed as its clear from this discussion human rights not only existed in Africa, but duties were also emphasized. In conclusion, historical development of international human rights encompasses honest examination of all civilizations, and certainly not just the Western civilization. Though the Western has dominated the development of the principle of human rights and monopolized its internationalization, the idea of dignity is universal and cannot come from one particular civilization. The international human rights system at the United Nations enshrines the values of all humanity.

Bibliography

Books and Articles

Bennett, T. W. "Human Rights & the African Cultural Tradition." *Transformation Journal* No. 22 (1993): 30–40.

Bennett, Thomas William. "Maintenance of minor children: a problem of adapting customary law to meet social change." *Acta Juridica* (1980): 115–25.

Brownlie, Ian. *Principles of Public International Law*. 4th ed. Oxford: Clarendon Press, 1990.

Burman, Sandra. *Chiefdom Politics and Alien Law*. London and Basingstoke: The MacMillan Press, 1981.

Dalacoura, Katerina. *Islam, Liberalism and Human Rights*. London: I. B. Tauros and Co, 2003.

Donnelly, Jack. *International Human Rights. Dilemmas in World Politics*. 2nd ed. Colorado/ Oxford: Westview Press, 1998.

Donnelly, Jack. "The Relative Universality of Human Rights." *Human Rights Quarterly* 29, No. 2 (2007): 281–306.

Elechi, O. Oko. "Human Rights and The African Indigenous Justice System." A Paper for Presentation at the 18th International Conference of the International Society for the Reform of Criminal Law, 8–12 August 2004, Montreal, Quebec, Canada.

60 Joseph Oloka-Onyango, "Human Rights and Sustainable Development in Contemporary Africa: A New Dawn, or Retreating Horizons?" *Human Development Report 2000 Background Paper*.

61 Claude E. Welch, Jr, "The African Charter and Freedom of Expression in Africa," *Buffalo Human Rights Law Review* 4 (1999): 105.

Fortes, Meyer. *Kinship and the Social Order*. London: Routledge and Kegan Paul, 1969.
Fox, Diana J. "Women's Human Rights in Africa: Beyond the Debate Over the Universality for or Relativity of Human Rights." *African Studies Quarterly* 2, Issue 3 (1998), http://web.africa.ufl.edu/asq/v2/v2i3a2.htm
Gluckman, Max. *The Ideas in Barotse Jurisprudence*. Manchester: Manchester University Press, 1963.
Hamnett, Ian. *Chieftainship and Legitimacy, an Anthropological Study of Executive Law in Lesotho*. London: Routledge and Kegan Paul, 1975.
Hammond-Tooke, W. D. *Command or Consensus: the Development of Transkeian Local Government*. Cape Town: David Philip, 1975.
Holleman, J. F. *Issues in African Law*. The Hague: Mouton, 1974.
Jr, Claude E. Welch. "The African Charter and Freedom of Expression in Africa." *Buffalo Human Rights Law Review* 4 (1999): 101–22.
Lauren, Paul Gordon. *The Evolution of International Human Rights: Visions Seen*. Philadelphia: University of Pennsylvania Press, 1998.
Locke, John. *Two Treatise On Government*. London: Printed for R. Butler, W. Reid, W. Sharpe, and John Bumpus, 1821 (1689).
Machlem, Patrick. *What is International Human Rights Law? Three Applications of a Distributive Account*. Texas: Bernard and Andre Rapoport Center for Human Rights and Justice University of Texas School of Law, 19 November 2007.
Matua, Makau Wa. "The Banjul Charter and the African Cultural Fingerprint: An Evaluation of the Language of Duties." *Virginia Journal of International Law* 35 (1995): 339–380.
Mutua, Makau. *Human Rights: A Political and Cultural Critique*. Philadelphia: University of Pennsylvania Press, 2002.
Nirmal, Chiranjivi J. *Human Rights in India*. New Delhi: Oxford University Press, 2000.
Nsereko, DDN. *Victims of Crime and their Rights. In Criminology in Africa*. Edited by Tibamanya mwene Mushanga. Rome: United Nations Interregional Crime And Justice Research Institute (UNICRI), 1992.
Peledda, Salvatore. *On being Human. Interpretations of Humanism from The Renaissance to the Present*, 1997.
Rajawat, Mamta. *Burning Issues of Human Rights*. Delhi: Kalpaz Publications, 2001.
Schapera, Isaac. *Government and Politics in Tribal Societies*. London: C. A. Watts and Co, 1956.
Schapera, Isaac. *A Handbook of Tswana Law and Custom*. 2nd ed. Oxford: Oxford University Press, 1955.
Shaw, Malcolm N. *International Law*. 4th ed. Cambridge: Cambridge University Press, 1997.
Steiner, Henry J., and Philip Alston. *International Human Rights in Context. Law, Politics and Morals*. 2nd ed. Oxford: Oxford University Press, 2000.
Wilson, Monica and Leonard Thompson, eds. *The Oxford History of South Africa*. Vol. I. Oxford: Clarendon Press, 1969.

Websites

www.unhchr.org
www.au.org

Chapter Two

Civil and Political Rights

*Joshua Castellino**

1. *Introduction*

When the Universal Declaration of Human Rights was proclaimed in 1948, it articulated the notion that human rights were to accrue to every individual human being in a bid to protect their inherent dignity.[1] In this context it identified human rights as were implicitly understood as 'indivisible' consisting of civil, political, economic, social and cultural rights, all of which would need due attention if the goal of creating an effective human rights regime was to be achieved. The task of codifying the aspiration expressed in the Universal Declaration of Human Rights fell to the United Nations Commission of Human Rights, a subsidiary body to the Economic and Social Council of the United Nations. This body was tasked with coming up with the requisite laws, processes and institutions that would be able to turn the promise of human rights into an objective deliverable within the respective domestic jurisdictions of all States.[2]

However in the deliberations within the Commission two very different ideas of human rights began to emerge: one which viewed human rights as a fundamental part of the liberal State, and the other which viewed human rights as part of the obligations to be delivered upon by an interventionist State. These two polar views were represented in the debate across the classical East-West divide. Western ideologies of rights drew heavily on the notion of civil liberties and the rights of individual freedom as expressed in the liberal philosophies of the seventeenth and eighteenth century. Proponents schooled in this view

* Prof. Joshua Castellino, Professor of Law & Head of Law Department, Middlesex University, London, UK.

[1] For an exposé of the issues at the time of the framing see Johannes Morsink, *The Universal Declaration of Human Rights: Origins, Drafting and Intent* (Philadelphia: University of Pennsylvania Press, 1999).

[2] Henry Steiner and Philip Alston, *Human Rights in Context* (Oxford: Oxford University Press, 2007).

were keen to restrict the role of the State in public life and to seek to regulate the extent to which the State could intrude on personal liberties. On the other hand Eastern ideologies represented in this particular discussion by the Soviet Union, believed in an interventionist State with significant presence in the public realm where economic and social rights were considered fundamental to the well-being of the population. The clash between these ideologies took place within the deliberations at the Commission on Human Rights and resulted in the bifurcation of the human rights agenda into civil and political rights on the one hand, and economic, social and cultural rights on the other.[3]

The fundamental problem that many Western States had with economic and social rights in particular was that they were seen as intangible and difficult to enforce. They were thus labelled by some as 'provision' rights: and for many it was not the job of the State, but rather of the individual to 'provide'. It was the job of the State to 'protect'; but to protect effectively, it would be necessary to have tangible rights that could be judicially enforced. The result of this ideological split was an overt emphasis on civil and political rights to the detriment of economic, social and cultural rights throughout the latter part of the twentieth century. The human rights movement has only recently recovered from this narrow divisive idea of rights, and once again embraces the idea of human rights as indivisible. Thus to classify rights on the basis of their nature as civil and political or economic, social and cultural is no longer acceptable currency. Bearing in mind this important caveat this chapter will seek to show the impact of the division of the human rights agenda, and will seek to portray the regimes for civil and political rights as they have evolved out of that first discussion at international level about the efficacy of human rights between 1948 and 1966. To fulfil this aim this chapter is divided into three further parts. The first of these will discuss the International Covenant on Civil and Political Rights adopted by the Commission at the end of the discussions described above, in 1966. The second section will select a few key rights from the Covenant in a bid to show the parameters of the rights identified as 'civil and political'; while the final section will seek to offer a commentary on the challenges for implementation that lie ahead.

[3] For more on this discussion see Daniel M. Thomas, *The Helsinki Effect: International Norms, Human Rights, and the Demise of Communism* (Princeton, New Jersey: Princeton University Press, 2001).

2. *The Covenant*

With the prospect of a unified Bill of Rights becoming increasingly unlikely within deliberative discussions in the Commission on Human Rights, work began toward the articulation of two separate Covenants: one focussed on economic, social and cultural rights, and the other emphasizing civil and political rights. Both documents were put to the General Assembly via the Third Committee, adopted and opened for signature in 1966. The International Covenant on Civil and Political Rights came into force on the 23rd of March 1976, in accordance with the provisions of Article 49.[4] Together with the International Covenant on Economic, Social and Cultural Rights, and the Universal Declaration of Human Rights of 1948, it formed what is referred to as the International Bill of Rights. In addition between 1948 and 1976 when the Covenants came into force, a number of discussions were also underway, some of which led to multilateral treaties addressing civil and political rights.

The International Covenant on Civil and Political Rights (henceforth 'the Covenant') could be understood as the codification of the civil and political rights' aspirations expressed in the Universal Declaration of Human Rights in 1948, into legally binding provisions. The document is viewed by many as the foundation of human rights law: its importance derived from the large number of rights contained within the document[5] and its extensive scope of application to 'all persons'.[6] Over the years significant jurisprudence has developed under its auspices, which has helped to shape the contours of the rights contained in the document. In keeping with the growing consensus on specific human rights issues the Covenant has been supplemented by two further optional protocols.

The Covenant itself is divided into four parts, with a detailed preamble. Part I contains a single article: the right to self-determination. This article is also common to the International Covenant on Economic and Social Rights, in reflection of the fact that unless a people are in a position to determine their own future in a spirit of freedom, the articulation of further human rights

---

[4] REGISTRATION: 23 March 1976, No. 14668. TEXT: United Nations, Treaty Series, vol. 999, p. 171 and vol. 1057, p. 407 (procès-verbal of rectification of the authentic Spanish text). STATUS: Signatories: 60. Parties: 144 [1].

[5] As opposed to instruments that address specific rights such as the Convention on the Prohibition of All Forms of Torture, Cruel or inhuman degrading Treatment or Punishment or the Genocide Convention.

[6] In contrast to Conventions that focus on a specific group such as the Convention for the Elimination of All Forms of Discrimination Against Women or the Convention on the Rights of the Child, among others.

would be meaningless. Part Two articulates the nature of the state obligations' in upholding the promises of the Covenant, and includes provision (under article 4) for derogations from its provisions in times of public emergencies. Part Three consists of a series of substantive rights that accrue to individuals, including pure protection rights such as the rights against torture and slavery, but also other rights designed to promote a democratic society, such as the right to free and fair elections and to due process. These rights are guaranteed by the provisions contained in Part II which seeks guarantees from the State to put in place the mechanisms that would enable the realization of the rights contained in Part III. Part IV of the Covenant sets up the mechanism though which the Covenant will be monitored, articulating the mandate of the Human Rights Committee: a body consisting of eighteen independent experts, elected by State Parties to the Treaty, who have the role of refereeing its implementation, interpreting its mandate in a dynamic manner, and safeguarding its provisions.

In addition there are two protocols appended to the Covenant, both of which are optional i.e. States need to ratify these if they are to be binding on the State. The first of these Protocols, referred to as Optional Protocol I (or OP1) creates an individual complaint mechanism. States that sign and ratify this protocol provide competence to the Human Rights Committee to examine individual complaints that may emanate within the State over any of the rights contained within the Covenant. The Second Optional Protocol focuses on the abolition of the Death Penalty: States that ratify this protocol have undertaken to abolish the death penalty as a punishment from their jurisdictions.

The principle on which the Covenant works is relatively simple and is the same as for every other of the United Nations' multilateral human rights treaties. Each article in the Covenant is binding upon the States that have signed and ratified it (with the exception of those that have entered reservations against particular provisions). States are required to implement these obligations by making the necessary legislative, judicial or administrative changes that would enable realization of the rights within their State. To ensure that the process is monitored effectively the Human Rights Committee, set up under Article 28 of the Covenant, has the duty to supervise implementation. It does this in a variety of different ways. By far a significant component of its work is in the scrutiny of State reports submitted under Article 40 of the Covenant. This article requires that States submit to a periodic review of their performance by the Human Rights Committee on each of the grounds identified in the Covenant. After the submission of an initial report once the State becomes a party to the Treaty, regular reports are required to be submitted to keep the Committee abreast of the developments within the State. The Committee is required to scrutinise these reports and to address questions to the State parties *vis-à-vis* its contents. The final views adopted by the Committee, called Concluding Observations are then addressed to the State party with a view to providing constructive criticism of how human rights can be better protected within the State.

Citizens of States who have ratified Optional Protocol 1 can approach the Human Rights Committee with a petition in the case of a violation of their rights.[7] There are some fundamental conditions that need to be fulfilled before a petition will be entertained: it needs to have exhausted domestic remedies, it needs to be within the statute of limitations set for the Covenant, cannot be anonymous or constitute an abuse of the right to petition, must refer to a specific article from the Covenant, and could not be submitted to more than one international procedure of this nature. On receiving such a petition the Human Rights Committee determines its eligibility under the grounds identified above, and then, if eligible, asks States to respond to the allegations made within the complaint. Both parties have a chance to argue their case before the Human Rights Committee adopts Views on the petition. These views, like the Concluding Observations to State Reports are not binding on the State in the manner that a Court order would be, but nonetheless have significant value in highlighting potential State violations and drawing attention to them in an international forum.

In its role as guardians of the Covenant the Human Rights Committee also undertakes discussion that are aimed at clarifying the parameters of the rights contained or on other issues it feels are hindering the effective implementation, or monitoring of Covenant rights. These discussions often lead to 'General Comments': often based on the learned experience of functioning of the Covenant, but also containing important clarifications about the nature of the rights contained in the document. Like the Concluding Observations and Views on Individual complaints these Comments are seen as authoritative though not legally binding.

There are several ways to interpret the provisions contained in the Covenant. The plain meaning of the text of the Covenant, agreed in the six official languages of the United Nations (English, French, Spanish, Arabic, Russian and Chinese) is the most usual and reliable manner of interpretation. However should there be disagreements over the particular interpretations to be attributed to the words, jurists seek to unearth the rationale for the words. In other words, to return to the discussions undertaken in order to agree the set of words that appear in the text. These deliberations, contained in a document called the *travaux preparatoires* clearly show the intention of the drafters and to that extent are considered an important guide in unlocking nuances of the document. The

---

[7] An updated list of the States that have ratified the optional protocol is available at: http://www.bayefsky.com/./html/ccpr_opt_ratif_table.php (accessed 15 September 2008).

views of the Human Rights Committee, as guardians of the Covenant not only provide further assistance in the interpretation of the language of the Covenant, but also allows a dynamic modern interpretation that is in keeping with the spirit of the Covenant if not its literal provisions.[8]

3. *The Rights Package*

The substantive provisions of the Covenant can be grouped into the following five categories.[9] Indeed it could be argued that the provisions contained in this Covenant provide a basic guide to the civil and political rights that exist in international human rights law.

1. Self-Determination (Art. 1)
2. Rights Concerning Protection of Physical Integrity (Art. 6, Art. 7, Art. 8, Art. 10, Art. 16)
3. Procedural Rights (Art. 2(1), Art. 3, Art. 9, Art. 11, Art. 13, Art. 14, Art. 15, Art. 16, Art. 26)
4. Fundamental Freedoms (Art. 12, Art. 17, Art. 18, Art. 19, Art. 20, Art. 21, Art. 22)
5. Protection of Individual belong to Identifiable Groups (Art. 23, Art. 24, Art. 25, Art. 27)

3.1. *Self-determination*

This 'right' framed in the same language in the two Covenants, is one of the most controversial of human rights, encompassing civil and political rights and also economic, social and cultural rights. Essentially the Covenant suggests, in the words of Article 1(1) that 'All Peoples have the right to Self-determination'. It goes on to articulate that this right basically entails a people to make deliberative decisions over their civil, political, economic, social and cultural future. The second part of the article posits that no people may be deprived of the means to their livelihood, while the third part [i.e. Article 1(3)] imposes a duty for the realization of the right to self-determination on all States including those with Non-Self-Governing and Trust Territories.

---

[8] For more on the drafting of the Covenant and the role of the Human Rights Committee in its interpretation see Dominic McGoldrick, *The Human Rights Committee: Its Role in the Development of the International Covenant on Civil and Political Rights* (Oxford: Oxford University Press, 1991).

[9] Various commentators suggest alternative classifications. E.g. see Sarah Joseph, Jenny Schultz, and Melissa Castan, *The International Covenant on Civil and Political Rights; Cases, Materials and Commentary* (Oxford: Oxford University Press, 2005).

The article, framed in the context of United Nations decolonisation, is aimed at furthering that process and ensuring that the States emerging from it possess the full capability and political independence to adopt appropriate human rights standards as contained in the rest of the document.[10] However in using the term 'peoples' the Covenants entered into a long-ranging discussion, namely 'who' are the peoples. The *travaux preparatoires* to the Covenant clearly indicates that 'people' in this context is to be interpreted as a 'colonial people' whereby colonialism was understood as the classical European domination over non-European populations on other continents. This view has been implicitly verified by the Human Rights Committee, though many groups around the world seek to be accepted as 'people' with the right to self-determination.

In terms of public international law self-determination is identified as consisting of any one of three options: a) integration with an existing State, b) free association with an existing State or c) secession from an existing State to form an independent State.[11] Many groups see option c) as the only justifiable option and to that extent look to the Covenant to provide moral support for their cause of 'national' liberation. Against this, the view of the Human Rights Committee is clear: it interprets 'people' narrowly, has in the past, failed to find individual petitions under this right eligible on the grounds that it is a collective and not an individual rights, and where it does entertain petitions is concerned more about the 'subsistence' of grounds such as indigenous peoples whose lands and livelihoods may be under threat.[12]

3.2. *Rights concerning Protection of Physical Integrity*

These rights are traditionally considered civil rights, were in the Magna Carta of England and, along with the fundamental freedoms, examined below, have been crucial rights around which civil libertarian movements have grown.[13] In the context of the classification offered here the following rights are included: a) the right to life (Art. 6), b) the prohibition of torture, or cruel, inhuman

---

[10] For more on self-determination see Antonio Cassese, *Self-determination of Peoples: A Legal Reappraisal* (Oxford: Oxford University Press, 1995); James Crawford, *The Rights of Peoples* (Cambridge: Cambridge University Press, 1995); Hurst Hannum, *Autonomy, Sovereignty & Self-determination: The Accommodation of Conflicting Rights* (Philadelphia: University of Pennsylvania Press, 1990); Joshua Castellino, *International Law & Self-Determination: The Interplay of Politics of Territorial Possession with Formulations of National Identity* (The Hague: Martinus Nijhoff Publishers, 2000).

[11] As articulated in General Assembly Resolution 1541 (XV).

[12] See S. James Anaya, *Indigenous Peoples in International Law* (Oxford: Oxford University Press, 2004).

[13] For a general introduction to 'civil liberties' see Connor Gearty, *Civil Liberties* (Oxford: Oxford University Press, 2001).

or degrading treatment or punishment, (Art. 7) c) the prohibition of slavery, servitude or forced labor (Art. 8), and d) the humane treatment of detainees (Art. 10).

Many argue that this category of rights as a whole may in time be considered norms of *jus cogens* in public international law.[14] That is, that these rights have come to be recognized throughout history as rights that constitute minimum recognizable legal standards with no exceptions permissible. To that extent they are inalienable, or to use the language of human rights law are 'non-derogable'. That is, no restrictions upon these rights would be permissible even in the context of a declaration of a state of emergency and the restriction of other rights.[15] The reason for the importance given to these rights is that they concern basic guarantees to the physical integrity of human person, which are often particularly vulnerable in the context of national emergencies such as wars or political upheavals. Thus while human rights law allows the suspension or curtailment of other rights in the context of national emergencies (as contained in Article 4 of the Covenant), no justification is permissible for the violation of these rights. It needs to be also made clear that norms of *jus cogens* are binding upon States irrespective of their consent: i.e. unlike other human rights contained in documents such as the Covenant which are only binding upon those States that have signed and ratified the Covenant or Treaty in question, norms of *jus cogens* are binding on every State, irrespective of their consent.

In the contemporary context of the so-called 'War Against Terror' many sought to question the importance given to these rights. The argument put forward at one stage by the Department of State of the United States of America was that 'terrorism' constituted a new kind of threat, which had resulted in a state of emergency, and where it was necessary to suspend such rights. Thus it would be permissible to use a form of torture to extract a confession from an alleged terrorist, and such use of force against the physical integrity of an individual would be justifiable in the context of the potential saving of hundreds of lives. International society as a whole however refused to endorse this view:

---

[14] Some doubt could be expressed as to whether Article 10 fits into this category, however if read in conjunction with article 7 this objection could be overcome). In addition the existence of the death penalty in several States would suggest that the right to life does not fit into this category easily either. For a right to be considered a norm of *jus cogens* there would have to be clear evidence of it being universally accepted as such both in terms of legal opinion as well as in terms of consistent State practice.

[15] For more on the notion of 'derogation' from human rights treaties see the classical text by Jaime Oraa, *Human Rights in States of Emergency in Public International Law* (Oxford: Oxford University Press, 1990). A more contemporary piece of writing, especially taking into account September 11th and focussing on its perception in the public realm is: Patricia R. Zimmermann, *States of Emergency: Documentaries, Wars, Democracies* (Minneapolis: University of Minnesota Press, 2007).

for fear that erosion of physical integrity rights would claw-back the significant gains made by human rights law in the context of the inherent dignity and worth of every human being including potential terrorists. As a result the United States of America reversed its position, though significant violation of physical integrity rights have continued at its illegal detention facility at Guantanamo Bay and in other CIA detention camps across the world. The phenomenon of Extraordinary Renditions – whereby alleged terror suspects may be abducted by security forces in any jurisdiction and then transported to secret detention camps for questioning is also a clear violation of the kinds of physical integrity rights contained in this section of the Covenant.

The international community has made inroads into the use by States of the death penalty as a punishment distributed through its criminal justice system. While the text of Article 6 of the Covenant allows restricted room for the use of the death penalty against strict conditions, the Optional Protocol to the Covenant described above has created a specific obligation upon signatories to abolish the use of the death penalty altogether. The trend among States at international level is clearly toward recognition that the use of the death penalty is barbaric; and that the State ought not to have the power to extinguish life, even in the unlikely event that this decision is arrived at through a perfect criminal justice system. The few States that still exercise the death penalty, including certain States of the United States of America are under pressure to justify such action and commentators express belief that the death penalty will be abolished in time. In the few States around the world where the death penalty is in use it is restricted to the most heinous crimes with exemptions for juveniles and pregnant women. However like every rights violation State killings continue to be a significant factor depriving hundreds of individuals of their life each month.

The Atlantic Slave Trade conducted between 1440 and 1870 was one of the most dramatic violations of human rights in history. Unlike slavery that existed before in ancient Greece it violated the basics of human dignity and also transported and transplanted them in terrible conditions to locations far removed from their origins. International consciousness against slavery, led by William Wilberforce is considered by many to be the first real human rights struggle on the basis that it posited the inherent dignity and worth of every human being, including that of the slaves. Since then the prohibition of slavery, servitude and forced labor has become a key norm of *jus cogens* with several international conventions that touch on some or all of its constituent elements. Its reflection in the Covenant, while a historical statement against the phenomenon, also has contemporary relevance. Labelled 'contemporary forms of slavery', this consists of the phenomenon of individuals trafficked for profit by non-State actors, for the payment of significant sums of money, in dangerous conditions, with those who arrive in a new State left without protection due to their status as illegal immigrants. They often live as the slaves of the trafficker or their new overlord with no access to rights. The phenomenon of 'bonded labor' is also widespread, whereby generations of an individual who incurred a debt to an overlord are required to work *ad infinitum* for little monetary compensation in conditions that are often worse than those imposed on Atlantic Slave Trade victims.

3.3. *Procedural Rights*

For the rights contained in the document are to be meaningfully codified, implemented and monitored it is crucial that certain procedural safeguards are put in the place. The rights contained in this sub-section enable the realization of other civil and political rights. To that extent while they also constitute rights, they are particularly important in laying down the kinds of standards that are necessary to create effective processes or mechanisms through which other rights are made realizable. The rights that fall under this rubric can be grouped as follows: a) the principle of non-discrimination (as contained in Articles 2(1), 3 and 26); b) principles surrounding the criminal justice system (as contained in Articles 9, 11, 13, 14 and 15); c) the principle governing accrual of rights (Article 16).

The principle of non-discrimination lies at the foundation of human rights law. Simply stated, it posits that human rights accrue to every human being irrespective of any personal identifiers such as gender, race, religion, ethnicity, nationality, descent, class, caste, membership of a minority or indigenous group, age or disability. In addition it applies irrespective of the current personal/ civil status or circumstances of the individual. The fundamental importance of this principle lies in the fact that it guarantees rights without exclusion: a particularly important facet in the context of vulnerable groups whose human rights are often violated. While States are allowed to make distinctions where these may be necessary, (e.g. in determining standards that may be necessary for the fulfilment of certain roles in society) these can never be arbitrary or targeted against any members of a particular group. In terms of the civil and political rights identified in the Covenant this principle is reflected in Article 2(1), where each State that is member to the Covenant is required to respect and ensure the human rights recognized in the Covenant for each individual within its territory. It highlights that such enjoyment of rights cannot be hampered on grounds of 'race, sex, language, religion, political or other opinion, national or social origin, property, birth or other status'.[16] This guarantee is reiterated in the context of gender in Article 3 of the Covenant. The unequal enjoyment of rights between men and women is widespread throughout the globe and

[16] Article 2(1), ICCPR.

remains a fundamental weakness of the extent to which the human rights promises can be fulfilled. The non-discrimination provision contained in Article 26 is specific in that it seeks to guarantee this principle *vis-à-vis* legal protection. The human rights system is embedded within law: domestic law is seen as the ultimate guarantor of the rights articulated, with some residual, perhaps remedial role for international law should domestic law fail. However for this notion to be realized it becomes fundamental that all are treated equally by the law especially in the context of the enjoyment of rights. A failure to enshrine this principle would result in differential treatment in the context of the available of remedies, and to that extent would defeat the human rights project.

Ensuring that the criminal justice system of States offers adequate protection to every individual has traditionally been a significant component of the civil rights movement. Since the State possesses the means to punish individuals it can prove that they are guilty of wrongdoing; it becomes important to ensure that the determination of individual guilt or innocence is undertaken with the best possible guarantees of fairness. The Covenant seeks to articulate a number of rights that ensure that individuals are treated in a manner that upholds their human dignity at a time when they may be particularly vulnerable to an abuse of this dignity. First, it guarantees the security and liberty of every individual by protecting them from arbitrary arrest or detention. Where detention occurs it seeks to introduce fundamental guarantees that such detention is undertaken with due care, through a process that is legal and with respect to the rights of the individual. Among the guarantees sought are, full disclosure of charges at time of arrest, prompt appearance before judicial authorities and an entitlement to take proceedings against the detention. In addition in the case of wrongful arrest provision is made to ensure that due compensation is paid.

The provisions of Article 11 state that failing to fulfil a contractual obligation should not be adequate grounds leading to imprisonment. The rationale behind the article was to combat the phenomenon of 'debtors' prisons' prevalent in some parts of the world. The salience of this right has become a key element in the context of Migrant Workers' rights and is reflected in Article 20 of the International Convention on the Rights of all Migrant Workers and Members of their Families. Article 13 also puts in place a procedural guarantee in the context of aliens, whether or not they are migrant workers. The purpose of this article is to make sure that in the instance that an individual has to be expelled from a territory, there would be adequate safeguards of her/his rights. There have been two general comments from the Human Rights Committee that have sought to offer clarification on how this article is to be interpreted.[17] Inevitably, the salience of this article has become relevant in the context of refugee and

[17] See General Comment 15 and General Comment 28.

asylum issues, and has also come to the fore more in the context of expulsions on the grounds of alleged 'national security' interests in the aftermath of September 11th.

In many ways the key procedural article in the Covenant is the notion of fair trial as articulated in the text of Article 14 of the Covenant. There are several important dimensions to this article including the question as to what could be considered a 'suit at law', the principle of equality before the courts, the issues of access to the court, the characteristics of the court in question as well as the elements that need to be in place for a trial to be considered free and fair. The article also stresses some fundamental rules of criminal justice as they have evolved over the centuries such as rules concerning the presumption of innocence, against compulsory self-incrimination and double jeopardy. This is arguably the civil right in international human rights law over which there has been the most discussion, with several cases in various forms at national and international tribunals. The Human Rights Committee itself has entertained a range of cases concerning a whole set of different issues related to the right to a fair trial.[18] Article 15 of the Covenant also builds on the edifice of procedural rights contained in the Covenant by seeking guarantees over the determination of guilt based on the passage of retrospective criminal laws. The article is based on the long standing principles in criminal law of *nullum crimen sine lege* (no crime without its prior existence in law) and *nulla poena sine lege* (no punishment without its prior existence in law) and can be considered a fundamental principle to the guarantee of a system of law that is fair and not open to abuse.

3.4. *Fundamental Freedoms*

Prior to the United Nations regime of human rights, then President of the United States of America Franklin D Roosevelt made a famous speech that is referred to as the 'Four Freedoms Speech'. Delivered to the USA Congress in the context of the Annual State of the Union Address in January of 1941, Roosevelt is accredited with articulating four freedoms that have since become a cornerstone within international human rights law. The four freedoms were identified as the freedom of speech and expression, freedom of belief, freedom from want and freedom from fear. His speech set against the stark backdrop of the World War Two prophesized:

> That is no vision of a distant millennium. It is a definite basis for a kind of world attainable in our own time and generation. That kind of world is the very antith-

[18] For a list of the relevant cases grouped under theme see Joseph, Schultz, and Castan, *The International Covenant on Civil and Political Rights*, 389–461.

> esis of the so-called new order of tyranny which the dictators seek to create with the crash of a bomb.[19]

The prophecy was remarkable for several reasons, most importantly because it articulated an early vision of human rights that was indivisible, and secondly because of the importance it placed on the development of such a system of guarantees, as a bulwark against tyranny by force. The history of human rights reflects how this vision was brought to bear on the creation of the human rights regime, through the personal mission and leadership of First Lady Eleanor Roosevelt in the context of the framing of the Universal Declaration of Human Rights in 1948. The subsequent erosion of rights by the more contemporary regimes of the United States of America bears sad testimony of how rights can be defeated even in countries with a relatively high level of freedom.

In the context of civil and political rights the freedoms articulated in the Covenant include the freedom of movement (Article 12), the right to privacy (or the freedom from interference in issues within the private realm, Article 17), the freedom of thought, conscience and religion (Article 18), the freedom of expression (Articles 19 and 20) and the freedoms of assembly and association (Articles 21 and 22). While these freedoms are vital to the creation of a society that respects human dignity and worth, they have been eroded with a degree of regularity by States around the world. It sometimes appears that these freedoms are, in practice, very much third in terms of the human rights priorities of States i.e. behind the norms of *jus cogens* that have to be obeyed and behind the procedural rights that are considered clear indicators of human rights violations. By contrast the freedoms are rights that are derogable: i.e. it is possible to suspend them at times of emergency, albeit only to the strict extent necessary. This discussion has come to the fore in the context of events in the aftermath of September the 11th when in the name of anti-terror legislation States have placed severe restrictions of many of the freedoms, often differentiating the freedoms of one individual as against that of another on the basis of their ethnicity or religion. The text of these articles makes it clear that limitations can be placed on them, usually, of those…

> …provided by law, are necessary to protect national security, public order (*ordre public*), public health or morals or the rights and freedoms of others, and are consistent with the other rights recognised in the present Covenant.[20]

There is a lack of consensus in terms of what the freedoms may constitute and the extent to which the State needs to intervene to protect them or to protect

[19] Franklin D. Roosevelt, *State of the Union Address*, 6 January 1941.

[20] See e.g. Article 12(3). Also see Articles 18(3), 19(3), 21 and 22(2) of the International Covenant on Civil and Political Rights, 1966.

exercise of them from affecting other rights. Thus the question of the freedom of expression has instigated debates of the extent to which insulting or hate speech could be tolerated, and in the context of the right to privacy, over the extent to which violations that occur in private such as genital mutilation, wife-battery or child abuse should merit State intervention. The freedom of religion has generated important questions as to the extent to which the rights of certain groups (often women, children or lower 'castes' or professions) within the religion can be violated in the name of religious belief, and in terms of the freedom of association as to the extent to which proscribed groups, be they terrorist or supremacist or racist groups can be allowed to form and associate in the public realm.

While the text of the articles make it clear that the rights are not absolute, the extent to which they have been violated, especially in the context of States' battles against 'terrorists' has led to serious questions about how close the international community is to realizing Roosevelt's dream. Indeed the last decade has shown that rather than terror itself it is often the draconian response of States, to the potential use of terror that has caused serious human rights violation, leading to what some commentators have called a culture of 'fear'. It is clear that the freedom to live one's life in security, without the threat of terrorism is fundamental to human rights: but when the quest for the realization of this 'right' begins to target and impinge unduly on the other freedoms it is time to question the impact of these measures on civil and political rights. This process of questioning has been underway in several of the highest domestic courts led by activists and lawyers who are determined that the freedoms won through human rights law over centuries of struggle will not be surrendered to the State in the name of what it might label a 'war' against terror. After all, one of Roosevelt's freedoms articulated above was the freedom from fear: and fear is generated just as easily by excessive and arbitrary State interference as it is through the actions of terrorist groups.

3.5. *Protection of Individuals belong to Identifiable Groups*

The final category of civil and political rights articulated in the Covenant could be classified under the heading of the rights of individuals who belong to certain identified groupings. There has long been a debate in human rights law as to the extent to which human rights are 'individual' or 'collective'. Many have argued that 'collective' rights may be more appropriate, but even among those that agree with this notion it has been difficult to frame a collective right in such a manner that it would allow an individual to opt out. The failure to guarantee such an exit to an individual would be to condemn them to potential violation of their rights by the group to which they belong, going against the fundamental promise of human rights guaranteeing the dignity and worth of every individual.

Against this there has historically been recognition in public international law of the vulnerability of certain groups, prime among these of 'national' minorities, women and children. International society has made various attempts to seek to protect the rights (usually civil and political) of such groups. In the Covenant itself such rights are manifest in Article 23 (protection of the family), Article 24 (protection of children), Article 25 (rights of political participation) and Article 27 (rights of minorities). While 'women' as a group have not been identified with specific rights, the general non-discrimination provision on the basis of gender contained in Article 3, emphasizes the importance in guaranteeing all the rights contained in the Covenant to all women on par with men.

The protection for the rights of the family and the rights of minorities as civil and political rights transcends the traditional debate of individual versus collective rights. The language of the Covenant makes it clear that the rights contained accrue to the individual on the basis of their membership of a particular named group. Thus the rights contained remain individual rights to be accessed individually rather than collectively. There is significant jurisprudence before the Human Rights Committee over the rights of minorities, though in the main the more successful arguments that have been put forward have been in the context of groups that are 'indigenous' rather than minorities.[21] The intersection of the rights of minorities with the claim for self-determination, as enshrined in Article 1 has also been the cause of some controversy. In this context the Human Rights Committee clearly posits that the right to self-determination in the external, political sense is not a right that is available to minorities. It has nonetheless entertained the rights of indigenous peoples as to what can be called 'subsistence' rights.[22]

The one political right of minorities that can be considered of fundamental importance is contained in Article 25: *vis-à-vis* political participation. While the text of Article 25 is general it could be argued that this important right provides a key to ensuring that minority voices are effectively articulated within the public sphere. It is for this reason that Article 25 has been grouped with collective rights.

The protection of the rights of children is framed in general terms by Article 24, but like in the case of women's rights, it has also been the subject of a separate regime, namely the Convention on the Rights of the Child. There is some debate over the extent to which the rights of children can be considered 'civil and political' rights since they would tend toward guarantees of freedoms and

---

[21] For the distinction between 'minorities' and indigenous peoples' see Working Paper on the Relationship & Distinction between the Rights of Persons Belonging to Minorities & Those of Indigenous Peoples' UN Doc. E/CN.4/Sub.2/2000/10.

[22] Joshua Castellino and Jérémie Gilbert, "Self-determination, Indigenous Peoples and Minorities," *Macquarie Law Journal* Special Issue: Self-determination 3 (2003): 155–78.

provision of socio-economic conditions in which the child might thrive. The Convention on the Rights of the Child however, in identifying four founding principles to that Convention has shown the importance to be placed on the civil and political rights dimension of children. The four cornerstone principles under the Convention on the Rights of the Child are identified as being the principle of non-discrimination (Article 2), the principle of ensuring the best interest of the child (Article 3), the importance of the life, survival and development of the child (Article 6) and the respect for the views of the child (Article 12).[23] In addition there have also been two additional protocols that have been appended to the Convention covering the area of the sale of children and child pornography and the specific context of children in armed conflict especially those forced into child soldiery.

Overall it could be argued that the fundamental conceptual difficulties that impacted the development of collective civil and political rights have been overcome. There still remain questions of the extent to which the rights of individuals belonging to groups can be protected against the collective will of the group, but by and large it would appear that courts and tribunals over the world have been unafraid to interpret these against existing human rights principles such as non-discrimination.

4. *Future Challenges*

The resurgence of the view that human rights are indivisible may be seen by some as downplaying the importance of civil and political rights and giving credence to socio-economic and cultural rights. However to see the resolution of that debate in such negative terms would be to reiterate the debate in the human rights community that, it could be argued, has hindered the overall efficacy of the regime since 1966. It is clear that for the human rights regime to be cogent, civil and political rights need to be enshrined and guaranteed alongside economic, social and cultural rights. Many cultural relativists have argued that socio-economic rights are more important than civil and political rights. This argument is usually encapsulated in slogans such as 'You can't eat the right to vote' to justify the emphasis on socio-economic rights rather than civil and political rights. It is important to stress that this debate can only be resolved in one way: to stress the unity and indivisibility of all human rights, without a hierarchy of one type of rights over the other. It is only when all the

[23] For more on child rights see Sharon A. Detrick, *A Commentary on the United Nations Convention on the Rights of the Child* (The Hague: Martinus Nijhoff Publishers, 1999).

human rights can be guaranteed in unison to every human being that international society will be anywhere near the dream of human rights that was so effectively articulated by Roosevelt and then translated into an international vision in the Universal Declaration of Human Rights. Having finally seen the resurgence of socio-economic rights the challenge would now be to strengthen the extent to which the rights can be considered in a more harmonious and mutually symbiotic relationship.

In terms of civil and political rights there has been significant progress made in terms of the codification of the rights themselves. Laws, at international and national level, make the dimensions of the fundamental civil and political rights clear, and also explain the extent to which they may be derogable. However as we have seen in the aftermath of the events of September 11th clear-cut consensus on the contours of the rights has not in and of itself been enough to ensure their potency in guaranteeing protection. In the context of fighting terrorism, many rights including that of torture, that had hitherto been considered resolved issues, suddenly came under attack. While the response of the human rights community has been to reinforce the importance of these rights, the manner in which it was possible to abrogate them suggests that no rights are as strong as they ought to be. The challenge going forward has to focus on the extent to which these rights are reaffirmed and strengthened against challenge.

A second challenge that has been identified in terms of civil and political rights is to shore up the extent to which the fundamental freedoms can be abrogated. As we have seen above, these have come under some pressure in the context of the law enforcement battle against terror networks, but there are also important questions that need to be asked and answered about the extent to which the freedoms sit alongside some of other rights: especially in the context of where the freedoms may conflict with some of the rights. Human rights regimes need to guarantee the rights of different cultures, but it is equally clear that particularly manifestations of cultures is leading to a violation of important human rights. The question of the interpretation of religion (rather than religion itself) lies at an important junction of this debate, and while the international community clearly cannot prescribe or interpret religious rights, on occasion the manifestation of religion has begun to have a negative impact on human rights. Handling this issue in a manner that is sensitive and respectful, but that does not compromise on human rights values would be a key element to the future success at creation a regime that guarantees the rights of all.

Without a doubt the biggest challenge in terms of civil and political rights, but arguably also in terms of socio-economic rights, lies in ensuring wide implementation and monitoring. It could be argued that the phase of 'codification' of rights must be brought to a close, with a greater emphasis on implementation i.e. the manner in which States put the rights agreed into practice within their domestic jurisdiction. This step is crucial in being able to realize an effective bulwark of protection: without this human rights are reduced to mere statements of intent since the international standards, while binding upon States, are difficult to enforce. Needless to say the mechanisms for the monitoring of the extent to which States fulfil their human rights obligations is also important. There has been a debate raising in the context of the politics of human rights at international level as to whether the process of 'naming and shaming' can yield effective dividend. This process of 'naming and shaming' is all that is available by way of sanctions in the human rights world. Thus the only way in which recalcitrant States can be encouraged to implement human rights within their jurisdictions is under the threat of international embarrassment that accompanies 'naming and shaming'. However many States have been arguing for sometime that this process is an undue infringement of State sovereignty and that the human rights agenda should instead be pursued through 'technical cooperation' and knowledge transfers.

While there is some merit to the suggestion that States need actual help: monetary, technological and intellectual, in overcoming the hurdles that exist to an effective human rights system, to suggest that the little pressure that may be exerted at the moment ought not to be, would be to provide States with undue protection from censure which is not warranted. The reiteration of the indivisibility of rights has made an important contribution in removing the key ideological distinctions that had previously provided agnostic States with the opportunity to label the human rights agenda as western and to opt out of its mechanisms on the grounds that they were too focussed on civil and political rights and not on the immediate pressing concerns that were faced in some of these States. It is now important for the international community to reiterate the importance of human rights at the highest level and to do so by addressing criticism to every State that violates human rights whether the most powerful or the weakest. With some key ideological battles won, with the important achievement of reiterating human rights in the face of security threat overcome, the future of human rights would undoubtedly lie in convincing all States of how the implementation of human rights for every citizen, lies in their best interests. When States overstep the mark it is of utmost importance that the international community unites to criticize the State and insist that they uphold the consensual values. Thus there has to be consistency in criticizing the United States of America and focussing on it adhering to human rights values as much as there needs to be a focus on Sudan and its rights violations. After all, a Sudanese life is worth just as much as an American, Afghani or Iraqi life, with the same inherent dignity.

Bibliography

Anaya, S. James. *Indigenous Peoples in International Law*. Oxford: Oxford University Press, 2004.

Cassese, Antonio. *Self-determination of Peoples: A Legal Reappraisal*. Oxford: Oxford University Press, 1995.

Castellino, Joshua. *International Law & Self-Determination: The Interplay of Politics of Territorial Possession with Formulations of National Identity*. The Hague: Martinus Nijhoff Publishers, 2000.

Castellino, Joshua, and Jérémie Gilbert. "Self-determination, Indigenous Peoples and Minorities." *Macquarie Law Journal* Special Issue: Self-determination 3 (2003): 155–78.

Crawford, James. *The Rights of Peoples*. Cambridge: Cambridge University Press, 1995.

Detrick, Sharon A. *A Commentary on the United Nations Convention on the Rights of the Child*. The Hague: Martinus Nijhoff Publishers, 1999.

Gearty, Connor. *Civil Liberties*. Oxford: Oxford University Press, 2001.

Hannum, Hurst. *Autonomy, Sovereignty & Self-determination: The Accommodation of Conflicting Rights*. Philadelphia: University of Pennsylvania Press, 1990.

Joseph, Sarah, Jenny Schultz, and Melissa Castan. *The International Covenant on Civil and Political Rights; Cases, Materials and Commentary*. Oxford: Oxford University Press, 2005.

McGoldrick, Dominic. *The Human Rights Committee: Its Role in the Development of the International Covenant on Civil and Political Rights*. Oxford: Oxford University Press, 1991.

Morsink., Johannes. *The Universal Declaration of Human Rights: Origins, Drafting and Intent*. Philadelphia: University of Pennsylvania Press, 1999.

Oraa, Jaime. *Human Rights in States of Emergency in Public International Law*. Oxford: Oxford University Press, 1990.

Steiner, Henry, and Philip Alston. *Human Rights in Context*. Oxford: Oxford University Press, 2007.

Thomas, Daniel M. *The Helsinki Effect: International Norms, Human Rights, and the Demise of Communism*. Princeton, New Jersey: Princeton University Press, 2001.

Zimmermann, Patricia R. *States of Emergency: Documentaries, Wars, Democracies*. Minneapolis: University of Minnesota Press, 2007.

Documents

General Assembly Resolution 1541 (XV)
General Comment 15 and General Comment 28
UN Doc. E/CN.4/Sub.2/2000/10.

Website

http://www.bayefsky.com/./html/ccpr_opt_ratif_table.php

Legal Instruments

Convention for the Elimination of All Forms of Discrimination Against Women, 1979
Convention on the Prevention and Punishment of the Crime of Genocide, 1948
Convention on the Prohibition of All Forms of Torture, Cruel or inhuman degrading Treatment or Punishment, 1984
Convention on the Rights of the Child, 1989

Chapter Three

An Introduction to Economic, Social and Cultural Rights: Overcoming the Constraints of Categorization through Implementation

*Vinodh Jaichand**

1. *Introduction*

On 10 December 2008, the United Nations General Assembly adopted by consensus the Optional Protocol to the International Covenant on Economic, Social and Cultural Rights, paving the way for individual complaints of economic, social and cultural rights against States Parties. It now seems to be an appropriate time to reflect on why it has taken so long for these developments to occur. The Protocol will open for ratification by States Parties on 24 September 2009. Before any high expectations are placed on the Optional Protocol for the delivery of better implementation of economic, social and cultural rights, there is a need to temper that expectation with reference to some realities of the past. At the same time there is tremendous optimism that economic, social and cultural rights obligations can no longer be ignored or wished away by many States.

I make this contribution with a modest objective, as a mere introduction of the subject to international human rights law because the study of economic, social and cultural rights is now very wide with a strong focus on a number of substantive areas which have, because of space constraints, been omitted. The growth in research and study of this area is vast. The objective I have alluded to above is directed as a retrospect and a prospect of these rights. The historical context of the development of human rights law is where I begin because that explains the block or hesitancy in the practice of many States, in the hope that jurisprudence and practice from others parts of the world will fire the enthusiasm for domestic law reform. My explanation of the content and implementation of economic, social and cultural rights is cursory and brief. Any longer indulgence on my part would have unduly lengthened this contribution. For similar reasons, the discussion on regional systems of protection of economic, social and cultural rights has been directed to the only example where the dichotomy between civil and political rights and economic, social and cultural rights does not exist. The discussion on the domestic enforcement through justiciability is also skewed in favour of the cases from States which have begun to protect economic, social and cultural rights. Here too the range is not wide but extends to two countries' experiences.

I have taken essentially a chronological approach from the international to the domestic with a view to illustrate how an initial false categorization has been utilized to create tiers in the protection of human rights. Further reliance on that categorization is detrimental to the rights of the majority of the world's population.[1]

2. *Historical Developments*

There are a number of States who, despite ratifying the International Covenant on Economic, Social and Cultural Rights,[2] do not treat the rights contained therein as real human rights but rights to be realized. To understand why there is a neglect of this obligation and a relegation of these rights, an examination of the historical development of human rights provides a few markers. While the Cold War had a role to play in the development of social, economic and cultural rights it was Franklin D. Roosevelt who in 1941 articulated the Four Freedoms[3] in which the freedom from want was one which, "translated into universal terms, means economic understandings which will secure to every nation a healthy peacetime life for its inhabitants-everywhere in the world."[4]

No doubt that freedom found its way to the United Nations Commission on Human Rights which was originally tasked with the duty in 1947, in parallel with the drafting of the Universal Declaration of Human Rights (hereinafter UDHR), to draft the international Covenant. This Covenant and the Declaration were to be presented to the United Nations General Assembly simultaneously.[5] However, the polarization of the world over the Cold War had a

---

* Dr Vinodh Jaichand is Deputy-Director at the Irish Centre for Human Rights at the National University of Ireland, Galway, Ireland. My thanks go to Dr S. Darcy for his useful comments.

1 Henry J. Steiner, Philip Alston, and Ryan Goodman, "Economic and Social Rights," in *International Human Rights in Context*, ed. Henry J. Steiner, Philip Alston, and Ryan Goodman (New York: Oxford University Press. 2008), 262–72.

2 Opened for signature, ratification and accession on 16 December 1966, entered into force 3 January 1976, 993 UNTS 3, http://www2.ohchr.org/english/law/cesr.htm

3 The others were the freedom of speech, the freedom from fear and the freedom of faith.

4 Annual Message to Congress, 6 January 1941.

5 Mashood A. Baderin and Robert McCorquodale, "The International Covenant on Economic, Social and Cultural Rights: Forty Years of Development," in *Economic, Social and Cultural*

major influence. It resulted in the drafting of the Covenant being difficult as the United Nations Commission on Human Rights prepared a text that paralleled the UDHR. In 1952 the General Assembly instructed the Commission on Human Rights to prepare two covenants as they gave in to the pressure of the western liberal Member States of the United Nations.[6] The result was that the human rights provisions were bifurcated into the International Covenant on Civil and Political Rights (hereinafter ICCPR) and the International Covenant on Economic, Social and Cultural Rights (hereinafter ICESCR), even though the original intention was to have a single one. These two Covenants and the UDHR are often referred to as the International Bill of Rights.

The lengthy drafting and ratifying processes are indicative of the reluctance of States to permit their sovereign powers to be curtailed by human rights obligations. The Human Rights Commission submitted the two draft Covenants to the United Nations General Assembly in 1954. The Third Committee took more than a decade to review these draft texts and the final versions were adopted by the General Assembly in 1966, 19 years after drafting had begun. It was another decade before the Covenants come into force in 1976. The whole process of establishing the International Bill of Rights lasted nearly 30 years in total before completion. In addition, it took another 33 years to afford State Parties the opportunity to ratify an optional protocol which permits individual complaints to be submitted for adjudication at the international level.

Apart from the time taken in the process of drafting the content of the International Bill of Rights, the comparisons between the two Covenants have led to a steady drift over the years in the full understanding of the protection of all human rights.[7] Civil and political rights have been unfortunately referred to as the 'first generation' of human rights while economic, social and cultural rights are the so-called 'second generation'. The so-called 'third generation' refers to collective rights such as the right to development. This nomenclature is unfortunate because it has the effect of prioritizing rights, one right over the other and which is detrimental to all human rights. The language has been attributed

---

Rights in Action, ed. Mashood A. Baderin, and Robert McCorquodale (Oxford: Oxford University Press, 2007), 4.

6 Asbjorn Eide and Allan Rosas, "Economic, Social and Cultural Rights: A Universal Challenge," in *Social, Economic and Cultural Rights*, ed. Asbjorn Eide, Catarina Krause, and Allan Rosas (Netherlands: Kluwer Law International, 2001), 3. See also Baderin and McCorquodale, "The International Covenant on Economic, Social and Cultural Rights," 6.

7 Scott Leckie, "Another Step Toward Indivisibility: Identifying the Key Features of Violations of Economic, Social and Cultural Rights," *Human Rights Quarterly* 20, no. 1 (1998): 81–124 quotes Richard Falk's belief that the deliberate refusal to attend to the basic human needs amounted to type of "severe human rights violation" but that this refusal was not generally accepted as a violation of human rights by many, at 86.

to Karel Vasak and two commentators have been critical of these conclusions when they analyzed the history of human rights:

> The history of the evolution of human rights at the national level does not make it possible to place the emergence of different human rights into clear-cut stages. Efforts to do so would in any case make it necessary to distinguish also between civil and political rights, since the political rights were accepted as human rights much later than some of the civil rights, in some countries even later than economic and social rights.[8]

The Vasak classification, albeit useful in an abstract academic way of categorization, also contains an inaccurate reflection of the historical development of international human rights in which the original intention was to have one Covenant support one universal Declaration as early as 1947. To be fair to Karel Vasak, the 'generations' language was latched onto by the States looking for neat classifications which justified their lack of protection of all human rights for all persons, thereby continuing a phoney battle over a war that has since long ceased. In 1993 the Vienna Declaration and Programme of Action sought to correct this misperception by restating the original intent that "all human rights are universal, indivisible and interdependent and interrelated."[9] Any discussion of human rights, of necessity, draws us into comparisons between the ICCPR and ICESCR to illustrate the rightful location of economic, social and cultural rights.[10]

3. *Similarities and Differences in Content of ICCPR and ICESCR*

The two international Covenants do indeed have similarities and differences in the language which purports protection. Both have exactly the same language in the first paragraph of the first articles[11] which recognizes the right to self-determination. But Article 2, paragraph 1 is patently different where the ICCPR obliges each State Party "to respect and to ensure…the rights" in the Covenant[12] while the ICESCR permits State Parties "…to take steps…to

[8] Eide and Rosas, "Economic, Social and Cultural Rights," 4.

[9] World Conference on Human Rights: Vienna Declaration and Programme of Action, UN doc. A/CONF.157/23, Part I, paragraph 5.

[10] See Craig Scott, "Reaching Beyond (Without Abandoning) the Category of 'Economic, Social and Cultural Rights,'" *Human Rights Quarterly* 21, no. 3 (1999): 633–60 where he 'argues for the return of the original purpose of the UDHR…'

[11] 1. All peoples have the right to self-determination. By virtue of that right they freely determine their political status and freely pursue their economic, social and cultural development.

[12] 2.1 Each State Party to the present Covenant undertakes to respect and to ensure to all individuals within its territory and subject to its jurisdiction the rights recognised in the present

the maximum of its available resources...to achieve progressively...the full realisation of the rights..."[13] There is little equivocation in the ICCPR protection while the ICESCR permits progressive realization dependent on state resources. Indeed, the normative language of the ICESCR norms is wide and presents challenges when there is an attempt to implement them as legal principles.[14] While the Committee on Economic, Social and Cultural Rights have clarified that State Parties may not rely on the lack of funds as an excuse for doing nothing to protect economic, social and cultural rights, most States take the approach that these are not really rights as they not justiciable. This feeds into the contention that these are so-called 'second generation' rights. The question of justiciability will be addressed below.

One argument for non-justiciability is based on the doctrine of the separation of powers in a democratic State where the courts are not empowered to encroach into the legislative arena which makes policy for the State. In this line of argument, where a court of law decides which policy is more appropriate or how much more money should be allocated to a state programme, that would violate the separation of powers doctrine it is said.[15] According to this reasoning, the court is ill-suited, and perhaps not trained, to perform this function.[16] The argument continues that courts are better suited to protect civil and political rights where States have a negative duty like permitting the freedom of speech or the right to demonstrate. In any case, the democratically elected persons in the legislature are responsible for state policy, not the judges who are appointed to their positions, the proponents hold. In an economic, social and cultural right the State has a positive duty to act and such action is likely to be costly.

In addressing these lines of argument, it is important to note that the State has some duty to act positively, and not always negatively, in civil and political cases when it protects the right of a detained person, for example. In such

---

Covenant, without distinction of any kind, such as race, colour, sex, language, religion, political or other opinion, national or social origin, property, birth or other status.

[13] 2.1 Each State Party to the present Covenant undertakes to take steps, individually and through international assistance and co-operation especially economic and technical, to the maximum of its available resources, with a view to achieving progressively the full realisation of the rights recognised in the present Covenant by all appropriate means, including particularly the adoption of legislative measures.

[14] As Professor Hunt has already pointed out, the language of certain ICCPR rights, for example freedom from torture, is also inexact and subject to interpretation.

[15] See Kevin Hopkins, "Shattering the divide-when judges go too far," http://www.derebus.org.za/archives/2002Mar/articles/dicide.htm; Craig M. Scott and Patrick Macklem, "Constitutional Ropes of Sand or Justiciable Guarantees? Social Rights in a New South African Constitution," *University of Pennsylvania Law Review* 141 (1992): 1–148.

[16] See the Comments of the former Minister of Justice of Ireland in footnote 18 below.

cases the court may dictate to the State to spend money to permit the convicted person to access newspapers or books while she is imprisoned. Indeed, all of the administration of justice costs money because they amount to necessary expenditure because that is deemed to be a feature of a democratic state. When the Supreme Court of the United States of America ordered that its judgment in *Brown* v. *Board of Education of Topeka*[17] be enforced, the 101st Airborne Division from Fort Campbell, Kentucky was deployed to Arkansas. Does this expenditure amount to the court "meddling" in the business of another branch of government?

On the issue of the competence of the judges,[18] there are many instances where the lack of knowledge on substantive issue before the court are attended to by the presence of expert witnesses, from finance to space technology, and that does not handicap the administration of justice. The function of courts is dispute resolution and disputes around economic, social and cultural rights should not be exempt from adjudication simply because the issue before a court does not form part of the syllabus for the training of a judge.

To leave economic, social and cultural disputes to democratic self-correction, as we do when we vote out the government we dislike at the end of a four or five year terms under our political rights, is to relegate the plight of the disadvantaged, marginalized and vulnerable as being trivial and not as relevant. These rights also have urgencies which demand that they be attended to in a timely manner. Finally, on the question of elections as part of representative democracy, many States do not elect their judges but follow a set appointments procedure, it is true. Whatever the nature of that appointment procedure, once completed it attributes legitimacy to judges. The political representative and the judge each have different competencies but both are public servants, albeit one is more independent than the other. Each has a different role, however appointed, and if those elected fail to take appropriate action, the dispute resolution system envisaged through the courts may be used to break the deadlock.

[17] 347 US 483.

[18] In a speech by the former Minister for Justice, Equality and Law Reform, Mr Michael Mc Dowell on 5 April 2003 the Minister said the following on justiciability:

> ...If the judiciary arrogate to themselves, or have arrogated to them, the resolution of social and economic issues, then the democratic process is usurped, as is the legislature and the executive. One must also consider the fact that they are not examined as to the content of their social and economic opinions when appointed, judges who then trespass on the proper sphere of the legislature or the executive do so without a mandate. It is a trespass on the entitlement of the people, in the last analysis, to determine social and economic issues in accordance with their view of the common good as expressed through the ballot box.

It must be conceded that active economic, social and cultural rights protection will cost more money because so small a percentage is being spent currently on them by so many State Parties to the ICESCR. In some cases there are many people to whom that right might have to be granted. The current priority or urgency may not be present to deal with this in the public interest. When they are mooted by civil society organizations in those States for example, the spectre of higher taxes is raised. Yet recent examples of the usage of tax payer's funds to shore up reckless private corporations financially indicate that where there is the political will,[19] State Parties will use all the tax-payers resources to justify public interest, yet continue to ignore basic economic, social and cultural rights. A full discussion of these types of action is outside my brief.

There is a further point of difference between the protections of rights in the international Covenants. Derogations from obligation are permissible under certain circumstances in time of emergency which might threaten the existence of the State under the ICCPR in Article 4. This clearly recognizes the need to suspend some rights under special circumstances as a reality that the State Party might find itself. Whatever the circumstances might be, derogations from the obligations of ICESCR are not permitted as there is no comparable provision in the ICESCR. Put in another way: all economic, social and cultural rights are always protected in all circumstances. Therefore the requirement to protect rights in the ICESCR, in this respect, is much higher one might argue.

A cursory look at the substantive rights in ICESCR is necessary. There are overlapping provisions in both the ICCPR and ICESCR. Both Covenants deal with trade union rights (ICCPR Article 22 and ICESCR Article 7). In addition the International Labour Organization also provides for protection of a number of rights related to work and conditions of work under cultural rights, schools for ethnic minorities are protected in both (ICCPR Articles 18, paragraph 4 and 27 and ICESCR Article 26). Under Article 6 of the ICCPR, according to a more liberal interpretation of the right to life, such a right includes a minimum level of subsistence which entails engaging rights protected under the ICESCR. It is worth noting that the Convention of the Rights of the Child (CRC), now with 193 States Parties, provides for the protection of civil and political, and economic, social and cultural rights in the same document. Also the International Convention on the Elimination of All Forms of Discrimination against Women, with 186 States Parties, makes a similar contribution in protecting economic, social and cultural rights.

[19] The provision of billions of dollars to support ailing banks in the United States of America, Britain, Ireland, Iceland, Germany and France in September 2009 as a result of the over-priced housing market is one example. Similar assistance was provided to AIG, a multinational insurance corporation in the United States of America.

A summary of the main differences between the protections in both Covenants is that, it is said, the ICCPR norms create respect for these rights usually under sanction of the law. They are sometimes described as 'absolute' or immediate. They are justiciable in the courts of State Parties and as they are negative rights, they do not cost much, it is articulated. A significant feature of the ICCPR is that the Optional Protocol permitting individual complaints from States Parties was opened for signature some 43 years ago and came into force 33 years ago.

On the other hand, the differences between the covenants include the rights protected under ICESCR are to be fulfilled through a gradual realization over a period of time. The justification continues that these are not really rights but are more political or social objectives and therefore are not justiciable. They are likely to be more costly as positive obligations on the State and are best left to charity or welfare organizations who are specialists in dealing with these issues. In this instance, the State may well provide some funds to such organizations to front the provision of that service, as an act of generosity, they might add.

4. *The Norms and Enforcement*

A schematic summary of the International Bill of Rights that protect economic, social and cultural rights appears as below, where the article is listed after the abbreviation for the international instrument:[20]

4.1. Economic Rights
- Right to property: UDHR 17– **not** in ICCPR **or** in ICESCR
- Right to work: UDHR 23, ICESCR 6
- Right to social security: UDHR 23.3 & 25, ICESCR 9, CRC 26

4.2. Social Rights
- Adequate standard of living: UDHR 25, ICESCR 11, CRC 27
- Rights of families to assistance: ICESCR 10, CRC 27

4.3. Cultural Rights
- Right to education: UDHR 26, ICESCR 13 & 16, CRC 28 & 29
- Right to preserve cultural identity of minority groups: CRC 30, ICCPR 27
- Right to take part in cultural life: UDHR 27, ICESCR 15.1a
- Right to benefit from scientific progress: ICESCR 15.1b
- Right to benefit from moral and material interest: ICESCR 15.1c

The oversight function of both the ICCPR and ICESCR are left to committees. States Parties to the ICESCR submit reports to a monitoring body every

[20] Asbjorn Eide, "Economic, Social and Cultural Rights As Human Rights," in *Social, Economic and Cultural Rights*, ed. Eide, Krause, and Rosas, 11.

five years.[21] While originally States Parties under the ICESCR did not report to such a committee, but to the United Nation Economic and Social Council, this was changed. In the understanding of many of the Soviet states, who drove the drafting process of the ICESCR, implementation of the rights would take place with minimal international interference.[22] In the State reports both committees for the ICESCR and ICCPR rely on "naming and shaming" as a device to correct deficiencies in state practice. The Committee on Economic, Social and Cultural Rights has issued reporting guidelines to assist States, conducts on-site visits, engages in constructive dialogue with States Parties and issues concluding observations. Many of the States Parties have been unwilling to co-operate with the Committee on the constructive dialogue and by May 1996, there were 97 overdue reports from 88 States and 17 States had failed to submit a single report in 10 years.[23] The articulations of the monitoring body of ICESCR[24] on broader issues relating to all States parties are seen as authoritative interpretations of the Covenant as States Parties account for their progress before them.[25]

For example, the nature of State Parties obligations have been addressed in General Comment 3 which dealt with the implementation of the rights under Article 2 of ICESCR. There is the obligation of conduct by the State Party which means that the State Party guarantees that the rights will be exercised without discrimination. Also there is an obligation of result in which the State Party is committed to take action within a reasonably short time in which the steps are deliberate, concrete and targeted towards meeting the obligation. To

---

[21] Matthew Craven, "The UN Committee on Economic, Social and Cultural Rights," in *Social, Economic and Cultural Rights*, ed. Eide, Krause, and Rosas, 457.

[22] Ibid., 455.

[23] Ibid., 464.

[24] They sometimes take the form of General Comments, but usually there are state reports also. General Comments by the Committee have been issued on: Reporting by States Parties; International technical assistance measures (Art. 22); The nature of States parties' obligations (Art. 2(1)); The right to adequate housing; The economic, social and cultural rights of older persons; The right to adequate housing: forced evictions (Art. 11(1)); The relationship between economic sanctions and respect for economic, social and cultural rights; The domestic application of the Covenant; Persons with disabilities; The role of national human rights institutions in the protection of economic, social and cultural rights; Plans of action for primary education (Art. 14); The right to adequate food (Art. 11); The right to education (Art. 13); The right to the highest attainable standard of health (Art. 12); The right to water (Arts. 11 and 12); The equal right of men and women to the enjoyment of all economic, social and cultural rights (Art. 3); The right of everyone to benefit from the protection of the moral and material interests resulting from any scientific, literary or artistic production of which he is the author (Art. 15(1)(c)); The Right to work (Art. 6); and the right to social security.

[25] See also Allan Rosas and Martin Scheinin, "Implementation Mechanisms and Remedies," in *Social, Economic and Cultural Rights*, ed. Eide, Krause, and Rosas, 425–53.

satisfy the obligation to take steps all appropriate measures are expected to be taken including legislative action. The Committee drew the attention of States Parties to the fact that the obligation under the Covenant is not confined to the respect of human rights, but that States Parties have also undertaken to ensure the enjoyment of these rights to all individuals under their jurisdiction.

5. *On Justiciability: An Example of the Protection of ESC Rights in a Region*

The regional protection of economic, social and cultural rights with civil and political rights in one convention is best illustrated in the example of the African Charter on Human and Peoples' Rights which is the youngest regional system and came into force in 1986.[26] In this document there is no bifurcation of rights into civil and political on the one hand and economic, social and cultural on the other. The right to dignity[27] is a cross-cutting right which make all rights inter-connected and seamless. There is also protection for groups such as "all peoples" and the family for example, that is collective rights, together with the rights of the individual. The African Commission on Human Rights, in exercising its interpretive role on the provisions of the African Charter,[28] has

[26] The European Convention on Human Rights was signed on 4 November 1950 and it came into force on 3 September 1953. The European Social Charter was signed in 1961 and may be described as aims for social policy for the European State Parties who would "make every effort in common to improve the standard of living and to promote the social well-being of both their urban and rural populations by means of appropriate institutions and actions." The Additional Protocol to the American Convention on Human Rights in the area of Economic, Social, and Cultural Rights (more commonly known as the "Protocol of San Salvador"), was opened for signature on 17 November 1988. It entered into force on 16 November 1999. Both the European and American Conventions followed the bifurcated rights path of Europe. For additional material on these areas, see Robin R. Churchill and Urfan Khaliq, "Violations of Economic, Social and Cultural Rights: The Current Use and Future Potential of the Collective Complaints Mechanism of the European Social Charter," 195–240; Colin Warbrick, "Economic and Social Interests and the European Convention on Human Rights," 241–56 and Veronica Gomez, "Economic, Social and Cultural Rights in the Inter-American System," in *Economic, Social and Cultural Rights in Action*, ed. Baderin and McCorquodale.

[27] Article 5.
Every individual shall have the right to the respect of the dignity inherent in a human being and to the recognition of his legal status. All forms of exploitation and degradation of man particularly slavery, slave trade, torture, cruel inhuman or degrading punishment and treatment shall be prohibited.

[28] For a fuller discussion on this topic see Mashood A. Baderin, "The African Commission on Human and Peoples' Rights and the Implementation of Economic, Social and Cultural Rights in Africa," in *Economic, Social and Cultural Rights in Action*, ed. Baderin and McCorquodale,

pronounced its clear intention to enforce all the rights contained in the African Charter including economic, social and cultural rights, as it expressed in the *Social and Economic Rights Action Center and the Center for Economic and Social Rights* v. *Nigeria*[29] case. The case arose from the environmental degradation as a result of the oil industry in Ogoniland granted by the President Abacha where the Commission said:

> The uniqueness of the African situation and the special qualities of the African Charter on Human and Peoples' Rights imposes upon the African Commission an important task. International law and human rights must be responsive to African circumstances. Clearly, collective rights, environmental rights, and economic and social rights are essential elements of human rights in Africa. The African Commission will apply any of the diverse rights contained in the African Charter. It welcomes this opportunity to make clear that there is no right in the African Charter that cannot be made effective. As indicated in the preceding paragraphs, however, the Nigerian Government did not live up to the minimum expectations of the African Charter.

When the African Court on Human and Peoples' Rights begins to hear cases in the not too distant future, it is likely that its judgments on these types of cases will be path-breaking given the wide range of rights protected by the African Charter.

6. *On Justiciability: Domestic Enforcement*

When the normative principles of the international protection of all human rights, including economic, social, and cultural rights, are included in the constitution of a country then the proponents of justiciability of economic social and cultural rights have an effective mechanism. Examples from two countries mainly are discussed here: one where there was constitutional space, another where the space for litigation was created. I will begin with the example of the South African experience.[30]

139–66 and Chidi Anselm Odinkalu, "Analysis of Paralysis or Paralysis by Analysis? Implementing Economic, Social and Cultural Rights Under the African Charter on Human and Peoples' Rights," *Human Rights Quarterly* 23, no. 2 (2001): 327–69.

[29] (27 May 2002), African Commission on Human and Peoples' Rights, Decision 155/96, Fifteenth Annual Activity Report of the African Commission on Human and Peoples' Rights, 2001–2002.

[30] Jeanne M. Woods, "Justiciable Social Rights as a Critique of the Liberal Paradigm," *Texas International Law Journal* 38, no. 4 (2003): 763–74, where she writes about the power of the language of rights which has arisen from struggles and that economic, social and cultural rights, through examples of cases in South Africa, will mirror that kind of struggle for human dignity by those who do not have.

Since South Africa became a constitutional state[31] it protects economic, social and cultural rights together with civil and political rights. The International Covenant on Economic, Social and Cultural Rights has been signed but South Africa is not yet one of the 160 State Parties.[32]

The approach of the Constitutional Court to the economic, social and cultural rights has been classified into three main categories by one commentator.[33] The first would be 'basic' rights unqualified by references to resource constraints or notions of progressive realization and would include children's socio-economic rights,[34] the right to basic education and the rights of the detained and prisoners' socio-economic rights. The second category includes 'access rights' or the right of everyone to have access to adequate housing, health care, food, water and social security. The duty of the State is limited to taking "reasonable legislative and other measures within its available resources, to achieve the progressive realisation of each of these rights." The third category imposes a prohibition on the State with regard to the right to shelter in that no eviction may be made without an order of court[35] and the right not to be refused emergency health care.

---

[31] The Interim Constitution of 1994 first made provision for this under Chapter 3, Fundamental Rights, which would "apply to all law in force and all administrative decisions taken and acts performed during the period of operation of this Constitution". Section 2 of the Constitution of the Republic of South Africa, Act 108 of 1996 (hereafter referred to as the 1996 Constitution) states that the "…Constitution is the supreme law of the Republic: law or conduct inconsistent with it is invalid, and the obligations imposed by it must be fulfilled."

[32] According to Christof Heyns and Frans Viljoen, "The Impact of the United Nations Human Rights Treaties on the Domestic Level," *Human Rights Quarterly* 23, no. 3 (2001): 495, this is "due to bureaucratic bungling, caused by the responsibility for the ratification being transferred from one department to another." As of October 2008, this has not been corrected through ratification.

[33] Sandra Liebenberg, "The Protection of Economic, Social and Cultural Rights in Domestic Legal Systems," in *Economic, Social and Cultural Rights*, ed. Eide, Krause, and Rosas, 61–62.

[34] In *Khosa* v. *Minister of Social Development*; *Mahlaule* v. *Minister of Social Development*, permanent residents in South Africa from Mozambique brought the application on behalf of their children, other affected persons, the class of permanent residents and in the public interest. They challenged sections of the Social Assistance Act 59 of 1992 which disqualify persons who are not South African citizens from receiving welfare grants. Justice Mogoro, for the majority of the Court, held that the exclusion of permanent residents was not a reasonable way to achieve the right to social security. The State had to find a less drastic method of reducing the risk of permanent residents on becoming a burden on the State than mere exclusion.

[35] In *Port Elizabeth Municipality* v. *Various Occupiers*, 2004 (12) BCLR 1268, a number of persons who were unlawfully occupying private land were evicted by the municipality. Justice Sach, in an appeal by the municipality, that for the Court to be persuaded that it was "just and equitable" to evict people from their homes, the State would have to show that serious consideration was given to the possibility of providing alternative accommodation to the occupiers.

The jurisprudence of the South African Constitutional Court with regard to social and economic rights has been set out initially in the well-known trio of "reasonableness review"[36] cases of *Soobramoney* v. *Minister of Health, KwaZulu-Natal*, 1998 (1) SA 765 (CC), *Government of the Republic of South Africa* v. *Grootboom*, 2001 SA 46 and *Minister of Health* v. *Treatment Action Campaign*, 2002 (5) SA 721 (CC).[37] The central issue that appears to preoccupy the Constitutional Court in these types of cases is whether the policy chosen by the organs of state can reasonably be expected to deliver the rights in question.

From a cautious start, with some deference paid to the executive and legislature in *Soobramoney*, the Constitutional Court became quickly aware of the framework of its inquiry into the reasonableness of state policy. As a result of limited funds being available for dialysis treatment, which the Constitutional Court found did not fall within the ambit of the "right to emergency treatment", Mr Soobramoney was denied the right to that treatment. It said:

> A court will be slow to interfere with rational decisions taken in good faith by the political organs and medical authorities whose responsibilities it is to deal with such matters.[38]

In yet another eviction case, *President of the Republic of South Africa* v. *Modderklip Boerdery (Pty) Ltd*, 2005 (8) BCLR 786 (CC) private landowners were unable to secure a conviction order granted against 40,000 occupiers on his land. When they approached the sheriff's office they were asked to deposit R1.8 million, more than the value of the land, to engage a private security company. In an appeal against the High Court decision for the land owner, the Constitutional Court held that the State had failed to take reasonable steps to assist the property owner. The Court found that in these circumstances it is unreasonable of the State to stand by and do nothing. It found this to be a violation of the principle of the rule of law as well as the right of access to the courts. The Court held that the State compensate the landowners for the unlawful occupation of their property. In addition, the occupiers were to continue living there until alternative accommodation was found by the State.

36 Sandra Liebenberg, "Needs, Rights and Transformation: Adjudicating Social Rights," (New York: Centre for Human Rights and Global Justice Working Paper Economic and Social Rights Series No. 8, 2005), 18.

37 For a general overview, see Steiner, Alston, and Goodman, *International Human Rights*, 327–47.

38 At paragraph 29. See also *Campaign for Fiscal Equity* v. *State of New York*, 2006 WL 3344731(N.Y), 2006 N.Y Slip Op.08630 where the majority of the Court of Appeals of New York restated its earlier opinion in the same case: "[W]e expressed the necessity for courts to tread carefully when asked to evaluate state financing plans. On the one hand, the Judiciary has a duty "to defer to the Legislature in matters of policymaking, particularly in a matter so vital as education financing, which has a core element of local control. We have neither the authority nor the ability, nor the will, to micromanage education financing. On the other hand, "it is the province of the Judicial branch to define, and safeguard, rights provided by the New York State Constitution, and order redress for violation of them." Paragraph III.

In the *Grootboom* case, Mrs Grootboom, her children and number of similarly affected neighbors, moved from their home which had flooded during the winter rains onto land earmarked for low-cost housing. They were evicted from this land when the matter went before the High Court who found in their favor. The State appealed to the Constitutional Court which explained the ambit of the Court's inquiry within the standard of reasonableness of the state policy in the context of the separation of powers doctrine:[39]

> The precise contours and content of the measures to be adopted are primarily a matter for the legislature and the executive. They must, however, ensure that the measures they adopt are reasonable. A court considering reasonableness will not enquire whether other more desirable or favourable measures could have been adopted, or whether public money could have been better spent. The question would be whether the measures that have been adopted are reasonable. It is necessary to recognize that a wide range of possible measures could be adopted by the state to meet its obligations. Many of these would meet the requirement of reasonableness. Once it is shown that the measures do so, this requirement is met.

As the highest court in the land, it reiterated[40] that it had the power to adjudicate on socio-economic rights because the Constitution gave them that power. It also said that, within the debate around the separation of powers, it was entitled to examine this issue even if it had a financial implication.[41] It repeated that if it ordered legal aid to an accused individual, as a civil right, that too would have a financial implication. That would appear to be an adequate answer to those who maintain that the enforcement of civil and political rights, as a negative duty on the State, does not have cost implications, as discussed earlier. One commentator sees the political dimension of this debate clearly as privileging negative liberty and the existing economic *status quo*.[42]

In *Grootboom*, the Constitutional Court stated that reasonableness can be evaluated at the level of legislative programming and its implementation:

> Legislative measures by themselves are not likely to constitute constitutional compliance. Mere legislation is not enough. The state is obliged to act to achieve the

[39] At paragraph 41. In *Campaign for Fiscal Equality* v. *State of New York*, 2006 WL 3344731 (N.Y), 2006 N.Y. Slip Op.08630 the majority of the Court of Appeals of New York said: "The role of the courts is not, as Supreme Court assumed, to determine the best way to calculate the cost of a sound basic education in New York City schools, but to determine whether the State's proposed calculation of that cost is rational." Paragraph II.

[40] *Soobramoney* v. *Minister of Health, KwaZulu-Natal*, 1998 (1) SA 765(CC); 1997 (12) BCLR 1969 (CC) and *Government of the Republic of South Africa and Others* v. *Grootboom and Others*, 2001 (1) SA 46 (CC); 2000 (11) BCLR 1169 (CC).

[41] Ex parte Chairperson of the Constitutional Assembly: in re Certification of the Constitution of the Republic of South Africa 1996 (4) SA 744 (C).

[42] Liebenberg, "Needs, Rights and Transformation," 13.

> intended result, and the legislative measures will invariably have to be supported by appropriate, well-directed policies and programmes implemented by the executive. The programme must also be reasonably implemented. An otherwise reasonable programme that is not implemented reasonably will not constitute compliance with the state's obligations.[43]

The Constitutional Court also explained the meaning of reasonableness by linking it to the three democratic values of human dignity, equality and freedom[44] in the South African constitution:

> Reasonableness must also be understood in the context of the Bill of Rights as a whole. The right of access to adequate housing is entrenched because we value human beings and want to ensure that they are afforded their basic needs. A society must seek to ensure that the bare necessities of life are provided to all if it is to be a society based on human dignity, freedom and equality. To be reasonable, measures cannot leave out of account the degree and extent of the denial of the right they endeavour to realise. Those whose needs are the most urgent and whose ability to enjoy all rights therefore is most in peril, must not be ignored by the measures aimed at achieving realisation of the right. It may not be sufficient to meet the test of reasonableness to show that the measures are capable of achieving a statistical advance in the realisation of the rights. Furthermore, the Constitution requires that everyone must be treated with care and concern. If the measures, though statistically successful, fail to respond to the needs of those most desperate, they may not pass the test.[45]

The usual thinking on social policy matters is that they are solely legislative and executive functions[46] and the courts have a limited or no role to play there. In the *Treatment Action Campaign* case, the Constitutional Court said that:

> ...although there are no bright lines that separate the roles of the legislature, the executive and the courts from one another, there are certain matters that are pre-eminently within the domain of one or other arms of government and not others. All arms of government should be sensitive to and respect this separation. This does not mean, however, that courts cannot or should not make orders that have an impact on policy.[47]

---

43 See note 40, at paragraph 42.

44 Section 7 (1) of the 1996 Constitution.

45 See note 40, at paragraph 44.

46 Etienne Mureinik, "Beyond a Charter of Luxuries: Economic Rights in the Constitution," *South African Journal of Human Rights* 8 (1992): 464–71; Dennis Davis, "The Case Against the Inclusion of Socio-Economic Demands in a Bill of Rights Except as Directive Principles," *South African Journal of Human Rights* 8 (1992): 475–90; Vinodh Jaichand, "The Promise in the Right to Vote," *Comparative and International Law Journal of Southern Africa* 26 (1993): 1–16.

47 *Minister of Health* v. *Treatment Action Campaign*, 2002 (5) SA 721 (CC) at paragraph 98.

Indeed the issues before the Constitutional Court were not about whether economic and social rights are justiciable or not, but how they can be enforced. In the *Treatment Action Campaign* case the government's policy of failing to provide Nevaripine, an anti-retroviral drug used in reducing mother to child transmission of HIV/Aids at all state health facilities, was under scrutiny under the rights of children to medical care. The government appealed against the decision of the High Court. The Constitutional Court found in favor of Treatment Action Campaign when it held that the government's programme to prevent mother to child transmission was unreasonable.

The Constitutional Court, in this case, was mindful of its role in adjudicating upon socio-economic rights in the context of the separation of powers doctrine when it said:

> Courts are ill-suited to adjudicate upon issues where court orders could have multiple social and economic consequences for the community. The Constitution contemplates rather a restrained and focused role of the court, namely, to require the state to take measures to meet its constitutional obligations and to subject the reasonableness of these measures to evaluation. Such determination of reasonableness may in fact have budgetary implications, but are not in themselves directed at rearranging budgets. In this way the judicial, legislative and executive functions achieve appropriate balance.[48]

The development of the domestic jurisprudence in South Africa based on the review of the reasonableness of state policy has resonance in the Optional Protocol to the International Covenant on Economic, Social and Cultural Rights[49] where under the provisions for the Examinations of Communications it is stated:

> When examining communications under the present Protocol, the Committee shall consider the reasonableness of the steps taken by the State Party.... In doing so the Committee shall bear in mind that the State Party may adopt a range of

[48] 2002 (5) SA 721 at paragraph 38; 2002 (10) BCLR 1033 (CC). This argument is not antithetical to the views of Minister Mc Dowell (see footnote 18) who values the separation of powers as "the cornerstone of our society. Our form of Government does not relegate distributive issues of social and economic justice by making them the exclusive care of the Parliament and Government. Parliamentary democracy is by far the best agency to make value judgements on such issues. And Parliament is best suited by far to decide on resourcing and vindicating entitlements in the social and economic sphere." At best the Irish separation of powers model is but one, which excludes government accountability through the courts, and the South African another which is inclusive. The judiciary is one but branch of that power whose duty is to mediate disputes between all parties, including the State and the individual.

[49] Optional Protocol (GA Resolution A/RES/63/117) to the International Covenant on Economic, Social and Cultural Rights unanimously adopted by the general assembly on 10 December 2008. As of 30 March 2010, it has attracted 32 signatures but no ratifications or accessions.

> possible policy measures for the implementation of the rights set forth in the Covenant.[50]

In India, the Directive Principles of State Policy in the Constitution appeared to bar the courts from reviewing state action on economic, social and cultural rights.[51] However, the Indian Supreme Court has held that those Principles are of essential importance in interpreting the content of fundamental rights. It has used the civil right to life to interpret economic, social and cultural rights.[52] In *Keshavananda Bharati* v. *State of Kerala*[53] the Supreme Court said:

> Fundamental rights have themselves no fixed content; most of them are empty vessels into which each generation must pour its content in the light of its experience. Restrictions, abridgement, curtailment and even abrogation of these rights in circumstances not visualised by the constitution makers might become necessary; their claim to supremacy or priority is liable to be overborne at particular stages in the history of the nation by the moral claims embodied in Part IV [which contain the Directive Principles of State Policy].

In *Tellis* v. *Bombay Municipal Corporation*,[54] a case about pavement dwellers, the right not to be deprived of life was included to include the right to livelihood. In a similar way, the right to life included the right to basic necessities of life such as adequate nutrition, clothing and reading facilities in the case of *Francis Coralie Mullin* v. *The Administrator, Union Territory of Delhi.*[55] In *Ahmedabad Municipal Corporation* v. *Nawab Khan Gulab Khan*[56] the right to life included the right to shelter. In *Paschim Banga Khet Mazdoor Samity* v. *State of Bengal*[57] the right to life included the right to health and in *Mohini Jain* v. *State of Karnataka*[58] the right to life included the right to education.

---

[50] Article 8, paragraph 4.

[51] It states that the provision shall not be enforced by any court of law, "but the principles therein laid down are nevertheless fundamental in the governance of the country and shall be the duty of the State to apply these principles in making laws." Ireland, Papua New Guinea and Nigeria have similar provisions in their constitutions.

[52] This is not a unique approach and has been undertaken in numerous other jurisdictions in Europe. See Martin Scheinin, "Economic and Social Rights as Legal Rights," in *Social, Economic and Cultural Rights*, ed. Eide, Krause, and Rosas, 32 where he discusses the "integrated approach" of the protection of ESC rights through treaties on civil and political rights.

[53] 4 SCC 225 at paragraph 6.

[54] (1985) 3 SCC 545.

[55] (1981) 2 SCR 516.

[56] (1997) 11 SCC 123.

[57] (1996) 4 SCC 37.

[58] (1992) 3 SCC 666.

7. Conclusion

While the historical analysis does indicate a clear division on ideological lines between the western liberal States and the socialist States on the nature and protection of human rights, for States to continue that way is not only futile but also irresponsible. One reason for the growth in this area of study is the impact of non-implementation of economic, social and cultural rights is more discernable, and the United Nations has responded to the extent that its Member States have permitted it to. That response has been through the Millennium Development goals, which are laudable in their objective, but which in fact dilute the responsibility of States Parties to ICESCR which contain international human rights obligations that States parties have ratified and are obliged to uphold. In attempting to reach the Millennium goals, the failure of certain States to meet their obligations must not be excused.

The other reason for the growth is that the study of economic, social and cultural rights must be an inter-disciplinary one in which law would be but a component. Many other branches, other than law, continue to make major contributions. Therefore the whole discussion on justiciability must be seen as one vehicle for the delivery of human rights but not the only one. An understanding of economic principles is necessary for a complete comprehension on how to deal with these rights. Our law-makers need to be educated in the better ways to introduce these rights through law reform. The democratic process requires vigilance by civil society on issues of governmental accountability, including the ways in which budgets are devised and prioritized.

In the introduction I alluded to the Optional Protocol which will eventually permit individual and group petitions to Committee on Economic, Social and Cultural Rights which, when it comes into force, will track the path of the Optional Protocol on the International Covenant on Civil and Political Rights some 33 years later. This does raise the question about whether or not all best efforts in economic, social and cultural rights are being placed in creating parity with civil and political rights. Or is the central issue still pivoting around the enforcement of all human rights? Perhaps, it is time that economic, social and cultural rights shed the yoke of history and claimed their legitimate place as human rights in the legal systems of the world. To do otherwise would be to pay homage to an anachronistic State practice that has outlived its value or purpose.

Bibliography

Books and Articles

Baderin, Mashood A., and Robert McCorquodale. "The International Covenant on Economic, Social and Cultural Rights: Forty Years of Development." In *Economic, Social and Cultural Rights in Action*, edited by Mashood A. Baderin, and Robert McCorquodale, 3–24. Oxford: Oxford University Press, 2007.

Baderin, Mashood A. "The African Commission on Human and Peoples' Rights and the Implementation of Economic, Social and Cultural Rights in Africa." In *Economic, Social and Cultural Rights in Action*, edited by Mashood A. Baderin, and Robert McCorquodale, 139–66. Oxford: Oxford University Press, 2007.

Churchill, Robin R., and Urfan Khaliq. "Violations of Economic, Social and Cultural Rights: The Current Use and Future Potential of the Collective Complaints Mechanism of the European Social Charter." In *Economic, Social and Cultural Rights in Action*, edited by Mashood A. Baderin, and Robert McCorquodale, 195–240. Oxford: Oxford University Press, 2007.

Craven, Matthew. "The UN Committee on Economic, Social and Cultural Rights." In *Social, Economic and Cultural Rights*, edited by Asbjorn Eide, Catarina Krause, and Allan Rosas, 455–72. Netherlands: Kluwer Law International, 2001.

Davis, Dennis. "The Case Against the Inclusion of Socio-Economic Demands in a Bill of Rights Except as Directive Principles." *South African Journal of Human Rights* 8 (1992): 475–90.

Eide, Asbjorn. "Economic and Social Rights As Legal Rights." In *Social, Economic and Cultural Rights*, edited by Asbjorn Eide, Catarina Krause, and Allan Rosas, 29–54. Netherlands: Kluwer Law International, 2001.

Eide, Asbjorn, and Allan Rosas. "Economic, Social and Cultural Rights: A Universal Challenge." In *Social, Economic and Cultural Rights*, edited by Asbjorn Eide, Catarina Krause, and Allan Rosas, 3–7. Netherlands: Kluwer Law International, 2001.

Gomez, Veronica. "Economic, Social and Cultural Rights in the Inter-American System." In *Economic, Social and Cultural Rights in Action*, edited by Mashood A. Baderin, and Robert McCorquodale, 167–94. Oxford: Oxford University Press, 2007.

Heyns, Christof, and Frans Viljoen. "The Impact of the United Nations Human Rights Treaties on the Domestic Level." *Human Rights Quarterly* 23, no. 3 (2001): 483–535.

Hopkins, Kevin. "Shattering the divide-when judges go too far." http://www.derebus.org.za/archives/2002Mar/articles/dicide.htm.

Jaichand, Vinodh. "The Promise in the Right to Vote." *Comparative and International Law Journal of Southern Africa* 26 (1993): 1–16.

Leckie, Scott. "Another Step Toward Indivisibility: Identifying the Key Features of Violations of Economic, Social and Cultural Rights." *Human Rights Quarterly* 20, no. 1 (1998): 81–124.

Liebenberg, Sandra. "The Protection of Economic, Social and Cultural Rights in Domestic Legal Systems." In *Social, Economic and Cultural Rights*, edited by Asbjorn Eide, Catarina Krause, and Allan Rosas, 55–84. Netherlands: Kluwer Law International, 2001.

Liebenberg, Sandra. "Needs, Rights and Transformation: Adjudicating Social Rights." New York: Centre for Human Rights and Global Justice Working Paper Economic and Social Rights Series No. 8, 2005.

Mureinik, Etienne. "Beyond a Charter of Luxuries: Economic Rights in the Constitution." *South African Journal of Human Rights* 8 (1992): 464–71.

Odinkalu, Chidi Anselm. "Analysis of Paralysis or Paralysis by Analysis? Implementing Economic, Social and Cultural Rights Under the African Charter on Human and Peoples' Rights." *Human Rights Quarterly* 23, no. 2 (2001): 327–69.

Rosas, Allan, and Martin Scheinin. "Implementation Mechanisms and Remedies." In *Social, Economic and Cultural Rights*, edited by Asbjorn Eide, Catarina Krause, and Allan Rosas, 425–53. Netherlands: Kluwer Law International, 2001.

Scheinin, Martin. "Economic and Social Rights as Legal Rights." In *Social, Economic and Cultural Rights*, edited by Asbjorn Eide, Catarina Krause, and Allan Rosas, 29–54. Netherlands: Kluwer Law International, 2001.

Scott, Craig. "Reaching Beyond (Without Abandoning) the Category of 'Economic, Social and Cultural Rights.'" *Human Rights Quarterly* 21, no. 3 (1999): 633–60.
Scott, Craig M., and Patrick Macklem. "Constitutional Ropes of Sand or Justiciable Guarantees? Social Rights in a New South African Constitution." *University of Pennsylvania Law Review* 141 (1992): 1–148.
Steiner, Henry J., Philip Alston, and Ryan Goodman. "Economic and Social Rights." In *International Human Rights in Context*, edited by Henry J. Steiner, Philip Alston, and Ryan Goodman, 263–374. New York: Oxford University Press. 2008.
Warbrick, Colin. "Economic and Social Interests and the European Convention on Human Rights." In *Economic, Social and Cultural Rights in Action*, edited by Mashood A. Baderin, and Robert McCorquodale, 241–56. Oxford: Oxford University Press, 2007.
Woods, Jeanne M. "Justiciable Social Rights as a Critique of the Liberal Paradigm." *Texas International Law Journal* 38, no. 4 (2003): 763–74.

Constitution, Acts, Statutes, Declaration

African Charter on Human and Peoples' Rights, 1985
International Covenant on Economic, Social and Cultural Rights, 1966
Optional Protocol to the International Covenant on Economic, Social and Cultural Rights, 2008
Social Assistant Act, 1992
The Additional Protocol to the American Convention on Human Rights in the area of Economic, Social, and Cultural Rights (more commonly known as the "Protocol of San Salvador"), 1988
The Constitution of India, 1950
The Constitution of Ireland, 1937
The Constitution of Papua New Guinea, 1975
The Constitution of Nigeria, 1999
The Constitution of Republic of South Africa, 1996
The European Convention on Human Rights, 1950
The European Social Charter, 1961
The Interim Constitution of Republic of South Africa, 1994
World Conference on Human Rights: Vienna Declaration and Programme of Action, 1993
Universal Declaration of Human Rights, 1948

Website

http://www.ohchr.org/english/law/cesr.htm

Document

UN doc. A/CONF.157/23
A/HRC/8/l.2/Rev. 1/Corr.1 16 June 2008

Cases

Ahmedabad Municipal Corporation v. *Nawab Khan Gulab Khan* (1997) 11 SCC 123
Brown v. *Board of Education of Topeka*, 347 US 483
Campaign for Fiscal Equality v. *State of New York*, 2006 WL 3344731(N.Y.), 2006 N.Y. Slip Op.08630
Ex parte Chairperson of the Constitutional Assembly: in re Certification of the Constitution of the Republic of South Africa 1996 (4) SA 744 (C)
Francis Coralie Mullin v. *The Administrator, Union Territory of Delhi* (1981) 2 SCR 516
Government of the Republic of South Africa v. *Grootboom*, 2001 SA 46; 2000 (11) BCLR 1169 (CC)
Keshavananda Bharati v. *State of Kerala*, 1973 4 SCC 225
Khosa v. *Minister of Social Development* 2004 (6) SA 505; [2004] (6) BCLR 569
Mahlaule v. *Minister of Social Development, Port Elizabeth Municipality* v. *Various Occupiers*, 2004 (12) BCLR 1268

Minister of Health v. *Treatment Action Campaign*, 2002 (5) SA 721 (CC)
Mohini Jain v. *State of Karnataka* (1992) 3 SCC 666
Paschim Banga Khet Mazdoor Samity v. *State of Bengal* (1996) 4 SCC 37
President of the Republic of South Africa v. *Modderklip Boerdery (Pty) Ltd*, 2005 (8) BCLR 786 (CC)
Social and Economic Rights Action Center and the Center for Economic and Social Rights v. *Nigeria*, 27 May 2002, African Commission on Human and Peoples' Rights, Decision 155/96
Soobramoney v. *Minister of Health, KwaZulu-Natal*, 1998 (1) SA 765 (CC); 1997 (12) BCLR 1969 (CC)
Tellis v. *Bombay Municipal Corporation* (1985) 3 SCC 545
Treatment Action Campaign, 2002 (5) SA 721; 2002 (10) BCLR 1033 (CC)

Chapter Four

Women's Rights in International Law

*Mmatsie Mooki, Rita Ozoemana and Michelo Hansungule**

1. *Introduction*

Rights of women in international law took long to take root. This is partly due to the fact that states were reluctant to embrace what current United States Secretary of State and former first lady Hillary Clinton eloquently stated: 'women's rights are human rights'. For centuries, women all over the world were denied their full status. Despite historical advances in Europe towards individual freedom and liberty, beginning with the French and American Revolutions, the lot of women remained unsatisfactory. Women in Europe did not get the vote at the same time as men. In non-Western societies, the status of women continues to be defined by their sex and gender.

When the United Nations adopted the Convention on the Elimination of All Forms of Discrimination against Women (CEDAW), there was a deafening chorus of approval that the world was taking remedial action on this important matter. However, few States ratified the CEDAW without reservations. The fact that kings, presidents and prime ministers attached reservations to their instruments of ratification and accession clearly demonstrates that some of the most powerful people in the world are only reluctantly going along without conviction in the efforts towards an equal society.

Nevertheless, adoption of the United Nations Charter in 1945 set the stage for the current efforts at really getting to grips with the challenges facing women in particular translating women's rights as human rights.

* Mmatsie Mooki and Rita Ozoemana are both LL.D candidates at the Centre for Human Rights, Faculty of Law, University of Pretoria, South Africa.
Michelo Hansungule is Professor of Law in the Centre for Human Rights, Faculty of Law, University of Pretoria, South Africa.

2. *Recognition of Women's Rights: United Nations Charter and the International Bill of Rights*

The United Nations Charter (UN Charter) promotes universal respect for and observance of human rights and fundamental freedoms for all without distinction as to race, sex, language or religion.[1] It further stresses the equal rights of men and women,[2] and their eligibility to participate in the UN's principal and subsidiary organs.[3]

Following the UN Charter, three major international instruments commonly referred to as the International Bill of Human Rights were adopted. They are the Universal Declaration of Human Rights (UDHR); the International Covenant on Civil and Political Rights (ICCPR) and the International Covenant on Economic, Social and Cultural Rights (ICESCR). Though there is no explicit reference to women in the above mentioned instruments, all of them however, implicitly include women in the "equality context." Therefore, they reiterate the goal of achieving equality between the sexes.[4] Their common denominator is that first, they make reference to the provision of the UN Charter on the equal rights of men and women. Second, they specifically provide for sex as a prohibited ground of discrimination, therefore all rights found in these instruments are exercised without discrimination of any kind including on the basis of sex.[5] Third, the UDHR provides for equality before the law without any form of discrimination.[6] Fourth, they also make provision for special protection of mothers before and after birth.[7] Last, they also provide for the right of men and women of marriageable age to marry and found a family.[8]

3. *Women's Rights in other United Nations Conventions*

On realizing that important though it is, the International Bill of Rights was nevertheless insensitive to specific problems faced by women, the United

---

1 UN Charter, Articles 1(3) and 55(c).

2 UN Charter, Article 8.

3 UN Charter, Preamble.

4 Laura Reanda, "Human Rights and Women's Rights: the United Nations Approach," *Human Rights Quarterly* 3 (1981): 11.

5 UDHR, Article 2, provides that everyone is entitled to all the rights in the UDHR without distinction as to race, colour, sex, language or religion. This is also provided for in ICCPR, Article 2 and ICESCR, Article 2.

6 UDHR, Article 7.

7 ICESCR, Article 10 and UDHR, Article 25.

8 UDHR, Article 16 and ICESCR, Article 25.

Nations, under the sponsorship of the Commission on the Status of Women,[9] adopted three other international Conventions between 1952 and 1962. These are: the Convention on the Political Rights of Women,[10] Convention on the Nationality of Married Women[11] and Convention on the Consent to Marriage, Minimum Age of Marriage and Registration of Marriages (Convention on Consent to Marriage).[12] The feminist movement in Western countries in particular in the United States of America greatly assisted towards more 'women-specific' interventions in the form treaties and agreements solely focused towards advancing women's rights.

Given the noticeable political deficits faced by women and the importance of extending franchise to women, adoption of the Convention on the Political Rights of Women in 1952 was a natural sequence. The Convention gives women equal voting rights with men,[13] rights to stand for political office,[14] and access to public services.[15] It is common-cause that important though it is, marriage has the negative effect that it compromises the status of women. Consequently, the Convention on the Nationality of Married Women is concerned with the loss of nationality by women upon marriage or when their husband changes their nationality. It was drafted to address the problems of involuntary loss or change of nationality of women at the time of marriage or divorce.[16] It provides for the general principle that men and women have equal rights to acquire, change or retain their nationality. It stipulates that neither the celebration nor the dissolution of marriage between one of its nationals and a foreign national, nor the change of nationality by the husband during marriage, shall automatically affect the nationality of the wife.[17] On the other hand the Convention on Consent to Marriage explicitly state that "No marriage shall be legally entered into without the full and free consent of the parties."[18] It further mandates States to specify a minimum age of marriage.[19] However, Reanda rightly states that these

---

[9] Reanda, "Human Rights and Women's Rights," 19.

[10] The Convention was opened for signature and ratification by the General Assembly Resolution 640 (VII) of 20 December 1952 and entered into force 7 July 1954.

[11] The Convention was opened for signature and ratification by the General Assembly Resolution 1040 (XI) of 29 January 1957 and entered into force 11 August 1958.

[12] The Convention was opened for signature and ratification by General Assembly Resolution 1763 A (XVII) of 7 November 1962 and entered into force 9 December 1964.

[13] Convention on the Political Rights of Women, Article I.

[14] Ibid., Article II.

[15] Ibid., Article III.

[16] Natalie Kaufman Hevener, "An analysis of Gender Based Treaty Law: Contemporary Developments in Historical Perspective," *Human Rights Quarterly* 27 (1986): 85.

[17] Convention on the Nationality of Married Women, Article 1.

[18] Convention on Consent to Marriage, Article 1.

[19] Ibid., Article 2.

subsequent instruments have in common the limitation of their scope, and the absence of provisions for international measures of implementation.[20]

4. *Convention on the Elimination of all forms of Discrimination against Women*

4.1. *Background to the Women's Convention*

The most important international development in the promotion of gender and women's rights is the adoption of the Convention on the Elimination of all forms of Discrimination against Women (CEDAW). In 1967 the United Nations (UN) adopted the Declaration on the Elimination of all Forms of Discrimination against Women (Women's Declaration). It was only a statement of moral and political intent. Though the Women's Declaration was a considerable progress in women's rights, it did not however, have the contractual force of a treaty. In 1974 the Commission on the Status of Women decided to prepare a comprehensive and internationally binding instrument to eliminate the discrimination against women.[21] On the 18 September 1979 the UN adopted the Convention on the Elimination of All Forms of Discrimination against Women (in this chapter known for short as 'the Women's Convention').[22] It entered into force on 3 September 1981 and came into effect faster than any previous human rights Convention.[23] It is clear that the Women's Declaration set the stage for the elaboration and adoption of the Women's Convention.

The preamble of this Convention points out that despite existing human rights conventions adopted by the UN to promote equality of rights of men and women, extensive discrimination against women still exists.[24] This treaty marked the turning point in the history of international protection of women's human rights. It has been hailed as the international bill of rights for

---

[20] Reanda, Human Rights and Women's Rights," 19.

[21] See "Convention on the Elimination of all forms of Discrimination against Women" <www.lww-fairfax.org> (accessed 20 August 2008). This text was prepared by working groups within the CSW in 1976 and was deliberated by the Working group of the UN General Assembly between 1976 and 1979.

[22] It was opened for signature, ratification and accession by General Assembly Resolution 34/180 of 18 December 1979 and entered into force on 3 September 1981. Convention on the Elimination of All forms of Discrimination against Women UN Doc.A/Res/34/180 (1980).

[23] Sindiso Ngaba, "CEDAW: Eliminating Discrimination against Women," *Agenda* 27 (1995): 82.

[24] Women's Convention, Preamble paragraphs 5 and 6.

women.[25] It gives expression the non discrimination value in the international bill of rights instruments. As of April 2010, 186 States are party to the Women's Convention.[26] According to Cook, the Women's Convention is different from other international instruments as it develops the legal norm on non discrimination from a women's perspective.[27] Fayeeza Kathree indicates that the Women's Convention is the first international instrument which embodies the civil, political, social and cultural rights of women.[28] She further notes that the Convention is not concerned with formal equality of women with men but focuses on women's substantive equality.[29]

4.2. *Analysis of the substantive provisions of the Women's Convention*

The Women's Convention comprises of the preamble and 30 Articles divided into six chapters or sections. Articles 1 to 16 form the substantive provisions. The Women's Convention is divided as follows: Chapter I contains 6 Articles, Article 1 defines 'discrimination against women' and Articles 2 to 6 are the general provisions; Chapter 2 provides for the political rights of women in Articles 7 to 9; Chapter III addresses socio economic rights of women in Articles 7 to 14; Chapter IV provides for aspects of Civil law in Articles 15–16; Part V establishes a Committee on the Elimination of Discrimination against Women (CEDAW) and provides for a reporting system in Articles 17–22; Chapter VI deals with concluding issues like revisions, entry into force and reservations in Articles 23 to 30. It is not possible to discuss each one of the Convention Articles. However, reference will be made to substantive provisions of the Women's Convention as well as to the role that CEDAW plays.

4.2.1. *Definition of "discrimination against women" and agenda of State Parties*

The Women's Convention condemns discrimination against women and set out an agenda that State Parties should take to end such discrimination.[30] Therefore,

[25] Harold Hongju Koh, "Why America Should Ratify the Women's Rights Treaty (CEDAW)," *Case Western Reserve Journal of International Law* 34 (2002): 266; Carmel Shalev, "Rights to Sexual and Reproductive Health: The ICPD and the Convention on the Elimination of all forms of Discrimination against Women," *Health and Human Rights* 4 (2000): 43.

[26] Information received from <www.un/org/womenwatch/daw/cedaw/states.htm> (accessed 15 September 2008).

[27] Rebecca Cook "Women's International Human Rights Law: The Way Forward," *Human Rights Quarterly* 15 (1993): 239.

[28] Fayeeza Kathree, "Convention on the Elimination of all forms of Discrimination against Women," *South African Journal on Human Rights* 11 (1995): 421.

[29] Ibid., 425.

[30] Women's Convention, Article 2. Among others State Parties undertake to embody the principle of equality of men and women in their national constitutions; to adopt appropriate

the chief obligations are placed on individual countries. Article 1 defines discrimination against women as:

> Any distinction, exclusion or restriction made on the basis of sex which has the effect or purpose of impairing or nullifying the recognition, enjoyment or exercise by women irrespective of their marital status on the basis of equality of men and women, of human rights and fundamental freedoms in the political, social, cultural, civil or any other field.[31]

This definition merits further discussion in a number of respects. From this definition it is clear that even though a law or policy may not have the intention of denying women the enjoyment of rights, but if it has the effect of doing so then it constitutes discrimination. Feride Acar's interpretation of discrimination in Article 1 is discrimination of "effect" and "purpose," and covers both "direct" and "indirect" discrimination as well as "intentional" and "unintentional" discrimination.[32] In her elaboration of the definition of discrimination as provided in the Women's Convention Shalev stresses that the Women's Convention adopts an "effect" approach, meaning that discrimination will still be condemned even if it is not purposeful.[33] She further notes that the definition of discrimination applies to all women irrespective of their marital status.[34] Cook and Haws correctly point out that a violation of the Women's Convention arises when a State Party tolerates laws or practices that, on their face or in their application, expressly discriminate.[35] The preamble to the Women's Convention also indicates that its primary purpose is to "eliminate discrimination in all its forms and manifestation."[36] In Article 2 State Parties are called upon to adopt legislative measures including to embody the principle of non-discrimination in their constitutions and various legislations.[37] Further, State Parties must also undertake to refrain from practicing discrimination against women and to ensure that all public authorities and institutions similarly do so.[38]

---

legislative and other measures prohibiting all discrimination against women and to refrain from engaging in any act or practice of discrimination against women.

[31] Women's Convention, Article 1.

[32] Feride Acar, "Why CEDAW shows the way forward for the women's movement," <http://www.ww05.org/english3/speech/6.4.FerideAcar.pdf.> (accessed 20 August 2008).

[33] Shalev, "Rights to Sexual and Reproductive Health," 47.

[34] Ibid.

[35] Rebecca Cook and Jeanne Haws, "The United Nations Convention on the Rights of Women: Opportunities for Family Planning Providers," *International Family Planning Perspectives* 12 (1986): 49.

[36] Women's Convention, Preamble paragraph 15.

[37] Ibid., Article 2(a).

[38] Ibid., Article 2(d).

4.2.2. *General Provisions of Chapter I*
Article 3 mandates State Parties to take all appropriate measure including legislation to ensure the full development and advancement of women on the basis of equality with men.[39] Article 4 provides for affirmative action measures.[40] In addition, it also lays down certain conditions for such measures. Nqaba indicates that such measures should however be viewed as legitimate measures designed to redress historic inequalities and imbalances.[41] It is important to indicate that such measures are temporary and shall be discontinued when their objectives have been achieved.[42] States are also under an obligation to suppress both trafficking in women and exploitation of prostitution.[43]

Article 5 (a) requires State Parties to take all appropriate measures:

> To modify the social and cultural patterns of conduct of men and women, with a view to achieving the elimination of prejudices and customary and all other practices, which are based on the idea of the inferiority or the superiority of either of the sexes or on stereotyped roles for men and women.

The Women's Convention is the only UN Treaty to suggest that culture and tradition influence the formation of gender role in society. This is true as much of the discrimination against women goes behind multiple veils of family privacy, culture, religion and sovereignty.[44] Cook indicates how this article can be used to examine customary practices like female circumcision as it is a practice that arises from stereotypical perception that women are the principal guardians of a community's sexual morality.[45] Koh goes further and reveals examples of instances where women are subject to stunning abuses resulting from entrenched cultural and religious norms like genital mutilation,[46] "honor killing".[47] Female Genital Mutilation (FGM) or Female Circumcision is recognized internationally

---

39 Ibid., Article 3.

40 Ibid., Article 4 provides that State Parties shall adopt temporary special measures aimed at accelerating equality between men and women and such measures shall not be considered discrimination.

41 Ngaba, "CEDAW," 84.

42 Women's Convention, Article 4.

43 Ibid., Article 6.

44 Koh, "Why America Should Ratify the Women's Rights Treaty (CEDAW)," 267.

45 Rebecca Cook, "International Human Rights and Women's Reproductive Health." *Studies in Family Planning* 24 (1993): 78.

46 The World Health Organisation defines Female Genital Mutilation as comprising all procedures that involves partial or total removal of the external female genitalia or other injury to the female genital organs for non medical reasons. See WHO: Female Genital Mutilation <www.who.int/mediacentre/factsheet/fs241/en> (accessed 30 August 2008).

47 Koh, "Why America Should Ratify the Women's Rights Treaty (CEDAW)," 267. Honor killing is a practice whereby family members take it upon themselves to kill their sisters or cousins if they suspect them of bringing shame upon the family.

as a violation of the human rights of women and girl child. Reports by the World Health Organization (WHO) indicate that FGM has been documented in 28 countries in Africa and in several countries in Asia and the Middle East.[48] Some forms of the practice have also been reported among certain ethnic groups in Central and South America. There is also evidence of increasing numbers of girls and women living outside their place of origin, including in North America and Western Europe, who have undergone or may be at risk of undergoing FGM.[49] Article 5 therefore recognizes that the systemic nature of discrimination stems from the universal reality of patriarchy and foresees women's enjoyment of their human rights as contingent upon the dissolution of patriarchy in all its forms.[50] CEDAW is the first UN body to make a treaty recommendation on FGM in Recommendation No. 14 which called upon State Parties to eradicate the practice of Female Circumcision. However, Article 14 is one of the most reserved provisions of the Women's Convention. Such reservations compromise the object and purpose of the Women's Convention.[51] Reservations to Article 2 are mainly made by Islamic countries arguing that the provisions are in conflict with the *Sharia* or Islamic law.[52]

4.2.3. *Protection of Women's rights in political and public life*

In order to ensure equal participation of women and men in public and political life the Women's Convention outlines specific State Parties' obligation. States Parties are obligated to eliminate discrimination against women in public and political life. They must also ensure that women must be entitled to vote and be eligible for election on equal terms with men, to participate in the formulation of Government policy, and hold public office.[53] Women remain largely excluded from the Executive in their countries although there has been some progress.[54] It is indicated that between 1994 and 1998, the number of countries where women held at least 15 per cent of ministerial positions increased from

---

[48] See WHO, "FGM and harmful practices" < www.who.int/reproductive-health/fgm/ WHO > accessed 30 August 2008 and WHO, "Elimination of Female Genital Mutilation: an interagency statement by UNAIDS, UNDP, UNECA, UNESCO, UNFOA, UNHCHR, UNICEF, UNIFEN, WHO," 29.

[49] Ibid.

[50] Acar, "Why CEDAW shows the way forward for the women's movement," http://www.ww05.org/english3/speech/6.4.FerideAcar.pdf.

[51] Women's Convention, Article 2(f) requires States to take all appropriate measures, including legislation to modify or abolish existing laws, regulations, customs and practices which constitute discrimination against women.

[52] Ngaba, "CEDAW," 83.

[53] Women's Convention, Article 7.

[54] Department of Economic and Social Affairs, Statistics Division, *Report on the World Women Progress in Statistics*. United Nations: 2000.

16 to 28, and the number of countries where women held at least 20 percent of ministerial positions increased from 8 to16.[55] In the field of politics, many countries have introduced affirmative action measures to increase women's participation like a quota of 30 reserved seats for women in parliament. However, though there is progress in electing women to national parliaments, it is still far from the 30 per cent seen as a critical mass required to ensure that the interests of women are fully taken into account and reflected. Article 8 states that women should also be given equal opportunity to represent their Governments and participate in the work of international organizations, such as the United Nations, and its associated organizations.

4.2.4. *Socio-economic rights of women*

4.2.4.1. Equality in educational and employment opportunities

One area of particular concern for women is poverty. Due to unequal opportunities, women face disproportionate share of poverty relative to men. Therefore, international law provides for specific interventions to alleviate the lot of women in socio-economic field. Article 10 enjoins State Parties to ensure women's equal rights with men in the field of education. It underscores the need for the same conditions for access to studies,[56] to the same curricula and examinations,[57] same opportunities to benefit from scholarships and other study grants,[58] as well as reduction of female dropouts.[59] Hevener points out that reference to the reduction of female drop out is a new corrective action which was not mentioned in the 1962 Convention against Discrimination in Education.[60]

In Article 11 the State Parties obligate themselves to take steps to ensure the same rights on the basis of equality of men and women. These include the right to work; the right to the same opportunities for employment and the same criteria for selection and the right to free choice of profession and employment, to promotion, job security and vocational training and retraining.[61]

4.2.4.2. Equality in health care

Article 12 obliges State Parties to take all appropriate measures to eliminate discrimination against women in the field of healthcare and to ensure access to health care services, including those related to family planning. The importance

---

[55] Ibid.
[56] Women's Convention, Article 10(a).
[57] Ibid., Article 10(b).
[58] Ibid., Article 10(d).
[59] Ibid., Article 10(f).
[60] Kaufman, "An Analysis of Gender Based Treaty Law," 76.
[61] Ibid., 81.

of health care for women is evident from a number of provisions in the Women's Convention. For instance, it also guarantees the right of access to specific educational information and advice on family planning.[62] Women in rural areas should also have access to adequate health care facilities including information, counseling and family planning services.[63] This provision is important because the rates of maternal mortality are higher in rural areas since family planning and maternal health services are not as available as in urban places.[64] Cook and Haws reveal examples of requirement that inhibit equal access to family planning.[65] Among others: some nations allow husbands but not wives to obtain contraceptives without spousal authorization; in other countries unmarried men but not unmarried women may obtain contraceptive services; while in others availability of voluntary sterilization by women is managed differently from men.[66] The right to health is also linked to other rights provided for in the Women's Convention. For instance the Women's Convention also refers to the right of women to the protection of health and to safety in working conditions, including the safeguard of the function of reproduction.[67]

General Recommendation on women and health has elaborated CEDAW's understanding of Article 12.[68] According to this recommendation, States are encouraged to report on the most critical health issues affecting women in that country. Their reports should also reflect the health legislation, plans and policies for women relevant to health.[69] Furthermore, this recommendation indicates that the issues of HIV/AIDS and other sexually transmitted diseases are central to the rights of women and adolescent girls' sexual health.[70] In addition, States Parties should also include in their reports how they supply free services

62 Women's Convention, Article 10(h).

63 Ibid., Article 14(b).

64 Cook and Haws, "The United Nations Convention on the Rights of Women," *International Family Planning Perspectives* 12 (1986): 50.

65 Ibid.

66 Ibid., e.g. The availability of voluntary sterilization may be contingent on the number of cesarean sections that a woman has undergone or it may depend on the application of requirement like the "rule of 80" which permits a woman to be sterilized only when the number of her living children multiplied by her age exceeds 80.

67 Women's Convention, Article 11(1) f.

68 See General Recommendation No. 24 (20th session 1999).

69 General Recommendation No. 24, paragraph 9.

70 See General Recommendation No. 24, paragraph 18 which indicates that as a consequence of unequal power relations based on gender, women and adolescent girls are often unable to refuse sex or insist on safe and responsible sex practices. It also mentions that harmful traditional practices, such as female genital mutilation, polygamy, as well as marital rape, may also expose girls and women to the risk of contracting HIV/AIDS and other sexually transmitted diseases.

where necessary to ensure safe pregnancies, childbirth and post-partum periods for women. This is because many women are at risk of death or disability from pregnancy-related causes because they lack the funds to obtain or access the necessary services, which include ante-natal, maternity and post-natal services.[71]

4.2.4.3. Women in rural areas

Women in rural areas attracted the international community's particular attention in the women's Convention. Article 14 specifically acknowledges the particular problems women in rural areas face as well as the significant role which they play in the economic survival of their families and their work in the non-monetized sectors of the economy.[72] This indicates that the drafters of the Women's Convention where well aware of the serious issues posed by rural environments.[73] In the words of Claude Welch: "in rural areas, women face serious problems due to traditional land tenure systems, inheritance practices and lack capital." Article 14 recognizes rural women as particularly disadvantaged group.[74] This article goes further and sets out a programme of action to be followed by governments in addressing the plight of these women.[75] State Parties are therefore obliged to ensure among others that rural women participate in rural development planning,[76] they have access to adequate health care facilities,[77] education,[78] and access to agricultural credit and loans.[79]

4.2.5. *Aspects of civil law*

Often, women lack the minimum legal capacity and personality to required for them to advance and protect their legal rights. Article 15 elaborates upon rights to equality before the law and in all legal proceedings. It requires State Parties to accord to women in civil matters, a legal capacity identical to men, including equal rights to conclude contracts and to administer property.[80] When a woman cannot enter into a contract at all, or have access to financial credit, or can do so only with her husband's or a male relative's concurrence or guarantee, she is denied legal autonomy.[81]

---

[71] See General Recommendation No. 24, paragraph 27.

[72] Women's Convention, Article 14.

[73] Claude E. Welch, "Human Rights and African Women: A Comparison of Protection under Two Major Treatise," *Human Rights Quarterly* 15 (1993): 556.

[74] Ngaba, "CEDAW," 85.

[75] Women's Convention, Article 14(2) (a) – (h).

[76] Ibid., Article 14(2) (a).

[77] Ibid., Article 14(2) (b).

[78] Ibid., Article 14(2) (d).

[79] Ibid., Article 14(2) (g).

[80] Ibid., Article 15(2).

[81] See General Recommendation No. 21 (13th session 1996), paragraph 7.

Article 16 calls on State Parties to eliminate discrimination against women in all matters relating to marriage and family relations. This is one of the most reserved articles. In particular, State Parties must ensure among others: the same right to enter into marriage,[82] the same rights and responsibilities during marriage and at its dissolution,[83] and the same rights to decide freely the number and spacing of their children.[84] The issue of child marriage is addressed in non discriminatory language.[85] Most laws regulating the age of marriage prescribe a younger age for women to marry than men. Cook indicates how these laws violate provisions of Article 16 as well as Article 5 which prohibits laws and policies which are based on the "idea of inferiority or the superiority of either of the sexes."[86] The provisions of Article 16 are echoed in other UN Conventions.[87] In General Recommendation 21, CEDAW indicates that Article 16 (2) precludes States from permitting or giving validity to a marriage between person who have not yet attained the age of 18 for both man and woman. It further notes that early marriage not only affect health and impedes girl's education, it also limits the development of their skills and independence and reduces access to employment.[88]

4.2.6. *The Committee on the Elimination of Discrimination against Women*
The Committee on the CEDAW is the main Treaty-Body established to monitor compliance with the Women's Convention.[89] CEDAW is established "for the purpose of considering the progress made in the implementation of the Women's Convention."[90] It is also expected to report through the Economic and Social Council to the UN General Assembly on its activities.[91] It has the power to make general comments or recommendations based on the examination of reports and information received from State Parties.[92] Such comments or recommendations indicate ways in which State Parties should interpret and

---

[82] Women's Convention, Article 16(a).
[83] Ibid., Article 16(c).
[84] Ibid., Article 16(d).
[85] Ibid., Article 16(b) provides for the same right freely to choose a spouse and to enter into marriage only with the free and full consent.
[86] Cook and Haws, "The United Nations Convention on the Rights of Women," 51.
[87] UDHR, Article 16; Convention on Consent to Marriage, Articles 1 and 2; ICCPR, Article 23; ICESCR, Article 10 and Convention on the Elimination of all Forms of Racial Discrimination, Article 5(d)(IV).
[88] For further elaboration see General Recommendation No. 21 of 1994.
[89] Women's Convention, Articles 17–22 give details on the composition, the role and practices of CEDAW.
[90] Ibid., Article 17(1).
[91] Ibid., Article 21(1).
[92] Ibid.

apply the Women's Convention. The Concluding Observations or Comments are issued following the review of reports by State Parties and CEDAW consequently comments on the progress made by the State Parties in implementing its obligations under the treaty. Cook expounds that these comments can be particularly useful for elaborating the specific content broadly worded Treaty guarantees.[93] As of the end of 2007, CEDAW had issued 25 General Recommendations.[94]

It has been noted that one of the weaknesses pertaining to CEDAW is the absence of a provision in the Women's Convention which provides for the submission of individual complaints, thereby allowing it to receive petitions concerning alleged violation of the rights.[95] However, this shortcoming was remedied in 1999 by the adoption of the Optional Protocol to the Women's Convention (Optional Protocol).[96] An Optional Protocol is a legal instrument related to an existing treaty, which addresses issues not covered by or insufficiently developed in the treaty. It is described as "optional" because States are not obliged to become party to it, even if they have ratified or acceded to the related Convention. States that have become a party to the Optional Protocol recognize the competence of CEDAW to receive complaints from persons within their jurisdiction alleging violations of their right under the Convention.[97] The Optional Protocol also enables CEDAW to initiate inquiries if it has received reliable information indicating grave or systematic violation of the rights in the Convention.[98]

[93] Cook, "International Human Rights and Women's Reproductive Health," 76.

[94] Some of the groundbreaking recommendations made by CEDAW include General Recommendation No. 5 and No. 8 of 1988 which deals with the use of affirmative action measures to advance women's integration into education, economy, politics and employment; General Recommendation No. 12 of 1989 and No. 19 of 1992 addressing violence against women; General Recommendation 14 of 1990 on Female Circumcision; General Recommendation No. 22 of 1995 on equality in marriage and family relations as well as General Recommendation No. 24 of 1999 on measures to be taken to implement equality in women's right to health.

[95] Reanda, "Human Rights and Women's Rights," 22–23.

[96] It came into force on 22 December 2000.

[97] Optional Protocol, Article 2 which allows individual complaints by individuals or group of individuals who claim to be victims of any violation of rights in the Women's Convention.

[98] See Article 8, 9 and 10 of the Optional Protocol. Article 8 provides that if the Committee receives reliable information indicating grave or systematic violations by a State party of rights in the Convention, it shall invite that State party to cooperate in the examination of that information through the submission of observations. Article 10 enables State Parties to "opt out" of the inquiry procedure and therefore does not recognize the committee to initiate and conduct such inquiry.

4.2.7. *Concerns surrounding the Women's Convention/shortcomings*
A number of shortcomings are evident from the Women's Convention. First, one of its shortcomings is failure to directly address the issue of violence against women.[99] However, certain developments did take place hence the issue of violence against women will be discussed further in paragraph 5 below. Second, another concerning factor that has rendered the Women's Convention to be labeled "a Convention without teeth" is the difficulty in getting countries to report on compliance with its provision. This is evident from the status of submission of reports which indicates that State Parties whose reports where overdue by the 1st of December 2006 where 123 in total, and those whose reports where five years or more overdue where 36 in total.[100] Third, it is also criticized for not imposing an obligation on State Parties to act quickly or according to a time table. Fourth, despite wide ratification of the Women's Convention, many countries have entered the largest number of substantive reservations making it a Convention with the most reservations attached.[101]

Article 28 allows ratification subject to reservations, provided the reservations are not "incompatible with the object and purpose of the Convention."[102] The most reserved provisions relate to Articles 2, 9 and 16 and provide for rights relating to inheritance, marriage, divorce, citizenship and reproductive health.[103] Such reservations however, are not limited to procedural matters only but relates to substantive provisions which go to the core and purpose of the Women's Convention. The reasons cited by countries for such reservations relate to non conformity of domestic law with the Convention or due to religious based policies[104] or customary practices.[105] Reservations are therefore made on grounds that national law, tradition, religion or culture is not congruent with the Convention principles.[106] Brandt and Kaplan reveal that the problem is exacerbated

---

[99] Charlotte Bunch, "Women's Rights as Human Rights: Towards a Re-Vision of Human Rights," *Human Rights Quarterly* 12 (1990): 495.

[100] Committee on the Elimination of all Forms of Discrimination against Women, *Report of the Secretary – General on the status of submission of reports by State Parties under Article 18 of the Convention.* United Nations: 2003 <www.un.org.womenwatch/dew/cedaw/37sess.htm.> (accessed August 2008).

[101] Reservations are exceptions that State Parties make to a treaty, or provision to which they will not adhere to.

[102] Women's Convention, Article 28(1).

[103] See "Declarations, Reservations, Objections and Notification of withdrawal of reservations relating to the Convention on the Elimination of Discrimination against Women" <www.un.org.womenwatch/dew/cedaw/37session.htm> (accessed August 2008).

[104] This is normally the case in Arab or Islamic countries.

[105] This is the case in most African countries.

[106] See Convention on the Elimination of all Forms of Discrimination against Women (CEDAW), November 2005, *the league of women voters of the Fairfax Area Education fund* <www.lwv-fairfax.org.> (accessed August 2000).

by the fact that the Women's Convention provides no criteria for determining a reservation's incompatibility.[107]

5. *United Nations Groundbreaking Conferences*

Two of the most influential UN Conferences in the field of women's rights, the International Conference on Population and Development (ICPD)[108] and the Fourth World Conference on Women (Beijing conference)[109] were held in 1994 and 1995 respectively. The ICPD adopted the Cairo Programme of Action (Cairo Programme) and the Beijing Conference adopted the Beijing Declaration and Platform of Action (Beijing Platform). Both these conferences became virtually an agenda about the human rights of women and signaled the successful mainstreaming of women's rights as human rights.[110]

The Cairo Programme consists of 16 chapters. While it is not a Treaty with legally binding provisions, it remains a valuable international consensus document.[111] The Cairo Programme places the health and rights of women at the center of population and development programmes.[112] It states that the principles behind its provisions are to be found in existing international instruments.[113] This is clear from principle 8 of the Cairo programme which reiterates Article 12(1) of the Women's Convention on "the right of everyone to the enjoyment of the highest standard of physical and mental health." It further stresses "the right to decide freely and responsibly on the number and spacing of children.[114] It goes further and elaborates what the right to health means with respect to reproductive and sexual health.[115] Burrows rightly puts it when she identifies

[107] Michele Brandt and Jeffrey Kaplan, "The Tension between Women's Rights and Religious Rights: Reservations to CEDAW by Egypt, Bangladesh and Tunisia," *Journal of Law and Religion* 12 (1995): 107.

[108] The Conference took place on the 5–13 September 1994 in Cairo.

[109] The Conference took place on the 4–15 September 1995 in Beijing.

[110] Charlotte Bunch and Samantha Frost "Women's human rights: an introduction," *Routledge International Encyclopedia of Women: Women's issues and Knowledge* 2000, 8 available at Center for Women's Global Leadership. <http://www.cwgl.rutgers.edu/globalcenter/whr.html> (accessed August 2008).

[111] Francois Girard, "Cairo + Five: Reviewing Progress for Women Five Years after the International onference on Population and Development," *Journal of Women's Health and Law* 1 (1999): 2.

[112] Ibid.

[113] E.g. ICCPR, ICESCR, Women's Convention and the Convention on the Rights of the Child.

[114] This is also provided for in the Women's Convention, Article 16(e).

[115] See provisions of Chapter VII paras. 7.2 and 7.3 defining reproductive health as "a state of complete physical, mental and social well-being and not merely the absence of disease or

rights associated with reproductive choice and childbirth as central to the category of international women's rights.[116]

The Beijing Platform reiterates the same principles in paragraph 7.2 of the Cairo Programme.[117] These provisions are innovative and essential in realizing women's human rights. It further highlights 12 critical areas of concern for women which relate to Women and: poverty, education, health, violence, armed conflict, economy, power and decision making, institutional mechanisms for advancement, human rights, media, environment, and girl child. The importance of the Beijing Platform is evident from the fact that CEDAW now takes into account this 12 critical areas of the progress reports submitted by the States.

6. *Violence Against Women*

Violence against women is the greatest human rights scandal of all times. Women all over the world have witnessed violence perpetrated against them by the State through its officials, in the family by close relatives, by strangers and during armed conflict. Certain forms of violence occur because the women do not want follow certain rigid systems in their society such as female genital mutilation that occur mostly in Sub Saharan Africa, dowry related abuses as noted in Asia, forced marriages in certain cultures are unique to women. Domestic violence such as wife beating, battering and intimate partner abuse is suffered disproportionately by women. The effect of violence against women inhibits women from exercising and enjoying their rights as human beings and as women as noted in the Declaration for the Elimination of Violence against Women. Violence against women cuts across race, language, and status. It is not confined to any political or economic system but is prevalent in every society in the world. Religious observations in certain societies tend to limit women

infirmity, in all matters relating to the reproductive system and to its functions and processes. Reproductive health therefore, implies that people are able to have a satisfying and safe sex life and that they have the capability to reproduce and the freedom to decide if, when and how often to do so. Implicit in this last condition are the right of men and women to be informed and to have access to safe, effective, affordable and acceptable methods of family planning of their choice, as well as other methods of their choice for regulation of fertility which are not against the law, and the right of access to appropriate health care services that will enable women to go safely through pregnancy and childbirth and provide couples with the best chance of having a healthy infant."

[116] Noreen Burrows, "International Law and Human Rights: The Case of Women's Rights," in *Human Rights from Rhetoric to Reality*, ed. Campbell Tom et al. (Oxford and New York: Basil Blackwell, 1986), 85.

[117] See paragraphs 94 and 95 of the Beijing Platform.

from exercising and enjoying their rights as noted with women under Islam and some traditional belief system.

The UN has created initiatives aimed at eliminating all forms of violence and discrimination against women through the various agencies of the UN. The accession by most countries of the world to the Women's Convention and the UN Declaration on the Elimination of Violence against Women are some of the means of combating abuses against women by the world body. Despite the gains -made by women all over the world to bring attention to the issues of violence against women as a global scandal, more women still, suffer from all forms of abuse and discrimination.

6.1. *Forms of Violence against Women*

Violence against women has been defined as the kind of violence that inhibits the sexual, physical and psychological systems of women.[118] The unequal balance of power between men and women has contributed in the continued violation of the rights of women and further, the manner of socialization and ascribed gender roles have contributed to the subjugation of women. Women suffer abuses and violations in the following ways:[119]

- — Violence in the family in which battering occurs, sexual abuse of women and girl children, marital rape, female genital mutilation and other traditional practices that are harmful to women.
- — Violence against women in the community: this includes sexual abuse, sexual harassment in the work place, rape and trafficking of women and girl children for forced labour and forced prostitution.
- — Gender-based violence perpetrated by the State or State actors. This form of violence occurs mainly during armed conflict where women become 'war trophies' for the militants. Other perpetrators of violence against women in this category are armed officials who are supposed to protect the women but instead they turn around and abuse them.

It has been observed that in any of these categories of forms of violence, it may be physical, psychological and sexual. Acts of neglect or deprivation also forms part of the means of subjugating the woman. Discrimination against women forms the basis of all these aspects of violence experienced by women. It is on the basis of being treated differentially with regards to access to resources and opportunities that manifests into forms of violence that are experienced by women. The means of combating discrimination against women and ultimately violence is by way of ensuring gender equality or gender justice.

---

[118] Para 1 of Declaration for the Elimination of Violence against Women.

[119] Amnesty International Campaign, It's in our hands: Stop Violence against Women (2004) Amnesty International Publications, International Secretariat, London 3.

Gender justice is a concept that is believed to be the response against violence against women because it will ensure that women have equal access to opportunities on the basis of equality with men.[120] This idea finds more favor in certain parts of the world such as in Africa, South America and Asia. The reason is that more women in these areas face unequal power in terms of economic resources, right to reproductive and sexual right, right to inheritance and access to property. There are currently more challenges to combating violence against women in the African continent as opposed to Europe and America because of issues peculiar to Africa such as internal conflict and war, traditional belief systems that are opposed to human rights norms, and societal ideas of women's sexuality.[121]

6.2. *Violence against Women from an African Perspective*

Africans find expression in their cultural belief, customs and tradition. Majority of the people live in the rural towns and villages and are governed by the way of life in these areas which is basically communal in nature. To this extent, certain ceremonies are revered as a way of life for the people while in the modern society of the same country one would find that some of these cultures are not strictly observed.

In the traditional Zulu land of South Africa and Swaziland, it is common knowledge that the coming of age for young women is characterized by songs and dance before the royal king. Before these women celebrate their womanhood, they undergo virginity testing because only virgins partake in the annual reed dance. It is the culture of these people to perform the 'testing' and the reed dance. Young women take pride in the knowledge that they are respectable young women who have kept their chastity. On the other hand, human rights activists and children's rights advocates are against virginity testing because it is seen as a violation of the dignity of the young women. Most human rights instruments provide for the elimination of traditional practices that are harmful to women. The South African parliament passed the revised Sexual Offences Act in which virginity testing was outlawed.[122] The contention was that this

---

120 Rita Nkiruka Ozoemena, "African Customary Law and Gender Justice in a Progressive Democracy" (unpublished LLM thesis submitted to Rhodes University, Grahamstown, 2006), 36.

121 The manner in which the society views the role of women tends to aggravate the issue of violence against women. For example in South Africa, a young woman was assaulted by group of men for wearing a mini skirt at the Noord Taxi Rank in Johannesburg, South Africa. In this particular case, no one was arrested because it was a mob that attacked her and no one could be held responsible for the physical assault on this woman.

122 Section 12 Sexual Offences Act of 2006. In another development, Turkey rescinded from promulgating a law that allowed school girls who were having pre marital sex to undergo

testing was obtained without the explicit consent of the young women as sometimes many of them are below the age of 10. However, the protectors of this culture maintain that the submission to virginity testing is voluntary. To add to the protection of young women who attend the reed dance, King Zwelithini enjoined them to cover themselves because in African culture, overt exposure of women bodies is unacceptable. Within the African society there is usually the clash of culture and human rights principles because most of the revered traditions and culture of the people are being eroded by Eurocentric idea of human rights.

Another clash of human rights and culture in the African context involves the tradition of female genital mutilation. Most women in Africa have undergone genital mutilation.[123] This practice became a human rights issue because of the purpose for which it is performed. The cutting was not based on known health benefit as in the case of boys where it has been acknowledged by the WHO that circumcision can lower the risk of contracting the HIV/AIDS. For women the purpose for the cutting is aimed at limiting sexual libido and not for any known health benefit. For this reason, the tradition is a violation of the right to dignity of human person and bodily integrity as provided by most domestic and international law.[124]

Another way women's sexual behavior is controlled is also accomplished through determining how or whom they should have sexual relationship. For example, the idea of African women being lesbians is a taboo in many cultures. In some communities, women are expected to behave in a certain way. If such behaviors are in any way perceived to be contrary to the communities idea of an appropriate sexual behavior, those women are at the risk of being subjected to

---

virginity testing. From this view, the purpose of the testing is merely of a social nature to humiliate certain groups of women in Istanbul.

[123] Esther Kisaakye, "Women, Culture and Human Rights: Female Genital Mutilation, Polygamy and Bride Price," in *Human Rights of Women: International Instruments and African Experiences*, ed. Wolfgang Benedek, Esther M. Kisaakye, and Gerd Oberleitner (London: Zed Books, 2002), 271 where the writer stated that FGM is widely practised in at least 28 countries in Africa. It is estimated that about 136,797,440 women and girls in Africa had undergone one form or another of FGM by 1998. The estimated country prevalence ranges between 98 per cent in Djibouti to 5 per cent in Uganda and Democratic Republic of Congo.

[124] Most women who undergo genital mutilation in its various forms develop extensive health problems related to child bearing. A study conducted in Sierra Leone found that about 85 per cent of women who were circumcised required medical attention according to Frank Hosken at the 1988 International Seminar on Female Circumcision. Also the form of abuse where women's sexuality and behavior are controlled as in the case of female genital mutilation to curtail sexual expression is a violation of the right to bodily integrity. See Amnesty International Campaign: It's in our Hands, 18.

violence and degrading treatment.[125] Most of these women are forcibly confined in order to cure them of their sexual orientation. This kind of abuse occurs within the community where bringing the perpetrators to justice is usually difficult as the victims fear further discrimination and so do not report the abuse.[126] Although in countries like South Africa, gay and lesbians have won several cases in the Constitutional Court based on the discrimination clause in the Constitution.[127] However, the same frequency is not used in the cases of sexual abuse on women as a result of being lesbians.

Some of the sexual abuse that women are vulnerable to are sometimes based on cultural myths such as the idea that HIV/AIDS could be cured by having sex with a virgin.[128] This erroneous belief has sparked waves of rape of very young children in South Africa. Rape is one of the most violent and traumatic incidents that destroy the lives of women emotionally and psychologically. These days on the African continent, it is not just the violence of rape but now the intersection between rape and the contraction of HIV/AIDS.[129] Most of the women who are raped are at risk of contracting HIV/AIDS because of the high rate of infection on the continent. In Sub Saharan Africa, HIV/AIDS have reached an epidemic proportion where young women (15–24 years) account for

[125] See the Report of the Special Rapporteur on Violence Against Women, UN Doc. E/CN.4/1997/47, 12 February 1998, para. 8.

[126] In Zimbabwe, a young woman was locked in a room where a man was brought daily to rape her so that she can fall pregnant and be cured of her sexual orientation according to the interview conducted by Bev Clark, author of Lesbian Activism in Zimbabwe (1994). In South Africa, two women were also raped and killed because of their sexual orientation by a group of men. S. 9 of the South African Constitution prohibits discrimination based on sexual orientation.

[127] *National Coalition for Gay and Lesbian Equality*, 2000 (1) *BCLR* 39 (CC), *Fourie and Another* v. *Minister of Home Affairs*, 2006 (3) *BCLR* 355 (CC), *Satchwell* v. *President of Republic of South Africa*, 2002 (9) *BCLR* 986 (CC).

[128] Julie Stewart, "Arenas of Anguish-Tracking multiple, Perpetuating Trauma in HIV/AIDS and Gender-Based Violence Intersections," in *Gender-Based Violence in Africa: Perspectives From the Continent* published by the Centre for Human Rights, University of Pretoria, 113 where the writer argues that these beliefs are propagated by traditional healers who tend to benefit from exercising cultural power and who usually recommends this course of action. Other perpetrators other than the male perpetrator implicit in creating this cycle of trauma includes the State which fails to employ public education to disperse this kind of myth and also the failure to provide Antiretroviral and persons who collude to provide the young children that are raped.

[129] Report of the Special Rapporteur on Violence against Women on Intersections of Violence against Women and HIV/AIDS E/CN.4/2005/72 at 10 where she stated that over and above intimate partner violence in the home, or by strangers in the community, women are susceptible to risks of infection because in the cases of rape and sexual assault, they do not have control on where, when and how they should have sex therefore raising for women the significant high risk of contracting HIV/AIDS.

70 per cent of HIV which is three times more likely to be infected than young men of the same age.[130] Women are more at risk because of the unequal balance of power between men and women; the ability to seek protection through the use of condom which often times is not possible during rape. Also having many sexual partners on the part of the man puts women at risk although this kind of behaviour could possibly go both ways. Many women have lost their lives on violence arising from revealing their status. From indication, it is a vicious cycle of violence, discrimination and stigmatization for women on all turns. The situation is burdensome and draining for women especially those in the rural areas who are poor, illiterate and suffers tremendously from lack of access to medical care, home-based care may be insufficient and the victim would be unable to earn income due to hospitalisation as a result of the illness.[131]

Women are also at the receiving end during armed conflict which in the past decade has taken place in many countries of the African continent. Women are forcefully uprooted from their homes where they have security to become internally displaced persons and refugees fleeing their country or displaced in their own homes. For example, as a result of the economic meltdown in troubled Zimbabwe, young women and women of older age group left their homes in search of work in South Africa, others resorted to forced prostitution in order to put food on the table for their families.[132] In Sierra Leone, during the decade of conflict women were systematically raped because they become 'war trophies' for the militants or 'bush wives'. The use of sexual violence during armed conflict has been recognized as a form of genocide and a violation of the rights of women.[133] The militarization of the conflict region leaves very little means of escape for women who most times are fleeing with their children who are vulnerable to sexualized abuse. The nature of violent armed conflict further exacerbates the situation for women to get help to deal with the conflict let alone the associated sexual violence. In order to flee the conflict, they further

130 Violence against Women and HIV/AIDS: Critical Intersections, WHO Information Bulletin Series, Number 1. www.who.org.Violence against Women is both a cause and a consequence of the HIV/AIDS infection and as such is a driving force behind the high prevalence of the infection.

131 Stewart, "Arenas of Anguish- Tracking multiple, Perpetuating Trauma in HIV/AIDS and Gender-Based Violence Intersections," in *Gender-Based Violence in Africa*," 116.

132 SABC Special Assignment Programme on Zimbabwe 2007.

133 The International Criminal Tribunal for Rwanda in the case of *Prosecutor* v. *Mikaeli Muhimana*, Case No. ICTR-95-1B, Judgement and Sentence, 28 April 2005 recognized the violation implicit in rape during armed conflict as a way of subjugation, ethnic cleansing, domination and control. The systematic nature of rape during these times further exposes women to the scourge of HIV/AIDS. See Stewart, "Arenas of Anguish- Tracking multiple, Perpetuating Trauma in HIV/AIDS and Gender-Based Violence Intersections," in *Gender-Based Violence in Africa*, 112.

expose themselves to a cycle of violence that threatens their very lives such as hunger, rape and lack of access to hospital and medicines. Also the inability to know their status to HIV/AIDS after being raped leaves little option for access to medical care.[134] The situation in Darfur region of Sudan has been brought to the world attention by human rights organizations such as Amnesty International. The gross violation of human rights by the government sponsored janjaweed militia has been well documented where women are bearing the brunt of the war. Recently the International Court of Justice has issued a warrant of arrest for the Sudanese President Omar Bashir. This is a symbolic act on the part of the International community to recognize the war crimes that have been going on in Sudan in the last decade.

Most women in Africa are poor and lack professional skills that would enable them get gainful employment. Feminized poverty and the poor status of the socio-economic of women give rise to families sending their girl children away or these children are taken overseas by agents claiming to help the family come out of poverty. This form help actually involves trafficking in young children by syndicates who seek out these poor people and convince them to send their children overseas for a better life which in actual fact turn out to be sexual slavery, exploitation and forced labor of the girls. Although men suffer from trafficking for forced labor, the number of women and girls is by far the highest number of trafficked persons in the world.[135] Trafficking in persons has been recognized as a form of violence against women and the different dimensions of the issue have necessitated global response. The United Nations Protocol to Prevent, Suppress and Punish Trafficking (Palermo Protocol) was adopted in 2000 and entered into force in 2003. It is noteworthy that this Protocol exists, however, the majority of persons being trafficked are from rural areas and the nature of trade make it almost impossible for the government to put measures in place to deal with this form of violence against women. For example it has been noted that in 1999, 60 per cent of prostitutes in Italy or other sex related work are from Nigeria and about 80 per cent of these women are from the inland state of Edo in Nigeria.[136] The nature of these trafficking limits the power of women to negotiate safe sex and so puts them at the risk of sexually transmitted infections and HIV. In a survey conducted in South Africa which is also transit route in Southern Africa indicates that sex workers working at truck shops face violent reactions from clients, brutality and loss of income to as

---

[134] Amnesty International Campaign, Its' in our hands: Stop Violence against Women (2004) 61.www.amnestyinternational.org

[135] Bisi Olateru-Olagbegi, "State Response to Trafficking in Women and Children in Africa-The Nigerian Experience," in *Gender-Based Violence in Africa*, 154.

[136] Ibid., 160–61.

much as 25 per cent cut in income if they insist on condom use.[137] It is evident that violence against women in all its ramifications is always a cycle of violence, brutality and transmission of infections and diseases.

6.3. *Specific African mechanisms for combating violence against women*

In the African continent, most communities have means of dealing with societal issues which include family meetings where family problems are dealt with by the elders of the family and the greater community problems are dealt with by the chiefs in clan meetings. These problem-solving methods have helped most communities in dealing with treatment of women in the rural areas and even people who live in sub urban areas whose marriages are recognized by the traditional society sought to deal with matters in this form. It is argued that in the African society where communal living defines the people, these means of conflict resolution and problem-solving methods have yielded fruits in maintaining societal cohesion. Although it is common knowledge that the idea of any married woman being a wife and a daughter to the family she got married into, the transformation of this communal living to a more modern way of life brought about by colonialism and globalization have created rifts in the way of life of the majority of the African society. Communal living has given way to individualism on which most international instruments for human rights is based on. However, the African Charter on Human and Peoples' Rights gave impetus to the idea that the people and the family are an integral part of society hence the provisions in the Charter dealing with these groups.[138] The Draft Protocol to the African Charter on Women's Rights has consolidated the provisions in the Charter on the protection of women. Women and Children are seen as vulnerable within the society and thus require that their dignity and equality be protected and the State has a positive duty to ensure that these rights are protected by means of effective affirmative action.[139] The Charter has been criticized in its general format for the protection of women and the support given to family values and cultural traditions in one provision. This criticism is based on the fact that in the traditional African society, certain cultures discriminate against women such as wife inheritance, property inheritance and forced marriages. It is argued that culture evolves and thus in the African continent, these forms of discrimination may give way to equality and protection of

---

[137] Report of the Special Rapporteur on Violence against Women E/CN.4/2005/72 at para. 42.

[138] Henry Onoria, "Introduction to the African Syatem of Protection of Human Rights and the Draft Protocol," in *Human Rights of Women: International Instruments and African Experiences*, ed. Benedek, Kissakye, and Oberleitner, 231.

[139] Ibid., 326.

the dignity of women especially where the Charter seems to invoke the provisions of Convention for the Elimination of all Forms of Discrimination against Women (CEDAW) to give effect to the respect of women's dignity and equality. Also, the Charter seeks to ensure that women and children are protected from trafficking and forced labor.[140]

Other regional and sub regional mechanisms that seek to ensure that the rights of women are protected are initiatives such as the ECOWAS Plan of Action against trafficking and exploitative labour.[141]

The African Union (AU) in recognition of the unequal balance of power between men and women based on patriarchy acknowledged that gender justice or gender equality is the key to eradication of gender-based violence. To this effect, the Union adopted the Solemn Declaration on Gender Equality in Africa in July 2004. In its framework, the Declaration enjoins parties to deepen the understanding of the problem and target to eliminate gender-based violence by 2015.[142] States have dedicated resources to educating the public on gender-based violence, revising the laws and adopting new ones all aimed at eliminating gender-based violence. However, in the short time before the target year approaches, it is argued that States must ensure that the periodic reports are made to the AU ordinary summits consistently and the AU Assembly must dedicate resources to monitoring and evaluating positions. It is only where these mechanisms are made to be effective that results are achieved.

In recognition of the sexual and reproductive rights of women, the AU Conference of Ministers of Health in 2006 in Maputo produced a plan of action that would run from 2007 to 2010. The Maputo Plan of Action for the Operationalisation of the Continental Policy Framework for Sexual and Reproductive Health Rights is aimed at a collaborative effort on the intersection between violence against women and sexual and reproductive rights.[143] The high incidence of HIV/AIDS, sexually transmitted infections, and other health concerns of women require that governments develop strategies that would minimize the burden of these diseases on women. The effective implementation of these strategies would always remain key to eliminating violence against women.

[140] See generally Art. 1–5 of the Charter.

[141] 21 countries in West and Central Africa signed the Common Platform for Action in Libreville, Gabon on 24 February 2000. Each country was enjoined to take action to ensure the passing of comprehensive legislation to deal with human trafficking especially criminalizing traffickers, protecting victims including compensations and reparation rights. See Olateru-Olagbegi, "State Response to Trafficking in Women and Children in Africa-The Nigerian Experience," op. cit. (note 135), p. 173.

[142] Karen Stefiszyn, "The African Regional Response to Gender-based Violence," in *Gender-based Violence in Africa*, 22.

[143] Ibid., 29.

7. *Conclusion*

International rights of women is an important dimension of women's rights. Women's rights when they came to be recognized were largely limited to the domestic domain. It was not until the establishment of the UN Charter and subsequent developments on human rights that women's rights became concern of the international community. It is important that discrimination against women was given special focus as a particular problem area. This culminated in the adoption of the CEDAW. CEDAW to which all African States save for Somalia have subscribed is particularly important means of advancing the equal status of women. The CEDAW Committee responsible for the monitoring of implementation of commitments State Parties have assumed on becoming parties has assisted in developing the jurisprudence on women's rights through general comments and recommendations as well as decisions the Committee has taken when applying and interpreting the CEDAW in respect of individual complaints brought to its attention by complainants alleging violation of their rights under the 1999 CEDAW Optional Protocol. It is still a long way to go towards attainment of substantive equality between men and women but there is no doubt that post-Second World War international law has become sensitive to issues of gender and women's rights.

It is noteworthy that in terms of declaration and adopting plans of action for the continent, Africa has made great strides in combating violence against women. One of the major challenges towards effective elimination is poor governance, democratization and lack of political will on the part of the leaders to actually implement these strategies that they have adopted.

Public education remains one of the means of creating awareness of the new challenges to violence against women such as the intersection between violence against women and HIV/AIDS and bridging the gap between culture and human rights. Developing laws to be consistent with the value of equality and respect for the dignity of women would also be an appropriate means of eliminating violence against women.

Bibliography

Brandt, Michael, and Kaplan Jeffrey. "The Tension Between Women's Rights and Religious Rights: Reservations to CEDAW by Egypt, Bangladesh and Tunisia." *Journal of Law and Religion* 12 (1995): 105–42.

Bunch, Charlotte. "Women's Rights as Human Rights: Toward a Re-Vision of Human Rights." *Human Rights Quarterly* 12 (1990): 486–98.

Bunch, Charlotte, and Frost Samantha. "Women's Human Rights: An Introduction." *Routledge International Encyclopedia of Women: Global Women's issues and Knowledge.* Available at Center for Women's Global Leadership.<http://www.cwgl.rutgers.edu/globalcenter/whr.html>

Burrows, Noreen. "International Law and Human Rights: The Case of Women's Rights." In *Human Rights from Rhetoric to Reality*, edited by Campbell Tom, Goldberg David, Mc Lean Sheila and Muller Tom. Oxford / New York: Basil Blackwell, 1986.
Cook, Rebecca. "International Human Rights and Women's Reproductive Health." *Studies in Family Planning* 24 (1993): 73–86.
Cook, Rebecca. "Women's International Human Rights Law: The Way Forward." *Human Rights Quarterly* 15 (1993): 230–61.
Cook, Rebecca, and Jeanne Haws. "The United Nations Convention on the Rights of Women: Opportunities for Family Planning Providers." *International Family Planning Perspectives* 12 (1986): 49–53.
Cook, Rebecca. "International Human Rights and Women's Reproductive Health." *Studies in Family Planning* 24 (1993): 73–86.
Girard, Francoise. "Cairo + Five: Reviewing Progress for Women Five Years after the International Conference on Population and Development." *Journal of Women's Health and Law* 1 (1999): 1–14.
Koh, Harold Hongju. "Why America Should Ratify the Women's Rights Treaty (CEDAW)." *Case Western Reserve Journal of International Law* 34 (2002): 263–76.
Hevener, Natalie Kaufman. "An Analysis of Gender Based Treaty Law: Contemporary Developments in Historical Perspective." *Human Rights Quarterly* 27 (1986): 70–88.
Kathree, Fayeeza. "Convention on the Elimination of all Forms of Discrimination against Women." *South African Journal on Human Rights* 11 (1995): 421–37.
Ngaba, Sindiso. "CEDAW: Eliminating Discrimination against Women." *Agenda* 27 (1995): 81–89.
Olateru-Olagbegi, Bisi 'State Response to Trafficking in Women and Children in Africa-The Nigerian Experience' in Gender-Based Violence in Africa: Perspectives from the Continent published by the Centre for Human Rights, University of Pretoria.
Ozoemena, Rita Nkiruka. "African Customary Law and Gender Justice in a Progressive Democracy." Unpublished LLM thesis submitted to Rhodes University, Grahamstown, 2006.
Reanda, Laura. "Human Rights and Women's Rights: The United Nations Approach." *Human Rights Quarterly* 3 (1981): 11–31.
Shalev, Carmel. "Rights to Sexual and Reproductive Health: The ICPD and the Convention on the Elimination of All Forms of Discrimination against Women." *Health and Human Rights* 4 (2000): 38–66.
Stefiszyn, Karen. "The African Regional Response to Gender-based Violence."' In *Gender-based Violence in Africa: Perspectives from the Continent* Published by the Centre for Human Rights, University of Pretoria.
Welch, Claude. "Human Rights and African Women: A Comparison of Protection under Two Major Treatise." *Human Rights Quarterly* 15 (1993): 549–74.

Legal Instruments

Beijing Platform, 1995
Convention on the Consent to Marriage, Minimum Age of Marriage and Registration of Marriages (Convention on Consent to Marriage), 1962
Convention on the Elimination of all forms of Discrimination against Women (CEDAW), 1979
Convention on the Nationality of Married Women, 1957
Convention on the Political Rights of Women, 1952
Convention on the Rights of the Child
International Covenant on Civil and Political Rights, 1966
International Covenant on Economic, Social and Cultural Rights, 1966
Optional Protocol to the Women's Convention, 1999
Sexual Offences Act of 2006
UN Charter, 1945
Universal Declaration of Human Rights, 1948

Resolution and Recommendation

General Assembly Resolution 640 (VII) of 20 December 1952
General Assembly Resolution 1040 (XI) of 29 January 1957
General Assembly Resolution 1763 A (XVII) of 7 November 1962
General Assembly Resolution 34/180 of 18 December 1979
General Recommendation No. 8 of 1988
General Recommendation No. 12 of 1989
General Recommendation 14 of 1990
General Recommendation No. 19 of 1992
General Recommendation No. 21of 1994
General Recommendation No. 22 of 1995
General Recommendation No. 21 of 1996
General Recommendation No. 24 of 1999

Websites

www.Iww-fairfax.org
www.who.int/reproductive-health/fgm/ WHO
www.who.int/mediacentre/factsheet/fs241/en
www.un.org.womenwatch/dew/cedaw/37session.htm
www.lwv-fairfax.org.
www.who.org.
www.amnestyinternational.org
www.un.org.womenwatch/dew/cedaw/37sess.htm.

Reports

Report of the Special Rapporteur on Violence Against Women, UN Doc. E/CN.4/1997/47, 12 February 1998
Report of the Special Rapporteur on Violence against Women on Intersections of Violence against Women and HIV/AIDS E/CN.4/2005/72
Report of the Special Rapporteur on Violence againt Women E/CN.4/2005/72

Cases

Fourie and Another v. *Minister of Home Affairs*, 2006 (3) *BCLR* 355 (CC)
National Coalition for Gay and Lesbian Equality, 2000 (1) *BCLR* 39 (CC)
Prosecutor v. *Mikaeli Muhimana*, Case No. ICTR-95-1B, Judgement and Sentence, 28 April 2005
Satchwell v. *President of Republic of South Africa*, 2002 (9) *BCLR* 986 (CC)

Chapter Five

Globalization and Human Rights

*Heli Askola**

1. *Introduction*

This chapter discusses the various effects of globalization on human rights. Such an enquiry involves many questions. What exactly is globalization? Is it diminishing the power of the State to guarantee human rights, or indeed to violate them, or is it merely changing the ways in which this power is exercised? Does globalization raise entirely new human rights concerns or is it just transforming existing issues? Are the effects of globalization on human rights, generally speaking, detrimental or does globalization also facilitate efforts to implement human rights around the world? How and where do these effects occur?

The complex ways in which the increased (and increasing) interconnectedness and interdependence of global economic, political and social processes impact on the protection of human rights makes these questions difficult to answer conclusively. This chapter seeks to give a snapshot of some of the multiple relationships between globalization in its different forms and States' existing human rights obligations. On the one hand, it examines the challenges globalization poses to human rights and, on the other, discusses the opportunities globalization provides for better implementation of human rights. The chapter starts by briefly introducing the concept of globalization; it then presents some of the positive as well as negative effects of globalization on human rights, along two broadly defined axes: economic globalization and political, social and cultural globalization.

2. *Globalization*

What is globalization? The literature on the phenomenon of globalization has become increasingly abundant, yet the term itself remains emotionally loaded

* Dr Heli Askola, Senior Lecturer, Faculty of Law, Monash University, Melbourne, Australia.

and politically controversial. Many commentators, regardless of whether they are supporters of more globalization or critical of it, still disagree on exactly what the term covers.

In its most literal sense the term 'globalization' refers to a *process* (or processes) that transforms local or regional features, issues or phenomena into global ones. Even though globalization is often thought of as something relatively recent, it can be argued that globalization is actually a long process that can be traced back centuries to the discovery of America (maybe even the Silk Road or the Roman Empire).[1] Whilst there is a tendency, by some modern commentators, to portray globalization in progressive and linear terms, this process can more accurately be understood as a complex combination of economic, technological, socio-cultural and political forces that moves in fits and spurts.[2] The term itself, now in everyday use, started to become popular towards the late 1980s and early 1990s – but actually even the term itself is older than it is often assumed (it was used in social sciences in the 1960s and has been used by economists since the 1980s). What most current commentators tend to mean by globalization is the *intensification* of this transformational process, either since the Second World War or, even more recently, since the end of the Cold War. There are various analytical ways of defining and explaining these latest developments – this chapter focuses on two broad aspects: globalization that is purely economic/financial and globalization of political/ethical, social and cultural spheres.

If globalization is understood more narrowly in an economic sense, the term tends to be used to mean increasing economic integration and interdependence between countries – through trade, foreign direct investment, capital flows and so on – leading to the emergence of a global market for goods and services and capital. These processes have been driven by business interests and politicians and facilitated by advances in technology and science, which have reduced the cost of cross-border economic and financial transactions.[3] The founding of international institutions intended to oversee the processes of globalization after the Second World War has also been an influential factor in driving the processes of economic globalization around the world. The policies of the twin Bretton Woods institutions, the World Bank (which provides loans, credit and grants to developing countries) and the International Monetary Fund or IMF (which seeks to ensure global financial stability) have been promoting macro-economic adjustment policies in developing countries, involving greater open-

[1] See Alex MacGillivray, *A Brief History of Globalization* (London: Robinson, 2006), Ch. 1.

[2] See the discussion in David Held et al., *Global Transformations: Politics, Economics, and Culture* (Oxford: Polity, 1999), 1–28.

[3] Grahame Thompson, "Economic Globalization?" in *A Globalizing World? Culture, Economics, Politics*, ed. David Held (London: Routledge, 2004).

ness of national economies, deregulation and privatization. Negotiations on increasing trade flows originally took place under the auspices of the General Agreement on Tariffs and Trade (GATT) and lead to the establishment of the World Trade Organization (WTO) in 1995.

In a broader sense globalization can be seen as a phenomenon that goes beyond such economic processes. Broader perspectives focus on globalization as creating transformations in political, ethical, social, cultural, informational and environmental spheres and on the governance challenges posed by these transformations.[4] Often global transformations and local or regional developments overlap and intertwine with each other. In political terms globalization can be linked to regulating the increasingly manifold interrelationships of States and seeking to guarantee the human rights of individuals affected by economic and social globalization.[5] One of the most crucial social dimensions of globalization relates to increased migration, as opportunities offered by modern transport and fewer restrictions on travel (for some groups of people) have lead to a more global circulation of persons – which in turn has e.g. economic and cultural effects.[6] In cultural terms globalization increases cross-cultural contacts but also potential for 'culture clashes' – and it can also be discussed in terms of new forms of 'global consciousness'. This awareness of a shared planet can be linked to development challenges or, more recently, environmental issues (such as global climate change) which are seen to be in need of global solutions.[7] New technologies and inventions are crucial facilitators of most dimensions of globalization (e.g. economic, political and cultural) – but modern technologies also create new regulatory challenges.[8]

Globalization, both in a purely economic sense and in a broader political/social/cultural sense, can of course be viewed in a negative or positive light. The most vociferous critics of globalization have been those 'anti-globalization' activists who have condemned the impact of economic globalization in the developing world where, it has been argued, global capitalism has produced widespread inequality, slowed social development and detrimentally impacted

---

[4] See e.g. Joseph S. Nye Jr. and John D. Donahue, eds. *Governance in a Globalizing World* (Washington: Brookings Institution Press, 2000); Held et al., *Global Transformations*; Malcolm Waters, *Globalization*, 2nd ed. (London: Routledge, 2001).

[5] Held et al., *Global Transformations*, Ch. 1.

[6] Ibid., Ch. 6.

[7] Sheila Jasanoff, "Image and Imagination: The Formation of Global Environmental Consciousness," in *Changing the Atmosphere: Expert Knowledge and Environmental Governance*, ed. Clark A. Miller and Paul N. Edward (Cambridge: MIT Press, 2001).

[8] Roger Brownsword, "What the World Needs Now: Techno-Regulation, Human Rights and Human Dignity," in *Global Governance and the Quest for Justice. vol. IV; Human Rights*, ed. Roger Brownsword (Oxford: Hart Publishing, 2005).

on the protection of human rights. This has created hostility to the excesses of economic globalization which found expression in the anti-globalization protests at the Seattle WTO meeting in 1999 and again in Genoa in 2001.[9] However, the effects of globalization on human rights are uneven even in the economic sphere, and many certainly advocate for *more* legal, political and social globalization to address governance gaps in areas such as international justice and attempts to counteract global warming. The next sections map these tensions onto the framework of human rights.

3. *Economic Globalization and Human Rights*

States have established commitments to respect and ensure international human rights, as elaborated by e.g. the two United Nations Covenants.[10] Economic globalization impacts on these and other human rights commitments in a multitude of ways. Whilst much attention has focused on various negative impacts of globalization, the picture is more nuanced. Despite the fact that economic globalization raises many concerns, its effects are uneven: it has brought undeniable benefits to (some) low- and middle-income countries and (some) previously economically disempowered individuals as well. Economic globalization is therefore not necessarily unequivocally detrimental for human rights, even if the way in which it has been managed requires closer scrutiny.

Many commentators, especially economists, see economic globalization, in the form of increased trade, investment and competition, as essentially benign and beneficial for the world on the whole.[11] From this perspective free trade, privatization, increasing flows of capital across borders, deregulation and outsourcing are key factors in promoting economic development by making developing economies work more efficiently and by bringing individuals increased opportunities to improve their economic situation. In developing countries markets, if properly managed, can arguably be engines for accelerated economic development and thus, together with strides in production and scientific and technological progress, contribute to the eradication of poverty.[12] To the extent that holds true, the forces of economic globalization pull in the same direc-

[9] William F. Fisher and Thomas Ponniah, eds, *Another World is Possible: Popular Alternatives to Globalization at the World Social Forum* (London: Zed Books, 2003).

[10] International Covenant on Civil and Political Rights (999 U.N.T.S. 171); International Covenant on Economic, Social and Cultural Rights (993 U.N.T.S. 3).

[11] Martin Wolf, *Why Globalization Works* (New Haven: Yale University Press, 2004); Jagdish Bhagwati, *In Defense of Globalization* (Oxford: Oxford University Press, 2004); Jeffrey Sachs, *The End of Poverty: Economic Possibilities for Our Time* (New York: Penguin Press, 2005).

[12] See e.g. Sachs, *The End of Poverty*.

tion as many of the human rights obligations that States have undertaken. For instance, the WTO aim to 'raise standards of living' and provide for 'full employment'[13] can be seen as being closely are aligned with and contributing to the 'progressive realization' of economic and social rights, such as the right to work or the right to an adequate standard of living as guaranteed by the International Covenant on Economic, Social and Cultural Rights (ICESCR).[14] It has also been argued that, at least in the long term, economic globalization contributes to democracy and better respect for civil and political rights, or is at least compatible with efforts to promote these rights.[15]

This understanding of economic globalization as a progressive force for good both in economic and political terms can, however, be criticized for incorporating simplistic assumptions about how economic globalization works.[16] Indeed, the most important criticism of economic globalization relates to its asymmetric character *in practice*: in a world characterized by unequal access to wealth and resources, there is a lack of a level playing field. Thus any benefits generated by economic globalization are likely to be unequally distributed rather than to 'trickle down' and semi-automatically lead to respect for all human rights.[17] In particular, while economic liberalization typically benefits wealthier nations (leading Western developed States) and successful individuals and companies in these countries, this can take place at the expense of poorer nations (i.e. mostly developing States) and their (non-elite) citizens.[18] With regard to human rights, while global income has grown and some previously disempowered groups have benefited from this, because of historical inequalities and global structural factors it cannot be taken for granted that any wealth generated has a beneficial effect on human rights *overall*. On the contrary, new challenges are brought up e.g. because of declining capability of States which have been adversely affected by global economic forces to guarantee the human rights of their populations.[19]

---

[13] Marrakesh Agreement Establishing the World Trade Organization, preamble.

[14] Articles 2, 6 and 11 of the International Covenant on Economic, Social and Cultural Rights (1966).

[15] Rhoda Howard-Hassmann, "The Second Great Transformation: Human Rights Leapfrogging in the Era of Globalization," *Human Rights Quarterly* 27 (2005): 1–40.

[16] Jack Donnelly, "Human Rights, Democracy, and Development," *Human Rights Quarterly* 21 (1999): 608–32.

[17] Dean Baker, Gerald Epstein, and Robert Pollin, *Globalization and Progressive Economic Policy* (Cambridge: Cambridge University Press, 1998); Joseph Stieglitz, *Globalization and Its Discontents* (New York: W. W. Norton & Company, 2002); Lourdes Benería, *Gender, Development, and Globalization* (New York: Routledge, 2003).

[18] Adam Gearey, *Globalization and Law: Trade, Rights, War* (Lanham: Rowman & Littlefield, 2005).

[19] Alison Brysk, ed., *Globalization and Human Rights* (Berkeley: University of California Press, 2002); Wolfgang Benedek, Koen De Feyter, and Fabrizio Marrella, eds, *Economic Globalisation and Human Rights* (Cambridge: Cambridge University Press, 2007).

Unequal economic globalization may also create increased political instability and environmental degradation which in turn affect the human rights of vulnerable individuals.

Some fault for the threat that the present international economic system poses on human rights has been laid at the door of international financial institutions that control the processes of economic globalization and promote policies that affect human rights in the name of international economic adjustment.[20] The World Bank and the International Monetary Fund have faced broad criticism not only for their undemocratic decision-making structures (both have rules that favour industrialized lender nations)[21] but for commanding developing nations to adopt policies that constrain States' capacity to guarantee human rights without conflicting with international economic law. The World Bank, which funds large development projects, has been criticized for giving loans to governments with poor human rights records or rife with corruption as well as for funding projects that are environmentally and culturally disruptive and undermine the human rights of vulnerable individuals and groups.[22] Moreover, its funding not only targets large-scale infrastructure projects (e.g. building of dams) which may sideline investment in primary health care or basic education,[23] but also sometimes comes with requirements for structural adjustment, like privatization of services. Privatization of essential public services like water (or health) services can raise the prices for essential goods and services[24] and, if not carefully managed, lead to individuals not having access to clean water or essential sanitation.

With regard to economic adjustment, the International Monetary Fund has faced even more criticism than the World Bank over its policies that mostly ignore, yet can inadvertently undermine, human rights. The IMF, which gives loans to countries that require urgent financial assistance to avoid an economic catastrophe, insists on economic reform as a condition to its loans, and the conditions imposed by the IMF to implement 'free-market friendly' policies have arguably taken away some of developing countries' sovereignty.[25] The

---

[20] See e.g. Koen De Feyter, *Human Rights: Social Justice in the Age of the Market* (London: Zed Books, 2005).

[21] Ngaire Woods, "The Challenge of Good Governance for the IMF and the World Bank Themselves," *World Development* 28 (2000): 823–41.

[22] See e.g. the discussion of the Chad-Cameroon Oil and Pipeline project in Korinna Horta, "Rhetoric and Reality: Human Rights and the World Bank," *Harvard Human Rights Journal* 15 (2002): 227–44.

[23] Articles 12 and 13 of the International Covenant on Economic, Social and Cultural Rights (1966).

[24] Kate Bayliss, "Privatization and Poverty: The Distributional Impact of Utility Privatization," *Annals of Public and Cooperative Economics* 73 (2002): 603–25.

[25] Joseph Stiglitz, *Making Globalization Work* (New York: W. W. Norton & Company, 2006).

IMF, which aims to stabilize the global economy, is not (unlike the World Bank) a development bank and its decisions about investment are based almost exclusively on financial concerns (including generating profits). Therefore, in its lending activities non-financial concerns tend to be treated as internal problems of the debtor nation. However, as a result of these arrangements, debtor States may face a crippling debt that has to be prioritized – unless they refuse to cooperate with the IMF – and such states may also become unable to focus their efforts to realize economic and social rights.[26] The adverse human rights effects of these adjustments are often felt along class and gender lines so that e.g. women disproportionately bear the costs of adjustment.[27]

Moreover, the fact that economic adjustment programs advocating privatization and deregulation bring in non-State actors raises fresh human rights issues when these private actors challenge States' traditional roles as the guarantors of central public goods.[28] Privatization of water, electricity and telecommunications services has increased the influence and impact of non-State actors such as multinational corporations, which benefit from the increasing economic openness of developing countries and as a result often control vast segments of production and society. Unlike States, multinational corporations are not recognized by international human rights law as obligation holders. Therefore their practices in developing countries can have detrimental human rights impacts, involving e.g. threat to life and health, for which they themselves do not bear automatic responsibility.[29] The increasing presence and influence of multinational corporations has also contributed to infamous cases of environmental damage; and the activities of multinational corporations have also challenged core labour rights throughout Southeast Asia and many parts of Latin America.[30]

---

[26] The most famous example of a State default is the 2002 Argentinean crisis that resulted in the largest sovereign debt default in world history. See e.g. Stiglitz, *Making Globalization Work*, 220–25; Sabine Michalowski, "Human Rights in Times of Economic Crisis: The Example of Argentina," in *Global Governance and the Quest for Justice*, ed. Brownsword.

[27] Bharati Sadasivam, "The Impact of Structural Adjustment on Women: A Governance and Human Rights Agenda," *Human Rights Quarterly* 19 (1997): 630–65.

[28] Koen De Feyter and Felipe Gómez Isa, eds, *Privatisation and Human Rights in the Age of Globalisation* (Antwerp: Intersentia Uitgevers, 2005).

[29] Sarah Joseph, "An Overview of the Human Rights Accountability of Multinational Enterprises," in *Liability of Multinational Corporations under International Law*, ed. Menno Kamminga and Saman Zia-Zarifi (The Hague: Kluwer Law International, 2000); Karin Lucke, "States' and Private Actors' Obligations under International Human Rights Law and the Draft UN Norms," in *Human Rights and International Trade*, ed. Thomas Cottier, Joost Pauwelyn, and Elisabeth Bürgi (Oxford: Oxford University Press, 2005).

[30] Christine Kaufmann, *Globalisation and Labour Rights: The Conflict Between Core Labour Rights and International Economic Law* (Oxford: Hart Publishing, 2007).

Aspects of international trade, and the structures and practices of the WTO in particular, have also become the target of increasing human rights scrutiny.[31] One of the most common criticisms of the human rights impacts of economic globalization in this regard is that whilst free trade is advocated as a good-for-all, developing States have been short-changed in trade negotiations in ways that benefit multinational corporations and may endanger the human rights of populations in developing countries.[32] One of the instruments negotiated under the auspices of the WTO, the Agreement on Trade-Related Aspects of Intellectual Property Rights (TRIPS), which sets out minimum patent law requirements for WTO member States, is a good example of the tensions that can arise in this respect. Intellectual property rights protected by TRIPS benefit patent-rich agricultural and pharmaceutical industries in developed States but can threaten existing obligations under international human rights instruments in other States. For instance, TRIPS became controversial shortly after its adoption regarding the high costs of patented medicines which are needed to combat HIV or malaria in developing countries – obviously lacking access to affordable medicines can threaten the right to health and the right to life.[33] Similarly, TRIPS also requires developing countries to extend property rights to crops, potentially impacting on the right to adequate food.[34]

Whilst increasing global flows of capital and goods are seen as essential drivers of the world economy, deregulation with regard to the flow of people is firmly resisted by developed States. This is not to say that international migration has not increased – it has, as the number of global migrants has more than doubled since 1975 – but that industrialized countries and regions have been very concerned to manage and control these flows to their economic benefit, e.g. to 'skim the best and brightest' of the workers of developing countries rather than to encourage global labour mobility *per se*.[35] Restrictions on the movement of workers from the poorer areas to the richer, whilst factual opportunities for

---

[31] Wolfgang Benedek, "The World Trade Organization and Human Rights," in *Economic Globalisation and Human Rights*, eds. Benedek, Feyter, and Marrella.

[32] Stieglitz, *Globalization and Its Discontents*, Ch. 3.

[33] See e.g. Davinia Ovett, "Making Trade Policies More Accountable and Human Rights-Consistent: A NGO Perspective of Using Human Rights Instruments in the Case of Access to Medicines," in *Economic Globalisation and Human Rights*, ed. Benedek, Feyter, and Marrella; Frederick Abbott, "The Rule of Reason and the Right to Health: Integrating Human Rights and Competition Principles in the Context of TRIPS," in *Human Rights and International Trade*, ed. Cottier, Pauwelyn, and Bürgi.

[34] Christine Breining-Kaufmann, "The Right to Food and Trade in Agriculture," in *Human Rights and International Trade*, ed. Cottier, Pauwelyn, and Bürgi; Shelley Edwardson, "Reconciling TRIPS and the Right to Food," in ibid.

[35] Stieglitz, *Globalization and Its Discontents*, 89. Note that international human rights law only guarantees the right to leave a country (and to return to one's own country), not to enter

migrating have increased, has meant that growing numbers of undocumented labourers are vulnerable to exploitation and abuse e.g. by manipulative middlemen and unscrupulous employers in receiving industrialized States.[36] Often these effects are mapped along gender and class lines, impacting on the rights of those who are most vulnerable.[37] The potential problems with regard to workers in an otherwise globalizing economy are not limited to developing nations – whilst generally developed States have benefited from economic migration, some workers in advanced economies, particularly those in unskilled jobs, are being increasingly displaced by low-wage competition in developing countries.

Workers are different from other factors of production because they are human beings – and for that reason economic migration is a good example of a phenomenon that is in part linked to economic globalization but also has social and cultural dimensions (see the subsequent section). Indeed, the processes of economic globalization increasingly spill over to other walks of life. For instance, growing public discontent with the perceived injustices of global capitalism in developing countries can contribute to movements demanding radical economic and political change and erode of democracy and the rule of law. Such threats have lead to calls for reforming the international economic system. Much of this kind of work has focused on making the existing international financial organizations more accountable for their impact on human rights and on encouraging multinational corporations to be more socially responsible in their activities. For instance the World Bank has made some (albeit tentative) progress towards expansion into 'human rights territory' and evaluates its proposed activities from the point of view of human rights or labour rights.[38] On the whole, however, the more entrenched features of the global economic system, such as the global division of labour, still require more scrutiny to ensure that international human rights are adequately protected.

another country. See Article 12 of the International Covenant on Civil and Political Rights (1966).

[36] Patrick A. Taran, "Human Rights of Migrants: Challenges of the New Decade," *International Migration* 38 (2002): 7–51.

[37] Saskia Sassen, *Globalization and Its Discontents* (New York: New Press, 1998), esp. Section II.

[38] Jonathan Fox, "Transnational Civil Society Campaigns and the World Bank Inspection Panel," in *Globalization and Human Rights*, ed. Brysk; Laurence Boisson de Chazournes, "The Bretton Woods Institutions and Human Rights: Converging Tendencies," in *Economic Globalisation and Human Rights*, ed. Benedek, Feyter, and Marrella.

4. *Political, Social and Cultural Globalization and Human Rights*

As has already been indicated in the previous section, economic globalization does not take place in a vacuum. Its processes contribute to accelerated economic integration of productive forces which, together with scientific and technological advances, contributes to more intensive contact between States and peoples, increased migratory flows and cultural interaction. Globalization thus raises human rights implications in a growing number of policy areas outside the purely economic field. Complex political issues of global governance that arise relate to regulating the relationships between nations and between individuals in a globalizing world and to seeking to ensure global security through multilateral mechanisms. The growing interdependence of countries and peoples in every sphere raises social, cultural and ideological issues related to mobility, identity, multiculturalism and community. Global challenges – such as entrenched poverty in some developing regions, the HIV epidemic and other pandemics and global climate change – are increasingly seen as requiring worldwide solutions.

The political impact of globalization appears to involve a challenge to the foundational premise of the current international system, which places States as sovereign entities at the heart of the international order.[39] The system based on the United Nations Charter still forms the core of the international system, but it is increasingly obvious that States are progressively more interdependent and also interact with a multitude of powerful actors, such as international financial and other inter-governmental institutions and non-State actors such as multinational corporations. New levels of governance and authority (such as the European Union) are born out of regional political action. The human rights implications of these processes are contradictory and still unfolding. On the one hand, the interdependence of States means that powerful States or even private actors can take action that has far-reaching extraterritorial human rights consequences. On the other hand, there also exists more scope for interventions to stop human rights violations[40] or to mobilize universal jurisdiction to bring perpetrators of human rights violations, such as torture, to justice.[41] Yet many of these steps, though widely celebrated, have only been taken as a response to horrific genocides and crimes against humanity in the 1990s. The International

---

[39] Duncan French, "International Rhetoric and the Real Global Agenda: Exploring the Tension between Interdependence and Globalisation," in *Global Governance and the Quest for Justice*, ed. Brownsword.

[40] Wayne Sandholtz, "Humanitarian Intervention. Global Enforcement of Human Rights?" in *Globalization and Human Rights*, ed. Brysk.

[41] Chandra Sriram, "Globalisation of Justice: for Better or Worse?" in *Global Governance and the Quest for Justice*, ed. Brownsword.

Criminal Tribunals for Former Yugoslavia[42] and Rwanda[43] and the permanent International Criminal Court[44] are prime examples of this (reactive rather than proactive) trend.

In some ways, increased global attention to international human rights *per se* can be seen as part of the globalization of law and governance. Human rights are, after all, 'a global project' – one that can arguably be 'used to shape economic globalisation'[45] or that is a 'vehicle and expression of a global ethic'.[46] Global awareness of the Universal Declaration of Human Rights, the two UN Covenants and other human rights conventions has grown and 'human rights' has become *lingua franca* of international justice movements. Many proponents of these developments are civil society groups and transnational non-governmental organizations (NGOs), which themselves are part of the global trend, which was already mentioned with regard to economic globalization: the growing influence of non-State actors. Just as multinational corporations challenge the traditional role of the State as the guarantor but also the prime violator of human rights, the rise of activist civil society groups, some of them cross-border, highlights how their pursuit of their interests or values is increasingly transnational.[47] The success of individual local human rights campaigns (e.g. the Ogoni in the Niger delta) can depend on how well their concerns resonate with transnational human rights NGOs that might be willing to back local claims.[48] Activists are helped in their efforts to publicise and demand redress for human rights violations by modern communications technology – which however, is no panacea. Technology can also be used to impede efforts to implement human rights, for instance by fragmenting and distorting the message of human rights campaigners. It can even be used to track down

---

[42] The International Criminal Tribunal for the former Yugoslavia (ICTY) was set up by Security Council Resolution 827 of 25 May 1993.

[43] The International Criminal Tribunal for Rwanda (ICTR) was set up by Security Council Resolution 955 of 8 November 1994.

[44] The Rome Statute of the International Criminal Court (UN Doc. A/CONF.183/9 of 17 July 1998) entered into force on 1 July 2002.

[45] Koen De Feyter, "Introduction," in *Economic Globalisation and Human Rights*, ed. Benedek, Feyter, and Marrella, 5.

[46] George Ulrich, "Towards a Theory of Global Ethics in Support of Human Rights," in *Economic Globalisation and Human Rights*, ed. Benedek, Feyter, and Marrella, 39.

[47] On transnational social networks, see Margaret E. Keck and Kathryn Sikkink, *Activists beyond Borders: Advocacy Networks in International Politics* (Ithaca: Cornell University Press, 1998).

[48] Clifford Bob, "Globalization and the Social Construction of Human Rights Campaigns," in *Globalization and Human Rights*, ed. Brysk.

dissenters and crack down on freedom of expression in closed societies that allow little political freedom.[49]

Other non-State actors that have gained influence in the globalizing world are less benevolent than human rights NGOs. Transnational crime is seen as one of the new (or, at least, transformed) global challenges to ensuring international security.[50] Increasing awareness of transnational crimes with potentially severe human rights implications, such as trafficking and smuggling in human beings has led to the adoption of global crime-fighting cooperation instruments.[51] Perhaps even more pertinently, after the terrorist attacks on American and European soil, the treat of terrorism has climbed up the global security agenda as a sense of an insecurity has intensified in the West. What both transnational crime and terrorism have in common is not only that both may (obviously) affect their victims' human rights (e.g. freedom rights of those subjected to human trafficking or those targeted by bombings) but that also States' activities *against* both phenomena raise serious human rights issues. Both the 'War on Transnational Organised Crime' and in particular the 'War on Terror' have highlighted concerns about how traditional civil rights are threatened by repressive responses to crime and terrorism which are driven by a sense of collective insecurity. A wide range of human rights concerns emerges in this regard, ranging from the (im)permissibility of torture[52] and preventative detention of suspected terrorists to concerns over racial and religious discrimination.[53]

The divisive and simplistic language of the 'War on Terror' that demarcates a border between the 'good' (the supposedly morally superior West under attack) and the 'bad' (terrorists using despicable tactics) once more raises the social and cultural dimensions of globalization, such as the relationship between the growing movement of people across borders and identity formation, multiculturalism and integration.[54] Growing international migration has an obvious economic impact on both sending and receiving countries (see above) but also

---

[49] Shane Weyker, "The Ironies of Information Technology," in *Globalization and Human Rights*, ed. Brysk.

[50] Roy Godson and Phil Williams, "Strengthening cooperation against transnational crime," *Survival* 40 (1998): 66–88.

[51] See e.g. the United Nations Convention against Transnational Organized Crime (UN Doc. A/53/383 (2000)) and its protocols against human smuggling and human trafficking.

[52] Maureen Ramsay, "Can the torture of terrorist suspects be justified?" *The International Journal of Human Rights* 10 (2006): 103–19.

[53] Paul Hoffman, "Human Rights and Terrorism," *Human Rights Quarterly* 26 (2004): 932–55.

[54] Javaid Rehman, "Islam, 'War on Terror' and the Future of Muslim Minorities in the United Kingdom: Dilemmas of Multiculturalism," *Human Rights Quarterly* 29 (2007): 831–78.

affects politics, e.g. through the formation of ethnic minorities.[55] Ethnic diversity tests the limits of existing forms of citizenship and national identity as well as States' commitment to anti-discrimination. Continuing migration into developed countries, which treat migrants and asylum-seekers as a security threat or exploitable economic resource, has spawned policies that drive many vulnerable migrants into the hands of abusive middlemen and employers. Migration, especially when unauthorised, poses a direct challenge to States' commitment to fostering tolerance and guaranteeing the human rights (including labour rights) of *everyone* in their territory.[56] How to fight racial and religious discrimination and to guarantee respect for migrants' human rights by public as well as private actors is therefore becoming one of the crucial social questions posed by globalization.[57]

In terms of culture, globalization is intensifying the spread of cultural forms, ideas and values. Modern technologies (and global communication companies) are in one sense sweeping away cultural boundaries and homogenizing people's values and aspirations, just as the growth of tourism is increasing individuals' exposure to and understanding of other cultures, religions and customs.[58] Cultural exchange has the potential both to serve as an integrating and tolerance-inducing force and to undermine local traditions, to spread cultures of intolerance and to create 'culture clashes' between the 'the West and the Rest' (the latter aspect has again been brought into ever sharper relief by the threat of and response to terrorism). Criticism of cultural globalization as promoting 'Americanization', e.g. excessive consumerism or individualism, is well known, as is the charge that human rights (being a project stemming from the European Enlightenment) are not universal and may even be a form of Western cultural imperialism.[59] Insofar as cultural globalization promotes values and ideas with potential to destroy or fundamentally alter local cultural and religious traditions or to undermine local languages, it can be considered a threat to the cultural rights of those affected, such as indigenous groups. However, whilst the globalization of culture has given rise to politically or religiously inspired

---

55 Stephen Castles and Mark A. Miller, *The Age of Migration: International Population Movements in the Modern World*, 3rd ed. (New York: Guilford Press, 2003).

56 Kristen H. Maher, "Who Has a Right to Rights? Citizenship's Exclusions in an Age of Migration," in *Globalization and Human Rights*, ed. Brysk.

57 The International Convention on the Protection of the Rights of All Migrant Workers and Members of Their Families (G.A. res. 45/158, annex) is yet to be ratified by most States.

58 Hugh Mackay, "The Globalization of Culture?" in *A Globalizing World? Culture, Economics, Politics*, ed. Held; Held et al., *Global Transformations*, Ch. 7.

59 Jack Donnelly, "Cultural Relativism and Universal Human Rights," *Human Rights Quarterly* 6 (1984): 400–19; see also Abdullahi Ahmed An-Nai'im, "Islam, Islamic Law and the Dilemma of Cultural Legitimacy for Universal Human Rights", in *Asian Perspectives on Human Rights*, ed. Claude Welch and Virginia Leary (Boulder: Westview Press, 1990).

resistance, it has also led to creative interpretation and adaptation. It would be simplistic to characterize cultural globalization as a one-way street – whilst it may homogenize, it also engenders and supports plurality and differentiation that may in fact benefit marginalized sub-groups and individuals struggling for respect and recognition.

Finally, one of the most crucial future factors impacting on human rights in a globalized world is ecological. Environmental issues raised by economic globalization have been on the agenda for a while – it is common knowledge that the economic advances of globalization have come at a massive cost in terms of cross-boundary water and air pollution, over-fishing and the spread of invasive species.[60] The potential consequences of environmental degradation for the human rights of vulnerable populations have become even more evident as awareness of climate change has grown. In short, global environmental challenges have become a matter of human survival that cannot be solved without international cooperation. What makes environmental issues difficult in terms of global governance is that though climate change is a global problem with potentially dramatic global human rights implications (such as 'environmental refugee' flows), not everyone is equally responsible for causing it. Industrialized nations account for most of the past and current emissions (largely through the burning of fossil fuels) but the emissions of developing countries are rising. The question is how to equitably allocate the necessary reductions in emissions, without hindering the economic and social progress of developing countries. The human cost of failing to stop the planet warming places a great responsibility on States to reach a sustainable compromise, and reach it soon.

5. *Conclusion*

The net effect of globalization on international human rights is impossible to quantify. Globalization takes many forms and increasingly blurs the lines between different generations of rights. Proponents of economic globalization often assume the processes of globalization contribute to human rights via economic development; yet economic globalization has also resulted in deepened divisions in the level of enjoyment of human rights – between industrialized countries and developing nations, between elites and professionals and low-skilled workers, between the economically powerful and the economically marginalized. In a broader sense globalization involves a complex web of political, social, cultural, ideological processes that brings politics, people and ideas together and gives rise to new forms of global and regional governance. Yet

[60] Held et al., *Global Transformations*, Ch. 8.

the processes of globalization, involving increasing international insecurity and instability, have also intensified a number of human rights concerns and can engender new risks and challenges pertaining to migration, religion, culture and identity that have harmful effects.

The underlying basic assumption upon which all international human rights agreements are founded on is States' responsibility to ensure the human rights of those present in their jurisdiction – however, in a globalized world States' capacity to effectively guarantee observance of human rights across the board cannot be taken for granted. Yet the primary responsibility for respecting and ensuring human rights still remains with national governments who have to find new ways of regulating the conduct of new actors that play a role in the implementation of human rights. They have to adapt to new concerns that arise out of the changed international environment, transformed power relationships and multiple and sometimes conflicting legal obligations. The challenge that globalization entails for the protection of human rights is fundamental, and many of the effects of continuing globalization, be they positive or negative, still remain to be seen.

Bibliography

Abbott, Frederick. "The Rule of Reason and the Right to Health: Integrating Human Rights and Competition Principles in the Context of TRIPS." In *Human Rights and International Trade*, edited by Thomas Cottier, Joost Pauwelyn, and Elisabeth Bürgi, 279–300. Oxford: Oxford University Press, 2005.

An-Nai'im, Abdullahi Ahmed. "Islam, Islamic Law and the Dilemma of Cultural Legitimacy for Universal Human Rights." In *Asian Perspectives on Human Rights*, edited by Claude Welch and Virginia Leary, 31–54. Boulder: Westview Press, 1990.

Baker, Dean, Gerald Epstein, and Robert Pollin. *Globalization and Progressive Economic Policy*. Cambridge: Cambridge University Press, 1998.

Bayliss, Kate. "Privatization and Poverty: The Distributional Impact of Utility Privatization." *Annals of Public and Cooperative Economics* 73 (2002): 603–25.

Benedek, Wolfgang. "The World Trade Organization and Human Rights." In *Economic Globalisation and Human Rights*, edited by Wolfgang Benedek, Koen De Feyter and Fabrizio Marrella, 137–169. Cambridge: Cambridge University Press, 2007.

Benedek, Wolfgang, Koen De Feyter, and Fabrizio Marrella, eds. *Economic Globalisation and Human Rights*. Cambridge: Cambridge University Press, 2007.

Benería, Lourdes. *Gender, Development, and Globalization*. New York: Routledge, 2003.

Bhagwati, Jagdish. *In Defense of Globalization*. Oxford: Oxford University Press, 2004.

Bob, Clifford. "Globalization and the Social Construction of Human Rights Campaigns." In *Globalization and Human Rights*, edited by Alison Brysk, 133–147. Berkeley: University of California Press, 2002.

Boisson de Chazournes, Laurence. "The Bretton Woods Institutions and Human Rights: Converging Tendencies." In *Economic Globalisation and Human Rights*, edited by Wolfgang Benedek, Koen De Feyter and Fabrizio Marrella, 210–242. Cambridge: Cambridge University Press, 2007.

Breining-Kaufmann, Christine. "The Right to Food and Trade in Agriculture." In *Human Rights and International Trade*, edited by Thomas Cottier, Joost Pauwelyn, and Elisabeth Bürgi, 341–381. Oxford: Oxford University Press, 2005.

Brownsword, Roger. "What the World Needs Now: Techno-Regulation, Human Rights and Human Dignity." In *Global Governance and the Quest for Justice.* Vol. IV, *Human Rights,* edited by Roger Brownsword, 203–234. Oxford: Hart Publishing, 2005.

—— ed. *Global Governance and the Quest for Justice.* Vol. IV, *Human Rights.* Oxford: Hart Publishing, 2005.

Brysk, Alison, ed. *Human Rights and Private Wrongs. Constructing Global Civil Society.* New York: Routledge, 2005.

—— ed. *Globalization and Human Rights.* Berkeley: University of California Press, 2002.

Castles, Stephen, and Mark A. Miller. *The Age of Migration: International Population Movements in the Modern World.* 3rd ed. New York: Guilford Press, 2003.

Cottier, Thomas, Joost Pauwelyn, and Elisabeth Bürgi, eds. *Human Rights and International Trade.* Oxford: Oxford University Press, 2005.

De Feyter, Koen. "Introduction." In *Economic Globalisation and Human Rights,* edited by Wolfgang Benedek, Koen De Feyter, and Fabrizio Marrella, 1–14. Cambridge: Cambridge University Press, 2007.

——. *Human Rights: Social Justice in the Age of the Market.* London: Zed Books, 2005.

De Feyter, Koen and Felipe Gómez Isa, eds. *Privatisation and Human Rights in the Age of Globalisation.* Antwerp: Intersentia Uitgevers, 2005.

Donnelly, Jack. "Cultural Relativism and Universal Human Rights." *Human Rights Quarterly* 6 (1984): 400–19.

——. "Human Rights, Democracy, and Development." *Human Rights Quarterly* 21 (1999): 608–32.

Edwardson, Shelley. "Reconciling TRIPS and the Right to Food." In *Human Rights and International Trade,* edited by Thomas Cottier, Joost Pauwelyn, and Elisabeth Bürgi, 382–390. Oxford: Oxford University Press, 2005.

Fisher, William F. and Thomas Ponniah, eds. *Another World is Possible: Popular Alternatives to Globalization at the World Social Forum.* London: Zed Books, 2003.

Fox, Jonathan. "Transnational Civil Society Campaigns and the World Bank Inspection Panel." In *Globalization and Human Rights,* edited by Alison Brysk, 171–200. Berkeley: University of California Press, 2002.

French, Duncan. "International Rhetoric and the Real Global Agenda: Exploring the Tension between Interdependence and Globalisation." In *Global Governance and the Quest for Justice.* Vol. IV. *Human Rights,* edited by Roger Brownsword, 121–136. Oxford: Hart Publishing, 2005.

Friedman, Thomas. *The World is Flat: A Brief History of the Twenty-First Century.* New York: Farrar, Straus and Giroux, 2007.

Gearey, Adam. *Globalization and Law. Trade, Rights, War.* Lanham: Rowman & Littlefield, 2005.

Godson, Roy, and Phil Williams. "Strengthening cooperation against transnational crime." *Survival* 40 (1998): 66–88.

Held, David, Anthony McGrew, David Goldblatt, and Jonathan Perraton. *Global Transformations: Politics, Economics, and Culture.* Oxford: Polity, 1999.

Hoffman, Paul. "Human Rights and Terrorism." *Human Rights Quarterly,* Vol. 26 (2004): 932–55.

Horta, Korinna. "Rhetoric and Reality: Human Rights and the World Bank." *Harvard Human Rights Journal* 15 (2002): 227–44.

Howard-Hassmann, Rhoda. "The Second Great Transformation: Human Rights Leapfrogging in the Era of Globalization." *Human Rights Quarterly* 27 (2005): 1–40.

Jasanoff, Sheila. "Image and Imagination: The Formation of Global Environmental Consciousness." In *Changing the Atmosphere: Expert Knowledge and Environmental Governance,* edited by Clark A. Miller and Paul N. Edward, 309–337. Cambridge, Ma: MIT Press, 2001.

Joseph, Sarah. "An Overview of the Human Rights Accountability of Multinational Enterprises." In *Liability of Multinational Corporations under International Law,* edited by Menno Kamminga and Saman Zia-Zarifi, 75–93. The Hague: Kluwer Law International, 2000.

Kaufmann, Christine. *Globalisation and Labour Rights: The Conflict Between Core Labour Rights and International Economic Law.* Oxford: Hart Publishing, 2007.

Keck, Margaret E., and Kathryn Sikkink. *Activists beyond Borders: Advocacy Networks in International Politics*. Ithaca: Cornell University Press, 1998.
Lucke, Karin. "States' and Private Actors' Obligations under International Human Rights Law and the Draft UN Norms." In *Human Rights and International Trade*, edited by Thomas Cottier, Joost Pauwelyn, and Elisabeth Bürgi, 148–163. Oxford: Oxford University Press, 2005.
MacGillivray, Alex. *A Brief History of Globalization*. London: Robinson, 2006.
Mackay, Hugh. "The Globalization of Culture?" In *A Globalizing World? Culture, Economics, Politics*, edited by David Held, 47–84. London: Routledge, 2000.
Maher, Kristen H. "Who Has a Right to Rights? Citizenship's Exclusions in an Age of Migration." In *Globalization and Human Rights*, edited by Alison Brysk, 19–43. Berkeley: University of California Press, 2002.
Michalowski, Sabine. "Human Rights in Times of Economic Crisis: The Example of Argentina." In *Global Governance and the Quest for Justice*. Vol. IV. *Human Rights*, edited by Roger Brownsword, 33–52. Oxford: Hart Publishing, 2005.
Nye, Joseph S. Jr. and John D. Donahue, eds. *Governance in a Globalizing World*. Washington: Bookings Institution Press, 2000.
Ovett, Davinia. "Making Trade Policies More Accountable and Human Rights-Consistent: A NGO Perspective of Using Human Rights Instruments in the Case of Access to Medicines." In *Economic Globalisation and Human Rights*, edited by Wolfgang Benedek, Koen De Feyter, and Fabrizio Marrella, 170–209. Cambridge: Cambridge University Press, 2007.
Ramsay, Maureen. "Can the torture of terrorist suspects be justified?" *The International Journal of Human Rights* 10 (2006): 103–19.
Rehman, Javaid. "Islam, 'War on Terror' and the Future of Muslim Minorities in the United Kingdom: Dilemmas of Multiculturalism." *Human Rights Quarterly* 29 (2007): 831–78.
Sachs, Jeffrey. *The End of Poverty: Economic Possibilities for Our Time*. New York: Penguin Press, 2005.
Sadasivam, Bharati. "The Impact of Structural Adjustment on Women: A Governance and Human Rights Agenda." *Human Rights Quarterly* 19 (1997): 630–65.
Sandholtz, Wayne. "Humanitarian Intervention. Global Enforcement of Human Rights?" In *Globalization and Human Rights*, edited by Alison Brysk, 201–225. Berkeley: University of California Press, 2002.
Sassen, Saskia. *Globalization and Its Discontents*. New York: New Press, 1998.
Sen, Amartya. *Development as Freedom*. Oxford: Oxford University Press, 1999.
Sriram, Chandra. "Globalisation of Justice: for Better or Worse?" In *Global Governance and the Quest for Justice*. Vol. IV. *Human Rights*, edited by Roger Brownsword, 173–184. Oxford: Hart Publishing, 2005.
Stiglitz, Joseph. *Making Globalization Work*. New York: W. W. Norton & Company, 2006.
Stieglitz, Joseph. *Globalization and Its Discontents*. New York: W. W. Norton & Company, 2002.
Taran, Patrick A. "Human Rights of Migrants: Challenges of the New Decade." *International Migration* 38 (2002): 7–51.
Thompson, Grahame. "Economic Globalization?" In *A Globalizing World? Culture, Economics, Politics*, edited by David Held, 85–126. London: Routledge, 2000.
Ulrich, George. "Towards a Theory of Global Ethics in Support of Human Rights." In *Economic Globalisation and Human Rights*, edited by Wolfgang Benedek, Koen De Feyter, and Fabrizio Marrella, 39–66. Cambridge: Cambridge University Press, 2007.
Waters, Malcolm. *Globalization*. 2nd ed. London: Routledge, 2001.
Weyker, Shane. "The Ironies of Information Technology." In *Globalization and Human Rights*, edited by Alison Brysk, 115–132. Berkeley: University of California Press, 2002.
Wolf, Martin. *Why Globalization Works*. New Haven: Yale University Press, 2004.
Woods, Ngaire. "The Challenge of Good Governance for the IMF and the World Bank Themselves." *World Development* 28 (2000): 823–41.

International Legal Instruments

Marrakesh Agreement Establishing the World Trade Organization, 1994
International Covenant on Economic, Social and Cultural Rights (ICESCR), 1966

International Covenant on Civil and Political Rights (ICCPR), 1966
International Convention on the Protection of the Rights of All Migrant Workers and Members of Their Families, 1990
The International Criminal Tribunal for the former Yugoslavia (ICTY), 1993
The International Criminal Tribunal for Rwanda (ICTR), 1994
Agreement on Trade-Related Aspects of Intellectual Property Rights (TRIPS), 1994
The Rome Statute of the International Criminal Court (ICC), 1998
The United Nations Convention against Transnational Organized Crime, 2000

Resolution and Documents

Security Council Resolution 827 of 25 May 1993
Security Council Resolution 955 of 8 November 1994
UN Doc. A/53/383 (2000)
UN Doc. A/CONF.183/9 of 17 July 1998

Chapter Six

Role of the UN in the Promotion and Protection of Human Rights

*Elvira Domínguez-Redondo**

1. *Introduction*

Modern international law of human rights is the result of an evolving process where the responsibility of States -derived from their sovereignty- has been connected with one of the fundamental values of the international community after World War II: the dignity and consequent need for the protection of human beings. While the main responsibility for establishing regimes for the promotion and protection of human rights remains within domestic jurisdictions, a model of co-operation among different legal regimes has been developed. This model of co-operation identifies a responsibility for the International community to codify new human rights standards, and to establish international systems to monitor State behavior *vis-à-vis* those standards. The international law of human rights comprises both substantive norms (enunciating rights and duties) and procedural norms that mainly establish monitoring mechanisms to offer some protection against the State at international level. Both categories of norms (substantive and procedural) constitute the 'international systems or regimes of human rights'.

The international regimes of human rights can be categorized as 'universal' or 'regional', closely associated with existing international or regional organizations from which they derive their legitimacy. These organizations have provided specific ideological and institutional frameworks as well as the material support to guarantee the survival and autonomy of the different human rights regimes. In particular, the universal regime of promotion and protection of human rights has been conceived and grown under the auspices of the Organization of the United Nations.

The idea of creating a regime for the protection of human rights with universal scope was at the very essence of the creation of the UN Organization in

---

* Dr Elvira Domínguez-Redondo, Senior Lecturer in Law, Middlesex University, London, UK.

1945. At the 1945 San Francisco Conference, held to draft the *Charter of the United Nations*, a proposal to embody a "Declaration on the Essential Rights of Man" was put forward. The idea of promulgating an "international bill of rights" was also considered by many as basically implicit in the Charter. However, the founders of the UN were unable to overcome their reluctance at the time to accept any erosion of their sovereignty represented by a regime that might have implied conferring the Organization with powers to intervene in domestic affairs of the Member States.[1]

The UN Charter contains several references to human rights. Besides the preamble,[2] some of these references are enshrined in substantive provisions [Articles 1.3, 55 (c) and 56] while some are norms of an institutional nature that deal with competent organs in the field [Articles 13.1.(b), 60, 62.2 and 68]. The normative content of these references in the Charter made a significant contribution towards the insertion of the fundamental principle for the respect for human rights into the discourse of public international law.[3] However there are no explicit rights recognized within the Charter.

Nonetheless the rather innocuous references to human rights included in the Charter have been used as the basis of a growing UN human rights regime, permeating (at least nominally) all the spheres of activities and structures of the UN. In order to explore these issues depper, this Chapter will be divided in three sections: firstly, the different ideologies and geopolitical backgrounds that have guided and shaped the UN human rights activities throughout its existence will be analyzed; a second section will be devoted to outlining the main standards and processes moulding normative developments of the UN system for the protection and promotion of human rights. The chapter will conclude with an overview of the main UN charter-based and treaty-based mechanisms available to implement those standards.

---

[1] As reflected in Article 2.7 of the UN Charter: "Nothing contained in the present Charter shall authorize the United Nations to intervene in matters which are essentially within the domestic jurisdiction of any state or shall require the Members to submit such matters to settlement under the present Charter (...)".

[2] "We the people of the United Nations, determined... to reaffirm faith in fundamental human rights, in the dignity and worth of the human person, in the equal rights of men and women and of nations large and small."

[3] The commentary on Articles 55 and 56 is particularly useful in explaining the legal status and relevance of human rights provisions within the Charter. See Bruno Simma, ed., *The Charter of the United Nations: A Commentary*, 2nd ed. (Oxford: Oxford University Press, 2002); Jean-Pierre Cot and Alain Pellet (dirs), *La Charte des Nations Unies: commentaire article par article*, 3rd ed. (Paris: Economica, 2005).

2. *From Codification to Efficiency: The Different Phases of the Human Rights Discourse within the United Nations*

The meaning of the "universal" scope of UN action is not the same today as 60 years ago when the Organization was created. The UN that started its existence with the representatives of 51 countries had a different shape and prevailing political philosophy underpinning its actions compared with the contemporary version with its 192 State members. It is usual to divide the history of the UN in a variable number of periods dominated by different axis-ideologies. Focusing on UN human rights actions, and partially using Cassesse's timeframe division on the formative years of human rights doctrines,[4] these periods can be summarized as follows:

1) A period of primary attention to codification of international human rights standards, dominated by Western doctrine (from 1945 to late 1950s) and the confrontation characterizing the cold war between the capitalist and the socialist bloc. Primary importance was attached to civil and political rights; the drafting of new human rights treaties with monitoring mechanisms to evaluate their compliance; and the recognition of self-determination as a general principle of Law but not rights of peoples. After a period of exclusive attention on the drafting of the "International Bill of Human Rights",[5] in the mid-50s a "Plan of Action" was approved marking a tendency to address promotional human rights activities. This comprised: consultative services to provide advice to governments requesting them;[6] a (failed) system of periodic reports, and the study of rights or group of rights.[7]

2) From 1955 to 1974, socialist doctrines dominated the UN human rights debates: the socialist block provided leadership among the newly emerging post-colonial States and four new eastern European countries gained membership of the organization. This doctrine privileged economic, social, and cultural rights (over civil and political rights); the right of self-determination; and the right of equality (with the consequent prohibition of discrimination, especially racial

[4] Antonio Cassesse, *International Law* (Oxford: Oxford University Press, 2001), 353–57.

[5] The 'International Bill of Human Rights' is the term used to refer to three "core" normative documents: the Universal Declaration of Human Rights adopted by the UN GA in 1948 and two Covenants on which drafting commenced in this period but which were not approved until 1966: the International Covenant on Civil and Political Rights, and the International Covenant on Economic, Social and Cultural Rights.

[6] See UN doc. E/2731, (1955) *Report on the 11th session of the UN Commission on Human Rights* and UN General Assembly Resolution 926 (X) of 14 December 1955.

[7] UN Doc. E/2844-E/CN.4/731, *Report on the 12th session of the UN Commission on Human Rights* (1956), in particular Resolution I (Annual Reports on Human Rights) and II (Studies of Specific Rights or Groups or Rights).

discrimination).[8] The UN felt the effects of processes of decolonization with the appearance of the "Third World" with its own social, economic, politic and ideological characteristics.[9] After the *Bandung Conference* held in 1955, this new grouping of States would significantly influence international relations. Six years later, 25 States celebrated the first summit of the Non-Aligned Movement in Belgrade, where it was decided that, taking advantage of their large representation in the Organization,[10] the UN would be the common platform oriented to the attainment of their interest, especially to make the principle of self-determination effective in its economic and political variant. This had visible outcomes. United under what came to be known as the *Group of 77*, developing States instigated the first UN Conference on Trade and Development in 1964. The influence in the General Assembly was notable: the First Development Decade (1960–1970) was proclaimed; and very significant Declarations on the rights to self-determination approved.[11] Although not always in their best interest, the "Third-World" majority at the UN supported the creation of human rights monitoring mechanisms to avoid the risk of marginalization as second-rate countries with consequent reduction of foreign aid.[12]

This attitude of developing countries was crucial to the growth of human rights mechanisms. It came alongside a phase of distension between the East and West Group that facilitated decision-making processes within the UN.[13] Thus despite the dominance of the socialist doctrine with renewed emphasis

---

[8] Cassesse, *International Law*, 355.

[9] See Evan Luard, *A History of the United Nations*, vol. 2, *The Age of Decolonization, 1955–1965* (London (etc.): The Macmillan Press Ltd, 1989).

[10] Between 1945 and 1960, more than 40 countries and eight hundred million persons (a quarter of the inhabitants of the planet) achieved independence. New extensions of the membership of the UN reflected those changes. By 1967, 57% of the 127 States Member of the UN were Asian and African States.

[11] UN GA Resolution 1514(XV) of 14 December 1960, Declaration of Independence to Colonial Countries and Peoples; UN GA Resolution 1803 (XVII) of 14 December 1962 *on Permanent Sovereignty over natural resources*; and UN GA 2625 (XXV) of 24 October 1970, Declaration on Principles of International Law Concerning Friendly Relations and Co-Operation Among States in Accordance with the Charter of the United Nations.

[12] Maxime Tardu, "Human Rights Complaint Procedures of the United Nations: Assessment and Prospects," in *Des Menschen Recht zwischen Freiheit und Verantwortung. Festchrift für Josef Partsch zum 75. Geburtstag*, ed. Jekewitz Jürgen et al. (Berlin: Duncker & Humblot, 1989), 287–314.

[13] During the 60s the crisis of the Cuban Missile Crisis was resolved and a "red telephone" was installed directly connecting the White House and the Kremlin. In addition the USA and the Soviet Union started negotiations to agree on a regulation for the no-proliferation of nuclear weapons with salient outcomes such as The Treaty Banning Nuclear Weapons Tests in The Atmosphere, in Outer Space and Under Water (1963); The Treaty of Non-Proliferation of Nuclear Weapons (1968) and the Strategic Arm Limitation Treaty (SALT I, in 1972).

on the principle of non-intervention, this is the period when significant human rights monitoring mechanisms were created. The following are examples of this new direction: the General Assembly established several monitoring bodies; a Special Committee to monitor the implementation of the Declaration of Independence to Colonial Countries and Peoples[14] with competence to carry out its task by employment of *all available means*,[15] the first ever fact-finding mission to a country was sent to South Vietnam in connection with the allegation of human rights violations of the Buddhist community,[16] and the General Assembly established a Special Committee on the *apartheid* policies of the Government of South Africa.[17]

During this period the first human rights treaties setting up a monitoring body was inaugurated: namely, the Committee for the Elimination of All Forms of Discrimination and the Human Rights Committee.[18]

In 1966–7 the Economic and Social Council[19] and its then subsidiary body, the UN Commission on Human Rights, abandoned the doctrine of non-competence in addressing human rights violations. It instead created the first "charter-based" human rights procedures to review human rights violations in selected countries,[20] although at that time only the situation relating to *apartheid* and colonial territories had enough support to come under scrutiny.

3) From the 1970s to the end of the Cold War in 1989–90 the UN slipped deeper into its "eternal crisis" due to the intensification of the East-West conflict, a proliferation of new categories of armed conflicts to which the UN

---

[14] Resolution 1514 (XV) of 14 December 1960.

[15] UN GA Resolution 1654 (XVI) of 27 November 1961, The Situation with Regard to the Implementation of the Declaration on Granting of Independence to Colonial Countries and Peoples, paragraph 5.

[16] The report of the mission is contained in UN doc A/5630 (1963). For the precedents of this Mission, see Stephen Kaufman, "The necessity for rules of procedure in *ad hoc* United Nations Investigations," *American University Law Review*, no. 18 (1969): 752–55.

[17] UN GA Resolution 1761 (XVII) of 6 November 1962. See Theo van Boven, "Chartering New Grounds in Human Rights," in *Human Rights from Exclusion to Inclusion; Principles and Practice. An Anthology from the Work of Theo van Boven*, ed. Fons Coomans et al. (The Hague: Kluwer Law International, 2000), 5–15 and R.B. Ballinger, "UN Action on Human Rights in South Africa," in *The International Protection of Human Rights*, ed. Evan Luard (London: Thames and Hudson, 1967), 248–85, *esp*. 257–66.

[18] On those mechanisms see below, section IV.

[19] UN ECOSOC Resolution 1102 (XL) of 4 March 1966 and 1164 (XLI) of 5 August 1966 reinforced by the UN GA Resolution 2144 A (XXI) of 26 October 1966.

[20] The "official" birth of this mechanism is marked with the adoption of the UN ECOSOC Resolution 1235(XLL) of 6 June 1967 on the Question of the violation of human rights and fundamental freedoms, including politics of racial discrimination and of segregation and of apartheid, in all countries, with particular reference to colonial and other dependent countries and territories. For more on the "Charter-Based" procedures, see below section IV.

was unable to respond, the accusations of application of "double standards" in UN actions along with allegations of espionage within the secretariat, the disagreement on the role of the UN when dealing with human rights, and the claims of involvement in war crimes of a former UN Secretary General, Kurd Waldheim.[21]

During this phase the prevailing doctrine inspiring the debate on human rights activities was led by developing countries, benefiting from their numerical superiority in the Organization. For economic, political and cultural reasons as well as due to the need to protect the stability of their societies and territories after decolonization, many post-colonial countries showed indifference, or even hostility towards civil and political rights.[22] According to this doctrine, aside from exceptional cases (e.g. *apartheid* or the occupation of Arab territories), "naming and shaming" was deemed counterproductive. A co-operative approach was privileged instead, with an emphasis on development and its economic roots, and the need to change the international context propitiating differences among countries.

The decade of the 80s coincides with growing emphasis on international issues with the beginning of processes that would come to be labelled 'globalization'. Civil society organized around concrete segments of the population (children, women, disappeared, prisoners, etc.) gained status as relevant stakeholders in international relations demanding effective answers from the relevant institutions. This contributed to the proliferation of monitoring mechanisms and many new treaty-based and charter-based mechanisms were established. In addition to the entry into force of the monitoring mechanisms created in the previous period,[23] the following can be named: the Group of Three,[24] the Committee on the Elimination of Discrimination Against Women,[25] Commit-

[21] Adam Roberts and Benedict Kingsbury, "The UN's roles in a divided world," in *United Nations, Divided World. The UN's Roles in International Relations*, ed. Adam Roberts and Benedict Kingsbury (Oxford: Clarendon Press, 1988), 1–29, *esp.* 11–14.

[22] Cassesse, *International Law*, 356–57.

[23] Committee on the Elimination of all Forms of Racial Discrimination was the first to start its activities after the entry into force of the corresponding Convention in 1969. The Covenant on Civil and Political Rights and on Economic, Social and Cultural Rights entered into force in 1976, with their corresponding monitoring mechanisms. In addition the Second Protocol of the Covenant on Civil and Political Rights aiming at the abolition of death penalty was adopted on 15 December 1989 (in force since 11 July 1991).

[24] In charge of monitoring the International Convention on the Suppression and Punishment of the Crime of Apartheid, adopted in 30 November 1973 (entry into force 18 July 1976). As other UN monitoring mechanisms on this issue, the Group of Three suspended its activities with the abolition of *apartheid* in 1996.

[25] Monitoring body of the Convention on Elimination of All Forms of Discrimination Against Women (adopted on 18 September 1978, in force since 1981).

tee Against Torture,[26] Commission against *Apartheid* in Sports[27] and the Committee on the Rights of the Child.[28] Other human rights standards were drafted but encapsulated in non-binding legal instruments.[29]

4) The end of the Cold War brought with it a generalized optimism in the realm of international relations and the debate on the possibility of a "New International Order". Released from the East-West conflict and its paralyzing effects, the confidence in the capacity of the UN to act, grew. This trust came with accompanying demands on the UN to provide solutions to problems whose roots could be traced to earlier times, and new challenges such as the complete globalization of the economy, the eradication of poverty, the impact of the technological revolution, drug trafficking, demographic explosion and environmental issues. The efforts of the UN in human rights moved towards the implementation of existing norms and efficiency of monitoring systems on the ground.

This was reflected in the celebration of the Second World Conference on Human Rights held in Vienna in 1993, dominated by a pragmatic spirit. By then, the UN human rights system had become an autonomous subject of the international agenda. This Conference confirmed the UN's central role at international level for the promotion and protection of human rights. The debates during this Conference showed a move towards "operative" activities on human rights, i.e. an increased focus on moving away from UN Conference Rooms to concentrate on the implementation of UN activities in the field.[30] Following the guidelines of the Vienna Declaration and Programme of Action the UN engaged in a stronger debate and more significant efforts towards the implementation of economic, social and cultural rights. The favorable environment existing in the first years of the 90s is exemplified by the almost unexpected and immediate creation of the figure of the UN High Commissioner for Human Rights in 1993.[31]

---

[26] Monitoring body of the Convention Against Torture and Other Cruel, Inhuman and Degrading Treatment (adopted on 10 December 1984, in force since 1988).

[27] Monitoring body of the International Convention Against *Apartheid* in Sports, adopted on 10 December 1985 (in force between 1988 and 1996).

[28] Monitoring body of the Convention on the Rights of the Child, adopted on 10 December 1989 (in force since 1990).

[29] A list of universal human rights instrument (both treaties and declarations without legal force) is available at the website of the UN Office for Human Rights: http://www2.ohchr.org/english/law/index.htm#instruments (accessed 9 September 2009).

[30] Christian Strophal, "Human Rights Year 1998: The Challenges for the International Human Rights System," *Austrian Review of International and European Law* 2, no. 3 (1997): 392.

[31] Bhaswati Mukherjee, "United Nations High Commissioner for Human Rights: Challenges and Opportunities," in *International Human Rights Monitoring Mechanisms. Essays in Honour*

At normative level, fruits were scarce for many years. From 1990 to 2006 one human rights treaty,[32] and four Protocols to already existing treaties were approved. Otherwise, the UN only drafted and approved non- legally binding standards. This was not due to lack of interest in codification of new subjects, but to the difficulty of regulating some of the relevant issues at universal scale. Prime among these are difficulties of conceptualising "third-generation" rights – environment, development, peace-; challenges emanating from technological progress – trafficking of persons using internet, human genome and other bio-ethical issues-; and the adaptation of international law to the evolution of the economy – human rights and transnational corporations. The approval of a Convention on the Rights of Persons with Disabilities (and its Optional Protocol) and the Convention for the Protection of All Persons against Enforced Disappearances[33] in 2006 is linked to the intended revitalization of the UN human rights machinery discussed below.

While it can be said that the present stage is marked by "broad consensus on the need to consider respect for human rights a *sine qua non* for full international legitimization, that is, in order to participate in international intercourse",[34] the three above-mentioned doctrines (Western, Socialist and Developing countries) with many nuances[35] remain present in UN debates. This is visible in the conflictive visions of the different actors since the creation of the Organization towards fulfilment of its objectives of security, peace and development. The necessary link between these three components is present in the political discourse and conforms the so-called 'three pillars' of the Organization. In the context of the last attempt to reform the UN on occasion of its 60th anniversary, the former UN Secretary General, Kofi Annan emphasised that '. . . we will not enjoy development without security, we will not enjoy security without development, and we will not enjoy either without respect for human rights'.[36]

---

of Jakob Th. Möller, ed. Gudmundur Alfredson et al. (The Hague: Martinus Nijhoff Publishers, 2001), 391–94.

[32] International Convention on the Protection of the Rights of all Migrant Workers and Members of their Families adopted on 18 December 1990, establishing as monitoring body the Committee on Migrant Workers (entry into force on 1 July 2003).

[33] Both of them set up their own monitoring mechanism. While the Convention on Enforced Disappearance was not in force by August 2008, the Convention on the Rights of Persons with Disabilities and its Optional Protocol entered into force in May 2008.

[34] Cassesse, *International Law*, 354.

[35] See for instance the analysis on the "Asian values" debate *vis-à-vis* human rights in Joshua Castellino and Elvira Domínguez Redondo, *Minority Rights in Asia* (Oxford: Oxford University Press, 2006), 5–26.

[36] Report of the UN Secretary-General, *In Larger Freedom: Development, Security And Human Rights For All*, UN doc. A/59/2005, 21 March 2005 para. 17. See also paras. 13–16. Furthermore an important claimed element of the 'Plan of Action' designed by the OHCHR as

Mainstreaming human rights has been an answer to attempt to avoid conflict within the institution's competing interests. However, we are far from harmonic coexistence. The post September 11 scenario has renewed emphasis on security over human rights concerns and some of the Security Council actions on terrorism seem far away from the human rights standards established by the Organization. The Millennium Development Goals[37] are a milestone for development but did not follow a human rights approach to development and did not consider the pledge of the most vulnerable groups in their realization, due to the lack of disaggregated data.[38]

3. *Normative Development of the UN System of Protection and Promotion of Human Rights*

Since the UN Charter does not enumerate or define human rights, one of the first tasks facing the UN was to enumerate and define what human rights were, and to articulate the means for their recognition and protection at universal level. As mentioned above, codifying the "International Bill of Human Rights" was the exclusive focus of human rights activities in the UN for the first years of life of the Organization.

Since then, the UN has served as a privileged forum for the creation and crystallization of human rights standards as customary law, treaty law and general principles of laws. Some human rights standards are now well-established norms and principles (e.g. the right to self-determination, prohibition of torture, freedom of conscience, non-discrimination) while many others are still emerging customary law or remain in the drafting process before becoming new conventional law (e.g. right to democracy, global governance, environment, peace, collective rights link to minorities or indigenous people, etc.). The legally binding nature of these standards has implications but the boundaries

called for in the Secretary General report *In Larger Freedom* (and included as Addendum 3 of that Report) was to integrate human rights into UN development, peace and humanitarian activities. See also *High Commissioner's Strategic Management Plan 2008–2009 and 2007–2008* (Geneva: OHCHR, 2007/2008).

37 The Millennium Development Goals, derived from the Millennium Declaration approved by the UN GA Resolution 55/2 of 8 September 2008, consist of eight international development goals that 189 States have agreed to achieve by 2015. They include: eradication of poverty and hunger; universal education; gender equality; maternal health; combat HIV/AIDS; environmental sustainability; and Global Partnership.

38 For criticism on the Millennium Development Goal from a human rights perspective, see also, Philip Alston, "Ships passing in the night: The current state of the human rights and development debate seen through the lens of the Millennium Development Goals,"' *Human Rights Quarterly* 27, no. 3 (2005): 755–829.

are increasingly blurred. As will be emphasized below, some human rights monitoring mechanisms carry out their task taking into account non-binding instruments (special procedures or the Universal Periodic Review). Although the violation of legally binding norms contained in treaties or customary law raises the international responsibility of the State, UN monitoring human rights bodies have not been endorsed with enforcement powers and their decisions on violations are not binding on States. However, the possibility of claiming responsibility exists and the recent jurisprudence of the International Court of Justice focusing on human rights violations is showing itself as a useful tool to reinforce the authority of human rights treaties.[39]

3.1. *The International Bill of Human Rights*

The International Bill of Human Rights consists of the Universal Declaration of Human Rights, the International Covenant on Economic, Social and Cultural Rights and its Protocol and the International Covenant on Civil and Political Rights with its two Optional Protocols.

3.1.1. *Universal Declaration of Human Rights*

The Universal Declaration of Human Rights was adopted by General Assembly Resolution 217 A (III) of 10 December of 1948 (a day commemorated as "Human Rights Day" since 1950). Since it was passed as a resolution of the General Assembly the Declaration is not binding by itself. However, the full Declaration, or at least part of its content have, in supervening years, become part of customary law. The Declaration is the basic text of reference for the activity developed by UN organs in human rights.

The Universal Declaration, made up of a Preamble and thirty articles, enumerated and defined civil, political, economic, social and cultural rights for the first time at universal level. It commences by laying down the philosophy on which the Declaration is based, in Articles 1 and 2 (freedom and equality as inherent rights of the human beings).

The list of rights contained in the Universal Declaration can be grouped, according to Prof. René Cassin, one of its key drafters, into four different categories as follows:[40]

---

[39] Rosalyn Higgins, "Human Rights in the International Court of Justice," in *Essays in Honour of John Dugard. The Protection of the Individual in International Law*, ed. Thomas Skouteris and Annemarieke Vermeer-Künzli, Special Issue of *Leiden Journal of International Law*, 20–4 (2000): 745–75.

[40] "La Déclaration universelle et la mise en oeuvre des Droits de l'Homme," in *Académie de droit international de La Haye: Recueil des Cours* 79 (1951–II): 239–367.

1) Personal rights – *My right to be me* (Articles 3 to 11). This includes among others, rights such as: life, liberty and security; freedom from slavery and servitude; freedom from torture and cruel, inhuman or degrading treatment or punishment; the right to recognition everywhere as a person before the law; and the right to an effective remedy before competent national tribunals for acts violating the fundamental rights granted by the constitution or by law.
2) Rights that belong to the individual in his/her relationships with the social group and in his relations with things of the external world – *Do not interfere with us* (Arts. 12 to 17). Rights belonging to this category include: freedom from arbitrary interference with privacy, family, home or correspondence; freedom of movement and residence within the borders of each State and right to leave any country, including her/his own, and to return to her/his country; or the right to seek and to enjoy in other countries asylum.
3) Spiritual faculties, fundamental civil freedoms and political rights – *I can help* (Arts. 18 to 21). For instance, freedom of opinion and expression or the right to peaceful assembly and association.
4) Economic, social and cultural rights – *I need care and work* (Arts. 22 to 27) including the right to social security taking in accordance with the organization and resources of each State; the right to work; or the right to form trade unions.

The concluding Articles 28 and 30 recognize the right to a social and international order as well as duties towards the community, including the possibility of limitations of rights determined by law solely for the purpose of securing due recognition and respect for the rights and freedoms of others and of meeting the just requirements of morality, public order and the general welfare in a democratic society.

The Universal Declaration on Human Rights has important political, moral and legal significance and its programmatic value has had a major influence inside and outside the UN. Much of its content is framed as positive law and has since become customary law. Other contents (like the right to leisure or paid holidays) are disputed or still at the stage of *soft law*. Still others, such as the provision of Article 28 (right to a social and international order in which the rights and freedoms set forth in the Declaration can be fully realized), express a wish of transforming international law into a law informed by the principle of solidarity.

The importance of the Universal Declaration as a common reference point for the human rights system is reflected in the continuous allusion made to it in governmental declarations, and in resolutions of international organizations, particularly the UN General Assembly and the International Court of Justice. Many universal, regional and bilateral treaties, allude to the Universal Declaration and many domestic Constitutions include specific reference to it.

Until the adoption of the two Covenants of 1966 (which did not enter into force until 1976) the Universal Declaration was the only international instrument of universal scope laying down human rights normative standards.

Nowadays, despite the extensive codification of human rights norms, the Universal Declaration still merits reference in evaluating behavior in the fulfilment of human rights duties, particularly when a given State may not have ratified other more specific or relevant treaties. Non-conventional bodies charged with the monitoring of State compliance with human rights base their activities largely on the Universal Declaration; in terms of their evaluation of State conduct, as well as in legitimising their own tasks of monitoring.

The reiterative invocation to the Universal Declaration by international organizations and by States has helped to create the conviction that there is a general obligation to respect and implement the rights contained in its articles. Thus, the Universal Declaration has inspired and incited the promotion and protection of human rights at international level, and has consolidated itself as a universal parameter of reference to measure the degree of State compliance with human rights standards. In recent years, there has been a growing tendency for UN organs, in preparing international instruments in the field of human rights, to refer not only to the Universal Declaration, but also to other parts of the International Bill of Human Rights.

3.1.2. *The Covenants*

The conflicts between States of the two blocks of the Cold War, the different conceptions of human rights of these States, as well as the appearance of the new decolonized States, explains both the decision of adopting two Covenants, and the time lag in agreeing a final text. The decolonization process also led to the enshrinement of common Article 1 to both Covenants, the right to self-determination, as the first human right.

In general both Covenant recognize the rights of the Universal Declaration, although the language varies from that of the Declaration. Some Declaration rights were not included in the Covenants e.g. the right to property and the right to a nationality. Also, the preamble, Articles 3 (equality between men and women) and 5[41] (guarantees in case of derogations or limitations of rights) are almost identical in the Covenant on Civil and Political Rights and the Covenant on Economic, Social and Cultural Rights.

[41] Article 5: 1. Nothing in the present Covenant may be interpreted as implying for any State, group or person any right to engage in any activity or to perform any act aimed at the destruction of any of the rights or freedoms recognized herein, or at their limitation to a greater extent than is provided for in the present Covenant 2. No restriction upon or derogation from any of the fundamental human rights recognized or existing in any country in virtue of law, conventions, regulations or custom shall be admitted on the pretext that the present Covenant does not recognize such rights or that it recognizes them to a lesser extent.

3.1.2.1. International Covenant on Civil and Political Rights
One of the rights recognized in the Covenant, not contained in the Declaration, was the right of persons belonging to ethnic, linguistic and religious minorities to enjoy their own culture, to profess and practice their own religion and to use their own language (Art. 27). The rules banning propaganda for law and the advocacy of national, racial or religious hatred that constitutes incitement to discrimination, hostility or violence (hate speech) were also elaborated for the first time. In 1989 the Second Optional Protocol to the International Covenant on Civil and Political Rights, aiming at the abolition of the death penalty, was adopted, extending the Covenant's scope to ensure that no one within the jurisdiction of a State Party to the Protocol could be executed.

Article 4 of the Protocol allows States to suspend or limit temporarily the enjoyment of certain rights in cases officially proclaimed 'public emergencies' that threaten the life of the nation. Such limitations or suspensions are permitted only "to the extent strictly required by the exigencies of the situation" and may never involve discrimination solely on the ground of race, color, sex, language, religion or social origin (Art. 4). The limitations or suspensions must also be reported to the UN.

Only preceded by the Convention on the Elimination of All Forms of Racial Discrimination, the Covenant is one of the first treaties of universal scope establishing a mechanism of implementation in its articles 28 to 45[42] and has been the model followed by other treaties.

The relevance of the Covenant can be gleaned from the number of ratifications it has received. By April 2010, 165 States were Parties of this treaty. This number, lower than for other comparable human rights treaties, is affected by reservations entered by States and by the lower number of ratifications for its two Protocols (111 ratifications to the First Protocol and 66 to the Second).

3.1.2.2. International Covenant on Economic, Social and Cultural Rights
This Treaty is the universal reference point for elaborating recognized economic, social and cultural rights, particularly for further codification at international and domestic level.

While it has been proclaimed, since the adoption of the Universal Declaration on Human Rights that economic, social and cultural rights, and civil and political rights are interconnected and interdependent,[43] the truth reflected in this Covenant is that economic, social and cultural rights have been assigned

---

[42] See below Section IV.

[43] Among other examples this is explicitly proclaimed in the Proclamation of Teheran of 1968 (Art. 13), the Convention on the Elimination of all Forms of Discrimination (Art 5), Convention on the Elimination of All Forms of Discrimination Against Women (part II, part III,

less guarantees at universal and regional level[44] and are as a consequence, less protected. The language chosen by the drafters of the Covenant, particularly in Article 2(1) of the Covenant was used to argue that it was not legally binding as long as the States had not reached certain economic and social conditions. The monitoring body of the Covenant, its most authoritative interpreter, has reaffirmed that the Covenant provides for progressive realization and acknowledges the constraints due to the limits of available resources. However the Committee has repeatedly stated that the Covenant imposes various obligations of immediate effect. Of these, two are of particular importance: 1) the prohibition of undertaking steps of a regressive nature without a justified reason, and 2) the obligation of protecting those rights without discrimination.[45]

Of course, the different level of "obligation" that was intended for these rights has had consequences in the mechanisms of implementation: until recently this regime only had provision for the softest version of the existing monitoring procedures at international level (State reporting procedure). The adoption of a Protocol in 2008[46] has opened an international channel through which victims could complain about the violation on economic, social and cultural rights. In addition, the adoption of the Protocol ought to imply the existence in the near future of universal jurisprudence helping in the task of defining the content of the "minimum standard" and the means of implementation required from the States to fulfil their citizens' economic, social, and cultural rights.

3.2. *The UN as a Forum of Creation of New Universal Human Rights Norms*

Besides the International Bill of Human Rights, there are three key avenues through which the normative development of international human rights law has taken place under the auspices of the UN.

1. The adoption of major treaties on human rights: This refers to multilateral treaties that are potentially universal, i.e., all States can become part of them. Nine such treaties exist, referred to, in UN language as "The Core International Human Rights Instruments" because each has established a committee of experts to monitor the implementation of treaty provisions by its States Parties. Some of the treaties are supplemented by optional protocols addressing specific

---

etc.), Declaration on the Right to Development (Article 6.2), or in the Vienna Declaration and Program of Action (paragraph 1.5).

44 Among the regional existing regimes (European, American and African) only the African system of protection has provided adequate balance between economic, social and cultural rights and civil and political rights.

45 Magdalena Sepúlveda Carmona, The Nature of the Obligations under the International Covenant on Economic, Social and Cultural Rights (Antwerpen / NewYork: Intersentia, 2003).

46 At the time of writing the Protocol had been adopted by the Human Rights Council on 18 June 2008 and it was expected its final adoption by the UN General Assembly.

concerns or providing additional competences to the monitoring treaty-bodies. Among these are the two Covenants commented upon above and their additional Protocols, the International Convention on the Elimination of All Forms of Racial Discrimination,[47] the Convention on the Elimination of All Forms of Discrimination against Women,[48] the Convention against Torture and Other Cruel, Inhuman or Degrading Treatment or Punishment,[49] the Convention on the Rights of the Child,[50] the International Convention on the Protection of the Rights of All Migrant Workers and Members of Their Families,[51] the Convention on the Rights of Persons with Disabilities (and its Optional Protocol)[52] and the International Convention for the Protection of All Persons against Enforced Disappearances.[53]

Many other international human rights treaties of universal scope adopted under the auspices of the UN constitute a milestone on the development of human rights standards, despite the lack of specific mechanisms to monitor their compliance.[54]

2. Resolutions of the Organization of the UN (the most important adopted by the General Assembly) or other Specialized Agencies belonging to the so-called system of the UN, such as UNESCO, UNICEF or ILO. Some of the most important ones such as the Universal Declaration of Human Rights, the Declaration of Independence to Colonial Countries and Peoples have already been discussed above. Many others can also be included for their significance in the development and consolidation of human rights standards. This includes the Declaration on the Right to Development[55] and the Declaration on the Rights of Indigenous Peoples.[56] Most human rights treaties have been preceded

---

[47] Adopted on 21 December 1965, entry into force 4 January 1969.

[48] Adopted on 18 December 1979, entry into force 3 September 1981. Its Optional Protocol conferring to the Committee monitoring this treaty competence to deal with individual complaints was adopted on 10 December 1999 (entered into force 22 December 2000).

[49] Adopted on 10 December 1984, entry into force 16 June 1987. Its Optional Protocol was adopted on 18 December 2002 (entry into force 22 June 2006) establishing a system of preventive visits.

[50] Adopted on 20 November 1989 (entry into force 2 September 1990). Two additional Protocols to this Convention were adopted on 25 May 2000 on the rights on the sale of children, child prostitution and child pornography; and on the involvement of children in armed conflict. Both Protocols entered into force in 2002.

[51] Adopted on 18 December 1990 (entered into force 1 July 2003).

[52] Adopted on 13 December 2006 (entered into force 12 May 2008).

[53] Adopted on 20 December 2006 (not yet in force).

[54] A list of them can be found at the Website of the UN Office for Human Rights: http://www2.ohchr.org/english/law/index.htm#instruments (accessed 9 September 2009).

[55] Adopted by the General Assembly Resolution 41/128 of 4 December 1986.

[56] Adopted by the General Assembly Resolution 61/295 of 13 September 2007.

by Declarations. In addition, they have played a substantial role in the creation and crystallization of new customary law. It is also by acts of organs of the UN that the so-called charter-based monitoring mechanisms have been created.

3. International Conferences: The most usual way to run multilateral negotiations with the end of adopting a multilateral treaty of universal scope is to schedule a diplomatic conference under the auspices of the UN. The most recent and important result of this kind of initiative has been the adoption of the Statute of the International Criminal Court.[57] Many Conferences have been celebrated to address particular human rights questions.[58] Of particular relevance are the two International Conferences addressing human rights globally: the first celebrated in Teheran in 1968, resulted in the Proclamation of Teheran; the second, celebrated in Vienna in 1993, resulted in the Vienna Declaration and Plan of Action.[59]

These conferences, as open forums of discussion for governmental and non-governmental actors, have been important in generating consensus around human rights questions. The final declarations resulting from these conferences provide an important lens for a general vision of the state of the question. They contain guidelines on the need of codification, and recommendations on practical measures to enhance the effectiveness of the rights under consideration.

While the presence of civil society is granted in the UN through NGOs with consultative status, International Conferences allow much wider participation of all interested actors in the field.

4. *"Charter-based" and "Treaty-based" Monitoring Mechanisms: Public Special Procedures and the Work of the Committees*

The organs of experts (Committees) established by the "Core International Human Rights Instruments" are known in UN terminology as "treaty-based" mechanisms/procedures/institutions (or conventional mechanisms/procedures/institutions) since they were established and operate under the framework of a particular treaty. Conversely, other human rights monitoring mechanisms established by the decision of an organ of the UN are known as "charter-based" procedures. This is a wide concept that includes any:

[57] Many other examples, as all the relevant treaties of international humanitarian law or the Convention on the Status of Refugee.

[58] These include for instance: World Conference on Racism and Racial Discrimination, Xenophobia and Related Intolerance (Durban, South Africa, 31 August–7September 2001); and the Fourth World Conference on Women (Beijing, China, September 1995).

[59] Doc. A/CONF/157/23 12, endorsed by the UNGA Resolution 48/121 de 1993.

> ...organ, procedure, body or mechanism that is based on, set up within or set forth in the constitution or charter of an intergovernmental organization – or is based on decisions taken by the assembly or representative body of an IGO [intergovernmental organization] to so establish it.[60]

In practice, the term "charter-based" procedures is normally used to designate those mechanisms created by the now defunct UN Commission on Human Rights – replaced since March 2006, by the Human Rights Council: i.e. the public special procedures and the "complaint procedure" (until recently denominated "1503 procedure"). Since the "treaty-based" institutions are born from the adoption of internationally legally binding instruments (treaties) and the "charter-based" institutions owed their existence to a decision of a political (i.e. intergovernmental) body, the former have been categorized as "Legal" control mechanism to distinguish them from the "political" control mechanism (i.e. charter-based mechanisms).[61]

4.1. *Treaty bodies*

The nine instruments identified above belonging to the category of "Core international Human Rights Instruments" set up specific bodies to monitor their implementation within the jurisdiction of States Parties to the Treaties. Each Committee is composed of independent experts, ranging in number from 10 to 23 members. Except for the Committee on the Elimination of Discrimination Against Women (CEDAW) supported by its own secretariat in New York (the Division for the Advancement of Women, DAW), all the Committees were supported by the Office of the High Commissioner on Human Rights in Geneva.[62] This anomalous situation ended when the responsibility for servicing CEDAW was transferred to the Office of the High Commissioner in January 2008.

By ratifying or accessing the core treaties named above, States Parties agree to be bound by a range of monitoring systems:

Periodic Reports: All treaty bodies are mandated to receive and consider reports submitted by State Parties detailing their implementation of the treaty provisions in the country concerned. These reports are required to explain the

---

[60] Victor Condé, *A Handbook of International Human Rights Terminology* (Lincoln and London: University of Nebraska Press, 1999), 16. See also, Henry J. Steiner, Philip Alston, and Ryan Goodman, *International Human Rights in Context. Law, Politics, Morals*, 3rd ed. (Oxford: Oxford University Press, 2008), 737–42.

[61] Theo van Boven, '"Political' and 'Legal' Control Mechanisms: Their Competition and Coexistence," in *Human Rights in Perspective. A Global Assessment*, ed. Asbjørn Eide and Bernt Hagtvet (Oxford: Blackwell Publishers, 1992), 45–47.

[62] The OHCHR has a liaison office in New York too.

legislative, judicial, administrative or other measures that have been adopted that give effect to treaty provisions. The Committees have issued guidelines to assist States with preparation of their reports, have elaborated general comments interpreting the treaty provisions and organized discussions on themes related to the treaties.

Interstate complaints: Some treaties have a system of inter-governmental complaint which, owing to its immensely political nature, has never been used. All State Parties to the International Covenant on Elimination of All Forms of Racial Discrimination are bound by this procedure according to its Articles 11–13. All the other treaties setting up this procedure require the specific consent of the state parties: the International Covenant on Civil and Political Rights [Art. 41(1)]; the Convention Against Torture [Art. 21] and the International Convention on Migrant Workers [Art. 75] Although States remain reluctant to denounce other States for human rights violations before the Committees, they seem increasingly willing to take cases against other States for the violation of provisions of human rights treaties in other fora, particularly, the International Court of Justice.[63]

Individual complaints: Of the nine core treaties and accompanying protocols, all except the Committee on the Rights of the Child and the Committee on Economic, Social and Cultural Rights,[64] have the competence, subject to specific consent of the States Parties, to deal with complaints from individuals claiming to be victims of violations of any of the rights set forth in the treaties examined hereto.

Confidential Inquiries: One monitoring mechanism set up in Optional Protocol of the Convention on the Elimination of Discrimination against Women (Arts. 8–11) the Convention Against Torture (Art. 20) and the Optional Protocol of the Convention on the Rights of Persons with Disabilities (Arts. 6–7) is the possibility of the concerned Committees to examine information, investigate and make confidential inquiries when there are well-founded indications that systematic violations of the provisions set forth by these Treaties are in

[63] A recent relevant exponent is the institution of proceedings by the Republic of Georgia before the International Court of Justice against the Russian Federation on 12 August 2008 for its actions in breach of the International Convention on the Elimination of All Forms of Racial Discrimination. Although there is a specific provision (Art. 22) in this and other human rights treaties providing for the settlement of disputes regarding the interpretation or application of the Convention, only recently States seem to settle their disputes using this prerogative. See *Armed Activities on the Territory of the Congo: New Application. Democratic Republic of Congo* v. *Rwanda*, Judgment of 3 February 2006, ICJ Reports 2006, No. 126.

[64] As stated above, the adoption by the General Assembly of the Protocol to this Treaty (and its subsequent ratification by States) will also open this channel for the Covenant on Economic, Social and Cultural Rights.

practice in the territory of a State Party. This procedure is subject to specific consent of the States Parties (Art. 28 CAT; Art. 10 OP-CEDAW and Art. 8 Convention on Persons with Disabilities).

Domestic mechanisms: In order to prevent future violations and ensure the implementation and monitoring of the concerned treaties, the Optional Protocol of the Convention Against Torture and Art. 33 of the Optional Protocol of the Convention on the Rights of Persons with Disabilities, impose the duty on State Parties to designate a specific national mechanism.

Some Committees have developed follow-up of their recommendations, and early warning mechanisms.[65] In any case, the decisions of those Committees lack legally binding force. The lack of co-operation of many States who are unwilling or unable[66] to comply with the provisions of the treaties and their monitoring procedures is an issue of major concern. Overdue reports are a widespread malpractice among States, but the lack of resources and other UN dis-functionalities are to be blamed for the backlog of complaints and reports to be examined.[67] More relevant is the question of the impact of these treaties and their monitoring procedures in the domestic realm. Although sometimes focused on individual cases, the main purpose of these mechanisms is to change States behavior to being compliant with human rights standards.[68]

4.2. *Charter-Based Institutions*

4.2.1. *Human Rights Council*

The Human Rights Council is the only intergovernmental body of the system of the UN devoted exclusively to the promotion and protection of human rights. It consists of representatives of 47 different countries following equitable geographical distribution. This political body is a subsidiary organ of the General Assembly and was created on 15th March 2006[69] to replace what until

---

[65] Once the Convention Against Enforced Disappearance enters into force, its monitoring Committee will have competence to consider individual and inter-state complaints; to grant a humanitarian urgent procedure; power to undertake visits; and competence to bring to the attention of the UN General Assembly situations of systematic practice of enforced disappearance.

[66] For instance, many States claim a problem of lack of resources to justify their lack of reporting to the appropriate Committees.

[67] Anne Bayefsky, *The UN Human Rights Treaty System in the 21st Century* (Hague: Kluwer Law International, 2000).

[68] A survey of the main initiatives for measuring human rights performance (as well as an analysis of their main weaknesses) *vis-à-vis* commitment with human rights standards and institutions at international level, can be found in Todd Landman, *Protecting Human Rights: A Comparative Study* (Oxon, etc.: Routledge, 2005).

[69] General Assembly Resolution 60/251 of 15 March 2006.

then was the main organ of the UN addressing human rights issues: the UN Commission on Human Rights.[70] The Human Rights Council has inherited the main mechanisms to monitor human rights performance among the charter-based institutions from its predecessor: the public special procedures along with a confidential complaint procedure and other subsidiary bodies focused on standard-setting or other specific thematic issues such as development or the effective implementation of the Durban Declaration and Programme of Action.

The Council meets for no fewer than three times per year for a total period of no less than ten weeks. In addition, it can hold Special sessions when the emergency of the situation requires it.[71] While these sessions (also celebrated by the former UN Commission on Human Rights) have traditionally addressed country situations, the 7th special session, held in May 2008, was the first to address a thematic issue: "The Negative Impact on the Realization of the Right to Food of the Worsening of the World Food Crisis, caused Inter Alia by the Soaring Food Prices". This represents a remarkable milestone for the advancement of economic, social and cultural rights and the understanding of human rights "emergencies" beyond potential or actual armed conflicts.[72]

The Human Right Council mandate includes promotional and protective human rights powers. Its meetings are public and any State Members, Observers and NGOs with consultative status can participate in the discussions. The Human Rights Council is an intergovernmental organ, i.e. it works under political principles. Therefore its work results on many occasions in consequences that are openly contrary to the legal principle of equal treatment for the same facts.[73] However, the governmental composition also assures that human rights issues remain on the political agenda of the States.

In addition to public discussions,[74] the Council's scope of activities includes the approval of resolutions and decision with different purposes:

[70] Created in 1946 as a subsidiary body of the Economic and Social Council (ECOSOC) it consisted of representatives of 53 States and used to meet publicly once a year.

[71] By 30 August 2008, 7 Special Sessions had been held on the situation of the following territories: occupied Palestinian territories, Lebanon, Myanmar and Darfur.

[72] A commented summary of the session can be found in: Council Monitor, "Overview, Human Rights Council, 7th Special Session, 3–28 March 2008" *Human Rights Monitor Series* (Geneva: International Service for Human Rights, 2008) available at http://www.ishr.ch/component/option,com_docman/Itemid,/task,doc_download/gid,150/. (accessed 18 August 2008).

[73] Miko Lempinen, The United Nations Commission on Human Rights and the Different Treatment of Governments (Abo: Abo Akademy Press, 2005).

[74] This can also be followed by Webcast at http://www.un.org/webcast/unhrc/index.asp (accessed 9 September 2009).

a) To make general recommendations with regard to the promotion and protection of human rights, including recommendations to the General Assembly with the aim at approving new human rights standards that may be conceived within the Human Rights Council;
b) To determine the provision of advisory services, technical assistance and capacity-building in consultation and with the consent of the States concerned;
c) To create subsidiary bodies to assist the Council perform its tasks. Among these subsidiary bodies the Human Rights Council has assumed several mandates set up by its predecessor the Commission on Human Rights with investigatory and monitoring competences: the public special procedures and a confidential complaint procedure (formerly known as 1503 procedure). While the relevance of the later has been in decline and many have advocated for its disappearance, public special procedures have a primary position due to their large number (38 at the time of writing), permanence and the relevance of their activities on supervising the behavior of States *vis-à-vis* human rights.

4.2.2. *Public Special Procedures*

Public Special Procedures are human rights monitoring mechanisms endorsed to individual experts ("Special Rapporteurs", "Special Representatives" and "Independent Experts") since 1967, whose common mandate is the investigation and reporting of human rights situations either in a specific territory (country mandates) or with regard to a phenomena of violations (thematic mandates).[75] These procedures owe their existence to resolutions adopted by majority in the Human Rights Council and are not subject to specific consent of any State. The scope of their action is truly universal:[76] all the States of the world are monitored by these bodies and they cover civil, political, economic, social and cultural rights as well as "rights of solidarity" such as issues related to development and the environment. Individual as well as collective rights are under scrutiny. Mandate holders have developed flexible methods of work and their activities go beyond reporting on their activities and findings. Most of them accept complaints on human rights violations to which they can react expeditiously thorough "urgent appeals". Mandate holders carry out country visits to investigate the situation of human rights in a given domestic context.

[75] The list of existing special procedures is available at http://www2.ohchr.org/english/bodies/chr/special/index.htm (accessed 20 August 2008).

[76] Obviously this is not the case for country mandates whose competence is limited to the territory under study, although the usual practice is that any country mandate can monitor the situation of the country with regard to any human right.

This requires the consent of the State to be visited, but is premised on complete freedom of movement and respect for the immunity and independence of the experts. As of August 2008, sixty two States have issued standing invitations allowing any Rapporteur to visit their countries.

The universal scope of special procedures and their easy accessibility are particularly valuable in a world where many States are not covered by specific regional system of protection of human rights;[77] may not have ratified all the UN core international human rights instruments, or may have ratified them only partially (with reservations or accepting limited monitoring procedures). In addition, many special procedures cover rights (such as food, health, housing, poverty) or groups (minorities, indigenous peoples) for which international channels are limited or inexistent. Access to special procedures is also characterized by the lack of formal requirement, enabling swiftness and flexibility.[78]

Conversely, their pronouncements are not legally binding. The importance acquired by the special procedures is rooted in the publicity of their work under the stamp of the UN. First of all, the debates, resolutions and decisions within the Human Rights Council concerning these procedures are public. More decisively, the possibility of using publicity not only as a channel of information but also as a tool to exercise pressure over States and other concerned actors by the special procedures themselves is one of the most significant achievements in the work of these mechanisms particularly during the past decade.

However, it is the multiplicity of governmental and non-governmental actors involved in the daily work of special procedures and the constant publicity of their actions that prevents governments from being able to estimate and/or mitigate the political costs that the existence of special procedures has, over the monitoring of their behavior, even when they have managed to defeat the impact of their negative assessment within the Human Rights Council.

4.2.3. *Universal Periodic Review*

The only substantial change introduced in the mandate of the Human Rights Council from that of its predecessor, the UN Commission on Human Rights is the existence of a periodic review mechanism to evaluate the fulfilment of human rights obligations by all States: the so-called Universal Periodic Review (henceforth UPR). While all countries are under scrutiny by public special procedures regarding the issues under their competence, few country mandates

[77] Regional systems of protection exist in Europe, America and Africa, but still the majority of the world population do not reside in countries bound by regional systems, mainly due to the lack of regional institutions in Asia.

[78] For an overview of the work of special procedures see, *Draft Manual of the United Nations Special Procedures*, 2006 available at http://www2.ohchr.org/english/bodies/chr/special/index.htm (accessed 9 September 2009).

exist, and some countries have always been immune to specific country actions within UN intergovernmental forums.[79] The introduction of a UPR is the most dramatic answer to this criticism in a bid to overcome the application of double standards and selectivity within the Council.[80] Under the UPR, all countries are reviewed following a cycle of 48 States per year, to complete the review of all the countries of the world in a period of four years. States under review are required to report on the situation of human rights in their country and to engage in an interactive dialogue with Member States on the Council and others wanting to take the floor. In its current configuration, NGOs and National Human Rights Institutions can attend the interactive dialogue, provide reliable information as a basis for review, and take the floor before the adoption of the final outcome report of this process. However, the interactive dialogue among States and a non-confrontational approach remain the central feature of this mechanism. This mechanism is still in its infancy:[81] it thus remains unclear as to how it will contribute to the "depoliticization" of the Council, and more importantly – as with any other international human rights institutions – the extent to which this process is likely to impact on improving human rights at domestic level.

Bibliography

Alston, Philip, and James, Crawford, eds. The *Future of UN Human Rights Treaty Monitoring.* Cambridge: Cambridge University Press, 2000.

Alston, Philip. "Ships passing in the night: The current state of the human rights and development debate seen through the lens of the Millennium Development Goals." *Human Rights Quarterly* 27, no. 3 (2005): 755–829.

Ballinger, R.B. "UN Action on Human Rights in South Africa." In *The International Protection of Human Rights*, edited by Evan Luard, 248–85. London: Thames and Hudson, 1967.

Bayefsky, Anne. *The UN Human Rights Treaty System in the 21st Century.* Hague: Kluwer Law International, 2000.

Boven, Theo van. "'Political' and 'Legal' Control Mechanisms: Their Competition and Coexistence." In *Human Rights in Perspective. A Global Assessment*, edited by Asbjørn Eide and Bernt Hagtvet, 36–45. Oxford: Blackwell Publishers, 1992.

——. "Chartering New Grounds in Human Rights." In *Human Rights from Exclusion to Inclusion; Principles and Practice. An Anthology from the Work of Theo van Boven*, edited by Fons Coomans, Cees Flinterman, Fred Grünfeld, Ingrid Westendorp, and J.C.M. Willems, 5–15. The Hague (etc.): Kluwer Law International, 2000.

---

[79] See for instance Ann Kent, *China, the United Nations, and Human Rights. The Limits of Compliance.* (Philadelphia: University of Pennsylvania Press, 1999).

[80] Elvira Domínguez-Redondo, "The Universal Periodic Review of the UN Human Rights Council: An assessment of the First Session," *Chinese Journal of International Law* 7, issue 3 (2008): 721–34.

[81] The first session took place in May 2008.

Carmona Sepúlveda, Magdalena. *The Nature of the Obligations under the International Covenant on Economic, Social and Cultural Rights*. Antwerpen / New York: Intersentia, 2003.
Cassesse, Antonio. *International Law*. Oxford: Oxford University Press, 2001.
Cassin, René. "La Déclaration universelle et la mise en oeuvre des Droits de l'Homme." *Académie de droit international de La Haye: Recueil des Cours* 79 (1951–II): 239–367.
Castellino, Joshua, and Elvira Domínguez Redondo. *Minority Rights in Asia*. Oxford: Oxford University Press, 2006.
Clapham, Andrew. "Globalization and the rule of Law." http:// http://www.business-human-rights.org/Home.
——. "Creating the High Commissioner for Human Rights: The Outside Story." *European Journal of International Law* 5, no. 4 (1994): 556–68.
Condé, Victor. *A Handbook of International Human Rights Terminology*. Lincoln and London: University of Nebraska Press, 1999.
Cot, Jean-Pierre, and Alain Pellet, eds. *La Charte des Nations Unies: commentaire article par article*. 3rd ed. Paris: Economica, 2005.
Domínguez-Redondo, Elvira. "The Universal Periodic Review of the UN Human Rights Council: An assessment of the First Session." *Chinese Journal of International Law* 7, issue 3 (2008): 724–34.
Eide, Asbjørn, Gudmundur Alfredsson, Göran Melander Lars, Adam Rehof, and Allan Rosas, with the collaboration of Theresa Swinehart, eds. *The Universal Declaration of Human Rights: A Commentary*. Oslo: Scandinavian University Press, 1992.
Fatouros, Arghyrios A. "International Law in the Era of Global Integration." In *Mélanges en l'honeur de Nicolas Valticos. Droit et justice*, edited by René-Jean Dupuy, 131–48. Paris: A. Pedone, 1999.
Heyns, Christof, and Frans Viljoen. *Impact Study of the United Nations Human Rights Treaties in Twenty UN Member States*. The Hague, Martinus Nijhoff, 2002.
Higgins, Rosalyn, "Human Rights in the International Court of Justice." In *Essays in Honour of John Dugard. The Protection of the Individual in International Law*, edited by Thomas Skouteris, and Annemarieke Vermeer-Künzli, Special Issue of *Leiden Journal of International Law* 20–4 (2000): 745–75.
Jhabvala, Farrokh. "The Drafting of the Human Rights provisions of the UN Charter." *Netherlands International Law Review* XLV, no. 1 (1997): 1–31.
Johnson, Glen, and Janusz Symonides. *The Universal Declaration of Human Rights. A history of its creation and implementation 1948–1998*. Paris: UNESCO, 1998.
Kaufman, Stephen. "The necessity for rules of procedure in *ad hoc* United Nations Investigations." *American University Law Review*, no. 18 (1969): 739–65.
Kent, Ann. *China, the United Nations, and Human Rights. The Limits of Compliance*. Philadelphia: University of Pennsylvania Press, 1999.
Landman, Todd. *Protecting Human Rights: A Comparative Study*. Oxon, etc.: Routledge, 2005.
Lempinen, Miko. *The United Nations Commission on Human Rights and the Different Treatment of Governments*. Abo: Abo Akademy Press, 2005.
Luard, Evan. *A History of the United Nations*. Vol. 2, *The Age of Decolonization, 1955–1965*. London (etc.): The Macmillan Press Ltd, 1989.
—— ed. *The International Protection of Human Rights*. London: Thames and Hudson, 1967.
Mukherjee, Bhaswati. "United Nations High Commissioner for Human Rights: Challenges and Opportunities." in *International Human Rights Monitoring Mechanisms. Essays in Honour of Jakob Th. Möller*, edited by Gudmundur Alfredsson, Jonas Grimheden, Bertrand G. Ramcharan and Alfred de Zayas, 391–94. The Hague: Martinus Nijhoff Publishers, 2001.
Roberts, Adam, and Benedict Kingsbury. "The UN's roles in a divided world." In *United Nations, Divided World. The UN's roles in International Relations*, edited by Adam Roberts and Benedict Kingsbury, 1–29. Oxford: Clarendon Press, 1988.
Simma, Bruno, ed. *The Charter of the United Nations: A Commentary*. 2nd ed. Oxford: Oxford University Press, 2002.
Steiner, Henry J., Alston Philip, and Ryan Goodman. *International Human Rights in Context. Law, Politics, Morals*. 3rd. ed. Oxford: Oxford University Press, 2008.

Strophal, Christian. "Human Rights Year 1998: The Challenges for the International Human Rights System." *Austrian Review of International and European Law* 2, no. 3 (1997): 391–432.

Tardu, Maxime. "Human Rights Complaint Procedures of the United Nations: Assessment and Prospects." In *Des Menschen Recht zwischen Freiheit und Verantwortung. Festchrift für Josef Partsch zum 75. Geburtstag*, edited by Jekewitz Jürgen, Karl Heinz Klein, Jörg Detlef Kühne, Hans Petersmann, and Rüdiger Wolfrum, 287–314. Berlin: 1989.

International Legal Intruments

Charter of the United Nations, 1945

Convention on Enforced Disappearance

Convention on the Rights of Persons with Disabilities and its Optional Protocol, 2008

Convention on the Elimination of All Forms of Discrimination against Women, 1979

Convention against Torture and Other Cruel, Inhuman or Degrading Treatment or Punishment, 1984

Convention on the Rights of the Child, 1984

Convention on the Rights of Persons with Disabilities (and its Optional Protocol), 2006

Declaration of Independence to Colonial Countries and Peoples, 1960

Declaration on Principles of International Law Concerning Friendly Relations and Co-Operation Among States in Accordance with the Charter of the United Nations, 1970.

Declaration on the Right to Development

Durban Declaration and Programme of Action, 2001

International Covenant on Civil and Political Rights, 1966

International Covenant on Economic, Social and Cultural Rights, 1966

International Convention for the Protection of All Persons against Enforced Disappearances, 2006

International Convention on the Suppression and Punishment of the Crime of Apartheid, 1973

International Convention on the Protection of the Rights of all Migrant Workers and Members of their Families, 1990

International Convention on the Elimination of All Forms of Racial Discrimination, 1965

International Convention on the Protection of the Rights of All Migrant Workers and Members of Their Families, 1990

International Convention on the Elimination of All Forms of Racial Discrimination, 1965

Optional Protocol of the Convention on the Elimination of Discrimination against Women, 1999

Optional Protocol of the Convention on the Rights of Persons with Disabilities, 2006

Proclamation of Teheran of 1968

Second Protocol of the Covenant on Civil and Political Rights aiming at the Abolition of Death Penalty, 1989

The Strategic Arm Limitation Treaty (SALT I), 1972

The Treaty Banning Nuclear Weapons Tests in The Atmosphere, in Outer Space and Under Water, 1963

The Treaty of Non-Proliferation of Nuclear Weapons, 1968

Vienna Declaration and Program of Action, 1993

Universal Declaration of Human Rights, 1948

UN Commission on Human Rights, 1946

UN GA Resolution 926 (X) of 14 December 1955

UN GA Resolution 1514(XV) of 14 December 1960

UN GA Resolution 1654 (XVI) of 27 November 1961

UN GA Resolution 1803 (XVII) of 14 December 1962

UN GA Resolution 1761 (XVII) of 6 November 1962

UN GA Resolution 2144 A (XXI) of 26 October 1966

UN GA 2625 (XXV) of 24 October 1970

UNGA Resolution 48/121 de 1993

UN GA Resolution 60/251 of 15 March 2006

UN GA Resolution 55/2 of 8 September 2008
UN ECOSOC Resolution 1102 (XL) of 4 March 1966
UN ECOSOC Resolution 1164 (XLI) of 5 August 1966
UN ECOSOC Resolution 1235(XLL) of 6 June 1967
UN Doc. E/2844-E/CN.4/731
UN doc. E/2731, (1955)
UN doc A/5630 (1963)
UN doc. A/59/2005, 21 March 2005
Doc. A/CONF/157/23 12

Committee and Monitoring Body

Committee on the Elimination of all Forms of Racial Discrimination was the first to start its activities after the entry into force of the corresponding Convention in 1969.
Monitoring body of the Convention on Elimination of All Forms of Discrimination Against Women, 1978
Monitoring body of the Convention Against Torture and Other Cruel, Inhuman or Degrading Treatment, 1984
Monitoring body of the International Convention Against *Apartheid* in Sports, 1985
Monitoring body of the Convention on the Rights of the Child, 1989

Case

Armed Activities on the Territory of the Congo: New Application. Democratic Republic of Congo v. *Rwanda*, Judgment of 3 February 2006, ICJ Reports 2006, No. 126

Websites

http://www.ishr.ch/hrm/council/index.html
http://www2.ohchr.org/english/law/index.htm#instruments
http://www2.ohchr.org/english/bodies/chr/special/index.htm
http://www2.ohchr.org/english/bodies/chr/special/index.htm
http://www2.ohchr.org/english/law/index.htm#instruments

Chapter Seven

Attributes of Successful Human Rights Non-Governmental Organizations (NGOs) – Sixty Years After the 1948 Universal Declaration of Human Rights

*George E. Edwards**

1. *Introduction*

It is undisputed that human rights non-governmental organizations ("human rights NGOs") have proliferated dramatically in the sixty years since the United Nations ("UN") promulgated the Universal Declaration of Human Rights,[1] and that human rights NGOs play a critical role in promoting and protecting human rights in all corners of the globe.[2] However, the human rights community

---

* Carl M. Gray Professor of Law; *and* Executive Chair, Graduate Law Programs; *and* Director, Program in International Human Rights Law; *and* Faculty Director, Master of Laws (LLM) Track in International Human Rights Law of Indiana University School of Law – Indianapolis. gedwards@indiana.edu; gedwards97@yahoo.com. Thanks to the following: Professors Karen Bravo, Maria Lopez, and Fran Quigley of Indiana University School of Law – Indianapolis; Law Librarian Mr. Steven Miller; Research Assistants Mr. Colin Coons, Mr. Simeon Sungi, Mr. Chris Nancarrow, Mr. Mark Shope, Mr. Matthew Trick, Ms. Detra Mills, and Ms. Heidi Reed; and Faculty Assistant Ms. Michelle Davis.

1 UN General Assembly, *Universal Declaration of Human Rights*, G.A. Res. 217A (III), adopted 10 December 1948, U.N. Doc. A/810 (1948) (hereinafter UDHR); See Felice D. Gaer, "Reality Check: Human Rights Nongovernmental Organisations Confront Governments at the United Nations," Third World Quarterly 16 (1995): 389–404. See, e.g., United Nations Educational, Scientific and Cultural Organization (UNESCO), "Conclusions: The Increasing Role and Importance of Human Rights NGOs," www.unesco.de/c_humanrights/V.php. (accessed July 21, 2009) ("Over the last 57 years an almost explosive growth of NGOs for the promotion and the defence of human rights has taken place.")

2 Ved P. Nanda, "The Human Rights Era at Fifty: Looking Back and Looking Forward," *Willamette Journal of International Law and Dispute Resolution* 5 (1997): 72, 78–85 (on the 50th

cannot agree on what constitutes a "human rights NGO", how tidily to categorize them, or even that "NGO" is an appropriate moniker for such groups.[3]

Furthermore, despite the omnipresence of human rights NGOs, human rights community stakeholders[4] cannot agree on a framework for vetting NGOs to help ensure their legitimacy. Definitional and other problems make it difficult for stakeholders easily to distinguish between human rights groups deserving support and human rights groups deserving disbandment. The UN, other intergovernmental organizations, and national governments need to know which groups are lawful, legitimate, and worthy of accrediting, licensing, granting tax benefits to, or supporting. Individuals seeking to join an NGO and recipients of NGO largesse need to know which NGOs to trust. Donors need to know which NGOs to fund, and NGOs need to know with which other NGOs they might collaborate to protect human rights.

While this chapter does not purport to develop this much-needed, coherent framework, it advances the framework's development by identifying and analyz-

---

Anniversary of the Universal Declaration of Human Rights, recognizing positive NGO contributions in promoting and protecting human rights).

[3] Academics, diplomats, governmental bureaucrats, and jurists have struggled on what to call these groups – the Third Sector, the independent sector, the volunteer sector, civil society organizations ("CSO" – objectionable because includes corporations), non-state actors (NSAs – objectionable because includes terrorists, guerillas), private voluntary organizations (PVOs), citizen associations, grassroots organizations, transnational social movement organizations, citizen sector organizations, self-help organizations, or community based organizations (CBOs). See, e.g., Peter J. Spiro, "NGOs and Human Rights: Channels of Power," in *Research Handbook on Human Rights* (Edward Elgar Publishing, forthcoming 2009), 2 http://ssrn.com/abstract=1324971 (discussing NGO descriptor) (accessed July 20, 2009); John Samuel, "Civil Society in an Uncivil World," *Pambazuka News*, Issue 324, October 18, 2007, http://www.pambazuka.org/en/category/comment/43788 (accessed July 20, 2009); http://www.globalpolicy.org/component/content/article/177/31602.html (accessed July 19, 2009) ("The term 'Civil Society' is contested terrain. Over the last fifteen years it has been used to denote everything from citizens' groups and activist formations to highly institutionalized non-governmental organisations and foundations.")

[4] Herein, the term "stakeholder" broadly includes "any person or entity affected by or interested in human rights concerns", such as inter-governmental organizations (e.g., the UN), national governmental bodies with human rights competence (e.g., national human rights commissions), private organizations that engage in human rights work, academic institutions that teach human rights or provide human rights pro bono services, individual and group victims of human rights abuses, prospective victims, donors to human rights endeavors, and groups that receive human rights donations. This definition of "stakeholder" is not exhaustive and might include, for example, corporations (who are obligated to protect human rights), terrorist groups, unlawfully organized rebels groups or mercenaries – irrespective of whether the stakeholder is an NGO.

ing attributes shared by successful human rights NGOs. This chapter posits that human rights community stakeholders may assess human rights NGOs in part by determining whether they possess these shared characteristics.

This chapter proceeds in five parts. Part II briefly traces the history of the contemporary human rights NGO from anti-slavery and other social movement groups of the eighteenth century, through the participation of human rights NGOs in the creation of the UN, through the proliferation of human rights NGOs today.

Part III identifies and analyzes ten characteristics of successful human rights NGOs. These characteristics, which overlap and are not exhaustive, relate to the human rights NGO's: (1) mission; (2) adherence to human rights principles; (3) legality; (4) independence; (5) funding; (6) non-profit status and commitment to service; (7) transparency and accountability; (8) adaptability and responsiveness; (9) cooperative and collaborative nature; and (10) competence and reliability.

Part IV builds upon the attributes identified in Part III, and explores a selection of NGO Codes of Conduct from around the globe designed to promote NGO accountability and transparency and to help bolster NGO credibility. Though efficacy of these Codes may vary, they all contain criteria useful in assessing NGOs.

Part V concludes that although much has changed since the UN and modern human rights NGOs were born six decades ago, what has not changed is the disagreement over what constitutes a human rights NGO and how to categorize such groups. However, stakeholders in the international human rights law arena universally agree that human rights NGOs are meant to protect internationally recognized human rights at local, national, sub-regional, regional and global levels. Successful and effective human rights NGOs should possess basic attributes, as described herein, and self-regulate – possibly in part by following NGO Codes of Conduct – to overcome internal and external challenges. Concerted efforts of all relevant stakeholders are needed to ensure that human rights NGOs are able to fulfill their mandate to protect human rights.

2. *NGOs & Human Rights NGOs*

2.1. *NGO Definition and Pre-United Nations History*

Many scholars and practitioners agree that the term "non-governmental organization" ("NGO") may be more readily defined by what it *is not*, and that what an NGO *is* depends on context.[5] Furthermore, it is undisputed that a universally agreed definition of NGOs has proved elusive.[6]

Rather than seek to crystallize a universal definition of NGO, I will instead provide the following working definition for purposes of this chapter: An NGO is a private, independent, non-profit, goal-oriented group not founded or controlled by a government.

The broad term "NGO" may encompass research institutes, churches and other religious groups, cooperatives, literary or scientific organizations, credit unions, foundations, girl and boy scouts, sporting groups, service organizations, neighborhood associations, consulting firms, political parties or other political

[5] For example, an NGO *is not* a governmental organization. See, e.g., Peter R. Baehr, "Mobilization of the Conscience of Mankind: Conditions of Effectiveness of Human Rights NGOs" (presentation at a UNU Public Forum on Human Rights and NGOs, United Nations University, Tokyo, Japan, September 18, 1996. (www.gdrc.org/ngo/lecture14.html) (accessed July 20, 2009) ("Human rights organisations are part of the phenomenon known as...NGOs. Curiously enough, these NGOs are defined by what they are *not*. They emphasize their distance and independence from governments, yet at the same time it is mostly the actions and activities of national governments that are the very cause and purpose of their existence. Without governments there would be no non-governmental organizations.") (emphasis in original; citation omitted); See also Philip Alston, "The 'Not-a-Cat' Syndrome: Can the International Human Rights Regime Accommodate Non-State Actors? in *Non-State Actors And Human Rights*, ed. Philip Alston (New York: Oxford University Press, 2005), 1–36; Martin A. Olz, "Non-governmental Organizations in Regional Human Rights Systems," *Columbia Human Rights Law Review* 28 (1997): 307, 313 ("NGO" definition depends on context).

[6] Lynne M. Rudasil surveyed NGO definitions as follows:

> Michael O'Neill divides NGOs into nine types in the United States. (O'Neill, 1990) His view of the NGO rests on the organization's orientation – whether it is toward religion, private education and research, healthcare, arts and culture, social sciences, advocacy and legal services, international assistance, foundations and corporate funders, and mutual benefit organizations. Gerard Clarke (1998) from the University of Wales, Swansea, defines NGOs as "...private, nonprofit, professional organizations with a distinctive legal character, concerned with public welfare goals." Suter (2003) defines them as "any organization outside the government, such as the public service and the defense forces, and business." Reinalda and Verbeek (2001) identify two defining characteristics for the NGO in an analysis of power relations. They agree with the definition in the YEARBOOK OF INTERNATIONAL ORGANIZATIONS that identifies NGOs as "organizations which have not been founded, and are not formally controlled, by national governments." In going beyond the Yearbook's definition, they maintain that a second characteristic for these organizations is pursuit "by private means private objectives that are likely to have domestic or transnational public effects."

Lynne M. Rudasil, "NGO, Information Flow and Nation: An Exploration in Relationships" (presented at World Library and Information Congress: 70th IFLA General Conference and Council, Buenos Aires, Argentina, August 26, 2004), 2, http://www.ifla.org.sg/IV/ifla70/papers/079e-Rudasil.pdf (accessed July 20, 2009).

groups,[7] educational and training institutions, and trade unions and other professional associations. Goals of these groups could be equally as broad and could include protecting business interests of the group's corporate members,[8] protesting corporate behavior,[9] promoting sports, promoting political candidates or policies, promoting the interests of a specific industry, education and training, disseminating news, or generally protecting international human rights.

Private organizations such as religious orders, charities, foundations, and educational groups have existed for centuries, but scholars tend to trace the roots of contemporary NGOs to the late Renaissance era, pointing to groups of private individuals who formed to combat government policy on slavery and other social issues in the 1700s.[10] By the 1800s, NGOs increasingly lobbied governments,

---

[7] Scholars differ over whether certain political groups or groups struggling for self-determination are human rights NGOs. See, e.g., Makau wa Mutua, "Book Review: Claude E. Welch, Protecting Human Rights in Africa: Strategies and Roles of Non-Governmental Organizations." *Michigan Journal of International Law* 17 (1996): 591, 613, n 81. Dean Mutua states that:

> NGOs and Western human rights academics have not, as a general rule, treated liberation movements such as the African National Congress (ANC) of South Africa or the South West African Peoples Organization (SWAPO) of Namibia as human rights groups despite the fact that such groups have sought to vindicate the right to self-determination, which is in my view the most fundamental of all human rights. They see such groups as "political" organizations and not human rights NGOs, which they believe should be "neutral," "apolitical," or "non-partisan." To them a group is a human rights NGO only if it is not directly involved in the contest for state power, does not seek to form government, is not directly linked to a particular political party, and primarily uses human rights standards as a basis for its advocacy. See Steiner, supra note 60, at 5–15, 61–76 (discussing the characteristics of human rights NGOs). I do not think the hazy distinctions drawn by INGOs are helpful; they still leave open why certain groups are not categorized as human rights NGOs.

[8] Trade associations are an example of an NGO whose goals include protecting the interests of corporate members. Labor unions would also be NGOs, but with interests of workers paramount. Because private corporations are for profit, they would not qualify as NGOs.

[9] A broad range of NGOs focus on "corporate social responsibility" issues such as working conditions. See, e.g., Isabella D. Bunn, "Global Advocacy for Corporate Accountability: Transatlantic Perspectives From the NGO Community," *American University International Law Review* 19 (2004): 1265, 1266, n. 1 (listing over twenty such NGOs in Europe).

[10] *See* Gavin Keeney, "The Unbearable Lightness of NGOs," *CounterPunch*, May 24, 2002, http://www.counterpunch.org/keeney0525.html (accessed July 16, 2009) (noting that NGOs "in one form or another have been part and parcel of the theory of civil society since at least the 18th century"). In April 1775, The Society for the Relief of Free Negroes Unlawfully Held in Bondage is said to have been formed in Philadelphia as the first U.S. slave abolition society. See "First American abolition society founded in Philadelphia," *History.com*, http://www.history.com/this-day-in-history.do?action=Article&id=462 (accessed July 16, 2009). In 1784, the society changed its name to the Pennsylvania Society for Promoting the Abolition of Slavery and the Relief of Free Negroes Unlawfully Held in Bondage. Ibid.

molded public opinion, and effected change.[11] Those "early" NGOs included the British and Foreign Anti-Slavery Society (1839),[12] the International Committee of the Red Cross (1863), the International Worker's Association (1864), the International Peace Bureau (1892), the Union of International Associations (1907), the Federal Council of Churches (1908), the American Jewish Committee (1906), and the French-based League for Human Rights (1898).

NGOs continued to flourish through the World Wars and are abundant today, sixty years later.[13]

---

[11] In 1835 French commentator Alexis de Tocqueville famously noted about volunteer groups: "Americans of all ages, all stations of life, and all types of disposition are forever forming associations.... In democratic countries knowledge of how to combine is the mother of all other forms of knowledge; on its progress depends that of all the others." (Alexis de Tocqueville, *Democracy in America*, ed. J.P Mayer and Max Lerner, trans. by George Lawrence (New York: Harper & Row, 1966) 485–488; quoted in Michael Yaziji and Jonathan Doh, NGOs and Corporations: Conflict and Collaboration (Cambridge: Cambridge University Press, 2009), https://www.cambridge.org/us/catalogue/catalogue.asp?isbn=9780521866842&ss=exc (accessed July 16, 2009). See Theda Skocpo, "What Tocqueville Missed: Government made all that 'volunteerism' possible," *Slate*, November 15, 1996, http://www.slate.com/id/2081 (accessed July 20, 2009). See Francis Lieber, *On Civil Liberty and Self-Government*, enlarged ed. (Philadelphia: J.B. Lippincott and Company, 1859) (noting the "all-pervading associative spirit" in the US and elsewhere), quoted in Steve Charnovitz, "Nongovernmental Organizations and International Law," *The American Journal of International Law* 100 (2006): 348, 350, n. 8.

[12] In 1909, this group merged with the Aborigines' Protection Society, and in 1990 changed its name to Anti-Slavery International. Anti-Slavery International bills itself as "the world's oldest international human rights organisation". See "Introduction to Anti-Slavery: Anti-Slavery International Today," *Anti-Slavery International*, http://www.antislavery.org/english/what_we_do/antislavery_international_today/antislavery_international_today.aspx (accessed July 20, 2009). It fought to abolish the slave trade (achieved in Britain in 1807) and slavery throughout the British colonies (achieved in 1833, effective 1834) and helped draft the 1926 *Convention on the Abolition of Slavery* and the 1956 *Supplementary Convention on the Abolition of Slavery, the Slave Trade and Institutions and Practices Similar to Slavery*. In 1975, it worked for creation of a UN expert group dedicated to the elimination of slavery, now called the UN Working Group on Contemporary Forms of Slavery. Anti-Slavery International now focuses on forced and bonded labor, child labor, human trafficking, and traditional or 'chattel' slavery. Peter P. Hinks, John R. McKivigan, R. Owen Williams, Encyclopedia of Antislavery and Abolition 58 (Greenwood Press, 2006).

[13] Lynne M. Rudasil, *NGO, Information Flow and Nation*, (NGO growth "has been almost as exponential as the growth of the Internet and has sometimes been seen as part of the process of globalization.") 2; Kenneth Boulding, quoted in Akira Iriye, *Global Community: The Role of International Organizations in the Making of the Contemporary World*. (Berkeley: University of California Press, 2002), 159 (The rise of international NGOs is "perhaps one of the most spectacular developments of the twentieth century, although it has happened so quickly that it is seldom noticed.")

2.2. *Definition of a "Human Rights NGO"*

How appropriately to define, classify or categorize "human rights NGOs" has proved as elusive as if not more elusive than sorting out the definition of "NGO". At the very least, a human rights NGO must fit the definition of NGO – it must be a group that is private, independent, non-profit, goal-oriented, and not founded by or controlled by a government.

But a human rights NGO goes further by requiring that the group's primary concern must be to promote and protect internationally recognized human rights. Human rights NGOs must be guided by international human rights law norms as incorporated into the 1948 Universal Declaration of Human Rights,[14] the International Covenant on Civil and Political Rights,[15] the

---

[14] The UN intended the UDHR to be a "common standard of achievement for all peoples and all nations". Its thirty articles address human rights broadly in several categories: civil and political rights (Articles 3–21); economic, social and cultural rights (Articles 22–27); and third generation rights (e.g., article 28, including group or collective or solidarity rights related to, for example, peace and development). These rights form the bases for over 100 UN treaties, declarations and other instruments, and for many national constitutions and other domestic law sources. On December 10, 2008 (Human Rights Day), weeks after being elected President of the United States, Barack Obama reconfirmed that the UDHR is at the root of many international agreements the US supports and at the root of human rights policies and practices with which the US aligns itself:

> The United States was founded on the idea that all people are endowed with inalienable rights, and that principle has allowed us to work to perfect our union at home while standing as a beacon of hope to the world. Today, that principle is embodied in agreements Americans helped forge – the Universal Declaration of Human Rights, the Geneva Conventions, and treaties against torture and genocide – and it unites us with people from every country and culture.
>
> When the United States stands up for human rights, by example at home and by effort abroad, we align ourselves with men and women around the world who struggle for the right to speak their minds, to choose their leaders, and to be treated with dignity and respect. We also strengthen our security and well being, because the abuse of human rights can feed many of the global dangers that we confront – from armed conflict and humanitarian crises, to corruption and the spread of ideologies that promote hatred and violence.
>
> So on this Human Rights Day, let us rededicate ourselves to the advancement of human rights and freedoms for all, and pledge always to live by the ideals we promote to the world.

President-elect Barack Obama, "Statement of President-elect Obama on Human Rights Day," *Change.gov*, December 10, 2008, http://change.gov/newsroom/entry/statement_of_president_elect_obama_on_human_rights_day (accessed July 19, 2009).

[15] *International Covenant on Civil and Political Rights*, G.A. Res. 2200A (XXI), art. 17, adopted and opened for signature, ratification and accession, December 16, 1966, U.N. Doc. A/6316 (1966), entry into force 23 March 1976 (hereafter "ICCPR"), http://www.unhchr.ch/html/menu3/b/a_ccpr.htm (accessed July 20, 2009).

International Covenant on Economic, Social and Cultural Rights,[16] other international human rights law instruments, and the customary international law of human rights. The United Nations and other bodies have promulgated international instruments to protect the integrity of NGOs, including human rights NGOs.[17]

The concept of "international human rights norm" is broad, and it overlaps with rights protected under other areas of international and domestic law, including international humanitarian law, international criminal law, international environmental law, development law, labor law, refugee and asylum law, constitutional law, domestic criminal law and procedure, and even the law of the sea. All these areas of law seek, in one form or the other, to protect international human rights (including, for example, rights of criminal suspects and

[16] *International Covenant on Economic, Social and Cultural Rights*, G.A. Res. 2200A (XXI), adopted and opened for signature, ratification and accession, December 16, 1966, U.N. Doc. A/6316 (1966), entry into force 3 January 1976 (hereafter "Economic Covenant"), http://www.unhchr.ch/html/menu3/b/a_cescr.htm (accessed July 20, 2009).

[17] For example, the preamble of the *Declaration on the Right and Responsibility of Individuals, Groups and Organs of Society to Promote and Protect Universally Recognized Human Rights and Fundamental Freedoms* acknowledges:

> the important role of international cooperation for, and the valuable work of individuals, groups and associations in contributing to, the effective elimination of all violations of human rights and fundamental freedoms of peoples and individuals, including in relation to mass, flagrant or systematic violations such as those resulting from apartheid, all forms of racial discrimination, colonialism, foreign domination or occupation, aggression or threats to national sovereignty, national unity or territorial integrity and from the refusal to recognize the right of peoples to self-determination and the right of every people to exercise full sovereignty over its wealth and natural resources[.]

UN General Assembly, G.A. Res. 53/144, March 8, 1999, UN Doc. A/RES/53/144 (1999), http://www.unhchr.ch/huridocda/huridoca.nsf/(Symbol)/A.RES.53.144.En (accessed July 16, 2009). See also Council of Europe, *European Convention on the Recognition of the Legal Personality of International Non-Governmental Organisations*, European Treaty Series, No. 142 (Apr. 24, 1986), http://conventions.coe.int/Treaty/en/Treaties/Html/124.htm (accessed July 20, 2009) (convention designed to facilitate work of international NGOs); Martin A. Olz, "Non-governmental Organizations in Regional Human Rights Systems," (exploring NGOs in the UN, Inter-American, European and African human rights systems, and comparing definitions of "NGO" in the *Encyclopedia of Public International Law*, ECOSOC resolutions, and the European Convention on Legal Personality of INGOs); Rudolf Bernhardt, ed., *Encyclopedia of Public International Law* (Amsterdam: North-Holland, 1986).

A full discussion of how to differentiate among different NGO types, or a taxonomy or typology, is beyond the scope of this chapter. Attempts at such include that in Peter J. Spiro, "NGOs and Human Rights: Channels of Power," in *Research Handbook on Human Rights* (Edward Elgar Publishing, forthcoming 2009), 2, http://ssrn.com/abstract=1324971 (accessed July 20, 2009) (article seeks "to systematize NGO activity relating to human rights", and offer "a typology of human rights NGOs, distinguishing generalist from identity-oriented human rights NGOs and domestic from transnational" and further that "It is not clear, however, that these distinctions are meaningful".)

defendants, due process rights, environmental rights of indigenous peoples, rights of individuals to nourishment acquired from ocean fishing, or labor rights of refugees or asylees). The definition of "human rights NGO" is broad and includes NGOs that seek to protect human dignity rights in all these boundless substantive areas of law.[18]

2.3. *Categorization of Human Rights NGOs*

Although many attempts have been made systematically to categorize human rights NGOs, universal agreement does not exist on a cogent typology.[19] The table below reflects a very broad categorization:

NGO Taxonomy	
NGO Category	Category Description
Geographical emphasis of operations	Local, national, regional, sub-regional, or international
Staff or members' nationality	Single nation or territory; multi-national
Status of personnel	Volunteer, paid, professional
Geo-political and economic origin	E.g., originate in democratic versus totalitarian nation; North versus South or East versus West
Structure	E.g., project model (funds raised for specific projects only), academic model (attached to academic institutions with teaching, research & service goals), consultancy (e.g., charge fees for services), corporate (operate like a corporation), membership (that promote the interests of their members)

[18] The *Declaration on the Right and Responsibility of Individuals, Groups and Organs of Society* sheds light on NGOs that have competence in the area of human rights. For example, Article 18 provides:

18(2). Individuals, groups, institutions and non-governmental organizations have an important role to play and a responsibility in safeguarding democracy, promoting human rights and fundamental freedoms and contributing to the promotion and advancement of democratic societies, institutions and processes.

18(3). Individuals, groups, institutions and non-governmental organizations also have an important role and a responsibility in contributing, as appropriate, to the promotion of the right of everyone to a social and international order in which the rights and freedoms set forth in the Universal Declaration of Human Rights and other human rights instruments can be fully realized.

http://www.unhchr.ch/Huridocda/Huridoca.nsf/(Symbol)/ A.RES.53.144.En (accessed July 20, 2009).

[19] See, e.g., Spiro, *NGOs and Human Rights*, at 2.

Table (*cont.*)

NGO Category	Category Description
Size	E.g., *large* such as Save the Children, Oxfam, Human Rights Watch or Amnesty International, or *small* such as many local, grassroots groups
Substantive area of human rights concern	E.g., fair trial rights, freedom of expression & association, rights of women & children, sexual orientation rights, liberty & security of persons, torture, cruel, inhuman or degrading treatment or punishment, disability rights, race discrimination & xenophobia, economic & social rights, cultural rights, civil & political rights
Nature of mandates and work	E.g., identifying human rights violators & documenting abuses; monitoring & influencing laws, policies & practice of governments and non-state actors; shaming human rights violators to force compliance with law; human rights education; fact-finding with or without on-site visits; legal research; advocacy including domestic & international litigation;[20] information evaluation & dissemination; democratization; fund-raising; mobilizing & empowering locals to participate in civil society; designing and implementing development projects; providing humanitarian aid; establishing standards or norms to measure or judge the conduct of individuals, NGOs, states, & other international actors
Funding levels	For personnel, physical resources and programs
Funding sources	From services rendered or sale of goods; donations from private donors, foundations, governments, quasi-NGOs, or IGOs
How they lobby or consult domestic governments & IGOs	Testifying at hearings, participating in treaty negotiations, joining government panels & delegations, liaising among governments and other NGOs
How they gather information	From interviews with victims & other human rights NGOs, newspapers & other periodicals, web, visits & discussions with governments, inter-governmental organization representatives & private persons
How they share information	Through conferences, colloquia, seminars, human rights public awareness campaigns, position papers, government consultations
Their affiliations	E.g., affiliated with a law school human rights clinics or program, or a church, mosque, or temple

[20] See, e.g., *Filartiga v. Pena-Irala*, 630 F.2d 876 (2d Cir. 1980).

In all cases, human rights are and should be "on the frontline of the human rights struggle, fighting to promote human rights".[21]

2.4. *Human Rights NGOs and the United Nations System – General Background*

Human rights NGOs contributed significantly to the negotiation of the UN Charter[22] and to virtually all, if not all, the UN's major international human rights law instruments from the Universal Declaration of Human Rights to date.[23] This section of the chapter explores the legal bases for the relationship

[21] Gay J. McDougall, "A Decade in Human Rights Law: Decade of NGO Struggle," *Human Rights Brief* 11(Spring 2004): 12. Ms. McDougall states about human rights NGOs:

> Through their work, NGOs frame policies and influence key government decisions. They give voice to causes that have been ignored, forgotten, or marginalized. They raise legal awareness within targeted communities, often providing basic legal representation in high-risk or neglected human rights cases. NGOs generate expert analysis on the ground and are integral to both the field and headquarters-level operations of virtually every human rights mission, often working alongside staff of the United Nations, the Organization for Security and Cooperation in Europe, the Organization of American States, the African Union, the Economic Community of West African States, and other international peacekeepers in dangerous conflict environments.

See also Gay J. McDougall, "The World Conference Against Racism: Through a Wider Lens," *Fletcher Forum of World Affairs* 26 (2002): 135, 147 (noting that the closing declaration of the NGO Forum associated with the World Conference on Racism "is a valuable document" as the "vast majority of NGO representatives participating in the NGO Forum came with legitimate anti-racism agendas" and the NGO closing document is "overwhelmingly progressive and articulates the aspirations of civil society groups from around the globe – people who face racism in their daily lives and who have much to say about how to combat it.").

[22] See, e.g., William Korey, *NGOs and the Universal Declaration of Human Rights: "A Curious Grapevine,"* (New York: St. Martin's Press, 2001), 19 (discussing study showing NGOs instrumental "in making human rights a vibrant and major force on the agenda of international diplomacy and discourse.") The subtitle of this book alludes to statements of Eleanor Roosevelt, who was instrumental in the UDHR's negotiation and drafting, who referred to the "curious grapevine" that would carry word of the UDHR around the globe so it "may seep in even when governments are not so anxious for it". See Claude E. Welch, Jr., Book Review: *NGOs and the Universal Declaration of Human Rights: "A Curious Grapevine", Human Rights Quarterly* 22.1 (2000): 298–301.

[23] See, e.g., U.N. Office of the President of the Millennium Assembly, "Reference document on the participation of civil society in United Nations conferences and special sessions of the General Assembly during the 1990s" (Version 1, August 2001), http://www.un.org/ga/president/55/speech/civilsociety1.htm (accessed July 16, 2009). This document also outlines rules and procedures for NGO accreditation, modalities for NGO participation, and NGO documentation for various UN meetings and conference during the 1990s, and illustrates the significant participation and impact of NGOs on protecting human rights through the UN system. Ibid.

between the UN and NGOs, the history of the relationship, the duties of inter-governmental organizations to consult with NGOs, and specifics about an umbrella NGO working with UN-affiliated NGOs. Recent Secretaries General of the United Nations – including Ban Ki-Moon, Kofi Annan, and Boutros Boutros-Ghali – have heralded the "indispensable" contributions that NGOs have made to the protection of human rights in the UN system.[24]

---

[24] On the occasion of the UDHR's 60th Anniversary, UN Secretary General Ban Ki-Moon noted:

> Since 1948, human rights have been at the core of the work of the United Nations. At the same time, civil society has been on the front line. For six decades, human rights defenders have sacrificed liberty, comfort and even life to ensure that all human beings can enjoy the rights enshrined in the Declaration—irrespective of their race, religion, ethnicity, gender or other status.

"Secretary-General's Video Message For Historic Paris DPI/NGO Conference Stresses Duty To Ensure That Human Rights Are Living Reality," Transcript of video message to the 61st UN Department of Public Information-NGO Conference, Paris, France, UN Doc. SG/SM/11774, NGO/650, PI/1850, September 3, 2008. http://www.un.org/News/Press/docs/2008/sgsm11774.doc.htm (accessed July 16, 2009).

UN Secretary General Kofi Annan, at the closing session of the 58th Annual UN Department of Public Information-NGO Conference, remarked:

> Whatever is decided and achieved, the United Nations cannot move ahead on its own. You all have a key role to play and we depend on you. Just as you have closely watched and influenced the negotiations on the Summit outcome, so must you now closely review what happens next. The grass roots you represent will expect you to assess the outcome document, and to tell us whether the reforms the leaders adopt go far enough. And we all need you to monitor developments at the country level, in the streets, in the villages, and to ensure that the leaders of your countries produce real results in the months and years ahead. You must make yourselves the guardians of the reform of the international system.
>
> In this sixtieth anniversary year of the United Nations, let us again acknowledge the wisdom of the founders, who, in Article 71, made provision for consultations with NGOs. Close engagement with civil society was seen then as vital for the Organization's health and for people's well-being. That is as true today as it was then – if anything, even more so.
>
> The relationship between us can never be measured merely by the number of NGOs attending global conferences, or taking part in meetings at UN Headquarters. What really matters is what happens out there, in the world and on the ground. Whether your main activity is helping set policy at the global level, or working directly to help people, you give true meaning to the phrase "we the peoples". I am grateful to every one of you for your engagement, and count on your support in the crucial time ahead.

U.N. Secretary-General Kofi Annan, "Without Vital Role of NGOs, World Could Hardly Respond to Myriad Crises, UN Secretary-General Annan Tells DPI/NGO Conference." U.N. Doc SG/SM/10085, NGO/582, PI/1674 (September 9, 2005) http://www.un.org/News/Press/docs/2005/sgsm10085.doc.htm (accessed July 16, 2009).

Former UN Secretary General Boutros Boutros-Ghali stated that even "a cursory examination of the participation of NGOs in the decision-making systems and operational activities of the United Nations shows without any doubt that NGO involvement has not only justified

2.4.1. *Legal Bases for NGO Involvement with the UN*

Article 71 of the UN Charter and various Economic and Social Council (ECOSOC) resolutions provide the legal bases for the relationship through which NGOs receive UN "consultative status" and formally provide technical analysis and expertise to various UN bodies. Article 71, which marked the first time that the term "non-governmental organization" was referred to in a UN document,[25] provides for international and national organization consultative arrangements, with priority on international groups:[26]

> The Economic and Social Council *may make* suitable arrangements for consultation with non-governmental organizations which are concerned with matters within its competence. Such arrangements *may be made* with international organizations and, *where appropriate*, with national organizations after consultation with the Member of the United Nations concerned. [emphasis added]

ECOSOC granted NGOs consultative status as early as 1948, and it spelled out the first set of rules governing this relationship in resolution 288 B(X) of 1950.[27] The General Assembly (GA) reviewed these rules, and through GA resolution 1296 of 1968, the GA established criteria for NGO participation and provided for the UN to appoint NGO liaison officers.[28]

As domestic and international human rights NGOs proliferated from the 1950s to the 1990s and significantly contributed to the UN's work, the UN expressly invited national, sub-regional, regional and international NGOs to

---

the inclusion of Article 71 in the Charter of the United Nations, but that it has far exceeded the original scope of" the Charter's legal provisions permitting NGO participation. "General Review of Arrangements for Consultations with Non-governmental Organizations – Report of the Secretary-General," E/AC.70/1994/5 (May 26, 1994), para. 40.

[25] See Renate Bloem, Isolda Agazzi and Philippe Dam, "The Conference of NGOs (CONGO): The Story of Strengthening Civil Society Engagement with the United Nations," (paper presented for the Conference of NGOs (CONGO)). http://www.ngocongo.org/files/story_of_congo.doc, 4 (accessed June 13, 2009).

[26] UN Charter, art. 71. Article 71 appears to have been primarily focused on relations between the UN and international NGOs (INGOs), as opposed to national NGOs, as evidenced by the article's provision that national NGO arrangements should be made "where appropriate" and after "consultation with the Member [State] of the United Nations concerned" – restrictions that did not exist with INGO relations. See *Charter of the United Nations*, http://www.un.org/en/documents/charter/ (accessed July 20, 2009); ECOSOC Resolution 1996/31 (July 25, 1996) (entitled "Consultative Relationship Between The United Nations And Non-governmental Organizations") www.un.org/documents/ecosoc/res/1996/eres1996-31.htm (accessed July 20, 2009).

[27] By 1946, ECOSOC had granted consultative status to approximately 41 NGOs, http://esa.un.org/coordination/ngo/new/index.asp?page=intro (accessed July 19, 2009). Today over 3,000 NGOs are accredited. NGOs with consultative status are listed at www.un.org/esa/coordination/ngo (accessed July 17, 2009).

[28] Ibid.

participate. In 1996, after a multi-year review of the NGO relationship, ECOSOC adopted resolution 1996/31 to update that relationship and permitted national and regional NGOs to be accredited if "their aims and purposes are in conformity with the spirit, purposes and principles of the UN Charter".[29] This resolution, which defines NGO as "any international organization which is not established by a governmental entity or intergovernmental agreement", governs the NGO relationship today, including NGOs' relationship with the Human Rights Council, which began operating only in 2006.[30] NGOs, whose

---

[29] U.N. Economic and Social Council, "Resolution 1996/31 – Consultative Relationship Between The United Nations And Non-governmental Organizations," July 25, 1996, U.N. Doc. E/1996/31 (1996), http://www.un.org/documents/ecosoc/res/1996/eres1996-31.htm (accessed July 20, 2009).

Resolution 31 of 1996 establishes three categories of consultative arrangements for NGOs: (a) General consultative status for large international NGOs whose area of work covers most issues on the ECOSOC agenda; (b) Special consultative status for NGOs that have special competence in a few fields of the ECOSOC activity and that are known within the fields in which they have or seek consultative status; and (c) Roster inclusion, for NGOs whose competence enables them to make occasional and useful contributions to the work of the UN and that shall be available for consultation upon request. Ibid., Part III. The resolution also formulated guidelines for written statements, oral statements and meeting attendance. Ibid., Part IV. For a discussion on NGOs and the European Commission, see generally Prodi, Romano and Neil Kinnock, "The Commission and Non-Governmental Organisations: Building a Stronger Partnership," Commission of the European Communities Discussion Paper, COM(2000) 11 Final (January 18, 2000), http://eur-lex.europa.eu/LexUriServ/LexUriServ.do?uri=COM:2000:0011:FIN:EN:PDF (accessed July 20, 2009).

[30] Resolution 1296 supersedes ECOSOC Res. 288 B (X) of Feb. 27, 1950. See U.N. Economic and Social Council, "Resolution 1296 (XIV) – Arrangements for Consultation with Non-Governmental Organizations," May 23, 1968, U.N. Doc. E/RES/1968/1296 (1968), http://www.un-documents.net/1296.htm (accessed July 19, 2009). Notably, in 1998, the Secretary-General issued a report (A/53/170) elaborating NGO arrangements, and in 1999 issued another report that purported to reflect views of Member States, specialized agencies, observers, intergovernmental organizations and NGOs. See Report of the Secretary-General of the United Nations, "Arrangements and practices for the interaction of non-governmental organizations in all activities of the United Nations system," U.N. Doc. A/53/170 (1998), http://www.un.org/documents/ga/docs/53/plenary/a53-170.htm (accessed July 20, 2009); Report of the Secretary-General of the United Nations, "Views of the Member States, members of the specialized agencies, observers, intergovernmental and non-governmental organizations from all regions on the report of the Secretary-General on arrangements and practices for the interaction of non-governmental organizations in all activities of the United Nations system," U.N. Doc. A/54/329 (1999), http://www.un-ngls.org/orf/UN-SG%20report-1999.doc (accessed July 20, 2009).

In 2000, the Millennium Declaration (adopted by resolution 55/2), offered a new mandate to enhance the NGO relationship, as follows:

NGO accreditation applications are reviewed by the ECOSOC Committee on NGOs,[31] provide input to the UN at public meetings, during international conferences and their preparatory meetings, and informally. NGOs may offer insights on all critical matters concerning the UN's operations, including matters that directly threaten peace and security. Even if an NGO does not have ECOSOC consultative status, the NGO may still consult with the UN on an *ad hoc* basis or through procedures established by various UN affiliated bodies.[32]

> We also resolve... [t]o develop strong partnerships with the private sector and with civil society organizations in pursuit of development and poverty eradication. [para 20]
>
> We resolve... [t]o strengthen further cooperation between the [UN] and national parliaments through their world organization, the Inter-Parliamentary Union, in various fields, including peace and security, economic and social development, international law and human rights and democracy and gender issues...To give greater opportunities to the private sector, non-governmental organizations and civil society, in general, to contribute to the realization of the Organization's goals and programmes. [para 30]

See U.N. General Assembly, Resolution adopted by the General Assembly, United Nations Millennium Declaration (September 18, 2000). U.N. Doc A/RES/55/2 (2000) paras. 20, 30, http://www.un.org/millennium/declaration/ares552e.pdf (accessed July 20, 2009).

The follow-up resolution to the outcome of the Millennium Summit (A/RES/55/162) provides:

> *Calls* for enhanced partnership and cooperation with national parliaments as well as civil society, including non-governmental organizations and the private sector, as set out in the Millennium Declaration, to ensure their contribution to the implementation of the Declaration; Declaration[.]

U.N. General Assembly, "Resolution adopted by the General Assembly – Follow up to the outcome of the Millennium Summit," December 18, 2000, U.N. Doc. A/RES/55/162 (2000) para. 14, ftp://ftp.fao.org/unfao/bodies/council/cl120/Y0556e2.pdf (accessed July 20, 2009).

31 The UN Committee on NGOs is an ECOSOC standing committee that was established by resolution 3(II) on 21 June 1946. http://esango.un.org/paperless/Web?page=static&content=committee (accessed July 19, 2009). The Committee, which reports directly to ECOSOC, has 19 member States, meets annually for several weeks in New York, and has occasional other sessions. The Committee's original terms of reference were set out in ECOSOC resolution 288 B (X) of 27 February 1950, which was superseded by ECOSOC resolution 1296 (XLIV) of 25 May 1968. The Committee's current terms of reference are outlined in Resolution 1996/31 of 25 July 1996. http://esango.un.org/paperless/Web?page=static&content=committee (accessed July 20, 2009). After the Committee reviews and approves an NGO's application, "it is only considered recommended for consultative status". Ibid. The ECOSOC reviews the recommendations, "takes note of the Committee's report and makes the decisions final". Ibid. "It is only after the recommendation becomes an ECOSOC decision that the NGO is granted the consultative status." Ibid.

32 For example, various U.N. specialized agencies grant their own accreditation for NGOs working in the agencies' areas of specialization. See U.N. Department of Economic and Social Affairs, "NGO related Questions and Answers," http://esa.un.org/coordination/ngo/new/index.asp?page=faqs (accessed June 12, 2009). Examples include: the International Labor Organization (ILO) in Geneva, the Food and Agriculture Organization of the UN (FAO) in

The 1993 Vienna Declaration and Program of Action provides further authority for NGOs to participate in UN affairs, proclaiming that NGOs "should be free to carry out their human rights activities, without interference, within the framework of national law and the Universal Declaration of Human Rights."[33] The Vienna Declaration confirmed "the promotion and protection of human rights" as "a matter of priority for the international community" and called on "States and international organizations, *in cooperation with non-governmental organizations,* to create favourable conditions at the national, regional and international levels to ensure the full and effective enjoyment of human rights."[34] The Vienna Declaration also recognized "*the important role of non-governmental organizations* in the promotion of all human rights...at national, regional and international levels...and to the...protection of all human rights and fundamental freedoms."[35]

2.4.2. *Conference of Non-Governmental Organisations in Consultative Relationship with the United Nations (CONGO)*

As a principal NGO membership organization associated with the UN since the 1940s, the Conference of Non-Governmental Organisations in Consultative Relationship with the United Nations (CONGO)[36] has recognized that the historical relationship between the UN and NGOs has been divided into three "generations".[37] In the first generation, from 1945 to the end of the Cold War,

Rome, UN Educational, Scientific and Cultural Organization (UNESCO) in Paris, the World Health Organization (WHO) in Geneva, the International Telecommunication Union (ITU) in Geneva, the International Maritime Organization (IMO) in London, the World Intellectual Property Organization (WIPO) in Geneva, the UN Industrial Development Organization (UNIDO) in Vienna, and the UN Conference on Trade and Development (UNCTAD) in Geneva. Ibid.

33 Vienna Declaration and Programme of Action, July 12, 1993, U.N. Doc. A/CONF.157/23 (1993), http://www.unhchr.ch/huridocda/huridoca.nsf/(Symbol)/A.CONF.157.23.En (accessed July 19, 2009) (adopted at the World Conference on Human Rights, 25 June 1993) para. 38.

34 Ibid. preamble, para. 13 (emphasis added).

35 Ibid., para. 38 (emphasis added).

36 In 1948, CONGO was founded as "an independent, international, non-profit membership association of" NGOs. See "About CONGO," http://www.ngocongo.org/index.php?what=about (accessed July 19, 2009). Since 1948, CONGO has facilitated NGO participation in UN debates and decision-making. It assists NGOs to support the UN Charter and enhance their relationship and cooperation with the UN and provides a forum for NGOs to study, plan, support and act on issues relating to UN principles and program. Members represent a wide range of human rights interests. Ibid.; www.ngocongo.org/index.php?what=about&start=1 (accessed July 17, 2009).

37 See Renate Bloem, Isolda Agazzi and Philippe Dam, "The Conference of NGOs (CONGO): The Story of Strengthening Civil Society Engagement with the United Nations," (paper

the UN Economic and Social Council (ECOSOC) permitted formal relationships principally to a handful of international NGOs.[38] In the second generation, a wave of national NGOs emerged, and the UN modified its consultative process to permit them to become accredited.[39] In the third generation, accredited international and national NGOs, both individually and in concert with each other, were able to contribute even more to the work of the UN.[40]

The NGO Branch of the UN Department of Economic and Social Affairs (DESA), through a network called "United Nations NGO Informal Regional Network" (UN-NGO-IRENE), coordinates collaboration between the UN and NGOs.[41] The UN-NGO-IRENE network interfaces between the UN headquarters in New York, UN organizations at the country level and non-UN organizations including academia, NGOs, business organizations, and philanthropic foundations.[42] Today, the United Nations has opened its doors to NGOs in many ways, for example, by its UN-NGO-IRENE Best Practices Network, which is an interactive website forum for NGOs to share and discuss best practices.[43]

2.4.3. *The United Nations Duty to Consult NGOs*

The United Nations, other inter-governmental bodies, and national governments facilitate NGO participation in those bodies' deliberations, negotiations, and decision-making. An emerging body of literature debates whether governments, inter-governmental organizations, and national governments have a duty to consult with NGOs, or whether these consultations are only permissive.[44]

presented for the Conference of NGOs (CONGO)). http://www.ngocongo.org/files/story_of_congo.doc, 4 (accessed July 17, 2009) (citing Tony Hill, "Three Generations of UN-Civil Society Relations: A Quick Sketch" (Background Paper for the Secretary-General's Panel of Eminent Persons on United Nations Relations with Civil Society, remarks by Coordinator, United Nations Non-Governmental Liaison Service); see generally http://www.ngocongo.org/index.php?what=about; www.ngocongo.org/index.php?what=about&start=1) (accessed July 17, 2009); http://www.un-ngls.org/orf/UNreform.htm (accessed July 17, 2009).

[38] Tony Hill, "Three Generations of UN-Civil Society Relations: A Quick Sketch".

[39] Ibid.

[40] Ibid.

[41] U.N. Department of Economic and Social Affairs, "Non-Governmental Organizations Branch," http://www.un.org/esa/coordination/ngo (accessed July 17, 2009).

[42] UN-NGO-IRENE works with the International Association of the Economic and Social Councils and Similar institutions (AICESIS) spread over 5 continents with activities in 65 countries involving over 3000 NGOs. Ibid.

[43] Ibid.

[44] See generally Steve Charnovitz, "Nongovernmental Organizations and International Law," 348–372 (citing treaties, non-treaty international instruments, and writing and teachings of scholars and jurists on the issue of the duty to consult). Professor Charnovitz defines

The two principal traditional sources of international law – treaties and customary international law – assist in the resolution of this question.

No treaty specifically addresses the issue of whether the duty to consult is a rule of international law.[45] Thus, we turn to the next source, customary international law, for which proof would need to be adduced in the form of state practice and *opinio juris*. These two elements exist, proving that the duty to consult is a binding norm of customary international law.

The state practice prong is easily satisfied. As Charnovitz notes, "consulting with NGOs is widespread and continues to expand", even in bodies that had "appeared to be off-limits for NGOs", such as the UN Security Council.[46] NGOs are routinely consulted in proceedings of many United Nations bodies, including the UN treaty bodies, the UN Forum on Forests, the Food and Agricultural Organization, the World Health Organization, the International Labor Organization, ECOSOC and the Human Rights Council.[47]

The state practice prong for the duty to consult is bolstered by treaty language that requires NGO consultation, such as provisions that NGOs "shall be admitted",[48] which is mandatory language, and not permissive.

Furthermore, the UN General Assembly promulgated a Declaration in 1999 that provides that "everyone has the right, individually and in association with others, at the national and international levels:…(c) To communicate with non-governmental or intergovernmental organizations".[49]

"consultation" as "a duty to listen" with a "good faith commitment to consider the information provided by the consulting partner." Ibid., 368 (citations omitted). Consultations could also include advisory groups, notice and comment, stakeholder dialogues, and general NGO access. Ibid.

[45] See ibid., 368.

[46] Ibid.

[47] NGOs have been consulted less routinely in proceedings of other inter-governmental bodies such as the UN General Assembly, the International Monetary Fund, and the World Bank. See Ibid.

[48] *Convention on International Trade in Endangered Species of Wild Fauna and Flora (CITES)*, Mar. 3, 1973, entry into force July 1, 1975, Art. XI(7)(a), 993 UNTS 243,12 ILM 1085 (1973) ("Any [NGO] technically qualified in protection, conservation or management of wild fauna and flora, in the following categories, which has informed the [CITES] Secretariat of its desire to be represented at meetings of the Conference by observers, *shall be admitted* unless at least one-third of the Parties present object"). See also http://www.cites.org/eng/disc/what.shtml (accessed July 17, 2009) (emphasis added).

[49] Declaration on the Right and Responsibility of Individuals, Groups and Organs of Society, Art. 5(a).

Similarly, the *opinio juris* prong has been satisfied.[50] Numerous legal scholars and practitioners have supported a right to consult.[51]

2.5. *Activities (Selected) of Human Rights NGOs in the International and Domestic Arenas*

Illustrating comprehensively the wide variety of human rights NGO types, and the wide range of activities in which they engage, would require substantially more space than this chapter permits. Thus, this section of the chapter will merely identify and examine a somewhat random cross-section or sampling of activities engaged in by a selection of human rights NGOs that operate in the international and domestic arenas. Highlighted are human rights NGOs participating in the United Nations system,[52] including NGOs participating

---

[50] The UN has stressed the importance of consultation in the promotion and protection of human rights. For example, in Agenda 21, the United Nations states:

> 23.2 One of the fundamental prerequisites for the achievement of sustainable development is broad public participation in decision-making. Furthermore, in the more specific context of environment and development, the need for new forms of participation has emerged. . . .
>
> 23.3 Any policies, definitions or rules affecting access to and participation by non-governmental organizations in the work of United Nations institutions or agencies associated with the implementation of Agenda 21 must apply equally to all major groups.

U.N. Conference on Environment and Development, "Agenda 21 – Rio Declaration on Environment and Development," U.N. Doc. A/CONF.151/26 (1992) (Vol III), http://www.un-documents.net/agenda21.htm (accessed July 21, 2009) Part III of Agenda 21 – Chapters 23 – 32 – is entitled "Strengthening the Role of Major Groups".)

[51] Professor Charnovitz wrote that "[o]ver the past several years, several commentators have suggested that international decision makers have an obligation to provide consultative opportunities for private groups, or contended that NGOs have a right to render advice. Steve Charnovitz, "Nongovernmental Organizations and International Law," 371 (citing Janne Elisabeth Nijman, *The Concept of International Legal Personality* 469 (2004) (suggesting that when groups "'are silenced or suppressed, the international community has a duty to accommodate these groups on stage and to be an audience to them'"); Laurence Boisson de Chazournes and Philippe Sands, Introduction to *International Law, The International Court of Justice and Nuclear Weapons* (Cambridge: Cambridge University Press, 1999) 1, 10 (seeing a "growing entitlement of individuals and non-governmental organisations to a more formal and informal involvement in international judicial and quasi-judicial proceedings"); Peter Willetts, "From 'Consultative Arrangements' to 'Partnership': The Changing Status of NGOs in Diplomacy at the UN," *Global Governance* 6 (2000): 191–212, 205 (suggesting that UN Charter Article 71 has risen to customary international law).

[52] In 2003, the Secretary General appointed a Panel of Eminent Persons on United Nations-Civil Society Relations to examine "the modes of participation in UN processes of non-governmental organizations, as well as of other non-governmental actors such as the private sector and parliamentarians." "UN-Civil Society Relations Panel Established," *UN Press*, Feb. 13, 2003, http://www.globalpolicy.org/component/content/article/177-un/31845.html (accessed July 17,

in United Nations conferences, NGOs submitting "shadow reports" and making oral presentations to UN treaty bodies about human rights violations in different countries, human rights "major groups" operating in the UN Forum on Forests, and NGOs participating in international complaint mechanisms. Also discussed are academic institutions engaging in human rights promotion and protection, and human rights NGOs operating outside the UN and intergovernmental human rights systems.

2.5.1. *NGOs Participating in United Nations Conferences*
Since the 1945 San Francisco conference in which NGOs played a major role in influencing world powers in shaping the United Nations, NGOs have continued to play a major role in UN conferences, and have made substantial contributions to the work of the UN in many areas, including development, peace, nutrition, health, rights of women and children, international crimes, racism and race discrimination, global finance, and human settlements – all of which directly or indirectly concern international human rights issues.[53]

2.5.2. *NGOs Presenting Shadow Reports to United Nations Treaty Bodies*
Pursuant to various United Nations international human rights law treaties, states parties to the treaties are required to report periodically on how the states

2009). In response to the Panel's findings, the UN Secretariat agreed that increased involvement of NGOs should "become a regular component of the General Assembly's work", and that the Security Council should "find ways to strengthen further its relationship with civil society." "Report of the Secretary-General in response to the report of the Panel of Eminent Persons on United Nations-Civil Society Relations," U.N. Doc. A/59/354 (2004), paras. 10, 14 http://www.undg.org/archive_docs/5244-SG_s_Response_to_the_Report_of_the_Panel_of_Eminent_Persons_on_UN-Civil_Society_Relations.doc (accessed July 17, 2009). Further, the Secretary General agreed to establish a trust fund to increase participation of representatives of non-governmental organizations from developing countries. Ibid., Part III.

[53] United Nations Conferences with major NGO participation have included: United Nations Conference on Environment and Development (UNCED/Earth Summit/Rio Summit) (1992, Rio de Janeiro); International Conference on Population and Development (ICPD) (1994, Cairo); World Conference on Human Rights (1993, Vienna); World Summit for Social Development (1995, Copenhagen); Fourth World Conference on Women: Action for Equality, Development and Peace (1995, Beijing); United Nations Conference on Human Settlements (Habitat II) (1996, Istanbul); World Conference Against Racism, Racial Discrimination, Xenophobia and Related Intolerance (2001, Durban); International Conference on Financing for Development (2002, Mexico); Special Session of the General Assembly for the Overall Review and Appraisal of the Agenda 21 (Earth Summit + 5) (1997, New York). See U.N. Office of the President of the Millennium Assembly, 55th session of the UN General Assembly. "Reference document on the participation of civil society in United Nations conferences and special sessions of the General Assembly during the 1990s." (Version 1, August, 2001), http://www.un.org/ga/president/55/speech/civilsociety1.htm (accessed July 16, 2009).

are complying or not complying with the human rights mandates incorporated into the treaties.[54] States submit their reports to UN "treaty bodies", which are groups of United Nations independent experts who review the states' reports and render "concluding observations" on whether the states comply or fail.[55] Human rights NGOs have, through express treaty language or by practice of treaty bodies, been permitted to participate in this process by, for example, submitting "shadow reports" that are "alternative to" and that counter states' own reports, and then traveling to the United Nations in New York or Geneva and orally presenting the reports to the UN treaty bodies.[56] Human rights NGO shadow reports have positively impacted the work of the treaty bodies, whose members have, for example, referred to shadow reports when posing questions to or raising issues with government representatives who appear for

---

[54] For example, pursuant to article 40 of the ICCPR, the Human Rights Committee will receive reports States Parties "undertake to submit…on the measures they have adopted which give effect to the rights recognized herein and on the progress made in the enjoyment of those rights". www.unhchr.ch/html/menu3/b/a_ccpr.htm (accessed July 17, 2009).

[55] The eight UN human rights treaty bodies are: The Human Rights Committee; the Committee on Economic, Social and Cultural Rights; the Committee on the Elimination of Racial Discrimination; the Committee on the Elimination of Discrimination against Women; the Committee Against Torture; the Committee on the Rights of the Child; the Committee on Migrant Workers; and the Committee on the Rights of Persons with Disabilities. See *Human Rights Bodies*, http://www.ohchr.org/EN/HRBodies/Pages/HumanRightsBodies.aspx (accessed July 17, 2009). Other international human rights bodies exist in regional systems, including the African Commission on Human and Peoples' Rights, the European Commission and the European Court of Human Rights, the European Committee for the Prevention of Torture, the Inter-American Commission and the Inter-American Court of Human Rights, and the ILO Committee on the Application of Conventions and Recommendations.

[56] For example, the Program in International Human Rights Law (PIHRL), based at Indiana University School of Law – Indianapolis, has authored or facilitated through the research and drafting of law students numerous Shadow Reports related to human rights abuses in many countries. See www.indylaw.indiana.edu/humanrights/UNshadow.html (accessed July 21, 2009). Representatives of the PIHRL and affiliated student groups from the school have traveled to Geneva and New York and formally and informally presented Shadow Reports to UN Treaty Bodies, and have witnessed their Shadow Report issues incorporated into questions that UN Treaty Body Experts asked government representatives in hearings and that Committees incorporated into their Concluding Observations post-hearings. The law students, faculty, and staff – with the collaboration and assistance of outside NGOs and others – tendered and presented Shadow Reports to the UN Human Rights Committee for countries and issues that include: Australia (rights of women, March 2009), Chad (rights of women and girls, March and July 2009); Panama (indigenous peoples, 2008); Zambia (press freedom, 2007); Chile (sexual orientation discrimination, 2007); USA (Hurricane Katrina, 2006); USA (sexual orientation discrimination, 2006); and Hungary (Roma, 2001). Ibid. Shadow Reports were submitted to the UN Race Discrimination Committee on: USA (discrimination against Muslims, Arabs, Middle Easterners, and South Asians, 2008); USA (Hurricane Katrina, 2008); Nepal (Dalit People, 2000). Ibid. In 2009, a report was submitted to the Committee Against

treaty body hearings. Sometimes treaty body members raise these issues during the formal, on-the-record hearings, and other times they may raise the issues informally with government representatives outside of meetings. At times, the treaty bodies incorporate into their concluding observations recommendations raised by NGOs in the NGO shadow reports. NGOs are a valuable resource for information for UN treaty bodies.[57]

Human rights NGOs can facilitate states' treaty compliance by urging states to include the citizenry in the compliance process. Human rights NGOs can encourage states to disseminate copies of the relevant human rights treaties, to disseminate draft government periodic reports, to hold wide consultative sessions, to permit NGO and other feedback, to fund NGO participation at treaty body hearings in New York or Geneva, and to disseminate widely any treaty body's concluding observations. Also, NGOs can encourage states to withdraw

---

Torture on other cruel, inhuman or degrading treatment or punishment in the Philippines. The PIHRL has also worked with the National Bar Association – International Law Section (NBA – ILS) in submitting Shadow Reports.

Students and faculty from other law schools have also submitted Shadow Reports, and collaborated on other treaty body advocacy projects, in collaboration with Indiana, on their own, or with other schools and NGOs. See, e.g., www.law.harvard.edu/programs/hrp/ (accessed July 20, 2009), www.law.columbia.edu/center_program/human_rights (accessed July 20, 2009), http://indylaw.indiana.edu/humanrights/shadowreports/USA%20Sexual%20Minorities.pdf and http://www.indylaw.indiana.edu/humanrights/UNshadow.html (accessed July 20, 2009) (Harvard Human Rights Program and Indiana submitted separate shadow reports on Panama during the same 2008 Human Rights Committee session; Stetson law student participated in Indiana report to Race Committee). NGOs that regularly submit shadow reports include Amnesty International (www.amnesty.org) (accessed July 18, 2009), Human Rights Watch (www.hrw.org) (accessed July 18, 2009), and The Centre for Civil and Political Rights (CCPR Centre) (http://www.ccprcentre.org/) (accessed July 18, 2009).

[57] An NGO participant at Human Rights Committee hearings in Geneva on implementation of the ICCPR in Hong Kong reflected:

> Many Committee members commented on the number of Hong Kong NGO representatives present at the hearings. As I sat and watched, and listened to the concerns of various members, I could not help but think about the member states that cannot send human rights advocates to these proceedings. Present and listening, human rights advocates from Hong Kong were able to provide immediate research and responses to any inaccurate representation the government made. Without this type of advocacy and physical presence, the Committee does not have adequate resources, or the same balance or diversity of input, to draft immediate concluding observations. This limitation, coupled with the fact that the Human Rights Committee cannot hold annual hearings on every member state, emphasizes the importance of on-site human rights advocacy.

Cheryl K. Moralez, *Seizing the Opportunity: Participation in the Fifth Periodic Report of the Hong Kong Special Administrative Region before the U.N. Human Rights Committee*, DePaul International Law Journal 4: (2000): 175, 180–181 (reflections by one of three DePaul law students who accompanied the author to these hearings in Geneva and worked with the Hong Kong Human Rights Monitor and other NGOs).

any treaty reservations and to submit overdue periodic reports. Furthermore, NGOs can urge states to encourage other states similarly to comply with treaty substantive and other rules.

2.5.3. *United Nations Bodies & "Major Groups" – The UN Forum on Forests – An Example of NGOs Working Within the UN System*

The United Nations Forum on Forests (UNFF)[58] is one of many UN bodies reaching out to NGOs and other non-state actors for participatory guidance and consultation. The UNFF is charged with protecting the world's exhaustible forests from environmental sustainability and human rights perspectives. The UNFF identified a range of forest-related stakeholders, called "major groups", who participate in UNFF proceedings as a key component of the body's work. NGOs are one of nine major groups[59] that are encouraged to participate actively in virtually all aspects of UNFF work.[60] The major groups are invited to full-day multi-stakeholder dialogues as part of UNFF regular sessions, are entitled to submit statements for the record, and can intervene orally at UNFF meetings.

Human rights fall within the competency of the UNFF as governmental and non-state actor policies and practices regarding forests may threaten economic, social, cultural, civil, and political rights of poor and marginalized indigenous

58 The UN Forum on Forests was created by ECOSOC Resolution 2000/35 as a UN subsidiary body instructed to promote "the management, conservation and sustainable development of all types of forests and to strengthen long-term political commitment to this end" based on, *inter alia*, the Rio Declaration, the Forest Principles, Chapter 11 of Agenda 21 and other milestones of international forest policy. See Resolutions and Decisions of the Economic and Social Council, UN Doc. ECOSOC Res 2000/35, October 18, 2000, http://www.un.org/esa/forests/pdf/2000_35_E.pdf (accessed July 18, 2009); U.N. Forum on Forests (UNFF), "About UNFF," http://www.un.org/esa/forests/about.htm (accessed July 18, 2009).

59 The nine Major Groups are: women; children and youth; indigenous people; local authorities; workers and trade unions; business and industry; scientific and technological communities; NGOs; and farmers and small forest landowners. http://www.un.org/esa/forests/about.htm (accessed July 18, 2009). Many of the Major Groups are represented by NGO leaders, and many of the representatives are heavily involved with NGOs independent of their involvement with the Major Groups.

60 See U.N. Forum on Forests (UNFF), "Participation of Major Groups." http://www.un.org/esa/forests/participation.html#1 (accessed July 18, 2009) ("Major groups organizations that are accredited with the Economic and Social Council of the UN (ECOSOC) and the Commission on Sustainable Development (CSD) are encouraged to participate in UNFF Sessions.... Organizations NOT accredited with ECOSOC or CSD may attend as part of the delegation of its country or as part of the delegation of an accredited organization."); See also U.N. Forum on Forests (UNFF), "UNFF Major Group Focal Points," http://www.un.org/esa/forests/contacts-major_groups.html (accessed July 18, 2009); U.N. Department of Economic and Social Affairs, "Agenda 21: Chapter 23 – Strengthening the Role of Major Groups," http://www.un.org/esa/sustdev/documents/agenda21/english/agenda21chapter23.htm (accessed July 18, 2009).

forest-dependent peoples.[61] The UNFF is charged with ascertaining how climate change and other forces deprive peoples of their human rights. Just like NGO stakeholders in cases involving human rights violations related to natural resources (such as conflict diamonds or conflict timber),[62] NGO stakeholders

---

[61] For discussions about human rights violations related to forests, see, e.g., Forest Peoples Programme, "Annual Report 2007," 2, http://www.forestpeoples.org/documents/ann_rep/fpprog_ar_07.pdf (accessed July 18, 2009). The Forest Peoples' Programme (FPP) stated:

> FPP's Legal and Human Rights Programme (LHRP) helps forest peoples to secure their rights through legal action and using international and national mechanisms set up to protect human rights. The LHRP provides information, training and capacity building so that people know their rights and how to defend them, and offers legal advice and litigation support for forest peoples pursuing complaints and cases through national courts and the international human rights system. FPP's detailed research and analysis, and submissions to international human rights bodies, help shape the evolution of international human rights standards and create a body of evidence and international opinion that supports indigenous peoples' advocacy in other areas such as multilateral banks and development agencies.

On November 28, 2007, after 10 years of work by FPP, the Inter-American Court of Human Rights recognized the human rights of indigenous peoples in *Saramaka People v. Suriname*, ruling that Suriname violated the Saramaka's human rights by not consulting and obtaining their consent before Suriname granted logging and mining concessions. http://www.corteidh.or.cr/docs/casos/articulos/seriec_172_ing.pdf (accessed July 18, 2009); http://www.forestpeoples.org/documents/ann_rep/fpprog_ar_07.pdf 4 (accessed July 18, 2009). For further discussion of the tie between human rights and forests, see, e.g., Global Witness, "Global Witness Testifies at the Liberian Truth and Reconciliation Commission on the role of national and international timber companies in fuelling Liberia's civil war," news release, February 19, 2009, http://www.globalwitness.org/media_library_detail.php/722/en/global_witness_testifies_at_the_liberian_truth_and) (accessed July 20, 2009) (human rights violations and abuse of forest resources); Stephen Then, "Logging, land clearing caused mass fish deaths in S'wak.," The Star Malaysia, February 20, 2009, http://thestar.com.my/news/story.asp?file=/2009/2/20/nation/20090220143652&sec=nation (accessed July 20, 2009) (The government noted the "unusual mass deaths" of fish in Malaysian rivers were caused by "suffocation due to siltation triggered by logging, plantations and land-clearing projects", and noted its desire "to balance the need for land development with the need to protect and conserve the environment and its natural resources because interior folks depended on these natural assets for their daily survival"); See generally, Stener Ekern, "Saving the Forest Through Human Rights: Indigenous Rights and Ethnic Tension in Guatemala," *International Journal on Minority and Group Rights*, 13 nos. 2–3 (2006): 171–186.

[62] NGOs such as Global Witness and Partnership-Africa Canada participated in and played a major role in the creation of the Kimberley Process, which is a scheme seeking to curb "conflict diamonds", which are "rough diamonds used by rebel movements or their allies to finance conflict aimed at undermining legitimate governments" in contravention of UN Security Council resolutions, the Kimberley Process Certification Scheme, and other norms. See "What is the Kimberley Process?" http://www.kimberleyprocess.com (accessed July 18, 2009). The Scheme obligates members to certify shipments of rough diamonds as "conflict-free" and prevent conflict diamonds from entering the legitimate trade. Diamonds must be in tamper-proof packaging and must be accompanied by a certificate guaranteeing they are conflict free. See

working on forest issues play a vital role in identifying those human rights violations, violators, and remedies.[63]

2.5.4. *NGOs Participating in International Complaint Mechanisms*

International human rights law treaties that permit individuals or states to file complaints include: the International Covenant on Civil and Political Rights; the Convention Against Torture; the Women's Convention, the Race Convention; the European Convention on Human Rights; the American Convention on Human Rights (Pact of San Jose);[64] and the African Charter on Human and Peoples' Rights.[65] Essentially three types of complaints have been used in the context of human rights treaties: (1) inter-state complaints, (2) individual complaints against a state, and (3) inquiries.[66] Generally, NGOs may file on

---

Ibid. For further discussion of the Kimberly process and the role of NGOs, see Ann C. Wallis, "Data Mining: Lessons from the Kimberley Process for the United Nations' Development of Human Rights Norms for Transnational Corporations," 4 *Northwestern University Journal of International Human Rights* (2005): 388, 397–398 (discussing conflict diamonds, NGOs and human rights in Angola, Democratic Republic of the Congo, and Sierra Leone).

For discussion of conflict timber, see, for example, Arthur G. Blundell, "Conflict Timber and Liberia's War", European Tropical Forest Research News 43–44: 32 (2005) (comment by Dr. Blundell of the UN Security Council Panel of Experts on Liberia); see also http://global-policy.org/security-council/dark-side-of-natural-resources/timber-in-conflict.html (accessed July 19, 2009); http://www.greenpeace.org/international/news/bloody-timber-off-the-market (accessed July 18, 2009).

63 See Frances Seymour, "Forests, Climate Change, and Human Rights: Managing Risk and Trade-offs," *Center for International Forestry Research*, October 2008, http://rightsandclimatechange.files.wordpress.com/2008/10/seymour-forests-cc-hr-0810021.pdf (accessed July 20, 2009).

64 *American Convention on Human Rights*, Adopted at the Inter-American Specialized Conference on Human Rights, San José, Costa Rica, November 22, 1969, http://www.cidh.oas.org/Basicos/English/Basic3.American%20Convention.htm (accessed July 20, 2009).

65 See *African Charter on Human and Peoples' Rights* (June 1981), *reprinted in* 21 I.L.M. 58 (1982), entered into force Oct. 21 1986, http://www.achpr.org/english/_info/charter_en.html (accessed July 20, 2009).

66 The UN Torture Committee and the UN Women's Committee may on their own initiative initiate an "inquiry" if they receive "reliable information containing well-founded indications of serious or systematic violations of the conventions in a State party." See U.N. Office of the High Commissioner for Human Rights, "Human Rights Bodies – Complaints Procedures: Inquiries," http://www2.ohchr.org/english/bodies/petitions/index.htm#inquiry (accessed July 20, 2009). The inquiry procedures and standards are set out in Article 20 of the United Nations Convention Against Torture and Other Cruel, Inhuman or Degrading Treatment or Punishment, www2.ohchr.org/english/law/cat.htm (accessed July 18, 2009) and articles 8–10 of the Optional Protocol to CEDAW, http://www.un.org/womenwatch/daw/cedaw/protocol/text.htm (accessed July 20, 2009). For a discussion of complaint procedures within the United Nations system, *see* Fact Sheet No. 7/Rev.1, Complaints Procedure, http://www2.ohchr.org/english/law/docs/Part_of_FS.No.7.pdf (accessed July 18, 2009).

behalf of themselves as aggrieved parties, or on behalf of individual or group victims. Furthermore, human rights NGOs may serve as legal advisors, experts, or amicus curiae in these cases.

2.5.5. *Academic Activities to Promote Human Rights*

Increasingly, academic institutions are promoting and protecting human rights through incorporating human rights research, teaching and service into their mission statements, and creating programs and centers to further those goals.[67] Law schools that have created human rights programs or clinics with these objectives include Indiana University School of Law – Indianapolis,[68] Harvard

[67] For a discussion of the academy's role in promoting and protecting human rights, see Henry J. Steiner, "The University's Critical Role in the Human Rights Movement", Harvard Human Rights Journal 15 (Spring 2002) http://www.law.harvard.edu/students/orgs/hrj/iss15/steiner.shtml (accessed July 18, 2009); Arturo J. Carrillo, "Bringing International Law Home: The Innovative Role of Human Rights Clinics in the Transnational Legal Process," Columbia Human Rights Law Review 35 (2004): 527; Stanley H. Hoffman, "Universities and Human Rights," *Human Rights Quarterly* 6, no. 1 (1984): 5, 5–13; see also Deena R. Hurwitz, "Lawyering for Justice and the Inevitability of International Human Rights Clinics," *The Yale Journal of International Law* 28 (2003): 505.

[68] The missions of the Indiana PIHRL, which was founded by the author in 1997, include: (1) to further the teaching and study of international human rights law at Indiana University School of Law – Indianapolis; (2) to promote scholarship in international human rights law; (3) to assist human rights governmental, inter-governmental, and non-governmental organizations on international human rights law projects; and (4) to facilitate student placements as law interns at domestic and overseas human rights organizations. See Program in International Human Rights Law, http://www.indylaw.indiana.edu/humanrights (accessed July 20, 2009).

The PIHRL has undertaken many human rights academic projects in the US and overseas. Since 1997, the PIHRL has facilitated over 100 U.S. law student placements as human rights law interns in over 50 countries on 6 continents. Students work for NGOs, IGOs (e.g., the UN), and governmental groups. Students receive law school scholarships for travel, housing, food and other internship expenses. Host organizations around the world incur no financial costs for interns.

The PIHRL researched and provided expert witness resources to defend US cases against Guantanamo Bay detainees Australian David Hicks and Canadian Omar Khadr, researched on behalf of former Yugoslav President Slobodan Milosevic (who was on trial at the UN International Criminal Tribunal for the Former Yugoslavia), researched for governments, advocated before the UN and other bodies, hosted UN and national leaders at campus conferences and seminars, and helped train judges in the U.S. and abroad.

The PIHRL, which is attached to an academic institution, through its human rights activities carries out its mission to teach its law students. Students receive academic credit for overseas and domestic intern work experiences, and for the research for criminal defendants, for Shadow Reports, for preparing position papers for governmental agencies, NGOs or the United Nations, and for other undertakings.

Law School,[69] Columbia Law School,[70] DePaul College of Law,[71] University of Buffalo School of Law,[72] University of New South Wales,[73] the University of Hong Kong (HKU) Faculty of Law,[74] and others in the U.S. and other countries.[75]

[69] The Harvard Law School Human Rights Program "fosters course work and participation of students in human rights activities through its summer fellowships, clinical work, speaker series, applied research and scholarship." See Harvard University Human Rights Program, http://www.law.harvard.edu/programs/hrp (accessed July 20, 2009). The Harvard Program was founded in 1984, and supported two overseas human rights internships for the author, who was a Harvard Law School student at the time.

[70] Since 1998, the Columbia Law School Human Rights Institute focused on international human rights education, scholarship and practice. http://www.law.columbia.edu/center_program/human_rights (accessed July 20, 2009).

[71] DePaul's International Human Rights Law Institute (IHRLI) was founded in 1990 and engages in human rights law research, documentation, training and advocacy. See http://www.law.depaul.edu/centers_institutes/ihrli/about_us (accessed July 20, 2009).

[72] The Buffalo Human Rights Center fosters coursework, research, scholarship and practical experience in the field of human rights. http://wings.buffalo.edu/law/BHRC (accessed July 20, 2009). It "aims to garner greater exposure and community support for the recognition, promotion, and protection of international human rights." Ibid.

[73] The Australian Human Rights Centre (AHRC) is an inter-disciplinary research and teaching institute based in the Faculty of Law at the University of New South Wales (UNSW). Founded in 1986, it has sought to increase public awareness about human rights procedures, standards and issues within Australia and the international community. It researches contemporary human rights issues, disseminates human rights information, and involves academics, research associates, student interns and volunteers in its programs. http://www.ahrcentre.org (accessed July 20, 2009).

[74] The HKU Centre for Comparative and Public Law was founded to "promote research in the fields of public and comparative law", but its main projects since the Centre's 1995 founding are essentially human rights in nature and include the international law implications of the resumption of Chinese sovereignty in 1997, immigration law and practice, equality and Hong Kong law, the Hong Kong Bill of Rights, and human rights protection under the Hong Kong Basic Law. See Centre for Comparative and Public Law, "About the Centre," *University of Hong Kong, Faculty of Law*, http://www.hku.hk/ccpl/about_centre/about_centre.html (accessed July 20, 2009).

[75] Much has been written about human rights work of academic institutions. See, e.g., Tamar Ezer and Susan Deller Ross, "Fact-Finding as a Lawmaking Tool for Advancing Women's Human Rights," *The Georgetown Journal of Gender and the Law* 7 (2006): 331–342 (discussing work of Georgetown's International Women's Human Rights Clinic and its transnational NGO partners: Law and Advocacy for Women – Uganda (LAW – Uganda); Leadership and Advocacy for Women in Africa – Ghana Alumnae, Inc. (LAWA – Ghana); and the Women's Legal Aid Centre in Tanzania (WLAC – Tanzania)).

2.5.6. *Human Rights NGOs Outside the UN and Other Inter-Governmental Systems*

Many thousands of local human rights NGOs in many different countries have no relationship with and seek no involvement with the United Nations or any other inter-governmental body. Those local NGOs may or may not use the language of "rights", "human rights", or "international human rights law", though the local issues fall squarely under conventional and customary international human rights law. These groups engage in international human rights endeavors, working at the domestic level.

An example of a human rights NGO that focuses on domestic issues is the Indiana Coalition Against Domestic Violence (ICADV), based in Indianapolis, Indiana, U.S.A. The mission statement of ICADV follows:[76]

> ICADV is committed to the elimination of domestic violence through: providing public awareness and education; advocating for systemic and societal change; influencing public policy and allocation of resources; educating and strengthening coalition members; and, promoting the availability of quality comprehensive services.

The ICADV works to protect domestic violence victims' internationally recognized human rights, such as the right to bodily and mental integrity, the right to health and the right to security. However, it tends to work on these issues through a domestic U.S. and Indiana lens, by referring to local criminal law or local social services, rather than by referring to international human rights law[77] even though the United States is bound to comply with the ICCPR and other international human rights law instruments and norms.

Domestic violence implicates not only domestic law, but also it implicates the internationally recognized rights to life, liberty, security, integrity, health, and a wide range of other international law protections. The nature of a group as a human rights NGO is not negated simply because that group may not adopt the moniker "human rights NGO" or may not use "international human rights law language". Local private social service agencies and other similar groups are "human rights NGOs" whether or not they identify themselves as such.[78]

---

[76] Indiana Coalition Against Domestic Violence, "Our Mission and Philosophy," http://www.violenceresource.org/mission.htm (accessed July 20, 2009).

[77] ICADV's training and resource materials point towards the local, domestic environment rather than towards international human rights law treaties. See ibid.

[78] Similarly, local groups would qualify as being human rights NGOs if they focus on other internationally recognized human rights at the domestic level, such as feeding or educating poor people in their village or community, or helping to protect neighbors' right to vote, to improve conditions in a local prison, or to promote equal rights for persons of all sexual orientations, clean air, or fair trials in local courts.

3. *Ten Characteristics of Successful Human Rights NGOs*

Successful human rights NGOs share many characteristics, far more than the ten listed and analyzed below. However, the characteristics identified and examined herein stand out as critical for human rights NGOs that seek to protect human rights in their chosen area(s) of work. This is not to say that every group that possesses these characteristics will be successful, or that every successful group fully incorporates all these characteristics. This chapter posits that the likelihood of an NGO's success is enhanced if it incorporates these characteristics into its structure and operations. These characteristics, which overlap and are not exhaustive, relate to the human rights NGO's: (1) mission; (2) adherence to human rights principles; (3) legality; (4) independence; (5) funding; (6) non-profit status and commitment to service; (7) transparency and accountability; (8) adaptability and responsiveness; (9) cooperative and collaborative nature; and (10) competence, reliability and credibility.

3.1. *Human Rights NGOs Must Have a Clear Mission to Promote and Protect Human Rights, and Be Result-Oriented*

Successful human rights NGOs carry out their mission to promote and protect a wide range of rights in many substantive areas. "Human rights", as broadly defined, includes rights and fundamental freedoms essential to the full lives of humans. Such rights include economic, social, cultural, civil, political and third generational rights enumerated in the Universal Declaration of Human Rights, other international human rights law instruments, and customary international human rights law.

An NGO's obligation to protect human rights is an "obligation of result",[79] which means that to fulfill its goal, the NGO must indeed protect human

[79] The United Nations Economic Committee, that oversees implementation of the UN Covenant on Economic, Social and Cultural Rights, alludes to obligations of conduct and obligations of result:

1. [W]hile the [Economic] Covenant provides for progressive realization and acknowledges the constraints due to the limits of available resources, it also imposes various obligations which are of immediate effect.
2. Thus while the full realization of the relevant rights may be achieved progressively, steps towards that goal must be taken within a reasonably short time after the [Economic] Covenant's entry into force for the States concerned. Such steps should be deliberate, concrete and targeted as clearly as possible towards meeting the obligations recognized in the [Economic] Covenant.

United Nations Economic Committee, "The Nature of States Parties Obligations – CESCR General Comment 3, Article 2, paragraph 1" (December 14, 1990), http://www.unhchr.ch/tbs/doc.nsf/(symbol)/CESCR+General+comment+3.En?OpenDocument, paras 1 & 2 (accessed July 20, 2009).

rights.[80] The nature of this obligation differs from that of an "obligation of conduct", which imposes an obligation "to take steps" or "to attempt" or "to try" to protect human rights, where compliance is realized when the conduct is undertaken. Mere steps, attempts or tries will not constitute fulfillment of an obligation of result.

All human rights NGOs advocate on behalf of human rights. They all endeavor to convince some actor – a local or national government, an intergovernmental organization like the UN or another non-state actor – to take some action or refrain from some action to protect the human rights of the NGO's constituency, those whose human rights the NGO seeks to protect. The NGO could be committed to advocating on behalf of prisoners of war, submitting reports to UN human rights treaty bodies, proposing plans to promote development in countries lacking food or health care, raising money for humanitarian aid, combating torture, providing adequate housing, or pursuing many other activities that would further human rights protection internationally or domestically.

A human rights NGO's objectives must be clearly defined. They must offer guidance to the NGO's workers, to victims seeking assistance, to donors wanting to know to what they are contributing, to other NGOs seeking collaboration, and to governments that license or monitor NGOs. The objectives must not be so broad as to be unattainable, such as a mission to eradicate all human rights violations of any nature in a particular country, which may not be a reasonably achievable goal. In addition, the objectives must not be overly narrow, since human rights overlap and are interrelated and do not exist in a vacuum.[81] Human rights NGOs that skip from project type to project type

[80] However, human rights NGOs can be "successful" even if they do not achieve all their stated goals, particularly if they fail due to forces outside their control. An NGO would be deemed successful, at least for purposes of this chapter, if it moves the human rights movement forward towards full protection of human rights. Sometimes the mere creation of a human rights NGO will move human rights protection forward, as its creation will spur individuals to recognize their rights and to take actions, even if small, to help in the realization of those rights.

[81] Vienna Declaration and Program of Action, paragraph 5 provides:

> All human rights are universal, indivisible and interdependent and interrelated. The international community must treat human rights globally in a fair and equal manner, on the same footing, and with the same emphasis. While the significance of national and regional particularities and various historical, cultural and religious backgrounds must be borne in mind, it is the duty of States, regardless of their political, economic and cultural systems, to promote and protect all human rights and fundamental freedoms.

Vienna Declaration and Programme of Action (July 12, 1993), U.N. Doc. A/CONF.157/23 (1993), (adopted by the World Conference on Human Rights on June 25, 1993), http://www.unhchr.ch/huridocda/huridoca.nsf/(Symbol)/A.CONF.157.23.En (accessed July 20, 2009).

may be unfocused, and may fail to acquire needed expertise in a particular substantive area.

Human rights NGOs should have "clean hands". They should be law-abiding, committed not only to protecting against violations of international human rights law, but also committed to complying with international human rights norms in their internal and external actions. That is, as explained more fully in Paragraph 3.2 below, human rights NGOs must adhere to human rights principles.

3.2. *Human Rights NGOs Must Adhere to Human Rights Principles*

Human rights NGOs must be guided by and must adhere to human rights principles as contained in the Universal Declaration of Human Rights, other human rights instruments, and customary international human rights law. An NGO that does not comply with human rights norms is hypocritical, loses credibility, and can become ineffective. It risks tainting the image or reputation of itself and of human rights NGOs generally, and it decreases the likelihood that it will be funded and will be able to carry out its mission to protect human rights.

To become affiliated with NGO networks, umbrella groups, and caucuses, NGOs must not only state that they abide by human rights norms in their structure and internal operations as well as externally in their human rights programs and projects, but also they must actually abide by human rights norms. To become accredited by inter-governmental organizations, NGOs must pledge to comply with UDHR rights.[82] Non-compliant NGOs can have their accreditation terminated.

NGOs pledge to be democratic,[83] consistent with the human right to representation. NGOs must comply with the UDHR right to non-discrimination in

---

[82] For example, for an NGO to become accredited with the United Nations Department of Public Information (UNDPI), "the NGO must support and respect the principles of the Charter of the UN and have a clear mission statement with those principles" and "should pursue the goals of promotion and protection of human rights in accordance with the spirit of the Charter of the United Nations, the Universal Declaration of Human Rights and the Vienna Declaration and Programme of Action". (ECOSOC Resolution 1996/31, para 25); http://www.un.org/dpi/ngosection/brochure.htm (accessed July 19, 2009); http://esango.un.org/paperless/Web?page=static&content=part3 (accessed July 18, 2009).

The UNDPI, which was created in 1946, recognized the importance of working with and through NGOs. This relationship was grounded in General Assembly Resolution 13(1) of 1946 and later on ECOSOC Resolution 1296 (XLIV) of May 23, 1968 and ECOSOC Resolution 1996/31 of July 25, 1996. See www.un.org/partners/civil_society/ngo/ngos-dpi; http://unic.un.org/aroundworld/unics/en/whoWeAre/aboutDPI/index.asp (accessed July 18, 2009).

[83] For example, the NGO Coordination Committee in Iraq (NCCI), which is an independent

hiring and firing employees and volunteers, and in assisting victims. This can prove challenging when cultural, societal, or religious differences – or distinctions based on gender or class – would ordinarily stifle mixing people of different groups. For example, in societies where tribal or ethnic differences are bases for conflict, mixed-membership NGOs may be difficult to form and operate, given looming questions of partiality, suspicion and distrust.

3.3. *Human Rights NGOs Must Be Legally Organized & Must Comply With Law*

A human rights NGO must comply with rules of its nation of incorporation, with the laws of the country in which it operates, and with international law, including international human rights law. Terrorists groups like al Qaeda may be disqualified from being considered an NGO due to illegal status or conduct under domestic or international law. Mafia, triads, and gangs could also be disqualified. Anarchists, such as those who use violence to demonstrate against World Trade Organization meetings or against the annual World Economic Forum in Davos, Switzerland, may be disqualified because of their conduct. Guerilla or rebel groups may be disqualified because they may not be legally formed or may engage in unlawful conduct.

Many countries require NGOs to register as non-profit organizations. In some countries, the registration process is fairly simple, and NGOs do not have great difficulty registering. In other countries, the governments impose significant hurdles to NGO registration generally.[84] In countries where NGOs face

initiative launched by Baghdad NGOs in April 2003, has a General Assembly composed of all NCCI members. See http://www.ncciraq.org (accessed July 19, 2009); http://www.ncciraq.org/spip.php?article6 (accessed July 18, 2009). The General Assembly is the primary decision maker and must identify issues for developing NCCI's strategic plan. Ibid. It votes on decisions, elects the Executive Board, approves the creation of working groups and endorses the appointment of the Executive Coordinator. Ibid.

[84] For example, in early 2009, the Ethiopian government proclaimed a law to regulate NGO creation, fundraising, and membership of trusts and endowments. See Federal Democratic Republic of Ethiopia, "Proclamation to Provide for the Registration and Regulation of Charities and Societies," Proclamation No. 621/2009, *Federal Negarit Gazeta*, No. 25, 4521, (February 13, 2009) http://www.crdaethiopia.org/Documents/Charities%20and%20Socities%20Legislation%20(Final%20Version)-Negarit%20Newspaper.pdf (accessed July 18, 2009). This Proclamation is reported to restrict activities in "human and democratic rights, gender or ethnic equality, conflict resolution, the strengthening of judicial practices or law enforcement" to Ethiopian NGOs with funding from "foreign sources" not exceeding 10% of their spending. See Hanibal Goitom, "Ethiopia: New law on charities passed despite objections," *Integrated Regional Information Networks (IRIN)*, January 6, 2009, http://www.loc.gov/lawweb/servlet/lloc_news?disp3_935_text (accessed July 19, 2009); http://www.unhcr.org/refworld/docid/49670b911a.html (accessed July 18, 2009); see also Equality Now, "Ethiopia: Proposed New Law Threatens to Shut Down Non-Governmental Organizations," December 2008, http://www.equalitynow.org/english/actions/action_2205_en.html (accessed July 20, 2009).

security and other difficulties, they may operate secretly, without registration. This may render those groups illegal under their national law, and this would make it very difficult for them to carry out their objectives because, for example, they could not openly raise funds or recruit for new members. Their capacity could be severely diminished, which begs the question of whether it is better to have a crippled human rights NGO than to have no NGO at all.[85]

NGOs should not accept contributions illegally or accept contributions from donors who acquired the funds illegally.

Registration and maintenance problems for human rights NGOs have occurred in many other jurisdictions, including Hong Kong, Malaysia, Russia, Kyrgyzstan, Cuba, Zambia, Zimbabwe, and Egypt.

85 This question is essentially answered in the affirmative, as evidenced by support given domestically and internationally to "human rights defenders", acting alone or as part of human rights NGOs, when those individuals and groups are challenged, harassed, or physically or otherwise harmed by governments or other repressors. The United Nations created a special procedure on human rights defenders, to help ensure their safety and ultimately their efficacy. In 2000, the UN Commission on Human Rights passed a resolution pursuant to which a UN Special Representative on the Situation of Human Rights Defenders was appointed, about which the Office of the High Commissioner for Human Rights reports:

> The Special Representative was mandated to report on the situation of human rights defenders in all parts of the world and on possible means to enhance their protection in full compliance with the Declaration. The main activities of the special representative shall be:
>
> (a) To seek, receive, examine and respond to information on the situation and the rights of anyone, acting individually or in association with others, to promote and protect human rights and fundamental freedoms;
>
> (b) To establish cooperation and conduct dialogue with Governments and other interested actors on the promotion and effective implementation of the Declaration;
>
> (c) To recommend effective strategies better to protect human rights defenders and follow up on these recommendations.

http://unhchr.ch/html/menu2/7/b/mdefintro.htm (citing Human Rights Defenders, Commission on Human Rights resolution 2000/61 (Apr. 26, 2000) (accessed July 18, 2009); http://www.unhchr.ch/huridocda/huridoca.nsf/(Symbol)/E.CN.4.RES.2000.61.En?Opendocument)) (accessed July 18, 2009).

Human rights NGOs that seek to protect human rights defenders – individuals and other NGOs – include Front Line, which is the International Foundation for the Protection of Human Rights Defenders. http://www.frontlinedefenders.org/about/frontline (accessed July 18, 2009). It was founded in Dublin in 2001, and seeks to protect human rights defenders at risk. Ibid. Front Line states that it "seeks to provide rapid and practical support to at-risk human rights defenders, including through a 24 hour emergency response phone line, and to promote the visibility and recognition of human rights defenders as a vulnerable group." Ibid.

3.4. *Human Rights NGOs Must Be Independent and Non-Partisan*

3.4.1. *Human Rights NGOs Serving Only One Master*

Human rights NGOs cannot afford to serve more than one master; they must be answerable to the needs of their constituents, who are the victims the human rights NGO are organized to protect. NGO administrators engage in a wide range of activities, not unlike that of for-profit administrators, and they must be strong and independent as they carry out mandates. NGO administrators set the NGO's policies and strategies, oversee its budget, operations and work methods, implement programs, make personnel decisions, and carry out the NGO's mission to protect human rights. Effective NGOs do not bow to undue outside influences, political or otherwise, from any source, including governments, political groups, corporations, or other human rights NGOs. A group that compromises its independence risks becoming a "fake NGO" or a "rogue NGO".[86]

Being independent and non-partisan does not mean that an NGO cannot collaborate with or support a political group or governmental agency, or cannot accept funds from such groups. Many NGOs assist governments (e.g., by providing humanitarian, consulting and other services to governmental agencies), and many NGOs collaborate with and brief governmental and political groups on a wide range of human rights issues (e.g., the Obama Presidential campaign

---

[86] The World Association of Non-Governmental Organizations (WANGO) in the Preamble to its Code of Ethics and Conduct for NGOs notes:

> Unfortunately, there are many actors in the NGO community that are neither responsible nor ethical. Alan Fowler, in his book *Striking a Balance*, utilized a collection of NGO acronyms to identify various NGO "pretenders," such as BRINGO (Briefcase NGO), CONGO (Commercial NGO), FANGO (Fake NGO), CRINGO (Criminal NGO), GONGO (Government-owned NGO), MANGO (Mafia NGO), and PANGO (Party NGO). Other NGOs may have started with the highest ideals, but now tolerate practices that were previously unacceptable. Many NGOs do not even understand the standards that they should be applying to their activities and governance.

World Association of Non-Governmental Organizations (WANGO), "Preface to Code of Ethics and Conduct for NGOs," March 5, 2005, http://www.wango.org/codeofethics.aspx?page=1 (accessed July 19, 2009). Other types include MANGOs (man controlled NGOs), BINGOs (business controlled NGOs), RINGOs (reactionary controlled NGOs or religious NGOs), TINGOs (tribal controlled NGOs) and DONGOs (donor-organized NGOs). For additional acronyms, see, for example, Norbert Götz, "Reframing NGOs: The Identity of an International Relations Non-Starter", *European Journal of International Relations* (2008): 14; 231 (http://ejt.sagepub.com/cgi/reprint/14/2/231.pdf) (accessed July 19, 2009); F. Halliday, "The Romance of Non-State Actors," in *Non-State Actors in World Politics*, ed. Daphne Josselin and William Wallace (New York: Palgrave Macmillian Publishers, 2002), 23. Others include QUANGO – quasi non-governmental organizations, or possibly TINGO – terrorist NGOs.

pre-election received feedback from NGO members, some of whom were part of Obama Steering Committee and Policy Groups).[87]

However, governments could impose conditions on NGOs that would compromise the NGO's independence. For example, it would compromise an NGO's independence if it accepted money from the U.S. government with the understanding that the NGO would promote the US government's position on political matters. Such an NGO would be acting as an extension of U.S. foreign policy and may find it difficult to criticize or take positions against declared or unstated US government positions. NGOs must be loyal to their causes and constituencies, which transcend loyalties to their donors and to themselves.[88]

3.4.2. *Human Rights NGOs Must Not Be Wedded to Public or Private Donors*

As mentioned, human rights NGOs must be independent. NGOs should not accept funding from sources that attach conditions to the funding, jeopardizing the NGO's independence in decision-making, internal operations, or programs or projects.[89] For example, until January 2009, the US government restricted

[87] For example, this author participated in two official Barack Obama Campaign Policy Groups: (a) the Obama Law & Justice Policy Group; and (b) the Obama LGBT Policy Group. Some members of each were affiliated with different outside groups, including academic institutions and human rights NGOs.

[88] These loyalties might color the attitudes and other behavior of other members of society, for example journalists, who are meant to be unbiased and non-partisans. If a journalist is embedded with US government soldiers on the battlefield as they were in Iraq, and the life of a journalist is literally in the hands of the US combatants, will the journalist be able to criticize his protector, or will he be biased by loyalty to his protector? See, e.g., Michael Massing, "Blind Spot: seeing Iraq through Uncle Sam's eyes," Columbia Journalism Review 43.3 (September-October 2008): 14; Paul McLeary, "Why Jon Lee Anderson Doesn't Like Embedding: The too-close-to-the-troops notion is flimsy," *Columbia Journalism Review* (Oct. 2007), http://www.cjr.org/behind_the_news/post_63.php (accessed July 19, 2009). NGOs, like journalists, must not be self-serving.

[89] The phenomenon where donors to NGOs, and even some NGOs themselves seek to dominate, manipulate and control NGOs' work has been seen as a form of neo-colonialism. But, not all instances of donor "attaching strings" to NGO funding should be refused. NGOs should consider whether accepting a donation might jeopardize the NGO's independence.

See Jay S. Ovsiovitch, "Feeding the Watchdogs: Philanthropic Support for Human Rights NGOs," *Buffalo Human Rights Law Review* 4 (1998): 341, 344. Funding should be avoided if it raises questions about an NGO's independence and objectivity. See, e.g., Howard B. Tolley, Jr., *The International Commission of Jurists: Global Advocates for Human Rights* (Philadelphia: University of Pennsylvania Press, 1994) 17. Professor Tolley notes that some question whether NGOs that accept government aid may be co-opted or lack credibility. Ibid. On the other hand, NGO reliance on funding from philanthropic organizations also raises questions of accountability and susceptibility to outside influence. David P. Forsythe, *Human Rights and World Politics*, 2nd ed. (Lincoln, Nebraska: University of Nebraska Press, 1989) 156–157 (noting Amnesty International refusing money to "project an image of neutrality").

funding to NGOs providing health-related human rights services overseas if those NGOs advocated for or provided abortion-related services, even if the services were provided using the NGOs' own, non-US resources.[90] If the US is the sole donor for a particular NGO or is one of only a few donors, and if the NGO heavily relies on the US for sustenance, that NGO would be wedded to the US and its policies.[91]

Many, if not most NGOs depend to some degree on their governments for direct or indirect assistance. Some NGOs are exempt from paying taxes to their governments, which translates into a subsidy of the NGOs. NGOs in many jurisdictions must be registered with the government, and they may feel pressure to comply with government demands for fear their licenses will be revoked.

Human rights NGOs should not be beholden to private donors. Private donors are not immune from seeking to control human rights NGOs. NGOs

[90] This is known as the "global gag rule" or "Mexico City Policy". See Center for Reproductive Rights, "Myths and Realities: Debunking USAID's Analysis of the Global Gag Rule," (January 15, 2009), http://reproductiverights.org/en/document/myths-and-realities-debunking-usaid%E2%80%99s-analysis-of-the-global-gag-rule (accessed July 19, 2009) (arguing that research shows that the global gag rule severely erodes family planning and related health-care services for rural women and interferes with NGOs' goal of helping secure locally responsive public health agendas). See also Patty Skuster, "Advocacy in Whispers: The Impact of the USAID Global Gag Rule Upon Free Speech and Free Association in the Context of Abortion Law Reform in Three East African Countries," Michigan Journal of Gender and Law 11 (2004): 97, http://www.reproductiverights.org/pdf/pub_art_skuster.pdf (accessed July 20, 2009) (noting rights deprivation in Uganda, Ethiopia, and Kenya); Rachael E. Seevers, "The Politics of Gagging: The Effects of the Global Gag Rule on Democratic Participation and Political Advocacy in Peru," *Brooklyn Journal of International Law* 31 (2006): 899, 899–900 (noting that "restrictions…prevent advocacy and civil participation by these recipient NGOs, and infringe on their right to free speech and their ability to speak out in a national democratic dialogue"). Some NGOs argue that the Global Gag Rule negatively affects human rights protections. See, e.g., Center for Reproductive Rights, "Breaking the Silence: The Global Gag Rule's Impact on Unsafe Abortion," (2003) http://www.reproductiverights.org/pdf/bo_ggr.pdf (accessed July 20, 2009); Population Action International, "Access Denied – U.S. Restrictions on International Family Planning," January 3, 2005 http://www.populationaction.org/globalgagrule/Summary.shtml (accessed July 20, 2009) (stating that the gag rule "forces a cruel choice on foreign NGOs", stifles free speech and public debate on abortion-related issues, and may jeopardize patients' health).

President Barack Obama reversed the Mexico City Policy on January 23, 2009, three days after his inauguration. He noted that the policy "undermined efforts to promote safe and effective voluntary family programs in foreign nations." See Rob Stein and Michael Shear, "Funding Restored to Groups That Perform Abortions, Other Care," *Washington Post*, p. A03, January 24, 2009, http://www.washingtonpost.com/wp-dyn/content/article/2009/01/23/AR2009012302814.html (accessed July 20, 2009).

[91] Similarly, NGOs should not attach unreasonable conditions to projects and programs they offer beneficiaries.

should inquire about whether any "strings are attached" to proposed contributions and should accept those contributions only if no strings are attached. For example, an NGO conducting work related to the right to health in developing countries might examine closely whether a pharmaceutical company that donates to the NGO may expressly or implicitly condition such donations on the NGO's advocacy positions or practices. The NGO should avoid actual impropriety and the air of impropriety.

3.5. *Human Rights NGO Funding Must Be Adequate & Appropriate*

Funding for an NGO must be adequate and appropriate so that the NGO will be able to carry out its projects and programs. Ascertaining what constitutes "adequate" or "appropriate" depends on many variables, making resolution of these questions the subject of much debate.

3.5.1. *Adequacy of Funding*

If an NGO's funding is not adequate, the NGO cannot fulfill its mandate of protecting human rights. The amount of funding that is adequate varies based on the NGO, its mission, and its operations. A large multi-national NGO may need millions of dollars to carry out its mission each year, while a small local NGO may only need a few hundred dollars.

3.5.2. *Appropriate Managing of Funding*

Several human rights NGOs lost sizeable amounts of money in the Bernie Madoff investment fraud scandal.[92] This has begged the question of what duty

---

[92] Bernard L. Madoff admitted that an "investment" fund he ran was essentially a $50 billion "Ponzi" scheme that bilked investors, and after pleading guilty, in June 2009 was sentenced to 150 years in prison. Tomoeh Murakami Tse, *Madoff Sentenced to 150 Years: Calling Ponzi Scheme 'Evil,' Judge Orders Maximum Term*, www.washingtonpost.com/wp-dyn/content/article/2009/06/29/AR2009062902015.html (accessed July 19, 2009).

MoveOn.org Civic Action (formerly known as MoveOn.org), is a U.S. registered 501(c)(4) nonprofit organization and focuses on education and advocacy on national issues. See "About the MoveOn Family of Organizations," http://www.moveon.org/about.html (accessed July 19, 2009). The organization sponsored a fundraiser for several NGOs negatively affected by illegal behavior admitted by Mr. Madoff. MoveOn describes these NGOs as follows: (a) *The Brennan Center for Justice*, that focuses on democracy and justice, voting rights and fair elections, checking presidential power in combating terrorism, and redistricting reform; (b) *Human Rights Watch*, that engages in "rigorous, objective investigations and strategic, targeted advocacy [to] build intense pressure for action and raise the cost of human rights abuse"; (c) *Advancement Project*, which is a policy, communications and legal action group committed to racial justice founded by veteran civil rights lawyers in 1998, and litigates to protect voters and support grassroots movements for education and immigrants' rights; and (d) *The Center for Constitutional Rights*, which was founded in 1966 by attorneys who represented civil rights an NGO has not to risk NGO assets in investments, and whether NGO fiduciary duties equal those in the for-profit world.

3.6. *Human Rights NGOs Must Be Committed to Service to Others & Be Non-Profit*

Human Rights NGOs goals should focus on service to others, emphasizing altruism, selflessness, and volunteerism. Those goals should not be on profit for the NGO, staff, or other stakeholders. However, that does not preclude NGOs from employing tools and mechanisms common in the profit-making business world, such as for administrative and fund-raising purposes.

---

movements in the South, and is a legal and educational organization committed to creatively using law as a positive force for social change in areas as diverse as illegal governmental wiretaps to Guantanamo. (See e-mail from Eli Pariser to G. Edwards, MoveOn.org Civic Action, December 29, 2008 (on file with author)) See https://civ.moveon.org/donatec4/dec_2008.html?id=15302–3191873-F2eyvdx&t=3 (accessed July 19, 2009).

Multiple foundations announced they closed because their funding was lost because of Madoff investments, including: (a) Robert I. Lappin Foundation, Salem, Massachusetts (announced $8 million loss on Dec. 12, 2008) (Gabrielle Birkner and Anthony Weiss, Madoff Arrest Sends Shockwaves Through Jewish Philanthropy, Forward: The Jewish Daily, Dec. 12, 2008, http://www.forward.com/articles/14725 (accessed July 20, 2009)); (b) the Chais Family Foundation (announced on Dec. 14, 2008) (http://ejewishphilanthropy.com/chais-family-foundation-closes (accessed July 20, 2009)); and (c) the Jeht Foundation (announced upon Madoff's arrest that "The JEHT Foundation, a national philanthropic organization, has stopped all grant making effective immediately and will close its doors at the end of January 2009. The funds of the donors to the Foundation, Jeanne Levy-Church and Kenneth Levy-Church, were managed by Bernard L. Madoff, a prominent financial advisor who was arrested last week for defrauding investors out of billions of dollars.") (http://www.jehtfoundation.org/news (accessed July 19, 2009)). The Jeht website provides:

> The [Jeht] Foundation was established in 2000. Its name stands for the values it holds dear: Justice, Equality, Human dignity and Tolerance. It supported programs that promoted reform of the criminal and juvenile justice systems; ensured that the United States adhered to the international rule of law; and worked to improve the voting process by enhancing fair representation, competitive elections and government transparency.
>
> The JEHT Foundation Board deeply regrets that the important work that the Foundation has undertaken over the years is ending so abruptly. The issues the Foundation addressed received very limited philanthropic support and the loss of the foundation's funding and leadership will cause significant pain and disruption of the work for many dedicated people and organizations. The Foundation's programs have met with significant success in recent years – promoting change in these critical areas in partnership with government and the non-profit sector. Hopefully others will look closely at this work and consider supporting it going forward.

http://www.jehtfoundation.org/news (accessed July 19, 2009). The American Civil Liberties Union stated that "two foundations that have been incredibly generous and longstanding supporters of [the ACLU's] national security and reproductive freedom work have been victimized by the Madoff scandal – forced to close their doors and terminate their grants" which means "that $850,000 in support we were counting on from these foundations in

3.7. *Human Rights NGOs Must Be Transparent & Accountable*

To be effective, human rights NGOs must be transparent and accountable.[93] Transparency would help avoid an air of impropriety and would inhibit actual impropriety because not only must NGOs be honest and trustworthy, but also they must appear to be such. To be credible, an NGO must share information about itself to stakeholders, including governments, victims they are aiding, donors, staff, consultants, advisors, relevant inter-governmental organizations, other relevant NGOs, umbrella groups or other similar structures in which the NGO participates, and the public at large.

Transparency and accountability do not necessarily require a human rights NGO to open all its financial, operational and other internal documents all the time. It does require an NGO to be cognizant of the sources of its funding and to inform interested stakeholders about internal decisions and records that would offer insight into agendas that an NGO might have that could conflict with the needs of the beneficiaries of the NGO's protection or conflict with donor or governmental requirements.[94]

2009 simply won't exist". (e-mail from Alma Montclair, ACLU Director of Administration and Finance to author, Dec. 23, 2008) (on file with author) (also noting that "As Director of Administration and Finance, it's my job to make sure that preparation includes prudently managing our organization's resources.")

[93] Hearty discussions have ensued about internal and external NGO accountability. See, e.g., NGO Coordination Committee in Iraq (NCCI), "Code of Conduct," Principle # 4, 3, http://www.ncciraq.org/IMG/pdf/NCCI_Charter_English_Sept05.pdf (accessed July 19, 2009) ("We hold ourselves accountable in the provision of assistance to our beneficiaries"). The UN Department of Public Information calls for NGOs to have statutes/by-laws providing for a transparent process of making decisions and electing officers and members. ECOSOC calls for NGOs to be accountable to its members.

[94] In 2008, Senator Hillary Clinton was nominated as Barack Obama's choice to be U.S. Secretary of State. Her husband, former U.S. President Bill Clinton, chairs a foundation – an NGO – in his name that focuses on human rights related to global climate change, HIV/AIDS in the developing world, childhood obesity and economic opportunity in the U.S., and economic development in Africa and Latin America. See William J. Clinton Foundation, http://www.clintonfoundation.org (accessed July 19, 2009). For transparency to protect the public good, President Obama's staff sought to examine the Foundation's activities and finances, including the identity of donors, to determine if Senator Clinton's appointment should be scuttled. See Peter Baker and Helene Cooper, "Clinton Vetting Includes Look at Mr. Clinton," *New York Times*, November 16, 2008, http://www.nytimes.com/2008/11/17/us/politics/17memo.html?_r=1&partner=%20rss&emc=rss&page%20wanted=all (accessed July 19, 2009). On December 18, 2008, the Clinton Foundation listed its donors to date. See "Press Release: William J. Clinton Foundation Publishes Names of All Contributors on Foundation Website," December 18, 2008, http://www.clintonfoundation.org/news/news-media/press-release-william-j-clinton-foundation-publishes-names-of-all-contributors-on-foundation-website (accessed July 19, 2009); Peter Baker and Charlie Savage, "In Clinton List, a Veil Is Lifted on Foundation," *New York Times*, December 18, 2008, http://www.nytimes.com/2008/12/19/us/politics/w19clinton.html (accessed July 19, 2009).

3.8. *Human Rights NGOs Must Be Adaptable and Responsive to Change*

An effective NGO needs to be open-minded, creative, and extremely flexible, and needs to be willing and able to adjust to changing needs and interests of donors, aid recipients, and governments. In particular, an effective NGO must be responsive and adaptable to changes in technology, substantive areas of human rights focus, and educational opportunities.

3.8.1. *Technology*

To carry out their missions today, many NGOs rely on the internet. Even in lesser-developed countries, NGOs use the internet to raise funds, to collaborate within NGO networks, to share information, to submit advocacy documents to the United Nations and other institutions, and to discuss better methods to protect human rights. Successful NGOs gain advantage through adapting to innovation, such as the internet, e-mail, mobile or cellular telephones, mail or post, fax, easier international travel, and tele-conferencing or video-conferencing.

A relatively new innovation in the electronic sphere is social networking, upon which NGOs increasingly rely. Social networking consists of individuals and groups connecting in online communities to communicate about topics of common interest. Of course human rights NGOs share interests in protecting human rights. Social networking sites include Facebook, LinkedIn, MySpace, Twitter, and many others. Through these sites, an individual creates a "user profile", which is used to connect with others with human rights interests, who in turn connect with others with that interest, and so on. What results are communities of networked individuals and groups with shared human rights concerns. These networks are used to exchange information, promote programs, solicit funding or other assistance, and solicit support for human rights causes. NGOs have found social networking sites useful, as evidenced by their recruiting staff to create and operate their networks.[95] Also, NGOs, human rights

[95] For example, an advertisement for the Campaign to Ban Torture appeared online for this position:

> The Campaign to Ban Torture seeks a self-motivated, innovative intern to advance our organizational goals through social networking on Facebook. The intern would be responsible for creating, designing and operating the Campaign to Ban Torture's Facebook page. The goal of this position will be to increase the organization's online presence by reaching a larger audience especially through our spreadable media.
>
> The internship can be preformed remotely beginning immediately. The Campaign will launch its Web site in late June and would like the Facebook page to be completed then to go live simultaneously.... Responsibilities include:
>
> 1. Design dynamic social network page on Facebook
> 2. In coordination with Senior Communications Manager, post, update and distribute informational materials, calendar listings, etc.;
> 3. Monitor the presence of similar nonprofits on social networking sites.

advocates, and victims have found such networks invaluable in instantly sharing with the world evidence of violations as they occur.[96]

Another relatively new phenomenon is "blogging". Human rights NGO blogs are websites on which human rights NGOs or their staff regularly post news and other items related to human rights and post comments about those items. Members of the general public can access NGO blogs of interest to them and may even be able to comment on them. These blogs serve many purposes, including to share information, to stimulate discussion and to prompt action.

Many other NGOs are adapting to the 21st Century and adopting other technologically innovative strategies to promote human rights.[97]

3.8.2. *Substantive*

Substantively, it is critical to assess whether and how responsive NGOs are to constantly changing values and mores, to conflicting advocacy strategy among

---

See Derechos: Human Rights Listings, "Social Networking Intern," posted on April 22, 2008, http://www.humanrightsblog.org/listings/2008/04/social_networking_intern.html (accessed July 20, 2009).

[96] See, e.g., Noam Cohen, Twitter on the Barricades: Six Lessons Learned, New York Times, (20 June 2009) (http://www.nytimes.com/2009/06/21/weekinreview/21cohenweb.html) (accessed July 20, 2009) (noting that "Social networking, a distinctly 21st-century phenomenon, has already been credited with aiding protests from the Republic of Georgia to Egypt to Iceland." Further, "Twitter, the newest social-networking tool, has been identified with two mass protests in a matter of months – in Moldova in April and in Iran last week, when hundreds of thousands of people took to the streets to oppose the official results of the presidential election."); Fran Quigley, Growing Political Will From the Grassroots: How Social Movement Principles Can Reverse the Dismal Legacy of Rule of Law Interventions, Columbia Human Rights Law Review 41.1 (Forthcoming 2009, on file with author).

[97] Groups such as NetSquared seek to help NGOs use "community empowering capabilities of the Internet to increase their impact and achieve social change." See NetSquared, "NetSquared's Goals: What are the Goals of NetSquared?" http://www.netsquared.org/about/netsquareds-goals (accessed July 19, 2009). The goals of NetSquared include to help "hundreds of thousands of" NGOs to: "Improve/increase advocacy efforts; Find new supporters (around the globe); Reengage the base; Have greater influence on national and global policy; Get more and better press; Increase value for [NGO] supporters…; Reinvent the possibilities of collaboration on a global scale; Build more and better partnerships; Help…NGO constituents become more active and accomplish more through [NGO] Internet communities." Ibid.

Another group, The Hub, has a participatory website through which individuals and NGOs around the world can post media such as videos, photos, and audio recordings to call attention to and mobilize action about human rights issues. See The Hub, "About the Hub," http://hub.witness.org/en (accessed July 19, 2009). Through the Hub's website, individuals and groups can connect to share human rights information. Ibid. The Hub is a project of WITNESS, which is a human rights NGO that uses video and online technologies to expose human rights violations around the globe. See WITNESS, "About WITNESS," http://www.witness.org/index.php?option=com_content&task=view&id=26&Itemid=78 (accessed July 19, 2009).

other NGOs working in the same subject area, or to the expanding interpretations or definitions of rights.

For example, a particular NGO might traditionally support civil and political rights (such as the rights to free expression, to bodily integrity, to a fair trial, and to vote), paying little if any attention to economic rights (such as the rights to food, to health care, and to shelter). That NGO may modify its strategy and incorporate economic rights, recognizing that civil, political and economic rights are inextricably intertwined, interrelated, and indivisible.

Human rights NGOs may adopt a comprehensive strategy, fighting for immediate full implementation of rights, or may adopt an incremental approach, fighting for rights in stages. For example, some groups combating sexual orientation discrimination may insist on full and immediate equality for persons of all orientations, whereas other similar groups may defer some claims such as equality of transgendered persons, until, for example, society is perceived to be more receptive.[98]

3.8.3. *Education*

Some human rights NGO workers or prospective workers may benefit from NGO educational opportunities in formal NGO degree programs or informal training programs on NGO management that cover topics such as creating and sustaining effective NGOs.[99]

---

[98] LGBT and other NGOs have long debated whether sexuality discrimination protections should be afforded to transgendered persons. See, e.g., Paul Schindler, "Tammy Baldwin Withholds Name From ENDA Stripped of Trans Protections," *Gay City News*, September 28, 2007, http://www.thetaskforce.org/TF_in_news/07_1009/stories/12_tammy_baldwin_withholds_name.pdf (accessed July 19, 2009) (discussing how LGBT groups differ over level and timing of protection for transgendered people, as the Employment Non-Discrimination Act, or ENDA, would be considered by the U.S. Labor and Education Committee without protections for transgendered Americans that were part of original bill). Some NGOs favor legislation that would immediately protect transgendered persons, and others believe that since there is more resistance to protecting transgender people than LGBT people, immediate emphasis should be on LGBTs with transgendered protection being sought incrementally. See ibid., noting, inter alia, statement by Congressman Barney Frank.

Twelve groups signed a letter stating that their "collective position remains clear and consistent" and they would "oppose any employment nondiscrimination bill that did not protect transgender people." Ibid. (listed groups included the National Gay and Lesbian Task Force (NGLTF), the National Center for Transgender Equality, the Empire State Pride Agenda, Lambda Legal, the National Center for Lesbian Rights, P-FLAG, the National Stonewall Democrats, Pride At Work, and the AFL-CIO).

[99] Several NGO educational programs are listed at www.gdrc.org/ngo/ngo-curriculum.html (accessed July 19, 2009), including: Cass Business School (London, Postgraduate Diploma & Masters in NGO Management); Rutgers University (New Jersey, USA, Non-Profit / NGO Management and Development); School for International Training (Vermont, USA, Master

3.9. *Human Rights NGOs Must Be Cooperative & Collaborative*

Human rights NGOs may not succeed if they work only within their own community or only with the constituency they serve, or are otherwise detached. Human rights NGOs must cooperate and collaborate with outsiders, including governments, inter-governmental organizations, other NGOs, the media, persons whose human rights the NGOs are seeking to protect, and others.

NGOs must cooperate with governments, that are charged with registering, monitoring, and granting tax and other benefits to them. Furthermore, NGOs collaborate with governments on projects and programs, and they may rely on governments for aid to help the NGOs carry out their missions. Similarly, NGOs cooperate and collaborate with inter-governmental organizations, such as the United Nations, that in essence vet the NGOs[100] to help ensure their credibility and viability, and then may fund them on projects, many of which involve doing collaborative work with UN agencies.[101]

---

of Science in Management); Imperial College at Wye (UK, NGO Management); International NGO Training and Research Centre (INTRAC) (United Kingdom, Short Course Training Programme for NGO Staff). See also NGO Management Courses in India, IndiaEdu Organization, http://www.indiaedu.com/career-courses/ngo-management (accessed July 19, 2009); NGO Management School Switzerland, "Programme Courses," http://www.ngoms.org/courses.htm (accessed July 19, 2009).

The London School of Economics and Political Science (LSE) offers a Master of Science degree in NGO Management for people seeking to work in the developing world as NGO analysts, policy-makers, researchers or practitioners. http://www.lse.ac.uk/collections/CCS/study/msc_devel_countries.htm (accessed July 19, 2009). The degree focuses on development, humanitarian, relief, and advocacy NGOs and examines: (a) NGO work, challenges, and the role they play in development, relief, and advocacy; (b) NGO relationships with other stakeholders including beneficiaries, communities, government, donors, social movements, transnational networks and other actors and how these relationships affect NGO work; (c) NGO internal organizational challenges, including evaluation, accountability, legitimacy, and planning; (d) changing policy contexts in which NGOs operate; and (e) theories of NGO public action. Ibid.

[100] Inter-governmental organizations "vet" NGOs through the NGO accreditation process. National governments "vet" NGOs when determining whether to bestow tax exempt status and other benefits.

[101] For example, UNDP engages a global network of development and human rights NGOs "at all levels to promote the Millennium Development Goals and support people in their efforts to build a better life." See United Nations Development Programme, "UNDP and civil society organizations," http://www.undp.org/partners/cso (accessed July 19, 2009). In addition, UNDP recognizes working with NGOs "is critical to national ownership, accountability, good governance, decentralization, democratization of development co-operation, and the quality and relevance of official development programmes." Ibid. UNDP partners with NGOs in six thematic areas: democratic governance; poverty reduction, crisis prevention & recovery, HIV/AIDS, energy & environment and Women's empowerment. Ibid.

NGOs charged with advocating for human rights must cooperate with governments and inter-governmental institutions to gain accreditation or a similar status to be able to present advocacy papers and participate in deliberations of those organizations. For example, the United Nations Economic and Social Council accredits NGOs who can assist ECOSOC on human rights and other issues. NGOs can also gain accreditation to national and regional human rights institutions.

Through cooperation with the United Nations, NGOs have been an instrumental part of treaty negotiations, such as for the Rome Conference on the ICC.[102] NGOs play a major role in the treaty monitoring process of United Nations treaty bodies, and indeed NGOs play an official role for some of the committees.[103] NGOs work very closely with academic institutions, whose professors and students lend expertise and person-power to NGO efforts, and who may hold key positions in the NGOs.[104]

Local and international NGOs working in the same geographic and substantive areas must cooperate with each other. The synergies can benefit victims and other constituents and communities who stand to be protected by human rights responses. Local NGOs on the ground may be more familiar with local victims and the extent of deprivations, and more familiar with political and legal

[102] *See* William R. Pace, "Civil Society Participation in the International Criminal Court: NGOs Advocacy for a Fair, Independent, and Effective ICC From Rome to Today," *Contribution to HURIDOCS Conference. 'Human Rights Council and International Criminal Court: The New Challenges for Human Rights Communications'*, February 25–27, 2009, Geneva. www.huridocs.org/involved/conference/presentations/Pace.doc (accessed July 19, 2009) (During the Rome ICC treaty conference 535 NGOs contributed to the delegations. Approximately 200 attended throughout the five weeks of negotiations. Their participation in "the ICC process will be regarded in history as one of the most successful human rights and human security international lawmaking initiatives ever. It has been uniquely effective due to the united efforts of many individuals and organizations pulling in the same direction.").

[103] *See, e.g.*, Mara R. Bustelo, "The Committee on the Elimination of Discrimination Against Women at the Crossroads," in Philip Alston and James Crawford (eds), *The Future of UN Human Rights Treaty Monitoring* (Cambridge University Press, 2000), 79, 107 (The Committee on the Elimination of Discrimination Against Women is a prime example of NGOs becoming increasingly involved in committee efforts. The CEDAW Committee has gradually increased the responsibility and opportunities of NGOs with regard to their participation in the session meetings. For example, NGOs are now "part of the Committee's formal process of preparing general recommendations, and formally part of the pre-sessional working group preparation for the review of periodic reports.").

[104] Tanya Lokshina, "NGO and Academia – A Liaison Between Amateurs and Professionals," (Presentation Text – Moscow Helsinki Group) http://programs.ssrc.org/gsc/gsc_activities/lokshina (Discussing the interplay between academia and NGOs. Human Rights NGOs benefit from their cooperation with academics involved in the fields of sociology, law, and psychology. "Academic lawyers [are] vital for the conduction of quality analysis of current legislation and development of legislative drafts and amendments in the interests of human rights.").

personalities and structures that fuel violations, and may be more familiar with local cultural, social and other community needs. International NGOs, many of whom may not be permanently located in the local regions to be served, must work with local NGOs, adapt to the community, recognize that the needs of the local community are paramount above the needs of the international NGOs, and refrain from actions that undermine successful local efforts. International NGOs must answer to their donors, some of whom are outsiders, who may disagree with local NGOs on how funds should be spent locally, or on which and the extent to which policies should be implemented locally. International NGOs should be cautious about attempting to impose their own will locally, which could alienate the victims sought to be protected, undermine community spirit, and even weaken local human rights protections. Also, international NGOs should be mindful that they may be competing with local NGOs for the same donations, diminishing the efficacy of the local NGOs.

NGOs must cooperate with media that can help disseminate information about human rights abuses and remedies and with human rights victims whose interests, needs and sensitivities must be taken into account before NGOs seek to act on victims' behalf.

NGOs will not always agree among themselves on policy, logistics, or other critical components of their work, and they may not all speak with one voice. But the more they collaborate, the better, as they work to promote and protect human rights with the best interests of the victims paramount.

3.10. *Human Rights NGOs Must Be Competent, Reliable & Credible*

To be effective, NGOs must be competent.[105] Many NGOs demonstrate high levels of competence and success.[106] World leaders, and many other people,

---

105 Dictionaries define "competent" as follows: having the necessary skill or knowledge to do something successfully; having requisite or adequate ability or qualities; capable; having the capacity to function or develop in a particular way; adequate for the purpose. See, e.g., Merriam Webster, http://www.merriam-webster.com/dictionary/competent (accessed July 19, 2009); Free Dictionary, http://www.thefreedictionary.com/competent (accessed July 19, 2009).

106 Competency in human rights NGO work is evidenced by the award of multiple Nobel Peace Prizes to NGOs and private individuals with NGO leadership, including: Wangari Maathai (founder of the Green Belt Movement "for her contribution to sustainable development, democracy and peace") (2004); Shirin Ebadi ("for her efforts for democracy and human rights. She has focused especially on the struggle for the rights of women and children;" co-founder of NGOs in Iran, including the Association for Support of Children's Rights and the Human Rights Defence Centre) (2003); Médecins Sans Frontières ("in recognition of the organization's pioneering humanitarian work on several continents") (1999); International Campaign to Ban Landmines, Jody Williams (1997); Rigoberta Menchú Tum (1992); Aung San Suu Kyi (1991); Mother Teresa (1979); Amnesty International (1977); Friends Service

have complimented NGOs for their contributions to the promotion and protection of human rights.[107]

If a human rights NGO is not competent, it does not mean that it is no longer an NGO. It simply failed in its mission to protect human rights. Some human rights NGOs may fail because they are mismanaged, suffer from bad decisions made by the board or employees, or underestimate the effort or resources needed for particular projects or programs. Some may fail because

Council, American Friends Service Committee (1947); International Committee of the Red Cross (1917, 1944, 1963). See The Nobel Foundation, "All Nobel Peace Prize Laureates," http://nobelprize.org/nobel_prizes/peace/laureates/index.html (accessed July 19, 2009).

[107] For example, former UN Secretary-General Kofi Annan, speaking to Iranian Nobel Peace Prize Laureate Ms. Shirin Ebadi, said "you, too, have shown us the impact that NGOs can have at home and on the global stage. Your richly earned Nobel Peace Prize continues a welcome trend of recognizing NGOs for their contributions to human rights, peace, disarmament and democracy." See "Without Vital Role of NGOs, World Could Hardly Respond to Myriad Crises, UN Secretary-General Annan Tells DPI/NGO Conference," U.N. Doc SG/SM/10085 (September 9, 2005), http://www.un.org/News/Press/docs/2005/sgsm10085.doc.htm (accessed July 16, 2009). The Secretary-General continued:

> Just two weeks ago in Niger, I saw United Nations agencies, funds and programmes doing what they do best: helping people in need. I was pleased to see how well they were working with their NGO partners. And I was impressed to see how quickly Médecins Sans Frontières was able to set up a nutrition centre, and treat more than 2,000 children, in a mere three weeks. I saw other humanitarian groups carrying out similarly valiant efforts. We have a long way to go in meeting the needs there, and a similar crisis looms in other parts of the Sahel and Africa. But without NGOs, we could hardly begin to respond to any of these crises. I thank you for the vital role you are playing.
>
> We also have much work to do in Sudan. There, too, NGOs have been our indispensable partners. When I visited Darfur in May, I was accompanied by Tom Arnold, Ken Bacon and George Rupp – the heads of Concern, Refugees International and the International Rescue Committee – who were able to offer invaluable perspectives on the situation. So let me pay tribute again, not only to the NGOs who have braved a threatening environment to deliver relief, but also to the others – local and international alike – who are working for reconciliation and human rights and making other essential contributions to the Sudanese peace process.
>
> The truth is that NGOs are working with us everywhere:...alongside us whenever crisis strikes...right behind us in advocating for women's rights, international criminal justice and action on global warming...and...often far out in front of us in identifying new threats and concerns. This is certainly one of your most important roles. You can often see what is not yet visible to diplomats, and think what still seems unthinkable to governments and their officials might not yet be able to admit. What you say may be unpalatable today, but often becomes the conventional wisdom of tomorrow, and, for that, I'm personally very grateful to you.

Ibid.

of corruption, embezzlement, or other illegal activity by employees[108] or outsiders.[109]

Not all competent NGOs succeed.[110] Some competent NGOs fail because governments place insurmountable hurdles in the NGOs' paths, making it impossible for those groups to succeed, particularly if the NGOs have no political or other leverage. For example, NGOs in oppressive countries may be subjected to impossibly demanding registration regulations, government harassment, reprisal, discrimination, threats, or intimidation. Some governments may restrict outside funding for NGOs, limit personnel and other outside assistance, and limit NGO freedom of expression, association, and peaceful assembly.[111] International human rights law permits governments to regulate NGOs, but some governments violate international human rights law by expressly banning NGOs or imposing regulations that *de facto* eliminate NGOs' ability to exist and function.

Many individual NGOs and groups of NGOs have successfully carried out their missions to protect human rights in a wide range of areas over the years. NGOs competently lobbied for human rights protections to be incorporated into the UN Charter and the Universal Declaration of Human Rights.

---

108 For example, American Red Cross employees were charged with defrauding the institution for padding a personal bank account with donations, embezzling to support a crack cocaine habit, forging signatures on purchase orders meant for disaster victims, and diverting other Red Cross funds to personal use. See, e.g., Jaime Holguin, "Disaster Strikes In Red Cross Backyard: Charity Fails To Get A Grip On Criminal Scandals At Local Chapters," *CBS Evening News*, July 29, 2002, http://www.cbsnews.com/stories/2002/07/29/eveningnews/main516700.shtml (accessed July 20, 2009).

109 For example, an NGO may invest funds through outsiders who handle the funds fraudulently, causing the NGO to lose large sums, as in the case of Mr. Madoff. A question would be raised as to whether and to what extent the NGO knew or should have known that the funds would be handled fraudulently, that is, should the NGO have invested the money elsewhere?

110 An NGO that does not complete its stated mission to protect human rights does not necessarily fail. All steps NGOs take towards protecting human rights are positive. Attempts to protect human rights will make victims, governments and others more aware of human rights norms, of state obligations to protect human rights, of human rights violations, and of steps that can be taken to promote human rights protection. NGOs serve a valuable human rights education function.

111 For example, recent attempts to restrict foreign financing are reported to have occurred in Moldova, Zimbabwe, Eritrea, Uzbekistan, and Belarus. See International Center for Not-for-Profit Law, "Recent Laws and Legislative Proposals to Restrict Civil Society and Civil Society Organizations," *Volume 8, Issue 4, The International Journal of Not-for-Profit Law*, (August 2006). www.icnl.org/knowledge/ijnl/vol8iss4/art_1.htm (accessed July 19, 2009) (noting that over the previous year "nineteen countries have reduced restrictive legislation aimed at weakening civil society. These countries join the more than 30 with existing laws, policies, and practices that stifle the work of civil society organizations." Such restrictions were also recently reported in Iran:

NGOs successfully lobbied for a new UN position for a High Commissioner for Human Rights (a post that had been opposed by UN leaders and many governments).[112] NGOs successfully lobbied for the international instrument promoting greenhouse gas control terms at the 1992 Earth Summit in Rio de Janeiro,[113] and were instrumental in the promulgation of the Landmine Treaty,[114] the Rome Treaty creating the International Criminal Court,[115] the Disabilities Convention,[116] and many other international law instruments that codify international human rights law.

> The laws on founding NGOs are often restrictive, funding is scarce, and many groups lack both experience and expertise. A majority of NGOs operate from a member's house or flat because they cannot afford an office.

Golnaz Esfandiari, "Iran: Growing NGO Community Offers Political Activism Where Government Does Not," *Pars Times: Greater Iran and Beyond* (2004) http://www.parstimes.com/news/archive/2004/rfe/ngos_activism.html) (accessed July 20, 2009).

[112] Sheikh Hafizur Rahman Karzon, "Human rights and non-state actors." *The Daily Star*, Issue 225, Feb. 4, 2006, http://www.thedailystar.net/law/2006/02/01/index.htm) (accessed July 20, 2009) (describing two NGO phases: the first phase is the emergence and development of international NGOs like Amnesty International; the second phase involves the creation and proliferation of domestic human rights monitoring and advocacy groups around the globe).

[113] Approximately 2,400 NGO representatives participated at the Earth Summit, and approximately 17,000 people attended the parallel NGO Forum in Rio de Janeiro. http://www.un.org/geninfo/bp/enviro.html (accessed July 19, 2009).

[114] The International Campaign to Ban Landmines (ICBL) "is a global network in over 70 countries that works for a world free of antipersonnel landmines and cluster munitions, where landmine and cluster munition survivors can lead fulfilling lives." http://www.icbl.org/index.php/icbl/About-Us (accessed July 19, 2009). The Campaign was awarded the Nobel Peace Prize for its efforts to bring about the 1997 Mine Ban Treaty. Ibid.

[115] For example, the Coalition for the International Criminal Court, which is a network of 2,500 NGOs, coordinated many efforts of diverse NGOs from all regions of the world who were active at all stages of the development of the ICC. http://www.iccnow.org/?mod=coalition (accessed July 19, 2009). In 2003, the ICC Assembly of States Parties adopted a resolution entitled "Recognition of the coordinating and facilitating role of the NGO Coalition for the International Criminal Court" (ICC-ASP/2/Res.8). Ambassador Allieu I. Kanu of Sierra Leone, Vice-President of the Assembly of States Parties introduced the resolution and noted: "In this journey, there are people who are generally seated on the sides or in the back of our assemblies, those who took the floor only occasionally, those who do not get the credit but nevertheless tirelessly sustain, defend and yes, set the spirit of the institution which we incarnate today. An organization that represented such people is the NGO Coalition for the ICC". Ibid.

[116] Janet E. Lord, "NGO Participation in Human Rights Law and Process: Latest Developments in the Effort to Develop an International Treaty on the Rights of People with Disabilities," *ILSA Journal of International and Comparative Law* 10 (2004): 311, 314 (noting that NGOs lobbied and received access to official bodies at all stages of the treaty negotiations, were permitted participation as observers, with rights to submit statements and make oral interventions) See, e.g., U.N. General Assembly, *Accreditation and participation of non-governmental organizations in the Ad Hoc Committee on a Comprehensive and Integral International Convention*

NGOs seemed to have been successful in campaigns directed against private corporations that allegedly violated human rights, such as Nestle regarding promoting its marketing artificial infant feeding around the world (rather than breast milk), Monsanto regarding distributing genetically modified food, and Starbucks, when after pressure of a "campaign for justice for coffee workers" Starbucks adopted a code of conduct for workers at its plantations in Guatemala.[117]

4. *NGO Self-Regulation Via Codes of Conduct and Ethics*

Some NGOs self-regulate through complying with Codes of Conduct, Codes of Ethics, or NGO Certification Schemes[118] proposed by individual NGOs, groups of NGOs, governments, inter-governmental organizations,[119] or commentators.[120] These Codes were designed for various reasons, including: to

---

on Protection and Promotion of the Rights and Dignity of Persons with Disabilities (July 26, 2002), U.N. Doc. A/RES/56/510 (2002), http://daccessdds.un.org/doc/UNDOC/GEN/N02/495/75/PDF/N0249575.pdf?OpenElement (accessed July 19, 2009). See also U.N. Ad Hoc Committee on a Comprehensive and Integral International Convention on Protection and Promotion of the Rights and Dignity of Persons with Disabilities, *Decision on the modalities of the participation of accredited non-governmental organizations in the Ad Hoc Committee to consider proposals for a comprehensive and integral international convention to promote and protect the rights and dignity of persons with disabilities*, August 2, 2002, http://www.unhchr.ch/disability/decparticipationNGOs.doc (accessed July 19, 2009).

[117] It is reported that U.S. labor rights NGOs advocating for Guatemalan coffee workers lobbied Starbucks to require business partners to "pay a living wage, respect freedom of association, provide sanitary housing, provide safe and healthy workplaces, and not practice discrimination." Lance Compa and Tashia Hinchliffe-Darricarrere, "Enforcing International Labor Rights through Corporate Codes of Conduct," *Columbia Journal of Transnational Law* 33 (1995): 663, 683. The Starbucks president is said to have initially refused to meet with the coalition and declined to adopt a code. Ibid., 683–684. The coalition reportedly initiated a public communication campaign, "including informational picketing at Starbucks stores, to pressure the company into adopting the proposed code". Ibid. Starbucks agreed to adopt a code of conduct. Ibid., 685 ("'[w]e accept the challenge to take the lead in adopting a Starbucks code of conduct'")(further citation omitted).

[118] In this chapter I refer to these codes and schemes as "Codes of Conduct" or "Codes".

[119] See, e.g., *Declaration on the Right and Responsibility of Individuals, Groups and Organs of Society.* See also John R. Crook, "Current Developments: The Fifty-First Session of the U.N. Commission on Human Rights," *American Journal of International Law* 90 (1996): 126 (citing Allan McChesny, "Protecting the Rights of all Human Rights Defenders," *The Review (International Commission of Jurists)* 55 (December 1995): 39).

[120] See, e.g., Ramon Mullerat, "The Need For Codes of Conduct in NGOs: The Experience of the Legal Profession," (paper presented at the American Bar Association Section of International Law, Washington, D.C., April 15, 2005), http://www.abanet.org/intlaw/calendar/

foster trust in NGOs; to help NGOs become more efficient; to defend against claims that NGOs are self-serving, corrupt and thus ineffectual; to stifle government attempts to impose regulations on NGOs; to codify standards of behavior among NGOs; and, to bolster credibility of NGOs who could advertise "seals of approval" awarded under the Codes.[121]

These Codes, some of which have not yet come into force, require NGOs to aspire to and comply with norms equal to or consistent with those contained in the list of attributes for successful human rights NGOs identified and analyzed earlier in this chapter.[122] A question remains as to how effective these Codes have been, but a full inquiry into their efficacy is beyond the scope of this chapter. They appear to be successful, generally, as evidenced as follows: by the proliferation of such Codes; by adherence thereto by longstanding, well-respected human rights NGOs; and by governments using Code participation as a criterion in determining whether to work with specific NGOs. Though the Codes discussed herein may not necessarily be the best-crafted, best-implemented, or most highly effective of the many Codes that exist, examining them is illustrative as all the Codes contain at least some attributes that any successful human rights NGO must possess.

---

spring2005/papers/31.09.doc (accessed July 19, 2009). Mullerat discusses, *inter alia*, the 1995 *Commonwealth Foundation NGO Guidelines for Good Policy and Practice* which contain "guidelines for governments dealing with NGOs, for NGOs themselves, for the policy and practice of those who fund NGO's [sic], along with a strategy action plan for the implementation of the guidelines." Ibid., 3. Mullerat argues that particularly post-scandals like Enron and WorldCom, NGOs, like private corporations, should have a code of ethics and a conflict-of interest policy. Ibid., 1. See also Anthony Adair, "Codes of Conduct are Good for NGOs Too," *IPA Review* (March, 1999) 26, http://www.ipa.org.au/library/review51–1%20 Codes%20of%20Conduct%20are%20good%20for%20NGOs%20too.pdf (accessed July 19, 2009) (noting that NGOs like commercial enterprises must "earn their role in society."); Robert Charles Blitt, "Who Will Watch the Watchdogs? Human Rights Nongovernmental Organizations and the Case for Regulation." *Buffalo Human Rights Law Review* 10 (2004): 261 (arguing that human rights NGOs need concrete rules to ensure credibility); Pieter H. Kooijmans, "The Nongovernmental Organizations and the Monitoring Activities of the United Nations in the Field of Human Right," in *The Role of Non-Governmental Organizations in the Protection of Human Rights, Symposium International Commission of Jurists* (1990), 15 (cited by Martin A. Olz, "Non-governmental Organizations in Regional Human Rights Systems," *Columbia Human Rights Law Review* 28 (1997): notes 1, 76.

[121] See Simon Heap, "Building Trust in NGOs," *The International Journal of Not-for-Profit Law*, Vol. 3, Issue 3 (2001), http://www.icnl.org/knowledge/ijnl/vol3iss3/sr_2.htm#_ftn18 (accessed July 20, 2009); see generally Catherine Shea and Sandra Sitar, Report and Recommendations – NGO Accreditation and Certification: The Way Forward? An Evaluation of the Development Community's Experience http://www.usaid.gov/our_work/cross-cutting_programs/private_voluntary_cooperation/conf_icnl.pdf (accessed July 19, 2009).

[122] See supra sections III(1) – (10).

4.1. *Afghan NGO Code of Conduct*

In Afghanistan in 2005, in response to accusations that NGOs had been abusing funds provided to rebuild the country post-war, aid groups in Afghanistan formulated the Afghan Code of Conduct[123] to regulate NGOs' in-country activities.[124] The Afghan Code of Conduct contains 21 articles to promote transparency, accountability and good management among NGOs by "voluntary self-regulation", to raise NGO standards of conduct and improve the quality of NGO services, and to help the public, governments, donors and media understand NGOs.[125]

The Afghan Code of Conduct has been signed by hundreds of the 2,400 national and international NGOs registered to operate in Afghanistan.[126] These groups are meant to be people-centered,[127] to be transparent and accountable,[128] and to be committed to sustainable positive impact,[129] to good internal

[123] The official name is the "Code of Conduct for NGOs Engaged in Humanitarian Action, Reconstruction, and Development in Afghanistan." See Agency Coordinating Body for Afghan Relief, http://www.acbar.org/downloads/Code%20of%20Conduct_English%20Version.pdf (accessed July 19, 2009).

[124] It had also been reported that the Afghan government and members of the public had confused NGOs working in Afghanistan with highly paid contractors and other profitable organizations "many of which are registered as NGOs with the country's ministry of economy". See Integrated Regional Information Networks (IRIN), "Afghanistan: New Code of Conduct to Regulate NGOs," May 31, 2005, http://www.irinnews.org/Report.aspx?ReportID=28641 (accessed July 20, 2009).

[125] Ibid., Afghan Code of Conduct, "Purpose of the Code."

[126] See Integrated Regional Information Networks (IRIN), "Afghanistan: New Code of Conduct to Regulate NGOs," May 31, 2005, http://www.irinnews.org/Report.aspx?ReportID=28641 (accessed July 20, 2009); http://www.acbar.org/display.php?page_id=66 (accessed July 20, 2009).

[127] The Afghan Code of Conduct provides that NGOs are primarily loyal, accountable and responsible to the people they serve whom they seek to help develop self-reliance. NGOs are to protect human rights, build trust, engage local people in conceiving and implementing projects and programs, and respect local values. Afghan Code of Conduct, "Principles of Conduct," section I(1).

[128] NGOs working in Afghanistan commit to being transparent and accountable to government and community partners, the public, donors and other interested parties. Afghan Code of Conduct, "Principles of Conduct," section I(3)(1). Accountability involves: sound financial policies, audits and systems for their accounts; complying with Afghan government regulations; being truthful in raising, using and accounting for funds; and sound financial, accounting, procurement, transport and administrative systems to ensure that resources are used for intended purposes. Ibid., sections I(3)3.2 & 3.3.

[129] NGOs working in Afghanistan commit to: being effective, including avoiding duplicative services; sustainability, including seeking durable, cost-effective solutions, building Afghan ownership and capacity, and focusing on long-term community goals; protecting Afghanistan's physical and natural environment and protecting the eco-system; and monitoring and evaluating program impact and sharing findings with relevant stakeholders. Ibid., section I(2).

governance,[130] to honesty, integrity and cost effectiveness,[131] to diversity, fairness and non-discrimination,[132] to building Afghan capacity,[133] and to independence.[134]

[130] NGOs working in Afghanistan commit to having written constitutions or memoranda to clearly define the NGOs' mission, objectives and organizational structures, developing policies and procedures to affirm a commitment to equal opportunities, applying hiring and termination practices that respect freedom of choice and human resource needs, offering positions based on merit, paying appropriate salaries, allocating job responsibilities appropriately, having appropriate notice provisions, and maintaining freedom from personal and professional conflicts. Ibid., section I(4).

[131] NGOs working in Afghanistan commit to honesty in activities, and to practices that do not undermine NGOs' ethical integrity, such as corruption, nepotism, bribery, and trading in illicit substances. Ibid., section I(5). NGOs will accept funds or donations only from those whose aims are consistent with the NGOs' mission and which do not undermine the NGOs' independence and identity. Ibid.

[132] Within their organizations, and within the scope of the NGOs' external programs and other initiatives, NGOs should seek gender, ethnic, geographic and religious diversity and equity, provide opportunities for the underserved, the vulnerable, the disabled, and other marginalized persons, and provide for affirmative action. Ibid., section I(6).

[133] NGOs working in Afghanistan are: to help build Afghan capacity to understand needs, establish priorities, and take effective action to ensure that Afghans meet humanitarian, development and reconstruction needs; to consult with local communities and the government when designing and implementing projects; to design projects to be taken over by target communities or the government to enhance sustainability; to prioritize Afghan nationals in recruiting, hiring and training; to maximize using appropriate local physical and technical resources; and to use appropriate locally owned and maintained technologies. Ibid., section I(7).

[134] NGOs working in Afghanistan commit: to not implement programs or gather information of a "political, military or economically sensitive nature for governments or other bodies that may serve purposes other than those directly consistent with [the NGOs'] "humanitarian or development missions"; to be autonomous according to Afghan and international law, and to resist imposing conditions that may compromise NGO missions and principles; to provide aid impartially based on need alone, regardless of race, religion, ethnicity, gender or nationality or political affiliation of recipients and not to tie humanitarian assistance to the embracing or acceptance of a particular political or religious creed; to be neutral and to not promote partisan national or international political agendas; to "not choose sides between parties to a conflict"; and to apply "SPHERE" – "We are knowledgeable about the SHPERE Humanitarian Charter and Minimum Standards in Disaster Response, and seek to apply these standards and the SPHERE indicators in the implementation, monitoring and evaluation of our humanitarian projects and programs." Ibid., section I(11); see http://www.sphereproject.org (accessed July 19, 2009); www.sphereproject.org/content/view/229/232 (accessed July 19, 2009).

4.2. *Ghanaian NGO Standards of Excellence*

In 2004, local Ghanaian NGOs, international NGOs working in Ghana, and donors began formally to address problems recognized in their mutual relations, including a lack of equity in their partnerships, accountability concerns, and concerns of NGO credibility flowing from reports of NGO "misdeeds" as well as lack of stakeholder commitments to building local capacity.[135] If NGOs met a certain standard, they would receive a "seal" or "certificate" which they could proudly display to show their commitment to complying with the Ghana NGO Standards of Excellence.

The Ghana NGO Standards sought to establish minimum standards, determined by the community, that enshrined "principles of good and ethical practice."[136] The regulatory framework for NGOs in Ghana was meant to help ensure that Ghana NGOs were accountable and transparent and were seen by the public and others to be accountable and transparent, and to enhance mutual trust and confidence among local NGOs, international NGOs, and donors.

The Standards were intended to demonstrate that NGOs could regulate themselves voluntarily, and that they had the ability: to promote internal organizational and institutional learning; to ensure transparency, accountability and good governance; to remain relevant and responsive to the needs of the Ghanaian people; to comply with internal guidelines; to improve the quality of their services; to improve relations and links between NGOs and stakeholders including the government and the private sector; and to encourage the development of mutually-beneficial strategic partnerships.[137]

The Standards were meant to reflect shared norms and rules of standardized behavior, all subject to NGO self-verification and quality control which would obviate governmentally imposed regulations. The Standards would apply to all NGOs working in Ghana, big or small, and irrespective of their specific remits.

---

[135] See Ghana NGO/CSO Standards Project, "Frequently Asked Questions (FAQs)," http://www.posdev.org/standards/faq_2007_eng.html (accessed July 19, 2009).

[136] Ibid. Sponsors of the Ghana NGO Standards included the Pan-African Organization for Sustainable Development (POSDEV) (serving as the Secretariat), Care International, the Ghana Association of Private and Voluntary Organizations in Development (GAPVOD), ActionAid Ghana (AAG), Ghana Center for Democratic Development (CDD), the Opportunities Industrialization Centres International (OICI), and the Democracy and Governance Department of the USAID Mission in Ghana.

[137] Ibid.

4.3. *Australian NGO Code of Conduct*

The Australian Council for International Development (ACFID)[138] administers a Code of Conduct for local and international human rights and development NGOs working in Australia.[139] Approximately 80 NGOs participate in this voluntary scheme and agree to conduct their activities with integrity and accountability. The Australian Code seeks to enhance standards and to ensure public confidence in the groups and their work to protect human rights through using overseas aid to reduce poverty through effective and sustainable development. NGOs need not be ACFID members to sign the Australian Code, but all members must sign and comply with it. Adherence to the Australian Code is required of all NGOs accredited with the Australian Agency for International Development (AusAID) to apply for Australian government funding.[140] The Australian Code sets out standards and requirements to which signatories are bound and against which complaints and compliance is assessed in areas including organizational integrity, governance, communication with the public, finances, and personnel and management practice.[141]

---

[138] The Australian NGO Code of Conduct has been operating ten years and was last amended in 2004. See Australian Council for International Development, *ACFID Code of Conduct for Non Government Development Organisations*, amended Oct. 5, 2004, http://www.acfid.asn.au/code-of-conduct/docs/code.pdf (accessed July 20, 2009).

[139] Ibid.

[140] The Australian NGO Code of Conduct is accompanied by a non-legally binding Guidance Document. The Guidance Document helps signatories interpret and apply the Code by offering suggestions for implementing the Code's provisions. See Australian Council for International Development (ACFID), "Code of Conduct Guidance Document," http://plone.acfid.asn.au/code-of-conduct/docs/guidance/12.08_full_doc.pdf 2 (accessed July 19, 2009). The Guidance Document was updated in December 2008. See http://www.acfid.asn.au/code-of-conduct/guidance (accessed July 20, 2009).

[141] In 2008, ACFID's Executive Committee appointed a committee to manage a formal review of the Australian NGO Code of Conduct and stakeholder activities in the decade of the Code's existence, and the committee is to make recommendations on the Code's objectives, governance and operational activities. The aim of the review of the content of the Code:

> is to update and where necessary develop the Code to ensure that it is continuing to meet all stakeholders' requirements and expectations. The revised Code will articulate the world's best practice standards against which the ethics, organisational integrity, governance, management, communication with the public, financial control and reporting, accountability and transparency of signatories can be measured and published.

See "Terms of Reference for the review of the content of the Australian Council for International Development's Code of Conduct," http://plone.acfid.asn.au/code-of-conduct/review/tor (accessed July 20, 2009). The Code Review Final Documents were meant to be disseminated on or about 28 August 2009. See "Review of the content of the Code of Conduct," http://plone.acfid.asn.au/code-of-conduct/review (accessed July 20, 2009).

4.4. *Iraqi NGO Code of Conduct*

The NGO Coordination Committee in Iraq (NCCI) is an independent initiative launched by NGOs present in Baghdad in April 2003.[142] The principal objectives of NCCI, which has expanded to a network of 80 International NGOs and 200 Iraqi NGOs,[143] include: (a) to be an independent, neutral and impartial NGO forum for coordination and information exchange among the NGO community on issues and activities related to Iraq and its population, irrespective of ethnicity, politics, gender and religion; (b) to advocate that human rights and international humanitarian law are respected and ensure humanitarian needs are identified, well lobbied for and met; and (c) to collaborate to enhance NGO capacity to deliver humanitarian and development assistance in Iraq.[144] All NCCI members are bound by its Code of Conduct incorporated into the NCCI Charter.[145]

4.5. *Ethiopian NGO Code of Conduct*

In 1997, NGO umbrella groups in Ethiopia appointed an Ad Hoc NGO Consultation Working Group which drafted a Code of Conduct for NGOs in Ethiopia, which was elaborated upon at consultative meetings in 1998 and adopted in September 1998 at a meeting attended by more than 200 NGO representatives.[146]

The Ethiopian NGO Code of Conduct was designed to promote NGOs' voluntary self-regulation to ensure transparency and accountability, to improve the quality of NGO services "by helping NGOs to adopt higher standards of conduct and to devise efficient decision-making processes," to "improve communication between the NGO community and the various stake holders," and

---

142 See generally NGO Coordination Committee in Iraq website (NCCI), http://www.ncciraq.org (accessed July 19, 2009).

143 Ibid.

144 http://www.ncciraq.org/spip.php?article6 (accessed July 19, 2009); http://www.ncciraq.org/IMG/pdf_NCCI_Presentation_2009_English.pdf (accessed July 19, 2009). NCCI's mission today further includes: "to optimise humanitarian assistance in Iraq through coordination;" to empower Iraq NGOs through "information sharing, knowledge exchange, creation of links, capacity building and sensitisation to humanitarian principles and approaches;" "to provide an independent and neutral space for NGOs operating in Iraq;" to "increase NGO capacities and knowledge to enhance the delivery of assistance on humanitarian grounds to Iraqi people in need;" and to "strengthen understanding amongst the various Iraq stakeholders." Ibid.

145 See NGO Coordination Committee in Iraq (NCCI), "NCCI Charter – Code of Conduct," http://www.ncciraq.org/spip.php?article6 (accessed July 19, 2009).

146 See "NGO Code of Conduct for NGOs in Ethiopia", http://www.crdaethiopia.org/Code%20of%20Conduct/CoC.htm (accessed July 19, 2009) (posted on website of Christian Relief and Development Association (CRDA)).

to improve NGO performance "by encouraging the exchange of experiences among its members and learning from proven best practices."[147]

4.6. *Philippine NGO Codes of Conduct and Ethics*

4.6.1. *Philippine Council for NGO Certification (PCNC)*

The Philippine Council for NGO Certification (PCNC)[148] was established in 1998 and entrusted by the Philippine government to: (a) certify NGOs for tax benefits and other purposes; (b) monitor NGOs with a Code of Conduct; and (c) recommend withdrawal of registration and tax privileges from NGOs who fail to comply.[149] Seeking to ensure that NGOs meet minimum criteria for greater transparency and accountability, the PCNC assesses NGOs based on the following criteria, which are also incorporated into the PCNC Guidebook on the Basics of NGO Governance: vision, mission, goals; governance; administration; program operations (including monitoring and evaluation systems); financial management; and partnering and networking.[150]

---

[147] Ibid., 3. The Ethiopian Code provides that NGOs working in Ethiopia: be people centered, be fair and equitable, have moral and ethical integrity, be transparent and accountable, have good governance; be independent; be communicative and collaborative; fostering gender equity; be environmentally conscious; promote sustainability; and have clear measurements for assessing impact. Ibid., pp. 3–6.

[148] The PCNC comprises 6 umbrella organizations: the Association of Foundations (AF) (composed of 135 foundations nationwide); the Bishops-Businessmen's Conference for Human Development (BBC) (among its leaders being Catholic bishops and business leaders); the Caucus of Development NGO Networks (CODE-NGO) (a network of 14 NGO networks with over 3000 NGO members throughout the country); the League of Corporate Foundations (organization composed of large and active corporate foundations); the National Council of Social Development Foundations (NCSD) (one of the country's oldest NGO networks comprising about 100 NGOs engaged in development and basic services); and the Philippine Business for Social Progress (PBSP) (a social development foundation set up and funded by 180 business corporations in the Philippines). http://www.pcnc.com.ph/aboutUs.php (accessed July 19, 2009). For a discussion of the PCNC, see generally Caroline Hartnell, "The Philippines: Self-Regulation on Trial," *Alliance Magazine* 8, No. 4, Dec. 2003, http://www.icnl.org/KNOWLEDGE/news/2004/01–09.htm (accessed July 19, 2009) (noting that the PCNC website states that PCNC Certification shall be a "'seal of good housekeeping'" that funders and donors may consider in choosing which organizations to support. Ibid. (citing http://www.pcnc.com.ph/background.php (accessed July 19, 2009)).

[149] Philippine Council for NGO Certification (PNCP), "About Us," http://www.pcnc.com.ph/aboutUs.php (accessed July 19, 2009). The PCNC website states that its "main function is to certify non-profit organizations that meet established minimum criteria for financial management and accountability in the service to underprivileged Filipinos". Ibid.

[150] See http://www.pcnc.com.ph/docs/PCNC_Guidebook_on_the_Basics_of_NGO_Governance.pdf (accessed July 19, 2009).

The PCNC writes about the significant role played by NGOs in Philippine society:[151]

> The Philippine NGO sector has developed a strong reputation for the delivery of basic services to the urban and rural poor. This has been recognized by national and local government, by other NGOs in the region, and by the donor community. In fact, NGO participation in all aspects of governance is enshrined in the Philippine Constitution. The past administrations of President Aquino and President Ramos have included NGOs in local and national consultations on important issues and have encouraged them to participate in the governance processes of the country.
>
> The newfound recognition of the role and contributions of the NGO sector in Philippine development has led to the spectacular rise in the number of NGOs in the country. Some reports state that there are as many as 60,000 non-profit, non-governmental organizations registered in the Philippines today.

4.6.2. *Philippine Caucus of Development NGO Networks (CODE-NGO)*

In 1990, the ten largest NGO networks in the Philippines established a coalition called the Philippine Caucus of Development NGO Networks (CODE-NGO).[152] In December 1991, 1000 NGOs attended CODE-NGO's first National Congress which ratified CODE-NGO's Covenant on Philippine Development and the Code of Conduct for Development NGOs.[153] CODE-NGO crafted the implementing rules for its Code of Conduct for Development NGOs,[154] and in 2000, the CODE-NGO National Board created the Commission on Internal Reform Initiatives (CIRI) to oversee creation of a mechanism to enforce member transparency and accountability. Enforcement is accomplished through the National Board, the CIRI, and the members themselves, and is meant to be rigorous, with concrete mechanisms for ensuring

[151] http://www.pcnc.com.ph/background.php (accessed July 19, 2009).

[152] See Caucus of Development NGO Networks (CODE-NGO), "History – How we started," http://code-ngo.org/home/index.php?option=com_content&view=article&id=84&Itemid=91 (accessed July 19, 2009).

[153] The CODE-NGO's Code of Conduct was implemented to promote professionalism, to better enable NGOs to self-regulate, to distinguish legitimate NGOs from untrustworthy groups that were abusing public trust, and to expand the reach of social development work in the Philippines. See ibid. See also Caroline Hartnell, "The Philippines: Self-Regulation on Trial," *Alliance Magazine* 8, No. 4, Dec. 2003, http://www.icnl.org/KNOWLEDGE/news/2004/01-09.htm (accessed July 19, 2009); The CODE-NGO Covenant on Philippine Development, http://code-ngo.org/home/images/stories/pdf/CODE-NGOCovenantonPhilippineDevelopmentandCodeofConduct.pdf (accessed July 19, 2009).

[154] http://code-ngo.org/home/index.php?option=com_content&view=article&id=84&Itemid=91 (accessed July 19, 2009). Also CODE-NGO created the Local Anti-Poverty Project (LAPP II), the Pork Barrel Project (PDAF Watch), a project for Economic Policy Reform and Advocacy (EPRA) and efforts at advocacy for federalism and constitutional reform. Ibid.

compliance.[155] For example, if members do not file certain reports or attend certain meetings, punishments may include: 1st Offense – Notice; 2nd Offense – Warning; 3rd Offense – Suspension of Benefits; and 4th Offense – Ground for termination.[156]

4.7. *South African National NGO Coalition (SANGOCO) NGO Code of Conduct*

The South African National NGO Coalition (SANGOCO) is an umbrella organization of NGOs from throughout the country formed in 1995 to coordinate NGO input into South African Government policy and ensure that NGOs continued to serve the people of South Africa.[157] SANGOCO believes that strong, informed, and effective NGOs are needed to contribute to government policy on all issues affecting South African human rights development, and that for NGOs to reach and maintain a high level, they must abide by a Code of Ethics promulgated by SANGOCO.[158] The Code of Ethics focuses on six core elements: values;[159] governance;[160] accountability;[161] management and human resources;[162] finance;[163] and resources.[164]

---

155 Ibid. at 13.

156 See The CODE-NGO Covenant on Philippine Development, 20. http://code-ngo.org/home/images/stories/pdf/CODE-NGOCovenantonPhilippineDevelopmentandCodeofConduct.pdf (accessed July 19, 2009).

157 http://www.sangoco.org.za/site/index.php?option=content&task=view&id=3&Itemid=25 (last accessed July 19, 2009).

158 http://www.sangoco.org.za/site/index.php?option=content&task=view&id=8&Itemid=30 (last accessed July 19, 2009).

159 SANGOCO Code of Ethics signatories "are committed to the following fundamental values that underpin the mission and objectives of signatories": Being responsive to needs and welfare of South Africans; Accountability and transparency; Participatory democracy; People-centred development; Respecting the rights, culture and dignity of all people within the framework of the Bill of Rights, as enshrined in the South African Constitution; enhancing race and gender equity; Ensuring SANGOCO remains true to its mission and objectives; Promoting voluntarism and active volunteer involvement at all levels; Mutual co-operation, collaboration and networking with other agencies around issues of mutual concern; and Striving for excellence, including efficient and effective service provision at all levels. See Ibid.

160 In the SANGOCO Code of Ethics, "governance" refers to ensuring that "the organization has a clear vision, mission, objectives and policies, and adheres to them;" specifying governance structures; developing and implementing conflicts of interest policy; ensuring independent auditing of accounts. It involves ensuring that members of the governance structure and staff excuse themselves from decisions where they have, or are perceived to have, a vested interest, and ensuring that "governance structure reflects the race and gender and composition of South African society." See ibid.

161 In the SANGOCO Code of Ethics, "accountability" refers to: ensuring internal democracy and transparency; enabling involvement of all stakeholders in planning programmes directly affecting them, and include stakeholders in regular evaluations of those programs; conducting regular sessions, including annual meetings; providing full disclosure of goals, programs, finances and governance; and inviting stakeholders to participate. See ibid.

4.8. *United States of America – InterAction Private Voluntary Organization (PVO) Standards*

InterAction, which is a membership association of U.S. NGOs, seeks to enhance the effectiveness and professional capacities of its members engaged in international humanitarian efforts.[165] InterAction claims to be the largest coalition of U.S.-based international nongovernmental organizations (NGOs) focused on the world's poor and most vulnerable people.[166] InterAction's 175 members collectively work in every developing country "expanding opportunities and supporting gender equality in education, health care, agriculture, small business, and other areas."[167]

---

[162] In the SANGOCO Code of Ethics, "Management & Human Resources" refers to: periodically reassessing the NGO's "mission, objectives and operations, in the light of changing context and constituents' needs;" analyzing "practices and implement changes needed to build a culture that encourages creativity, diversity, responsibility and respect;" developing clear, well defined written policies and procedures which relate to all employees, members and volunteers, with the policies adhering to law; establishing and maintaining "disciplinary and grievance procedures with clear lines of authority and accountability;" having clear and transparent development and other policies for staff; properly assessing skills, experience, qualifications, levels of responsibility and performance, and remuneration; and facilitating good internal communication. See ibid.

[163] In the SANGOCO Code of Ethics, "Finance" refers to: developing and maintaining proper financial management strategies; wherever possible ensuring that the funding base of the organisation is diversified; and ensuring clear and transparent accounting. See ibid.

[164] In the SANGOCO Code of Ethics, "Resources" refers to: managing organizational assets in a sustainable and cost-effective manner; developing "internal procedures and control mechanisms and implementing them to ensure the proper use of the assets;" properly monitoring the use of staff time; and conducting "cost-benefit analysis of projects and review resource allocations in the light of these." See ibid.

[165] See InterAction Organization, "Mission Statement," as revised March 2007, http://www.interaction.org/files.cgi/6014_PVOStandardsMarch2007.pdf#page=5 (accessed July 19, 2009). The InterAction Mission Statement notes InterAction's commitment to:

> Advocating and fostering human dignity and development; Striving for world justice through programs of economic and social development, relief, and reconstruction; Ameliorating the plight of refugees and migrants through relief, protection, settlement in place, voluntary repatriation, or resettlement to a third country; Helping people help themselves; Building public awareness and understanding as a necessary prerequisite for humanitarian assistance; Initiating a dialogue on public policy issues of importance to the membership; Being accountable to our individual constituencies, the American public, and the people we strive to assist; Respecting the diversity of perspectives and methods of operation of member agencies as a source of strength and creativity; Working in a spirit of collaboration and partnership as the most effective way to achieve common objectives; and Encouraging professional competence, ethical practices, and quality of service.

InterAction Statement of Commitment, 1–2.

[166] See InterAction Organization, "About Us," http://www.interaction.org/about (accessed July 19, 2009).

[167] Ibid.

Since 1994, all InterAction member organizations have had to certify compliance with the InterAction's Private Voluntary Organization (PVO) Standards.[168] Every other year, each member also self-certifies, using documented "evidence of compliance" to re-certify their compliance with the Standards.[169]

InterAction's PVO Standards were intended to ensure and strengthen public trust and confidence in the integrity, quality, and effectiveness of member organizations and their programs.[170] The Standards define the financial, operational, programmatic, and ethical code of conduct for InterAction and its member agencies, and encourages organizational learning, best practices, and InterAction members meeting the highest international non-profit standards.[171]

4.9. *The Sphere Project – Another Collaborative Effort for a Code of Ethics*

The Sphere Project was launched in 1997 by humanitarian NGOs, including the Red Cross and Red Crescent, and is based on two beliefs: first, that all possible steps should be taken to alleviate human suffering arising out of calamity and conflict; and second, that those affected by disaster have a right to life with dignity and therefore a right to assistance.[172] Sphere is three things: (a) a handbook entitled "Humanitarian Charter and Minimum Standards in Disaster Response"; (b) a broad process of collaboration; and (c) an expression of commitment to quality and accountability.[173] NGOs from around the world are linked by their adopting Sphere and applying it in national jurisdictions to protect human rights. The goals of Sphere are "to improve the quality of assistance to people affected by disaster and improve the accountability of states and humanitarian agencies to their constituents, donors and the affected populations".[174]

---

[168] http://www.interaction.org/pvostandards/index.html (accessed July 19, 2009).

[169] Ibid. The InterAction website notes that the Standards were "intended to ensure and strengthen public confidence in the integrity, quality, and effectiveness of member organizations and their programs", and that "the Standards were created when the overseas work of US NGOs was dramatically increasing in scope and significance. Defining the financial, operational, programmatic, and ethical code of conduct for InterAction and its member agencies, these high and objective standards, set InterAction members apart from many other charitable organizations." Ibid.

[170] See InterAction Organization, "InterAction's Private Voluntary Organizational Standards," http://www.interaction.org/pvostandards/index.html (accessed July 19, 2009).

[171] See ibid.

[172] http://www.sphereproject.org (accessed July 19, 2009).

[173] Ibid.

[174] Sphere is based on: (a) International Humanitarian, Human Rights, and Refugee law; and (b) The Code of Conduct: Principles of Conduct for the International Red Cross and Red Crescent Movement and NGOs in Disaster Response Programmes. The Sphere Project, "Sphere in Brief," www.sphereproject.org/content/view/229/232 (accessed July 19, 2009).

4.10. *World Alliance for Citizen Participation (CIVICUS) International Non-Governmental Organizations Accountability Charter*

In June 2006, World Alliance for Citizen Participation (CIVICUS) and ten other International NGOs launched the voluntary *International Non-Governmental Organizations Accountability Charter*, "publicly outlining their collective commitments to uphold the highest standards of professional and moral conduct".[175] CIVICUS sought to enhance NGO legitimacy, transparency and accountability, and lead by example. Charter signatories pledged to apply the Charter's provisions to all its policies, operations and programs, and it published a report outlining its level of compliance and intended steps to comply.[176]

The CIVICUS Civil Society Index (CSI) is a participatory needs assessment and action planning tool for global civil society, at the national level, aimed at creating a knowledge base and momentum for civil society strengthening initiatives.[177] The CSI seeks information about the state of civil society in a country, disseminates that information broadly to stakeholders (including government, donors, academics and the public at large), and seeks to enhance NGO capacity and sustainability and strengthen NGOs' contribution to positive social change.[178] CIVICUS also launched the International Advocacy Non-Governmental Organizations (IANGO) Workshop, in which IANGO leaders engage in reflection, learning and strategic thinking on accountability, transparency and other issues.[179] Other regulatory mechanisms include the Global Reporting Initiative (GRI), the NGO Sector Supplement, and the GRI Sustainability Reporting Guidelines.[180]

---

[175] See CIVICUS: World Alliance for Citizen Participation, "International Non-Governmental Organizations Accountability Charter, First Annual Compliance Report," June 2006-June 2007, 3, http://civilsociety.developmentgateway.org/uploads/media/civilsociety/CIVICUS%20INGOs%20Accountability%20Charter_%20Compliance%20Report.pdf (accessed July 19, 2009).

[176] Ibid. In June 2007, "Charter signatories agreed to work with the Global Reporting Initiative in the development of an NGO Sector Supplement, against which indicators signatories will report in the future." Ibid., 3. CIVICUS stated that it was "committed to complying with any external reporting requirements agreed-upon by Charter Signatories," and that it would "continue to strengthen its internal systems of accountability and reporting as it seeks to surpass the minimum external requirements and become a civil society leader in promoting the responsibilities of civil society organizations towards their different stakeholders." Ibid.

[177] Ibid., 8–10.

[178] Ibid.

[179] Ibid., 10, 11.

[180] Ibid., 3, 12.

4.11. *World Association of Non-Governmental Organizations (WANGO) Code of Ethics and Conduct for NGOs*

The World Association of Non-Governmental Organizations (WANGO), which is an international organization founded in 2000 by international NGOs and others,[181] seeks to unite NGOs worldwide to advance the human rights of peace and global well being. It "helps to provide the mechanism and support needed for NGOs to connect, partner, share, inspire, and multiply their contributions to solve humanity's basic problems."[182]

WANGO at its 2002 Annual Meeting in Washington DC initiated its Code of Ethics Project and appointed a committee to develop an NGO Draft Code of Conduct.[183] In March 2004, a preliminary draft was circulated, and in March 2005, after two and one half years of work, the current *WANGO Code of Ethics and Conduct for NGOs* was completed.[184] The Guiding Principles of the WANGO Code are: responsibility, service and public mindedness; cooperation

---

181 See World Association of Non-Governmental Organizations (WANGO), "About WANGO," http://www.wango.org/about.aspx (accessed July 19, 2009). The WANGO website provides:

> Concerned with universal values shared across the barriers of politics, culture, religion, race and ethnicity, the founding organizations and individuals envisioned an organization that would enable NGOs to work in partnership across those barriers, thereby weaving a selfless social fabric essential to establishing a worldwide culture of peace. By optimizing resources and sharing vital information, WANGO provides a means for NGOs to become more effective in completing their vital tasks.

Ibid.

182 Ibid.

183 World Association of Non-Governmental Organizations (WANGO), "Code of Ethics," http://www.wango.org/codeofethics.aspx (accessed July 19, 2009).

184 Ibid., (noting that the Code "remains an evolving work, which will be revised as necessary."). The Preface to the WANGO Code notes that in formulating the Code, numerous standards and codes of conduct and ethics from NGOs and NGO associations worldwide were consulted including the following: Association of Fundraising Professionals' *Code of Ethical Principles and Standards of Professional Practice*; Australian Council for Overseas Aid's (ACFOA) *Code of Conduct*; BBB Wise Giving Alliance's *Standards for Charity Accountability*; the *Code of Conduct for The International Red Cross and Red Crescent Movement and Non-Governmental Organizations in Disaster Relief*; the *Code of Conduct for NGOs (Earth Summit, 1992)*; the *Code of Conduct for NGOs in Ethiopia*; International Committee on Fundraising Organizations' (ICFO) *International Standards*; Maryland Association of Nonprofit Organizations' *Standards for Excellence: An Ethics and Accountability Code for the Nonprofit Sector*; Minnesota Council of Nonprofits' *Principles and Practices for Nonprofit Excellence; NGO Code of Conduct (Botswana); People in Aid's Code of Good Practice*; Star Kampuchea's *Code of Ethics: Goal, Mission and Roles of NGOs and POS*; and Transparency International's *Statement of Vision, Values and Guiding Principles*. World Association of Non-Governmental Organizations (WANGO), "Code of Ethics – Preface," http://www.wango.org/codeofethics.aspx?page=1 (accessed July 19, 2009).

beyond borders; human rights and dignity; religious freedom; transparency and accountability; and truthfulness and legality.[185]

4.12. *European Commission NGO Code of Conduct*

On July 22, 2005, the European Commission published a Draft Code of Conduct[186] which it stated would help prevent NGOs from being exploited for financing terrorism and other crimes of abuse. The Commission suggested that the voluntary Code would help protect NGOs, strengthen donor integrity and confidence, and promote high standards of transparency and accountability.[187] The Code was for NGOs working in the European Union that "engage in the raising and/or disbursing funds for charitable, religious, cultural, educational, social or fraternal purposes, or for the carrying out of other types of good works."[188] The Code required, *inter alia*, that NGOs prepare and maintain specific records (e.g., annual financial statements and annual reports), maintain audit trails of funds, and follow the "Know your beneficiaries, donors and associate" NGO rule, meaning that the NGO "should make best endeavours to verify the identity, credentials and good faith of their beneficiaries, donors and associate" NGOs.[189] The European Commission suggested that following these guidelines would "constitute a tool for [NGOs] to maintain public trust, to enhance credibility of their indispensable work and at the same time establish a framework for public authorities to identify and trace misuse of [NGOs] for terrorist financing and other criminal abuse".[190]

---

185 http://www.wango.org/codeofethics.aspx?page=2 (accessed July 19, 2009).

186 The discussion paper was titled "Draft Recommendations to Member States Regarding a Code of Conduct for Non-Profit Organisations to Promote Transparency and Accountability Best Practices." European Commission, Directorate-General for Justice, Freedom and Security, (July 22, 2005), European Commission Document No. JLS/D2/DB/NSK D(2005) 8208, http://ec.europa.eu/justice_home/news/consulting_public/code_conduct_npo/draft_recommendations_en.pdf (accessed July 20, 2009). However, the "discussion paper [was] drafted on the basis of preliminary consultations and does not reflect any official position of the European Commission." Ibid., 1.

187 Ibid. The European Commission stated that the Draft Code of Conduct "also responds to requests from EU Member State Governments and international bodies." Ibid. (citation omitted).

188 Ibid. (citation omitted) The European Commission refers to these NGOs as "NPOs" (Non-Profit Organisations). Ibid.

189 Ibid., 5.

190 Ibid., 4.

5. *Conclusion*

This chapter has shown that human rights NGOs – as defined herein as private, independent, non-profit, groups not founded by or controlled by a government, that have as a goal the promotion and protection of internationally recognized human rights – share common characteristics that help render them effective at carrying out their respective missions. Although sixty years have passed since the Universal Declaration of Human Rights was promulgated, and although scholars and practitioners still cannot agree on how to define or categorize human rights NGOs, it remains undisputed that successful, effective human rights NGOs play an instrumental role in helping to eradicate human rights abuses in every corner of the globe. Stakeholders at all levels rely on human rights NGOs, whether those NGOs possess the critical attributes discussed in this chapter, or whether they adhere to specific NGO Codes of Conduct, which themselves invariably incorporate the attributes. It is unfortunate that some human rights NGOs fail, but it is encouraging that many more human rights NGOs succeed, at least in part because of the attributes. The ten attributes identified and analyzed herein appear in successful human rights NGOs, whether they are small, one-volunteer, low-budget, locally-focused entities, or whether they are large, international groups with multi-million dollar operation budgets with staff and operations spread around the globe. These successful, effective human rights NGOs can and should be models for all human rights advocates and defenders.

Bibliography

Adair, Anthony. "Codes of Conduct are good for NGOs too." *IPA Review* (March, 1999): 26–27 (*available at* http://www.ipa.org.au/library/review51-1%20Codes%20of%20Conduct%20are%20good%20for%20NGOs%20too.pdf).

African Charter on Human and Peoples' Rights. June 27, 1981, 21 I.L.M. 58 (1982). http://www.achpr.org/english/_info/charter_en.html (accessed July 20, 2009).

Agency Coordinating Body for Afghan Relief. "Code of Conduct for NGOs Engaged in Humanitarian Action, Reconstruction, and Development in Afghanistan" http://www.acbar.org/downloads/Code%20of%20Conduct_English%20Version.pdf (accessed July 19, 2009).

Alston, Philip. "The 'Not-a-Cat' Syndrome: Can the International Human Rights Regime Accommodate Non-State Actors?" In *Non-State Actors And Human Rights*, edited by Philip Alston. New York: Oxford University Press, 2005.

American Convention on Human Rights, November 22, 1969, O.A.S.T.S. No. 36. http://www.hrcr.org/docs/American_Convention/oashr.html (July 20, 2009).

Annan, Kofi. "Without Vital Role of NGOs, World Could Hardly Respond to Myriad Crises, UN Secretary-General Annan Tells DPI/NGO Conference." U.N. Doc SG/SM/10085, NGO/582, PI/1674 (September 9, 2005) http://www.un.org/News/Press/docs/2005/sgsm10085.doc.htm (accessed July 16, 2009).

Anti-Slavery International. "Introduction to Anti-Slavery: Anti-Slavery International Today." http://www.antislavery.org/english/what_we_do/antislavery_international_today/antislavery_international_today.aspx (accessed July 20, 2009).

Australian Council for International Development (ACFID). "ACFID Code of Conduct for Non Governmental Development Organisations." Amended October 5, 2004, http://www.acfid.asn.au/code-of-conduct/docs/code.pdf (accessed July 20, 2009).

——. "Code of Conduct Guidance Document." (December, 2008). http://plone.acfid.asn.au/code-of-conduct/docs/guidance/12.08_full_doc.pdf (accessed July 20, 2009).

——. "Review of the content of the Code of Conduct." http://plone.acfid.asn.au/code-of-conduct/review (accessed June 13, 2009).

Australian Human Rights Centre. "About AHRC." *University of New South Wales, The Faculty of Law.* http://www.ahrcentre.org/ (accessed July 20, 2009).

Baehr, Peter R. "Mobilization of the Conscience of Mankind: Conditions of Effectiveness of Human Rights NGOs." Paper presented at the UNU Public Forum on Human Rights and NGOs, United Nations University, Tokyo, Japan, September 18, 1996. www.gdrc.org/ngo/lecture14.html (accessed July 20, 2009).

Baker, Peter and Charlie Savage. "In Clinton List, a Veil Is Lifted on Foundation." *New York Times*, December 18, 2008, http://www.nytimes.com/2008/12/19/us/politics/w19clinton.html (accessed July 19, 2009).

Baker, Peter and Helene Cooper. "Clinton Vetting Includes Look at Mr. Clinton." *New York Times*, November 17, 2008, A1. http://www.nytimes.com/2008/11/17/us/politics/17memo.html?_r=1&partner=%20rss&emc=rss&page%20wanted=all (accessed July 19, 2009).

Ban, Ki-Moon. "Secretary-General's Video Message For Historic Paris DPI/NGO Conference Stresses Duty To Ensure That Human Rights Are Living Reality." Transcript of video message to the 61st UN Department of Public Information-NGO Conference, Paris, France, UN Doc. SG/SM/11774, NGO/650, PI/1850, September 3, 2008. http://www.un.org/News/Press/docs/2008/sgsm11774.doc.htm (accessed July 16, 2009).

Bernhardt, Rudolf, ed. *Encyclopedia of Public International Law.* Amsterdam: North-Holland, 1986.

Birkner, Gabrielle and Anthony Weiss. "Madoff Arrest Send Shockwaves Through Jewish Philanthropy." *Forward: The Jewish Daily*, December 12, 2008. http://www.forward.com/articles/14725/ (accessed July 20, 2009).

Blitt, Robert Charles. "Who Will Watch the Watchdogs? Human Rights Nongovernmental Organization and the Case for Regulation." *Buffalo Human Rights Law Review* 10 (2004): 261–398.

Bloem, Renate, Isolda Agazzi, and Philippe Dam. "The Story of Strengthening Civil Society Engagement with the United Nations." Paper presented for the Conference of NGOs (CONGO). http://www.ngocongo.org/files/story_of_congo.doc (accessed July 17, 2009).

Blundell, Arthur G. "Conflict Timber and Liberia's War." European Tropical Forest Research News 43–44: 32 (2005).

Boisson de Chazournes, Laurence and Philippe Sands, eds. *International Law, The International Court of Justice and Nuclear Weapons.* Cambridge: Cambridge University Press, 1999.

Boutros-Ghali, Boutros. "General Review of Arrangements for Consultations with Non-governmental Organizations – Report of the Secretary-General." E/AC.70/1994/5 (May 26, 1994), para. 40.

Buffalo Human Rights Center. "Homepage." http://wings.buffalo.edu/law/BHRC.

Bunn, Isabella D. "Global Advocacy for Corporate Accountability: Transatlantic Perspectives From The NGO Community." *American University International Law Review* 19 (2004): 1265–1306.

Bustelo, Mara R. "The Committee on the Elimination of Discrimination Against Women at the Crossroads." In *The Future of UN Human Rights Treaty Monitoring*, edited by Philip Alston and James Crawford, 79–107. Cambridge University Press, 2000.

Carrillo, Arturo J. "Bringing International Law Home: The Innovative Role of Human Rights Clinics in the Transnational Legal Process." *Columbia Human Rights Law Review* 35 (2004): 527–587.

Caucus of Development NGO Networks (CODE-NGO). "About Us." http://www.code-ngo.net (accessed July 19, 2009).

——. "Covenant on Philippine Development and the Code of Conduct." (1991). http://www.code-ngo.net/Covenant.pdf (accessed July 19, 2009).

Centre for Civil Society. "MSc Management of Non-Governmental Organisations." *London School of Economics and Political Science.* http://www.lse.ac.uk/collections/CCS/study/msc_devel_countries.htm (accessed July 19, 2009).
Center for Reproductive Rights, The. "Breaking the Silence: The Global Gag Rule's Impact on Unsafe Abortion." (2003). http://reproductiverights.org/sites/default/files/documents/bo_ggr.pdf (accessed July 20, 2009).
Center for Reproductive Rights, The. "Myths and Realities: Debunking USAID's Analysis of the Global Gag Rule." (January 15, 2009). http://reproductiverights.org/en/document/myths-and-realities-debunking-usaid%E2%80%99s-analysis-of-the-global-gag-rule (accessed July 19, 2009).
Charnovitz, Steve. "Nongovernmental Organizations and International Law." *The American Journal of International Law* 100 (2006): 348–372.
Charter of the United Nations and Statute of the International Court of Justice. United Nations Publications, 1985, U.N. Sales No. DPI511 http://www.un.org/en/documents/charter/(accessed July 20, 2009).
CIVICUS: World Alliance for Citizen Participation. *International Non-Governmental Organizations Accountability Charter, First Annual Compliance Report, June 2006-June 2007.* http://civilsociety.developmentgateway.org/uploads/media/civilsociety/CIVICUS%20INGOs%20Accountability%20Charter_%20Compliance%20Report.pdf (accessed July 19, 2009).
Coalition for the International Criminal Court. "Homepage". http://www.iccnow.org/?mod=coalition (accessed July 19, 2009).
Cohen, Noam. "Twitter on the Barricades: Six Lessons Learned." *New York Times,* June 20, 2009. http:/www.nytimes.com/2009/06/21/weekinreview/21cohenweb.html (accessed July 20, 2009).
Columbia Law School. "Human Rights Institute." www.law.columbia.edu/center_program/human_rights (accessed June 14, 2009).
Compa, Lance A. and Tashia Hinchliffe-Darricarrère. "Enforcing International Labor Rights through Corporate Codes of Conduct." *Columbia Journal of Transnational Law* 33 (1995): 663–689.
Conference of NGOs in Consultative Relationship with the United Nations (CONGO). "About CONGO." http://www.ngocongo.org/index.php?what=about (accessed July 19, 2009).
Convention on International Trade in Endangered Species of Wild Fauna and Flora. (March 3, 1973) 993 U.N.T.S. 243,12 I.L.M. 1085. http://www.cites.org/eng/disc/text.shtml#top (accessed July 20, 2009); http://www.cites.org/eng/disc/what.shtml (accessed July 20, 2009).
Council of Europe. *European Convention on the Recognition of the Legal Personality of International Non-Governmental Organisations.* European Treaty Series, No. 142 (April 24, 1986): 1–5.
Crook, John R. "Current Developments: The Fifty-First Session of the U.N. Commission on Human Rights." *American Journal of International Law* 90 (1996): 126–138.
Derechos: Human Rights Listings. "Social Networking Intern." Posted on April 22, 2008. http://www.humanrightsblog.org/listings/2008/04/social_networking_intern.html (accessed July 20, 2009).
EJewishPhilanthropy: The Jewish Philanthropy Blog. "Chais Family Foundation Closes." Posted on December 15, 2008. http://ejewishphilanthropy.com/chais-family-foundation-closes/ (accessed July 20, 2009).
Ekern, Stener. "Saving the Forest Through Human Rights: Indigenous Rights and Ethnic Tension in Guatemala." *International Journal on Minority and Group Rights,* 13, no. 2–3 (2006): 171–186.
Equality Now. "Ethiopia: Proposed New Law Threatens to Shut Down Non-Governmental Organizations." December 2008. http://www.equalitynow.org/english/actions/action_2205_en.html (accessed July 20, 2009).
Esfandiari, Golnaz. "Iran: Growing NGO Community Offers Political Activism Where Government Does Not." *Pars Times: Greater Iran and Beyond,* 2004. http://www.parstimes.com/news/archive/2004/rfe/ngos_activism.html (accessed July 20, 2009).
European Commission, Directorate-General for Justice, Freedom and Security. "Draft Recommendations to Member States Regarding a Code of Conduct for Non-Profit Organisations to Promote Transparency and Accountability Best Practices." (July 22, 2005). *European Commission Document No. JLS/D2/DB/NSK D(2005) 8208.* http://ec.europa.eu/justice_home/

news/consulting_public/code_conduct_npo/draft_recommendations_en.pdf (accessed July 20, 2009).
Ezer, Tamar and Susan Deller Ross. "Fact-Finding as a Lawmaking Tool for Advancing Women's Human Rights." *The Georgetown Journal of Gender and the Law* 7 (2006): 331–342.
Federal Democratic Republic of Ethiopia. "Proclamation to Provide for the Registration and Regulation of Charities and Societies." Proclamation No. 621/2009, *Federal Negarit Gazeta*, No. 25, 4521, February 13, 2009. http://www.crdaethiopia.org/Documents/Charities%20 and%20Socities%20Legislation%20(Final%20Version)-Negarit%20Newspaper.pdf (accessed July 20, 2009).
Filartiga v. Pena-Irala. 630 F.2d 876 (2d Cir. 1980).
Forest Peoples Programme. "Annual Report 2007." http://www.forestpeoples.org/documents/ ann_rep/fpprog_ar_07.pdf (accessed July 18, 2009).
Forsythe, David P. *Human Rights and World Politics*. (2nd ed. Lincoln, Nebraska: University of Nebraska Press, 1989).
Free Dictionary, The. http://www.thefreedictionary.com/competent (accessed July 19, 2009).
Gaer, Felice D. "Reality Check: Human Rights NGOs Confront Governments at the UN." In *NGOs, the UN & Global Governance*, edited by Thomas G. Weiss and Leon Gordenker. Boulder, Colorado: Lynne Rienner Publishers, 1996.
Ghana NGO/CSO Standards Project. "Frequently Asked Questions (FAQs)." http://www.posdev.org/standards/faq_2007_eng.html (accessed July 19, 2009).
Global Witness. "Global Witness Testifies at the Liberian Truth and Reconciliation Commission on the role of national and international timber companies in fuelling Liberia's civil war." February 19, 2009. http://www.globalwitness.org/media_library_detail.php/722/en/ global_witness_testifies_at_the_liberian_truth_and (accessed July 20, 2009).
Goitom, Hanibal. "Ethiopia: New law on charities passed despite objections." *Integrated Regional Information Networks (IRIN)*, January 6, 2009, http://www.loc.gov/lawweb/servlet/lloc_news?disp3_935_text (accessed July 19, 2009); http://www.unhcr.org/refworld/ docid/49670b911a.html (accessed July 18, 2009).
Halliday, F. "The Romance of Non-State Actors." in *Non-State Actors in World Politics*, ed. Daphne Josselin and William Wallace (New York: Palgrave Macmillian Publishers, 2002), 23.
Hartnell, Caroline. "The Philippines: Self-Regulation on Trial." *Alliance Magazine* 8, No. 4, December 2003. http://www.icnl.org/KNOWLEDGE/news/2004/01-09.htm (accessed July 20, 2009).
Harvard Law School Human Rights Program. "Home page." http://www.law.harvard.edu/programs/hrp/(accessed July 20, 2009).
Heap, Simon. "Building Trust in NGOs." *The International Journal for Not-for-Profit Law* 3, Issue 3, 2001. http://www.icnl.org/knowledge/ijnl/vol3iss3/sr_2.htm#_ftn18 (accessed July 20, 2009).
Hill, Tony. "Three Generations of UN-Civil Society Relations: A Quick Sketch." (Background Paper for the Secretary-General's Panel of Eminent Persons on United Nations Relations with Civil Society, remarks by Coordinator, United Nations Non-Governmental Liaison Service).
Hinks, Peter P., John R. McKivigan, and R. Owen Williams. *Encyclopedia of Antislavery and Abolitio*n 58 (Greenwood Press, 2006).
History.com. "First American abolition society founded in Philadelphia." http://www.history. com/this-day-in-history.do?action=Article&id=462 (accessed June 11, 2009).
Hoffman, Stanley H. "Universities and Human Rights." *Human Rights Quarterly* 6, no. 1 (1984): 5–20.
Holguin, Jaime. "Disaster Strikes In Red Cross Backyard: Charity Fails To Get A Grip On Criminal Scandals At Local Chapters." *CBS Evening News*, July 29, 2002. http://www.cbsnews.com/ stories/2002/07/29/eveningnews/main516700.shtml (accessed July 20, 2009).
Hub, The. "About the Hub." http://hub.witness.org/en/AboutHub (accessed July 19, 2009).
Hurwitz, Deena R. "Lawyering for Justice and the Inevitability of International Human Rights Clinics." *The Yale Journal of International Law* 28 (2003): 505–550.
IndiaEdu Organization. "NGO Management Courses." http://www.indiaedu.com/career-courses/ ngo-management (accessed July 19, 2009).

Indiana Coalition Against Domestic Violence and the Resource Center. "Our Mission and Philosophy." http://www.violenceresource.org/mission.htm (accessed July 20, 2009).
Indiana University School of Law – Indianapolis, Program in International Human Rights Law (PIHRL). "United Nations Shadow Reports." www.indylaw.indiana.edu/humanrights/UNshadow.html; http://indylaw.indiana.edu/humanrights/shadowreports/USA%20Sexual%20 Minorities; pdf and http://www.indylaw.indiana.edu/humanrights/UNshadow.html (accessed July 21, 2009).
Integrated Regional Information Networks (IRIN). "Afghanistan: New Code of Conduct to Regulate NGOs." May 31, 2005. http://www.irinnews.org/Report.aspx?ReportID=28641 (accessed July 20, 2009).
InterAction Organization. "Mission Statement." Revised edition March 2007, http://www.interaction.org/files.cgi/6014_PVOStandardsMarch2007.pdf#page=5 (accessed July 19, 2009).
——. "PVO Standards – About Us." http://www.interaction.org/pvostandards (accessed July 19, 2009).
International Campaign to Ban Landmines, The. "About Us." http://www.icbl.org/index.php/icbl/About-Us (accessed July 19, 2009).
International Center for Not-for-Profit Law. "Recent Laws and Legislative Proposals to Restrict Civil Society and Civil Society Organizations." *The International Journal for Not-for-Profit Law, Volume 8, Issue 4* (August 2006). www.icnl.org/knowlege/ijnl/vol8iss4/art_1.htm (accessed July 21, 2009).
International Covenant on Civil and Political Rights. G.A. Res. 2200A (XXI), art. 17, adopted and opened for signature, ratification and accession, December 16, 1966, U.N. Doc. A/6316 (1966), entry into force March 23, 1976. http://www.unhchr.ch/html/menu3/b/a_ccpr.htm (accessed July 20, 2009).
International Covenant on Economic, Social and Cultural Rights. G.A. Res. 2200A (XXI), adopted and opened for signature, ratification and accession, December 16, 1966, U.N. Doc. A/6316 (1966), entry into force January 3, 1976. http://www.unhchr.ch/html/menu3/b/a_cescr.htm (accessed July 20, 2009).
International Foundation for the Protection of Human Rights Defenders. http://www.frontlinedefenders.org/about/frontline (accessed July 18, 2009).
International Human Rights Law Institute. "About Us." *DePaul University College of Law.* http://www.law.depaul.edu/centers_institutes/ihrli/about_us (accessed July 20, 2009).
Iriye, Akira. *Global Community: The Role of International Organizations in the Making of the Contemporary World.* Berkeley: University of California Press, 2002.
Karzon, Hafizur Rahman. "Human rights and non-state actors." *The Daily Star*, February 4, 2006, Issue 225. http://www.thedailystar.net/law/2006/02/01/index.htm (accessed July 20, 2009).
Keeney, Gavin. "The Unbearable Lightness of NGOs." *CounterPunch.* May 24, 2002. http://www.counterpunch.org/keeney0525.html (accessed July 16, 2009).
Kimberley Process. "What is the Kimberley Process?" http://www.kimberleyprocess.com/home/index_en.html (accessed July 18, 2009).
Kooijmans, Pieter H. "The Nongovernmental Organizations and the Monitoring Activities of the United Nations in the Field of Human Right." In *The Role of Non-Governmental Organizations in the Protection of Human Rights, Symposium International Commission of Jurists* (1990): 15–22.
Korey, William. *NGOs and the Universal Declaration of Human Rights: "A Curious Grapevine."* New York: St. Martin's Press, 1998.
Lieber, Francis. *On Civil Liberty and Self-Government.* Enlarged edition. Philadelphia: J. B. Lippincott and Company, 1859.
Lokshina, Tanya. "NGO and Academia – A Liaison Between Amateurs and Professionals." Presentation text for the GSC Fellows' Conference – by the Moscow Helsinki Group, September 2002. http://programs.ssrc.org/gsc/gsc_activities/lokshina.
Lord, Janet E. "NGO Participation in Human Rights Law and Process: Latest Development in the Effort to Develop an International Treaty on the Rights of People with Disabilities." *ILSA Journal of International and Comparative Law* 10 (2004): 311–318.
Massing, Michael. "Blind Spot: seeing Iraq through Uncle Sam's eyes." Columbia Journalism Review 43.3 (September-October 2008): 14.

McChesny, Allan. "Protecting the Rights of all Human Rights Defenders." *The Review (International Commission of Jurists)* Vol. 55 (December 1995): 39–57.
McDougall, Gay J. "A Decade in Human Rights Law: Decade of NGO Struggle." *Human Rights Brief* 11 (2004): 12–15.
——. "The Durban Racism Conference Revisited: The World Conference Against Racism: Through a Wider Lens." *Fletcher Forum of World Affairs* 26 (2002): 135–149.
McLeary, Paul. "Why Jon Lee Anderson Doesn't Like Embedding: The too-close-to-the-troops notion is flimsy." *Columbia Journalism Review* (Oct. 2007), http://www.cjr.org/behind_the_news/post_63.php (accessed July 19, 2009).
Merriam Webster's Online Dictionary. "Component." http://www.merriam-webster.com/dictionary/component (accessed July 19, 2009).
Moralez, Cheryl K. "Seizing the Opportunity: Participation in the Fifth Periodic Report of the Hong Kong Special Administrative Region before the U.N. Human Rights Committee." *DePaul International Law Journal* 4 (2000): 175–181.
MoveOn.org Civic Action. "About the MoveOn Family of Organizations." http://www.moveon.org/about.html (accessed July 19, 2009).
Mullerat, Ramon. "The Need For Codes of Conduct in NGOs: The Experience of the Legal Profession." Paper presented at the American Bar Association Section of International Law, Washington, D.C., April 15, 2005. http://www.abanet.org/intlaw/calendar/spring2005/papers/31.09.doc (accessed July 19, 2009).
Mutua, Makau wa. "Book Review: Claude E. Welch, Protecting Human Rights in Africa: Strategies and Roles of Non-Governmental Organizations." *Michigan Journal of International Law* 17 (1996): 591–613.
Nanda, Ved P. "The Human Rights Era at Fifty: Looking Back and Looking Forward." *Willamette Journal of International Law and Dispute Resolution* 5 (1997): 69–86.
NetSquared. "NetSquared's Goals: What are the Goals of NetSquared?" http://www.netsquared.org/about/netsquareds-goals (accessed July 19, 2009).
NGO Code of Conduct for NGOs in Ethiopia, (available on website of *Christian Relief and Development Association (CRDA))*, March 1999, http://www.crdaethiopia.org/Code%20of%20Conduct/CoC.Final.pdf.
NGO Coordination Committee in Iraq (NCCI). "Code of Conduct." Principle # 4, 3, http://www.ncciraq.org/IMG/pdf/NCCI_Charter_English_Sept05.pdf (accessed July 19, 2009)
——. "NCCI Charter – Code of Conduct." http://www.ncciraq.org/IMG/pdf/NCCI_Charter_English_Sept05.pdf (accessed June 13, 2009).
NGO Management School Switzerland. "Course Programme Courses." http://www.ngoms.org/courses.htm (accessed July 19, 2009).
Nobel Foundation. "All Nobel Peace Prize Laureates." *Nobelprize.com* http://nobelprize.org/nobel_prizes/peace/laureates/index.html (accessed July 19, 2009).
Obama, Barack. "Statement of President-elect Obama on Human Rights Day." *Change.gov*, December 10, 2008, http://change.gov/newsroom/entry/statement_of_president_elect_obama_on_human_rights_day (accessed July 19, 2009).
Olz, Martin A. "Non-governmental Organizations in Regional Human Rights Systems." *Columbia Human Rights Law Review* 28 (1997): 307–74.
Optional Protocol to the Convention on the Elimination of Discrimination against Women. http://www2.ohchr.org/english/law/cedaw-one.htm (accessed June 14, 2009).
Ovsiovitch, Jay S. "Feeding the Watchdogs: Philanthropic Support for Human Rights NGOs." *Buffalo Human Rights Law Review* 4 (1998): 341–363.
Pace, William R. "Civil Society Participation in the International Criminal Court: NGOs Advocacy for a Fair, Independent, and Effective ICC from Rome to Today." Contribution to *HURIDOCS Conference 'Human Rights Council and International Criminal Court: The New Challenges for Human Rights Communications.'* February 25–27, 2009, Geneva. www.huridocs.org/involved/conference/presentations/Pace.doc (accessed July 19, 2009).
Pariser, Eli. "MoveOn.org Civic Action." December 29, 2008 (e-mail from E. Pariser to G. Edwards on file with author).
Philippine Council for NGO Certification (PNCP). "About Us." http://www.pcnc.com.ph/aboutUs.php (accessed July 19, 2009).

Population Action International. "Access Denied – U.S. Restrictions on International Family Planning." January 3, 2005. http://www.populationaction.org/globalgagrule/Summary.shtml (accessed July 20, 2009).
Prodi, Romano and Neil Kinnock. "The Commission and Non-Governmental Organisations: Building a Stronger Partnership." Commission of the European Communities Paper, COM(2000) 11 Final (January 2000). http://eur-lex.europa.eu/LexUriServ/LexUriServ.do?uri=COM:2000:0011:FIN:EN:PDF (accessed July 20, 2009).
Quigley, Fran. "Growing Political Will From the Grassroots: How Social Movement Principles Can Reverse the Dismal Legacy of Rule of Law Interventions." Columbia Human Rights Law Review 41.1 (Forthcoming 2009, on file with author).
Rudasil, Lynne M. "NGO, Information Flow and Nation: An Exploration in Relationships." Presented at World Library and Information Congress: 70th IFLA General Conference and Council, Buenos Aires, Argentina, August 26, 2004. http://archive.ifla.org/IV/ifla70/papers/079e-Rudasil.pdf (accessed July 20, 2009).
Samuel, John. "Civil Society in an Uncivil World." *Pambazuka News*, Issue 324, October 18, 2007. http://www.pambazuka.org/en/category/comment/43788 (accessed July 20, 2009).
Saramaka People v. Suriname. Inter-American Court of Human Rights. (November 28, 2007), http://www.corteidh.or.cr/docs/casos/articulos/seriec_172_ing.pdf (accessed July 18, 2009); http://www.forestpeoples.org/documents/ann_rep/fpprog_ar_07.pdf 4 (accessed July 18, 2009).
Schindler, Paul. "Tammy Baldwin Withholds Name From ENDA Stripped of Trans Protections." *Gay City News*, September 28, 2007. http://www.thetaskforce.org/TF_in_news/07_1009/stories/12_tammy_baldwin_withholds_name.pdf (accessed July 19, 2009).
Secretary-General of the United Nations. "Arrangements and practices for the interaction of non-governmental organizations in all activities of the United Nations system." U.N. Doc. A/53/170 (1998). http://www.un.org/documents/ga/docs/53/plenary/a53-170.htm (accessed July 20, 2009).
——. "Report of the Secretary-General in response to the report of the Panel of Eminent Persons on United Nations-Civil Society Relations." U.N. Doc. A/59/354 (2004), paras. 10, 14 http://www.undg.org/archive_docs/5244-SG_s_Response_to_the_Report_of_the_Panel_of_Eminent_Persons_on_UN-Civil_Society_Relations.doc (accessed July 17, 2009).
——. "Views of the Member States, members of the specialized agencies, observers, intergovernmental and non-governmental organizations from all regions on the report of the Secretary-General on arrangements and practices for the interaction of non-governmental organizations in all activities of the United Nations system." U.N. Doc. A/54/329 (1999). http://www.un-ngls.org/orf/UN-SG%20report-1999.doc (accessed July 20, 2009).
Seevers, Rachael E. "The Politics of Gagging: The Effects of the Global Gag Rule on Democratic Participation and Political Advocacy in Peru." *Brooklyn Journal of International Law* 31 (2006): 866–935.
Seymour, Frances. "Forests, Climate Change, and Human Rights: Managing Risk and Trade-offs." *Center for International Forestry Research*, October 2008. http://rightsandclimatechange.files.wordpress.com/2008/10/seymour-forests-cc-hr-0810021.pdf (accessed July 20, 2009).
Shea, Catherine and Sandra Sitar, Report and Recommendations – NGO Accreditation and Certification: The Way Forward? An Evaluation of the Development Community's Experience http://www.usaid.gov/our_work/cross-cutting_programs/private_voluntary_cooperation/conf_icnl.pdf (accessed July 19, 2009).
Skocpol, Theda. "What Tocqueville Missed: Government made all that 'volunteerism' possible." *Slate*, November 15, 1996. http://www.slate.com/id/2081 (accessed July 20, 2009).
Skuster, Patty. "Advocacy in Whispers: The Impact of the USAID Global Gag Rule Upon Free Speech and Free Association in the Context of Abortion Law Reform in Three East African Countries." *Michigan Journal of Gender and Law* 11 (2004): 97–126. http://www.reproductiverights.org/pdf/pub_art_skuster.pdf (accessed July 20, 2009).
South African NGO Coalition (SANGOCO). "Code of Ethics." http://www.sangoco.org.za/site/index.php?option=content&task=view&id=8&Itemid=30 (accessed July 19, 2009).
Sphere Project. "Sphere in Brief." http://www.sphereproject.org/content/view/229/232 (accessed July 19, 2009).

Spiro, Peter J. "NGOs and Human Rights: Channels of Power." In *Research Handbook on Human Rights*. Edward Elgar Publishing, forthcoming 2009. http://ssrn.com/abstract=1324971 (accessed July 20, 2009).

Stein, Rob and Michael Shear. "Funding Restored to Groups That Perform Abortions, Other Care." *Washington Post*, January 24, 2009, A03. http://www.washingtonpost.com/wp-dyn/content/article/2009/01/23/AR2009012302814.html (accessed July 20, 2009).

Steiner, Henry J. and Mann, Jonathan. "International Human Rights and the University." Reprinted in *Symposium, Human Rights at Harvard: Interdisciplinary Faculty Perspectives on the Human Rights Movement*. Cambridge, MA: The Committee, 1995.

Then, Stephen. "Logging, land clearing caused mass fish deaths in S'wak." *The Star Malaysia*, February 20, 2009. http://thestar.com.my/news/story.asp?file=/2009/2/20/nation/20090220143652&sec=nation (accessed July 20, 2009).

Tocqueville, Alexis de. *Democracy in America*. Translated by George Lawrence. J.P Mayer and Max Lerner. Eds. (New York: Harper & Row, 1966).

Tolley, Howard B. Jr. *The International Commission of Jurists: Global Advocates for Human Rights*. Philadelphia: University of Pennsylvania Press, 1994.

Tse, Tomoeh Murakami, *Madoff Sentenced to 150 Years: Calling Ponzi Scheme 'Evil,' Judge Orders Maximum Term*, www.washingtonpost.com/wp-dyn/content/article/2009/06/29/AR2009062902015.html (accessed July 19, 2009).

United Nations Ad Hoc Committee on a Comprehensive and Integral International Convention on Protection and Promotion of the Rights and Dignity of Persons with Disabilities. "Decision on the modalities of the participation of accredited non-governmental organizations in the Ad Hoc Committee to consider proposals for a comprehensive and integral international convention to promote and protect the rights and dignity of persons with disabilities." August 2, 2002. http://www.unhchr.ch/disability/decparticipationNGOs.doc (accessed July 19, 2009).

United Nations Conference on Environment and Development. *Agenda 21 – Rio Declaration on Environment and Development*. United Nations Doc. A/CONF.151/26 (1992), UN Sales No. E.93.I.11 http://www.un.org/esa/sustdev/documents/agenda21/index.htm (accessed July 21, 2009).

United Nations Convention Against Torture and Other Cruel, Inhuman or Degrading Treatment or Punishment (December 10, 1984). U.N. Doc. A/RES/39/46 (1984). http://www.un.org/documents/ga/res/39/a39r046.htm (accessed July 20, 2009).

United Nations Department of Economic and Social Affairs. "Agenda 21: Chapter 23 – Strengthening the Role of Major Groups." http://www.un.org/esa/sustdev/documents/agenda21/english/agenda21chapter23.htm (accessed July 18, 2009).

——. "NGO related Questions and Answers." http://esa.un.org/coordination/ngo/new/index.asp?page=faqs (accessed June 12, 2009).

——. "Non-Governmental Organizations Branch." http://www.un.org/esa/coordination/ngo/ (accessed July 17, 2009).

United Nations Development Programme. "UNDP and civil society organizations." http://www.undp.org/partners/cso (accessed July 19, 2009).

United Nations Economic and Social Council. "Resolution 1296 (XLIV)." *Arrangements for Consultation with Non-Governmental Organizations*. May 23, 1968, U.N. Doc. E/RES/1968/1296 (1968). http://www.un-documents.net/1296.htm (accessed July 20, 2009).

——. "Resolution 1996/31." *Consultative Relationship Between The United Nations And Non-governmental Organizations*, (July 25, 1996), U.N. Doc. E/1996/31 (1996). http://www.un.org/documents/ecosoc/res/1996/eres1996-31.htm (accessed July 20, 2009).

——. "Resolution 2000/35." *Resolution and Decisions of the Economic and Social Council*. U.N. Doc. E/2000/99 (2000). http://www.un.org/esa/forests/pdf/2000_35_E.pdf (July 18, 2009).

United Nations Economic Committee. *The Nature of States Parties Obligations – CESCR General Comment 3*, December 14, 1990. http://www.unhchr.ch/tbs/doc.nsf/(symbol)/CESCR+General+comment+3.En?OpenDocument) (accessed July 20, 2009).

United Nations Educational, Scientific and Cultural Organization (UNESCO). "Conclusions: The Increasing Role and Importance of Human Rights NGOs." www.unesco.de/c_humanrights/V.php (accessed July 21, 2009).

United Nations Forum on Forests (UNFF). "About UNFF." http://www.un.org/esa/forests/about.html (accessed July 18, 2009).

——. "Participation of Major Groups." http://www.un.org/esa/forests/participation.html#1 (accessed July 18, 2009).

——. "UNFF Major Group Focal Points." http://www.un.org/esa/forests/contacts-major_groups.html (accessed July 18, 2009).

United Nations General Assembly. *Accreditation and participation of non-governmental organizations in the Ad Hoc Committee on a Comprehensive and Integral International Convention on Protection and Promotion of the Rights and Dignity of Persons with Disabilities* (July 26, 2002). U.N. Doc. A/RES/56/510 (2002). http://daccessdds.un.org/doc/UNDOC/GEN/N02/495/75/PDF/N0249575.pdf?OpenElement (accessed July 19, 2009).

——. *Declaration on the Right and Responsibility of Individuals, Groups and Organs of Society to Promote and Protect Universally Recognized Human Rights and Fundamental Freedoms.* U.N. Doc. A/RES/53/144 (1999). http://www.unhchr.ch/Huridocda/Huridoca.nsf/(Symbol)/A.RES.53.144.En (accessed July 20, 2009).

——. *Resolution adopted by the General Assembly – Follow up to the outcome of the Millennium Summit* (December 18, 2000). U.N. Doc. A/RES/55/162 (2000). ftp://ftp.fao.org/unfao/bodies/council/cl120/Y0556e2.pdf (accessed July 20, 2009).

——. *Resolution adopted by the General Assembly, United Nations Millennium Declaration* (September 18, 2000). U.N. Doc A/RES/55/2 (2000). http://daccess-ods.un.org/access.nsf/Get?OpenAgent&DS=A/RES/55/2&Lang=E (accessed July 20, 2009).

United Nations Office of the High Commissioner for Human Rights. "Complaint procedures within the United Nations system." Fact Sheet No. 7/Rev.1, Complaints Procedure, http://www2.ohchr.org/english/law/docs/Part_of_FS.No.7.pdf (accessed July 20, 2009).

——. "*Human Rights Bodies.*" http://www.ohchr.org/EN/HRBodies/Pages/HumanRightsBodies.aspx (accessed July 17, 2009).

——. "Human Rights Bodies – Complaints Procedures: Inquiries." http://www2.ohchr.org/english/bodies/petitions/index.htm#inquiry (accessed July 20, 2009).

United Nations Office of the President of the Millennium Assembly. "Reference document on the participation of civil society in United Nations conferences and special sessions of the General Assembly during the 1990s." (August 2001). http://www.un.org/ga/president/55/speech/civilsociety1.htm (accessed July 16, 2009).

United Nations Press. "UN – Civil Society Relations Panel Established." February 13, 2003, http://www.globalpolicy.org/component/content/article/177-un/31845.html (accessed July 17, 2009).

Universal Declaration of Human Rights. G.A. Res. 217A (III), U.N. Doc. A/810 (1948). http://www.un.org/en/documents/udhr/index.shtml (July 20, 2009).

University of Hong Kong, Faculty of Law Centre for Comparative and Public Law. "About the Centre." http://www.hku.hk/ccpl/about_centre/about_centre.html (accessed July 20, 2009).

Vienna Declaration and Programme of Action (July 12, 1993). U.N. Doc. A/CONF.157/23 (1993). http://www.unhchr.ch/huridocda/huridoca.nsf/(Symbol)/A.CONF.157.23.En (accessed July 20, 2009).

Wallis, Ann C. "Data Mining: Lessons from the Kimberley Process for the United Nations' Development of Human Rights Norms for Transnational Corporations." *Northwestern University Journal of International Human Rights* 4 (2005): 388–417.

Welch, Claude E., Jr. "Book Review: NGOs and the Universal Declaration of Human Rights: "A Curious Grapevine." *Human Rights Quarterly* 22.1 (2000): 298–301.

Willetts, Peter. "From 'Consultative Arrangements' to 'Partnership': The Changing Status of NGOs in Diplomacy at the UN." *Global Governance* 6 (2000): 191–212.

William J. Clinton Foundation. "Press Release: William J. Clinton Foundation Publishes Names of All Contributors on Foundation Website." December 18, 2008. http://www.clintonfoundation.org/news/news-media/press-release-william-j-clinton-foundation-publishes-names-of-all-contributors-on-foundation-website (accessed July 20, 2009).

Witness.org. "About WITNESS." http://www.witness.org/index.php?option=com_content&task=view&id=26&Itemid=78 (accessed July 21, 2009).

World Association of Non-Governmental Organizations (WANGO). "About WANGO." http://www.wango.org/about.aspx (accessed July 19, 2009).

——. "Code of Ethics." http://www.wango.org/codeofethics.aspx (accessed July 19, 2009).
——. Preface to *Code of Ethics and Conduct for NGOs*, March 5, 2005. http://www.wango.org/codeofethics.aspx?page=1 (accessed July 20, 2009).
Yaziji, Michael and Jonathan Doh, NGOs and Corporations: Conflict and Collaboration (Cambridge: Cambridge University Press, 2009), https://www.cambridge.org/us/catalogue/catalogue.asp?isbn=9780521866842&ss=exc (accessed July 16, 2009).

Chapter Eight

Do States have an Obligation under International Law to Provide Human Rights Education?

*Paula Gerber**

1. *Introduction*

Prior to 1948, human rights education (HRE) was exclusively a concern of domestic legal and education systems, as human rights were not considered to be an appropriate subject matter for international law. However, the development of the United Nations (UN) and the adoption of the Universal Declaration of Human Rights (UDHR)[1] saw this change, and for the first time HRE was included in an international instrument.

This chapter considers the historical background to HRE becoming part of international human rights law and analyzes what States are required to do in order to comply with international HRE obligations contained in treaties and other instruments. It concludes with a few observations about levels of compliance with international laws pertaining to HRE, and obstacles to the realization of those laws, before closing with some recommendations about how States might increase their adherence to international HRE mandates.

2. *Human Rights Education (HRE) in International Law*

The Preamble to the UNESCO Constitution declares that 'Since wars begin in the minds of men, it is in the minds of men that the defences of peace must be constructed'.[2] It is this philosophy that underpins human rights education, i.e. education about human rights, is one of the best ways of ensuring respect for

---

* Dr Paula Gerber is Deputy Director, Castan Centre for Human Rights Law, and Senior Lecturer, Faculty of Law, Monash University, Australia.

[1] Adopted and proclaimed by General Assembly Resolution 217 A (III) of 10 December 1948.

[2] Constitution of the United Nations Educational, Scientific and Cultural Organization, adopted in London on 16 November 1945.

human rights, and respect for human rights is one of the best ways of ensuring a culture of peace where human rights are respected. Thus, human rights education is akin to preventive medicine, in that it requires States to take proactive measures to stay 'healthy', thereby averting potential human rights crises, such as those witnessed in Kosovo, Darfur and Zimbabwe. Given that one of the main purposes of the UN is to maintain international peace and security,[3] it is not surprising that it has devoted significant efforts to promoting HRE. This section considers five initiatives of the UN to mandate and encourage greater HRE by States, namely:

(i) UDHR;
(ii) International Covenant on Economic Social and Cultural Rights;[4]
(iii) Convention on the Rights of the Child;[5]
(iv) UN Decade for Human Rights Education (1995–2004);[6] and
(v) World Programme for Human Rights Education (2005-ongoing).[7]

There are also provisions in other international instruments relating to HRE,[8] but the above are the most important HRE mandates, hence a detailed analysis of other instruments which refer to HRE is not included in this chapter.

2.1. *UDHR*

The first draft of the UDHR provided that everyone has the right to education, but made no reference to the content of such education.[9] Non-governmental organizations (NGOs) were actively involved in the drafting of the UDHR, and it was an NGO representative who first noted that:

---

[3] Preamble to the United Nations Charter signed at San Francisco on 26 June 1945, entered into force 24 October 1945.

[4] Adopted by General Assembly Resolution 2200A (XXI) on 16 December 1966, entered into force 3 January 1976.

[5] Convention on the Rights of the Child, adopted by General Assembly Resolution 44/25 on 20 November 1989, entered into force 2 September 1990.

[6] Proclaimed by the United Nations General Assembly in Resolution 49/184 on 23 December 1994.

[7] Proclaimed by the United Nations General Assembly in Resolution 59/113 on 10 December 2004.

[8] See for example, Article 10 in Convention on the Elimination of All Forms of Discrimination against Women, adopted by General Assembly Resolution 34/180 on 18 December 1979, entered into force 3 September 1981; Article 7 in Convention on the Elimination of All Forms of Racial Discrimination, adopted by General Assembly Resolution 2106 (XX) on 21 December 1965, entered into force 4 January 1969; and Article 5 in UNESCO Convention Against Discrimination in Education, adopted by the General Conference of the United Nations Educational, Scientific and Cultural Organization on 14 December 1960.

[9] Alex Easterman, a British journalist representing the World Jewish Congress. *United Nations Yearbook on Human Rights for 1947*, Lake Success, 1949, 484.

> The Article on education provided a technical framework but contained nothing about the spirit governing education which was an essential element. Neglect of this principle in Germany had been the main cause of two catastrophic wars.[10]

This view was endorsed by the UNESCO delegate, Pierre Lebar, who added that:

> [In] Germany, under the Hitler regime, education had been admirably organized but had, nevertheless, produced disastrous results. It was absolutely necessary to make clear that education to which everyone was entitled should strengthen respect of the rights set forth in the Declaration and combat the spirit of intolerance.[11]

As a result, the draft UDHR was amended to include Article 26(2) which provides that:

> Education shall be directed to the full development of the human personality and to strengthening of respect for human rights and fundamental freedoms. It shall promote understanding, tolerance and friendship among all nations, racial or religious groups, and shall further the activities of the United Nations for the maintenance of peace.

This language represents the first articulation of HRE in international law, and has become the foundation on which all subsequent proclamations regarding HRE have been built.

2.2. *International Covenant on Economic Social and Cultural Rights*

The UDHR, being a declaration, rather than a treaty, is not strictly speaking binding on States, and thus it was decided that the provisions of the UDHR should be incorporated into legally binding treaties. In the result, Article 26(2) of the UDHR was transformed into Article 13 of the International Covenant on Economic, Social and Cultural Rights (ICESCR). Three minor changes were made to the text, namely

1. The addition of a requirement that HRE include the development of a sense of dignity;
2. The call that individuals should have an education that enables them to participate effectively in a free society; and
3. The inclusion of a reference to ethnic groups, in addition to racial and religious groups.

The reference to dignity in Article 13(1) of ICESCR appears to be a recognition that HRE must make individuals aware of their own inherent worth and

---

[10] SR.8/p.4.

[11] SR.67/p.12.

of the human rights which accrue to them on this basis.[12] The addition of a requirement that education should enable a person to participate effectively in a free society requires that education is not only theoretical, but also practical, that is, HRE should teach students how to satisfy their practical needs in life.[13] Finally, the addition of the word 'ethnic' reflects the fact that discrimination occurs on more grounds than just race and religion, and thus ethnicity needed to be added.[14] Overall, the differences between Article 26(2) of the UDHR and Article 13(1) of ICESCR amount to little more than a 'fleshing out' of the norm relating to HRE.

The Committee on Economic, Social and Cultural Rights (CESCR), is the body of experts charged with monitoring States' compliance with, and implementation of, ICESCR.[15] One of the functions of the CESCR is to publish General Comments which:

> Provide authoritative interpretations of the general wording of the treaty text, thus assisting states parties to understand and fulfill their obligations under the treaties... they play an increasingly important role in promoting a shared understanding of treaty norms and developing agreement about the detail of their content.[16]

Thus, General Comments offer guidance on the interpretation and implementation of treaty provisions. General Comment No. 13[17] relates to Article 13 of ICESCR, and although it predominantly concentrates on the right to education, it does elaborate, to some degree, on the normative content of such education. In particular, it provides that:

> States parties are required to ensure that curricula, for all levels of the educational system, are directed to the objectives identified in article 13(1). They are also obliged to establish and maintain a transparent and effective system which monitors whether or not education is, in fact, directed to the educational objectives set out in article 13(1).[18]

---

[12] Klaus Dieter Beiter, *The Protection of the Right to Education by International Law: Including a Systematic Analysis of Article 13 of the International Covenant on Economic, Social, and Cultural Rights* (Leiden: Martinus Nijhoff Publishers, 2006), 95.

[13] Ibid.

[14] There is little detailed information available about what occurred during the drafting of Article 13 of ICESCR, in particular, who proposed these changes, and why. The leading texts on the drafting of ICESCR and Article 13 are silent when it comes to these changes, see Matthew Craven, *The International Covenant on Economic, Social and Cultural Rights: A Perspective on its Development* (USA: Oxford University Press, 1998).

[15] Established by ECOSOC Resolution 1985/17 of 28 May 1985.

[16] Dianne Otto, "'Gender Comment': Why Does the UN Committee on Economic, Social and Cultural Rights Need a General Comment on Women?" *Canadian Journal of Women and the Law* 14 (2002): 3.

[17] Committee on Economic, Social And Cultural Rights, E/C.12/1999/10, 8 December 1999.

[18] Ibid., paragraph 49.

Thus State Parties to ICESCR have a positive obligation to provide HRE, and States which permit schools to use a curriculum that is inconsistent with the requirements of Article 13(1) of ICESCR are violating this treaty norm.

Article 2 of ICESCR is relevant to a consideration of State Parties' obligation to provide HRE in accordance with Article 13(1). It provides that States are required to take steps to realize the rights set out in the ICESCR only to the *maximum of their available resources* and with a view to *progressively* fulfilling their obligations. Thus, State Parties are not required to immediately fulfill their obligation to provide HRE in accordance with Article 13, and non-compliance will be excused if it is due to budgetary constraints.[19] This is in stark contrast to State Parties' obligations under the corresponding provision in the International Covenant on Civil and Political Rights (ICCPR) which requires State Parties to immediately "respect and ensure" the rights set out in the ICCPR, with no scope for progressive realization.

General Comment No. 13 addresses this issue of progressive realization in two ways. First, while acknowledging that the obligation to implement Article 13(1) is progressive rather than immediate, State Parties are required to at least *take steps* to give effect to this norm. General Comment No. 3 elaborates on what "take steps" means, and notes that "such steps should be deliberate, concrete and targeted as clearly as possible towards meeting the obligations recognized in the Covenant".[20] Thus, although States are not required to immediately achieve HRE in accordance with Article 13, they are required to take action towards achieving that goal.

The second way in which General Comment No. 13 addresses a State Party's lack of resources to implement Article 13(1) is to note that *all* States, international organizations and NGOs must play a role in ensuring world-wide realization of the right to HRE. In particular, the committee refers to the need for a coordinated effort from "civil society, UNESCO, the United Nations Development Programme, UNICEF, ILO, the World Bank, the regional development banks and the International Monetary Fund".[21] Thus, the CESCR recognizes that many States lack the financial and technical ability to provide HRE and calls on members of the international community to assist those States to give effect to the HRE norm in Article 13(1).

Article 13(1) of ICESCR, read in conjunction with General Comment No. 13, provides a clear mandate for HRE that the 159 State Parties[22] are required to

[19] For further discussion on the meaning and application of Article 2 of ICESCR see General Comment No. 3 *The Nature of States Parties' Obligations*, 14 December 1990, E/1991/23.

[20] Committee on Economic, Social and Cultural Rights, E/1991/23, 14 December 1990, paragraph 2.

[21] General Comment No. 13, paragraph 60.

[22] As at 27 October 2008. Accessed at http://www2.ohchr.org/english/bodies/ratification/3.htm.

comply with, albeit, in a progressive, rather than immediate manner. It translates Article 26(2) of the UDHR into a binding legal obligation, and provides a solid legal foundation that later HRE initiatives have built upon.

2.3. *Convention on the Rights of the Child*

The International Year of the Child in 1979 was the impetus for creating the Convention on the Rights of the Child (CROC).[23] While it took only two years to draft the UDHR, it took ten years to finalize CROC.[24] This reflects the fact that CROC was drafted during the height of the Cold War, when there were significant tensions between East and West which made agreement on the final text difficult.

CROC was preceded by two earlier declarations on children's rights, namely, the 1924 Geneva Declaration on the Rights of the Child,[25] and 1959 UN Declaration on the Rights of the Child,[26] but unlike CROC, neither of these declarations dealt with education about human rights. Article 29(1) of CROC provides that:

> States Parties agree that the education of the child shall be directed to:
> (a) The development of the child's personality, talents and mental and physical abilities to their fullest potential;
> (b) The development of respect for human rights and fundamental freedoms, and for the principles enshrined in the Charter of the United Nations;
> (c) The development of respect for the child's parents, his or her own cultural identity, language and values, for the national values of the country in which the child is living, the country from which he or she may originate, and for civilizations different from his or her own;
> (d) The preparation of the child for responsible life in a free society, in the spirit of understanding, peace, tolerance, equality of sexes, and friendship among all peoples, ethnic, national and religious groups and persons of indigenous origin;
> (e) The development of respect for the natural environment.

The first thing to note about Article 29(1) is that the opening language is very weak. States do not *undertake* to provide HRE, nor are they required to *ensure* that children receive HRE; all that is required of States is that they *agree* that education should cover the matters set out in paragraphs (a) – (e). Thus, on the face of it, Article 29 does not compel States to provide HRE. Furthermore, just like Article 2 of ICESCR, Article 4 of CROC provides that State Parties

[23] Sharon Detrick, *The United Nations Convention on the Rights of the Child: A Guide to the Travaux Préparatoires* (Dordrecht: Martinus Nijhoff Publishers, 1992), 19.

[24] The drafting of CROC spanned a decade from 1979 to 1989.

[25] Geneva Declaration of the Rights of the Child of 1924, adopted 26 September 1924, League of Nations O.J. Spec. Supp. 21, at 43.

[26] General Assembly Resolution 1386(XIV) of 20 November 1959.

need only *progressively* implement Article 29 to the maximum extent of their available resources. Despite these weaknesses, Article 29(1) nevertheless makes a useful contribution to the international legal framework pertaining to HRE. For example, it expands on previous articulations of HRE by adding a requirement that HRE include education about respect for the environment. This is no doubt a reflection of the increasing concern about environmental degradation (something that was not a significant issue when the UDHR and ICESCR were drafted in the 1940s), and recognition of the interconnectedness of human rights and the environment.[27]

The meaning and interpretation of Article 29(1) was the focus of the Committee on the Rights of the Child's (CRC) first General Comment.[28] This General Comment emphasizes that the paragraphs in Article 29(1) are interrelated and that they reinforce, integrate and complement the other provisions in CROC, and cannot be properly understood in isolation from them.[29] Thus, this provision must be interpreted in a holistic manner that incorporates the fundamental principles of CROC, such as non-discrimination (Article 2), the best interest of the child (Article 3), and the right to participate (Article 12).[30]

General Comment No. 1 makes it clear that the HRE set out in Article 29(1) is aimed at sowing the seeds of harmonious relationships among all people, and helping to prevent the outbreak of violent conflicts and related human rights violations.[31] Overall, General Comment No.1 emphasizes that HRE must combat prejudice, racism, discrimination and xenophobia,[32] in order to promote peace and harmonious relationships amongst diverse peoples.

Article 29 of CROC is arguably the most significant international treaty provision relating to HRE because it is the one that binds the greatest number of States. This is because all States, with the exception of the United States and Somalia, have ratified CROC. As a result there are 193 States that have agreed to be bound by this provision pertaining to HRE.[33]

---

27 See for example Aaron Sachs and Jane A. Peterson, "Eco-Justice: Linking Human Rights and the Environment,"' (1995) Worldwatch Paper 127, Washington D.C., 1995), and Greg Maggio and Owen Lynch, "Human Rights, Environment, and Economic Development: Existing and Emerging Standards in International Law and Global Society," (1997) accessed at www.cedha.org.ar/docs/ENG38.doc on 23 July 2008.

28 Committee on the Rights of the Child, 'General Comment 1: The Aims of Education', CRC/GC/2001/1, 17 April 2001.

29 Ibid., paragraph 6.

30 Ibid.

31 Upendra Baxi, "Human Rights Education: The Promise of the Third Millennium?" in *Human Rights Education for the Twenty-First Century*, ed. George J. Andreopoulos and Richard Pierre Claude (Philadelphia: University of Pennsylvania Press, 1997), 146.

32 See for example General Comment No. 1, op. cit. (note 28), paragraph 11.

33 As at 29 October 2008. See http://www2.ohchr.org/english/bodies/ratification/11.htm.

It is worth noting that only two States have made reservations relating to Article 29. Both of these relate to State Parties interpreting and applying Article 29 (and a number of other Articles in CROC) in accordance with their constitutions.[34] Initially, three States ratified with reservations relating to Article 29, but Thailand has since withdrawn its reservation. It can therefore be said that HRE, as articulated in this treaty, enjoys broad international acceptance.[35]

2.4. *UN Decade for Human Rights Education (1995-2004)*

The international push for HRE extends beyond treaty provisions. By the early 1990s, the concept of HRE had been part of international human rights instruments for more than 40 years, yet there was concern about the extent to which States were actually taking steps to ensure that people were being educated about human rights.[36] To combat this perceived apathy, the UN General Assembly proclaimed the Decade for HRE (1995-2004), which called on all States to intensify their efforts regarding HRE, and to prepare and implement national plans of action for human rights education.[37] The Decade had five distinct objectives, namely to:

1. Assess the needs and formulate effective strategies for the furtherance of human rights education at the international, regional, national and local levels;
2. Build and strengthen programs and capacities for human rights education at these levels;
3. Coordinate the development of effective human rights education materials;
4. Strengthen the role and capacity of mass media in the furtherance of human rights education; and
5. Disseminate globally the UDHR in the maximum number of languages, and in other forms appropriate for various levels of literacy and for disabled.[38]

To assist States with preparing and implementing national plans of action, the Office of the High Commissioner for Human Rights (OHCHR) drafted Guidelines that included a set of principles, together with a step-by-step strategy for developing national plans of action in HRE.[39] These Guidelines called on States to establish a national committee for HRE, which should have responsibility for drafting the national plan of action for HRE; commissioning a baseline study

---

[34] Indonesia and Turkey ratified CROC with specific reservations concerning Article 29.

[35] See http://www2.ohchr.org/english/bodies/ratification/11.htm (accessed 21 August 2008).

[36] See for example Report of the Secretary-General on Human Rights Education, A/49/261-E/1994/110 and Add.1.

[37] General Assembly Resolution A/RES/49/184, 6 March 1995, paragraphs 5 and 6.

[38] Report of the United Nations High Commissioner for Human Rights on the implementation of the Plan of Action for the United Nations Decade for Human Rights Education (1995-2004), A/51/506/Add.1, 12 December 1996, paragraph 5.

[39] A/52/469/Add.1 and Add.1 /Corr.1, 20 October 1997.

of HRE; facilitating the implementation of the national action plan; conducting periodic evaluation and review; and finally preparing follow-up programs as required.[40]

Notwithstanding the call for States to prioritize HRE, at the end of the Decade, there was evidence that there was still a need for much more attention to be paid to education about human rights. The Report of the High Commissioner on achievements and shortcomings, listed the successes of the Decade as putting human rights education on the agenda, increasing awareness for HRE, and providing a framework for international cooperation in this area.[41] The shortcomings were said to be a failure to ensure the inclusion of economic, social and cultural rights as part of HRE; a tendency for urban populations to benefit from HRE more than rural populations; a failure to effectively coordinate HRE at all levels; and a lack of adequate resources – human, technical and financial.[42] The Report concluded with a recommendation that the General Assembly proclaim a second Decade for HRE with a strengthened coordination role for the UN, and more comprehensive support from the entire UN system.[43] It also supported the establishment of a voluntary fund for HRE,[44] and suggested that a convention on human rights education may be desirable.[45] Ultimately, none of these recommendations were adopted, the General Assembly preferring to proclaim an ongoing World Programme for HRE.

2.5. *World Programme for HRE (2005 – ongoing)*

As stated above, when the Decade for HRE was drawing to a close, there was a great deal of discussion about what should happen next. Ultimately the UN General Assembly decided that it would proclaim an ongoing World Programme for HRE.[46] The first phase of the World Programme was from 2005–2009, and focused on HRE in the primary and secondary school systems. States were encouraged to complete four distinct steps, namely:

(i) analyze the current situation of HRE in the school systems;
(ii) set priorities and develop a national implementation strategy;
(iii) implement and monitor HRE activities; and
(iv) carry out an evaluation of the program.[47]

[40] Ibid., paragraphs 4 and 23.
[41] E/CN.4/2004/93, 25 February 2004, paragraph 11.
[42] Ibid., paragraphs 24–28.
[43] Ibid., paragraph 32.
[44] Ibid., paragraph 42.
[45] Ibid., paragraph 44.
[46] Resolution 59/113 of 10 December 2004.
[47] General Assembly Resolution A/59/525/Rev.1, 2 March 2005, paragraph 26.

To achieve these steps, the OHCHR recommended that every Ministry of Education assign a relevant unit to be responsible for coordination with all relevant actors, and to serve as national focal point for school-based HRE initiatives. States were requested to advise the OHCHR of the identity of their focal point, and report on efforts to implement the plan of action for the first phase of the World Programme. Thus far, 50 States have submitted reports, with the majority coming from Europe and North American countries (although the United States is a notable absence).[48] This represents approximately a quarter of the UN membership, and is a disappointing response to such an important initiative. Furthermore, the reports indicate that many of these States have not progressed further than identifying the focal point for their national implementation of the first phase.[49] Of the States that have reported on more substantive efforts, there is evidence of a limited understanding of what HRE entails. For example, Australia refers only to civics and citizenship education,[50] which is just one narrow aspect of HRE, and does not include education about the broad spectrum of human rights, such as economic, social and cultural rights.[51]

2.6. *Conclusion Regarding International Efforts to Promote HRE*

The international push for HRE which began in the 1940s with the UDHR, has gathered increasing momentum in recent years. It is clear that in the international arena, HRE has been, and continues to be, the subject of much attention, and there is a strong push for increased education about human rights. However, this enthusiasm for HRE in the international arena does not appear to be replicated in the domestic sphere. For example, empirical research by the author into the extent of HRE in secondary schools in Melbourne, Australia and Boston, USA revealed low levels of HRE.[52] Similar studies in other jurisdic-

---

48 Eleven States are from Africa; 12 from Asia Pacific; 20 from Europe and North America; three from Latin America; and four from Middle East and North America. Accessed at http://www2.ohchr. org/english/issues/education/training/Summary-national-initiatives2005-2009.htm on 29 October 2008.

49 Accessed at: www.ohchr.org/english/issues/education/training/national-focal.htm on 22 March 2007.

50 http://www2.ohchr.org/english/issues/education/training/Summary-national-initiatives2005-2009.htm (accessed 29 October 2008).

51 For a more detailed discussion of the exact meaning of HRE see Paula Gerber, "Human Rights Education: A Slogan in Search of a Definition?" in *Research Handbook on International Human Rights Law*, ed. Sarah Joseph and Adam McBeth (UK: Edward Elgar Publishers, 2009) (forthcoming).

52 Paula Gerber, *From Convention to Classroom: The Long Road to Human Rights Education* (Germany: VDM Publishing, 2008).

tions have also exposed low levels of HRE in schools.[53] The lack of widespread HRE at the domestic level, in the face of a concerted international push for HRE, warrants further research into the possible causes. The next section considers some of the likely impediments to the incorporation of HRE into school curricula as well as some potential ways of overcoming these obstacles.

3. *Obstacles to the Realization of HRE*

The obstacles to compliance with international HRE laws tend to be in the nature political and financial barriers.[54] It is impossible for human rights education to become widespread if it is not embraced by governments as a priority. For many countries, not only is HRE not a priority, but it is actually perceived as a potential threat and destabilizing influence by the government. As one author notes:

> An educated and emancipated citizenry (such as students) may trigger calls for democratic change, respect for human rights and accountability of those in power, and cause political unrest. Such developments may ultimately lead to a loss of power of the ruling group in a society.[55]

Thus, governments may resist HRE in order to keep their citizens ignorant of their human rights, because they find it easier to violate a person's human rights if that person is ignorant of their rights, and how they can claim and enforce them. Even governments that are not motivated by a desire to keep their citizens ignorant of human rights, may chose not to prioritize HRE for other reasons. For example, organizations such as the Organisation for Economic Co-operation and Development (OECD) measure the quality of a country's

---

[53] See for example Ligia Neacsu-Hendry et al., "Implementing Human Rights Education in Three Transitional Democracies: Romani, Slovakia and Albania," in *Human Rights Education for the Twenty-First Century*, ed. Andreopoulos and Claude; Felissa Tibbitts, *Case Studies in Human Rights Education: Examples from Central and Eastern Europe* (Human Rights Education Associates & Council of Europe, 1997), accessed at www.hrea.org/pubs/HRECasestudies/index.html on 21 August 2008; Eva Dobozy, "Education in and for Democracy and Human Rights: Moving from utopian Ideas to Grounded Practice" (PhD thesis, Murdoch University, 2004), accessed at http://wwwlib.murdoch.edu.au/adt/pubfiles/adt-MU20050310.92906/01Front.pdf on 21 August 2008; and Penny Enslin, "Citizenship Education in Post-Apartheid South Africa," *Cambridge Journal of Education* 33, no. 1 (2003): 73–83.

[54] Fons Coomans, "Content and Scope of the Right to Education as a Human Right and Obstacles to its Realization," in *Human Rights in Education, Science and Culture: Legal Developments and Challenges*, ed. Yvonne Donders and Vladimir Volodin (Paris: UNESCO Publishing, and UK: Ashgate Publishing, 2007).

[55] Ibid., 212.

education system using factors such as the level of literacy and numeracy, rather than by whether HRE forms part of the standard curriculum.[56] Therefore, governments wanting to demonstrate that they have a high quality education system are likely to concentrate on the elements that global standards measure, rather than those, such as HRE which are not part of any evaluation of a State's education system.

For a State to provide HRE requires a financial commitment, and this may be an obstacle to HRE. Training teachers in human rights, developing resources for students and educators, and modifying the curricula to inculcate human rights, all place a financial burden on a State. However, it is not generally the case that States have no available financial resources, but rather that they use their budget on other priorities such as military spending.[57] Thus what can, at first glance, appear to be a financial obstacle to HRE, may in reality be a political obstacle, with governments preferring to finance their armed forces, rather than invest in human rights education. A lack of government resources available for HRE could be addressed by international funding bodies, such as the World Bank, IMF and international donors and aid agencies, requiring investment in HRE by the State as a condition to providing finance or aid.[58] Thus, it is suggested that external pressure could be used to influence governments' budgetary decisions in favor of HRE.

Although political and financial circumstances can be obstacles to HRE, so too can the lack of domestic human rights legislation. Empirical research has demonstrated that HRE is easier to achieve if there is a culture of human rights stemming from a domestic human rights instrument.[59] Having a Bill of Rights that is embedded in the culture of a country is one way of promoting HRE.[60] This can be seen in South Africa,[61] New Zealand[62] and the UK,[63] where HRE

---

[56] See OECD Programme for International Student Assessment at www.pisa.oecd.org/pages/0,3417,en_32252351_32235731_1_1_1_1_1,00.html (accessed 29 October 2008).

[57] K. Watkins, *Education Now: Break the Cycle of Poverty*, The Oxfam Education Report, Oxford, UK (2000).

[58] Coomans, "Right to Education as a Human Right," in *Human Rights in Education, Science and Culture: Legal Developments and Challenges*, ed. Yvonne Donders and Vladimir Volodin, 209.

[59] Gerber, *Human Rights Education.*

[60] See for example Charles N. Quigley and Center for Civic Education, *Preliminary Report on High School Students' Knowledge And Understanding Of The History And Principles Of The United States Constitution And Bill Of Rights* (Calabasas, California: Center for Civic Education, 1987).

[61] Constitution of the Republic of South Africa, 1996.

[62] Human Rights Act 1993 (NZ).

[63] Human Rights Act 1998.

increased following enactment of domestic human rights instruments.[64] The risk of relying on domestic instruments to promote HRE, is that the focus of the education is likely to be parochial rather than international,[65] and this is something that educators must guard against. In the age of globalization, it is important that HRE has a worldwide outlook. Notwithstanding that a Bill of Rights may have the effect of narrowing the scope of HRE, it is nevertheless suggested, that a strong domestic Bill of Rights can be a more effective tool in the push for increased HRE, than international initiatives calling for increased HRE. A 'home grown' call for HRE expressed in a domestic human rights instrument can have more impact that a distant call for HRE from 'foreign' diplomats in Geneva. Thus, it is recommended that promoting HRE in a country like Australia, that still has no Bill of Rights,[66] would best be achieved by pushing for a national Bill of Rights, rather than pushing for further UN action in this area.

Although this chapter has to a large degree focused on HRE in schools, the international mandates relating to HRE require much more than human rights education for children. Many other sectors of society require HRE, and other scholars have published literature on HRE in a diverse range of sectors, including the military,[67] police,[68] medical fraternity[69] and journalists.[70] Clearly, for HRE to have the most impact, it must reach all sectors of society.

64 Penny Enslin, "Citizenship Education in Post-Apartheid South Africa," 73, Andre Keet and Nazir Carrim, "Infusing Human Rights into the Curriculum: The Case of the South African Revised National Curriculum Statement," *Perspectives in Education* 23, no. 2 (2005): 99–110, and David Pitts, "Human Rights Education in Diverse, Developing Nations: A Case in Point – South Africa," *Issues of Democracy* 7, no. 1 (2002): 14–18.

65 Gerber, *Human Rights Education.*

66 Two jurisdictions within Australia do have local human rights legislation, namely Victoria with the Charter of Human Rights and Responsibilities Act 2006 (Vic) and the Australian Capital Territory with the Human Rights Act 2004 (ACT).

67 D. Michael Hinkley, "Military Training for Human Rights and Democratization," in *Human Rights Education for the Twenty-First Century*, ed. Andreopoulos and Claude, 296–309.

68 Marc DuBois, "Human Rights Education for the Police," in *Human Rights Education for the Twenty-First Century*, ed. Andreopoulos and Claude, 310–33.

69 Jonathan Mann et al., "Teaching Human Rights to Public Health Practitioners," in *Human Rights Education for the Twenty-First Century*, ed. Andreopoulos and Claude, 334–44.

70 Anita Parlow, "Beyond the "Official Story": What Journalists need to Know," in *Human Rights Education for the Twenty-First Century*, ed. Andreopoulos and Claude, 374–86.

4. *Conclusion*

This chapter has demonstrated that HRE has been a focal point of the UN since its inception, and almost all States have pledged themselves to providing HRE to a greater or lesser extent, depending on which treaties they have ratified, and which initiatives they have committed themselves to. Notwithstanding these efforts, there is still a significant gap between the right to HRE, as mandated in international law and the realization of such a right. The UN Human Rights Council has recognized this, and is exploring the possibility of drafting a Declaration on Human Rights Education and Training as the next step in promoting greater HRE.[71] A Declaration on HRE may provide greater clarity and certainty as to what is required and how it can be achieved. However, unless there is wide dissemination of such a Declaration – beyond just the community of diplomats and international lawyers – a Declaration on HRE is unlikely to accomplish anything more than the solid body of international law on HRE that already exists. This view is contrary to some NGOs who suggest that having a UN Declaration devoted to HRE would:

— enhance commitment to human rights education and training;
— codify human rights education as a human right;
— clarify definitions and practice;
— emphasize training of both duty-bearers and rights-holders;
— set benchmarks and indicators for HRE;
— create incentive and encouragement to States to implement the obligations they have undertaken; and
— provide a powerful tool for lobbying and advocacy by NGOs commited to HRE.[72]

However, this author argues that it is time for the international community to redirect its focus. The UN needs to concentrate less on standard setting, and more on monitoring and providing practical assistance to help States fulfill their obligation to provide HRE. If UN committees such as the CRC and the CESCR prioritize the scrutiny of States' HRE activities, this may help to muster the political will that is needed for the realization of HRE by States. Similarly, the UN Human Rights Council could also monitor States' HRE efforts as part of that body's Universal Periodic Review process. At the same time, practical and financial assistance is needed to enable many States to provide training for

---

[71] UN Human Rights Council Resolution 6/10, 28 September 2007. A Drafting Group of the Human Rights Council Advisory Committee met with NGOs in Geneva on Friday, 7 August 2008. The drafting committee will next meet in January 2009 during the next session of the Human Rights Council Advisory Committee.

[72] Human Rights Education Associates at: www.hrea.org/lists2/display.php?language_id=1&id=9562 (accessed 31 October 2008).

teachers, develop human rights curricula and create appropriate resources for students. UNESCO and the international aid and development community have a role to play in this area, so that in future no State can justify its failure to provide HRE on the basis of a lack of resources.

Bibliography

Books and Artilces

Baxi, Upendra. "Human Rights Education: The Promise of the Third Millennium?" In *Human Rights Education for the Twenty-First Century*, edited by George J. Andreopoulos and Richard Pierre Claude, 142-54. Philadelphia: University of Pennsylvania Press, 1997.

Beiter, Klaus Dieter. *The Protection of the Right to Education by International Law: Including a Systematic Analysis of Article 13 of the International Covenant on Economic, Social, and Cultural Rights*. Leiden: Martinus Nijhoff Publishers, 2006.

Coomans, Fons. "Content and Scope of the Right to Education as a Human Right and Obstacles to its Realization." In *Human Rights in Education, Science and Culture: Legal Developments and Challenges*, edited by Yvonne Donders and Vladimir Volodin, 183-230. Paris: UNESCO Publishing, and UK: Ashgate Publishing, 2007.

Craven, Matthew. *The International Covenant on Economic, Social and Cultural Rights: A Perspective on its Development*. USA: Oxford University Press, 1998.

Detrick, Sharon. *The United Nations Convention on the Rights of the Child: A Guide to the Travaux Préparatoires*. Dordrecht: Martinus Nijhoff Publishers, 1992.

Dobozy, Eva. "Education in and for Democracy and Human Rights: Moving from utopian Ideas to Grounded Practice." PhD thesis, Murdoch University, 2004. Accessed at http://wwwlib.murdoch.edu.au/adt/pubfiles/adt-MU20050310.92906/01Front.pdf

DuBois, Marc. "Human Rights Education for the Police." In *Human Rights Education for the Twenty-First Century*, edited by George J. Andreopoulos and Richard Pierre Claude, 310–33. Philadelphia: University of Pennsylvania Press, 1997.

Enslin, Penny. "Citizenship Education in Post-Apartheid South Africa." *Cambridge Journal of Education* 33, no. 1 (2003): 73-83.

Gerber, Paula *From Convention to Classroom: the Long Road to Human Rights Education* (2008) VDM Publishers, Germany.

Gerber, Paula. "Human Rights Education: A Slogan in Search of a Definition?" In *Research Handbook on International Human Rights Law*, edited by Sarah Joseph and Adam McBeth. UK: Edward Elgar Publishers, 2010.

Hinkley, D. Michael. "Military Training for Human Rights and Democratization." In *Human Rights Education for the Twenty-First Century*, edited by George J. Andreopoulos and Richard Pierre Claude, 296–309. Philadelphia: University of Pennsylvania Press, 1997.

Keet, Andre, and Nazir Carrim. "Infusing Human Rights into the Curriculum: The Case of the South African Revised National Curriculum Statement." *Perspectives in Education* 23, no. 2 (2005): 99–110.

Mann, Jonathan, Zita Lazzarini, Lawrence Gostin, and Sofia Gruskin, "Teaching Human Rights to Public Health Practitioners." In *Human Rights Education for the Twenty-First Century*, edited by George J. Andreopoulos and Richard Pierre Claude, 334–44. Philadelphia: University of Pennsylvania Press, 1997.

Neacsu-Hendry, Ligia Ivan Turek, Jana Kviecinska, Kozara Kati, and Theodore S. Orlin. "Implementing Human Rights Education in Three Transitional Democracies: Romani, Slovakia and Albania." In *Human Rights Education for the Twenty-First Century*, edited by George J. Andreopoulos and Richard Pierre Claude, 484–516. Philadelphia: University of Pennsylvania Press, 1997.

Otto, Dianne. "Gender Comment": Why Does the UN Committee on Economic, Social and Cultural Rights Need a General Comment on Women?" *Canadian Journal of Women and the Law* 14 (2002): 1–52.

Quigley, Charles N. and Center for Civic Education. *Preliminary Report on High School Students' Knowledge And Understanding Of The History And Principles Of The United States Constitution And Bill Of Rights*. Calabasas, California: Center for Civic Education, 1987.
Parlow, Anita. "Beyond the "Official Story": What Journalists need to Know." In *Human Rights Education for the Twenty-First Century*, edited by George J. Andreopoulos and Richard Pierre Claude, 374-386. Philadelphia: University of Pennsylvania Press, 1997.
Pitts, David. "Human Rights Education in Diverse, Developing Nations: A Case in Point – South Africa." *Issues of Democracy* 7, no. 1 (2002): 14–18.
Tibbitts, Felissa. *Case Studies in Human Rights Education: Examples from Central and Eastern Europe*. Human Rights Education Associates & Council of Europe, 1997. Accessed at www.hrea.org/pubs/HRECasestudies/index.html

Reports and Comment

General Comment No. 3 *The Nature of States Parties' Obligations*, 14 December 1990, E/1991/23.
Report of the Secretary-General on Human Rights Education, A/49/261-E/1994/110 and Add.1.
Report of the United Nations High Commissioner for Human Rights on the implementation of the Plan of Action for the United Nations Decade for Human Rights Education (1995–2004), A/51/506/Add.1, 12 December 1996.

Websites

www.cedha.org.ar/docs/ENG38.doc on 23 July 2008
http://www2.ohchr.org/english/bodies/ratification/11.htm.
http://www2.ohchr.org/english/bodies/ratification/11.htm
http://www2.ohchr.org/english/issues/education/training/Summary-national-initiatives2005-2009.htm
www.ohchr.org/english/issues/education/training/national-focal.htm
http://www2.ohchr.org/english/issues/education/training/Summary-national-initiatives2005-2009.htm
www.pisa.oecd.org/pages/0,3417,en_32252351_32235731_1_1_1_1_1,00.html
www.hrea.org/lists2/display.php?language_id=1&id=9562

Convention, Declaration and Act

Convention on the Elimination of All Forms of Discrimination against Women, 1979
Convention on the Elimination of All Forms of Racial Discrimination, 1965
Convention on the Rights of the Child, 1989
Constitution of the Republic of South Africa, 1996
Constitution of the United Nations Educational, Scientific and Cultural Organization, 1945
Human Rights Act 1993 (NZ)
Human Rights Act 1998.
International Covenant on Economic Social and Cultural Rights, 1966
The Charter of Human Rights and Responsibilities Act 2006 (Vic)
The Australian Capital Territory with the Human Rights Act 2004 (ACT)
UNESCO Convention Against Discrimination in Education, 1960
United Nations Charter, 1945
Universal Declaration of Human Rights, 1948

Committee, Decade, Programme

Committee on Economic, Social and Cultural Rights, E/1991/23, 14 December 1990
Committee on Economic, Social and Cultural Rights, E/C.12/1999/10, 8 December 1999
Committee on Economic, Social and Cultural Rights, General Comment No. 13
Committee on the Rights of the Child. 'General Comment 1: The Aims of Education.' CRC/GC/2001/1, 17 April 2001

General Conference of the United Nations Educational, Scientific and Cultural Organization, 1960
The Committee on Economic, Social and Cultural Rights (CESCR)
UN Decade for Human Rights Education (1995–2004)
World Programme for Human Rights Education (2005-ongoing)

Resolution

A/52/469/Add.1 and Add.1 /Corr.1, 20 October 1997
ECOSOC Resolution 1985/17 of 28 May 1985
E/CN.4/2004/93, 25 February 2004
Resolution 59/113 of 10 December 2004
United Nations General Assembly Resolution 217 A (III) of 10 December 1948
United Nations General Assembly Resolution 1386(XIV) of 20 November 1959
United Nations General Assembly Resolution 2106 (XX) of 21 December 1965
United Nations General Assembly Resolution 2200A (XXI) on 16 December 1966
United Nations General Assembly Resolution 34/180 of 18 December 1979
United Nations General Assembly Resolution 44/25 of 20 November 1989
United Nations General Assembly Resolution 49/184 of 23 December 1994
United Nations General Assembly Resolution A/RES/49/184, 6 March 1995
United Nations General Assembly Resolution 59/113 of 10 December 2004
UN Human Rights Council Resolution 6/10, 28 September 2007

Chapter Nine

Application of International Standards of Human Rights Law at Domestic Level

*Joshua Castellino**

1. *Introduction*

When the Universal Declaration of Human Rights was passed in 1948 it generated much excitement among human rights lawyers.[1] It was a first real statement at the highest echelons of international society, of the validity of human rights law and its pertinence to every corner of the global community. The Universal Declaration of Human Rights was framed as a series of aspirations, and the task then began, under the stewardship of Eleanor Roosevelt, to turn these aspirations into realizable human rights law.[2] As discussed in other contributions to this volume, this task initially consisted of the codification of international standards along the lines of the civil, political, economic, social and cultural iterations of the doctrine. The coming into existence of a recognizable regime of human rights law that is universal is vitally important: it sends out the clear message that individuals, no matter where they are, what national or ethnic group they belong to, what religion or belief they subscribe to, and whatever circumstances they may live in, are equal in the eyes of law, with equal dignity and worth attached to their being. Thus the rights of an individual in Sudan are as important as the rights of one in Sweden, with the universal regime of human rights law exhorting States to take the necessary steps to reflect this *de jure* position against the significantly more stark *de facto* situations.

---

* Professor Joshua Castellino, Professor of Law & Head of Law Department, Middlesex University, London, UK.

[1] See generally, Alfredsson Gudmundur and Eide Asbjörn, eds., *The Universal Declaration of Human Rights; A Common Standard of Achievement* (The Hague: Martinus Nijhoff Publishers, 1999).

[2] For an exposé of the issues at the time of the framing see Johannes Morsink, *The Universal Declaration of Human Rights: Origins, Drafting and Intent* (Philadelphia: University of Pennsylvania Press, 1999).

It is in the gap between the law and reality that vast numbers of human rights violations take place. The international human rights regime is not envisaged as being a tool that can be adjudicated upon with any real conviction at international level. If it was, some could argue that it would become a tool of neo-colonialism: preaching standards derived from western liberal tradition, imposed on other traditions. Instead the universal regime of human rights protection is created more as a network of minimal normative standards, that States are encouraged to accept and make realizable within their domestic systems, taking into account any cultural nuances that ought to be reflected. This contribution will seek to emphasize the importance of domestic regimes, first, by explaining the manner in which international standards are born and enter into reality and second, by emphasizing the manner in which international human rights regimes exhort States to implement the rights at domestic level. This contribution ends with a short conclusion on the extent to which this process has been successful.

2. *The Codification of International Human Rights Standards as Law*

It could be argued that there are at least seven discernible steps in how human rights law becomes applicable at domestic level. This series of steps assumes that no previous and appropriate regime for the protection of a given right existed in the country in question. This, naturally enough, is not always the case, with several domestic legal systems containing human rights norms that are considerably in advance of the minimal standards articulated in international instruments. However in terms of understanding how international human rights law comes into existence and how it is translated to domestic law, it is probably worth summarising these steps as follows:

1. Agreement about the need to create international norms
2. Creation of international norms
3. Codification of specific international standard in the form of a Declaration, Treaty or Convention
4. Signature/Ratification of the agreed International Instrument
5. Entry into Force
6. Legal Architecture of the State: Monist and Dualist States
7. The Additional Step for Dualist States

The quest for universal consensus over the need for creating an international standard is often the first point at which debate is instigated at international level on a given issue. International human rights laws have very often been initiated by a particular event or tragedy, such as the terrible events of World

War Two, which heightened the need for the creation of universal standards respecting human rights.[3] The treaty standards over issues concerning women and children's rights have come out of detailed discussions that were being conducted on these issues at international level by a variety of actors.[4] Most recently, international consensus has grown over the need to create specific standards around the rights of those with a disability, and those in conditions of enforced disappearance.[5] Other emerging issues include the push to codify standards on the rights of indigenous peoples.[6] Essentially these issues tend to emerge at international level through the actions of a range of actors lobbying for the instigation of an international debate on the subject. At this very first level of interest it is important that the issue benefits from a State that is willing to champion the cause and raise it in the various inter-governmental forums where such issues may be discussed.

In the context of the recent passage of the Declaration on the Rights of Indigenous Peoples there were several States and indigenous peoples' groups that voiced strong support for a Declaration that had previously risked being consigned to history. This support re-energized the discussion and resulted in the ultimate passage of the Declaration in the General Assembly of the United Nations. Of course, a Declaration does not create legally binding standards and to that extent does not generate any obligation upon States (other than that they should not undertake actions that defeat the object and purpose of the document). Nonetheless it is often an important second step in this process since declarations are often precursors to Conventions (i.e. legally binding standards creating specific state obligations). This has certainly been true in the context of the two Covenants which were preceded by the Universal Declaration of Human Rights, the Convention against Racial Discrimination which was preceded by the Declaration on the same subject, and the standards on women's rights, child rights, and migrant workers rights. It could be argued that the passage of a declaration could be the first significant step towards

---

3 For a general explanation of the acknowledgement of the need for standards see Egon Schwelb, *Human Rights and the International Community: The Roots and Growth of the Universal Declaration of Human Rights,1948–1963* (Michigan: Michigan University Press, 1964).

4 See Kelly D. Askin and Dorean M. Koenig, *Women and International Human Rights Law* (New York: Transnational Publishers, 2000). A particularly useful book in the context of the topic discussed here is the edited collection by Andrew Byrnes, Jane Connors, and Lum Bik, *Advancing the Human Rights of Women: Using International Human Rights Standards in Domestic Litigation* (London: Commonwealth Secretariat, 1997).

5 See International Convention for the Protection of All Persons from Enforced Disappearance (not yet in force). Full text available at: http://www2.ohchr.org/english/law/disappearance-convention.htm (accessed 5 September 2008).

6 See United Nations Declaration on the Rights of Indigenous Peoples. Adopted by the General Assembly, September 2007, UN Doc. A/RES/61/295 2nd October 2007.

articulating an international norm, even though this norm is not binding upon State Parties and is, to that extent, non-justiciable.

The third step in the process is often one of the most difficult in the context of generating agreed international standards with specific State obligations. At this stage the various 'rights' within a given subject are substantiated, in language that on the one hand protects and enshrines the meaning of the right at its heart, while on the other hand creating specific binding obligations upon those who undertake to uphold these rights. In the legalistic context in which international human rights sometimes operates, the precise framing of the right can be critical to the extent to which a right may be protected by the courts, be they at domestic or international level. It needs to be emphasized that should there be any discussion about the precise meaning of a phrase, courts and interpreters often seek to return to the discussions about the framing of the right, to seek to understand the intent of the drafters and give effect to these, since it was on this basis that the law was signed into existence by State Parties. From the perspective of the State Party the framing of any given right within a convention is crucial since this determines its own obligation *vis-à-vis* protecting or promoting that right. Once the text of every article has been agreed the Treaty may be said to be ready for signature and ratification. In the United Nations systems these treaties are approved by the General Assembly and States are invited to sign and ratify their contents, thus proceeding to the fourth step in the context identified here.

Depending upon the State concerned, signature and ratification could take place in one instance, or in separate instances. In broad terms a signature to a treaty indicates that the State is in favor of its object and purpose, while not necessarily being bound by the specifics contained in the actual text. Ratification on the other hand, is usually a formal act by which a State recognizes the full legal import of its obligation under the specific treaty or convention. In terms of the universal human rights instruments, the Convention on the Rights of the Child remains the most highly ratified international instrument with 193 ratifications. The United States of America has failed to ratify this Convention. While this is often used by activists to suggest that the United States does not take human rights seriously, it is perhaps, in actual fact, the reverse that is true. The United States of America, in the process of determining whether it can ratify an international instrument, is particularly mindful of the extent to which it can make it justiciable within its domestic regime. If it cannot do so, it will not ratify international instruments. This is in sharp contrast to many States that sign and ratify documents with seemingly little attention to making them applicable within their domestic regimes.

Most Conventions or Treaties have a pre-determined point at which the standard enters into force. This may be a specified date (as in the context of the International Covenants for Civil & Political and Economic, Social & Cultural

Rights) or could be a threshold such as the number of States that select to become bound by the standard, such as the in the case of the Migrant Workers Convention (which came into force after the twentieth instrument of ratification had been deposited). Once the Convention or Treaty enters into force all the State Parties that have ratified it are bound to respect the spirit and the letter of its text. The only two exceptions to this are in the case where a State Party has made a specific reservation (essentially a statement opting out of a particular provision, which usually needs acceptance by the other High Contracting Parties, and ought not to defeat the object and purpose of the Convention), or where a State Party has declared a state of emergency, suspending certain rights (with several conditions attached in terms of the type and length of the emergency, the necessity of the measures etc.). Outside these exceptions States who are party to the international standard are required to put in place the measures within their domestic legislation which will enable the Convention or Treaty rights to be justiciable.

The sixth criteria on the list identified above, is a reflection of the two types of legal systems that exist in broad global terms. There are States that believe that all legal standards are unitary, and others that make a distinction between national and other legal norms. In the case of the former, of which States such as Germany, the Netherlands, Spain and most civil law States are good exponents, ratification of an international covenant or treaty makes it automatically justiciable in domestic courts of law. However in dualist States, usually States that have had some connection with British common law, the belief in the absolute nature of parliamentary sovereignty means that any 'laws' passed by bodies other than the elected representatives of the State are not justiciable until the respective parliaments in these jurisdictions have taken the additional step of passing complementary legislation to make these laws operable within the jurisdiction. In many instances States that have signed and ratified the international documents either fail to pass domestic legislation, or modify the original document to the extent that makes it differ from the standards that it agreed to with its international partners. The efficacy of this process has a direct bearing on the extent to which domestic systems adequately reflect international standards.

3. *Domestic Implementation of Rights: The 'Engine Room' of Universal Instruments of Human Rights*

It could be argued that the growth of human rights law has eroded a crucial principle of public international law: the doctrine of State sovereignty. However this 'erosion' has come at the behest of States, who signed, ratified and brought the international standards into being, and in so doing, undertook to make the necessary changes to their domestic system to enable the rights contained in the international documents to be realizable within the State. Each of the seven operating universal human rights treaties contains a similar provision to this effect.

Article 2 of the International Covenant on Economic, Social and Cultural Rights is instructive, stating:

> 1. Each State Party to the present Covenant undertakes to take steps, individually and through international assistance and co-operation, especially economic and technical, to the maximum of its available resources, with a view to achieving progressively the full realization of the rights recognized in the present Covenant by all appropriate means, including particularly the adoption of legislative measures.
> 2. The States Parties to the present Covenant undertake to guarantee that the rights enunciated in the present Covenant will be exercised without discrimination of any kind as to race, colour, sex, language, religion, political or other opinion, national or social origin, property, birth or other status.
> 3. Developing countries, with due regard to human rights and their national economy, may determine to what extent they would guarantee the economic rights recognized in the present Covenant to non-nationals.

This particular Covenant is framed with the notion that States need to 'progressively realize' economic, social and cultural rights: a reflection that is crucial in the context of provision rights which are mindful of the capacity of the State to guarantee such rights.[7] The text of the Convention has this notion of progressive realization built into each right.[8] In addition the State obligation to give effect to these rights is contained this article. Article 2(1) as quoted above reflects the extent to which the achievement of socio-economic, and to a lesser extent cultural rights may need international assistance and co-operation. Irrespective of these caveats, it is clear that among the steps that States are expected to take, are 'all appropriate means, including particularly the adoption of legislative measures'.

Article 2(2) of the Covenant is a relatively standard non-discrimination clause through which States are required to guarantee that the rights actualized are available to all individuals, irrespective of their personal or group identity or other status indicators. The context for the expression of the notion of 'progres-

---

[7] For general reading on economic, social and cultural rights see Scott Leckie and Anne Gallagher, eds., *Economic, Social and Cultural Rights: A Legal Resource Guide* (Philadelphia: University of Pennsylvania Press, 2006).

[8] For an interpretation of these rights see Isfahan Merali and Valerie Ossterveld, eds., *Giving Meaning to Economic, Social and Cultural Rights* (Philadelphia: University of Pennsylvania Press, 2001).

sive realization' is once again reiterated in Article 2(3) where the text emphasizes the particular situation of developing countries, providing some leeway of the extent to which the States make socio-economic and cultural rights available to non-nationals.

Similarly, Article 2 of the International Covenant on Civil and Political Rights states:

> 1. Each State Party to the present Covenant undertakes to respect and to ensure to all individuals within its territory and subject to its jurisdiction the rights recognized in the present Covenant, without distinction of any kind, such as race, colour, sex, language, religion, political or other opinion, national or social origin, property, birth or other status.
> 2. Where not already provided for by existing legislative or other measures, each State Party to the present Covenant undertakes to take the necessary steps, in accordance with its constitutional processes and with the provisions of the present Covenant, to adopt such laws or other measures as may be necessary to give effect to the rights recognized in the present Covenant.
> 3. Each State Party to the present Covenant undertakes:
>   (a) To ensure that any person whose rights or freedoms as herein recognized are violated shall have an effective remedy, notwithstanding that the violation has been committed by persons acting in an official capacity;
>   (b) To ensure that any person claiming such a remedy shall have his right thereto determined by competent judicial, administrative or legislative authorities, or by any other competent authority provided for by the legal system of the State, and to develop the possibilities of judicial remedy;
>   (c) To ensure that the competent authorities shall enforce such remedies when granted.

As can be seen, the State obligation to implement international human rights law at domestic level is very different in the context of civil and political rights. The notion of progressive realization is conspicuously absent, on the grounds that these rights, consisting broadly of protection rights, ought to be realizable with immediate effect. Thus after the exhortation of non-discrimination similar to that expressed in Article 2(2) of the Economic, Social and Cultural Rights Covenant, the article calls upon States to provide the necessary measures that would enable the realization of the rights contained in this document at domestic level. Thus States are obliged to undertake the 'necessary steps' to give effect to Covenant rights at domestic level in accordance with their respective constitutional processes. The latter exhortation is particularly relevant in the context of Dualist States described above.

Unlike the language in Article 2 of the International Covenant on Economic, Social and Cultural Rights, in this Covenant the State obligations are further specified in Article 3, and include the provision of an effective remedy for rights violations [as contained in Article 3(a)], that this remedy be adjudicated upon by a competent authority [Article 3(b)], and that the remedies are enforceable [Article 3(c)].

The State obligation for the implementation of international human rights law into domestic law is framed differently in the context of the battle against racial and other discrimination. Article 2 of the International Convention for the Elimination of All Forms of Racial Discrimination states:

> 1. States Parties condemn racial discrimination and undertake to pursue by all appropriate means and without delay a policy of eliminating racial discrimination in all its forms and promoting understanding among all races, and, to this end:
>   (a) Each State Party undertakes to engage in no act or practice of racial discrimination against persons, groups of persons or institutions and to ensure that all public authorities and public institutions, national and local, shall act in conformity with this obligation;
>   (b) Each State Party undertakes not to sponsor, defend or support racial discrimination by any persons or organizations;
>   (c) Each State Party shall take effective measures to review governmental, national and local policies, and to amend, rescind or nullify any laws and regulations which have the effect of creating or perpetuating racial discrimination wherever it exists;
>   (d) Each State Party shall prohibit and bring to an end, by all appropriate means, including legislation as required by circumstances, racial discrimination by any persons, group or organization;
>   (e) Each State Party undertakes to encourage, where appropriate, integrationist multiracial organizations and movements and other means of eliminating barriers between races, and to discourage anything which tends to strengthen racial division.
> 2. States Parties shall, when the circumstances so warrant, take, in the social, economic, cultural and other fields, special and concrete measures to ensure the adequate development and protection of certain racial groups or individuals belonging to them, for the purpose of guaranteeing them the full and equal enjoyment of human rights and fundamental freedoms. These measures shall in no case entail as a consequence the maintenance of unequal or separate rights for different racial groups after the objectives for which they were taken have been achieved.

In this Convention the first obligation created is for condemning such discrimination and for taking all necessary measures to eradicate the phenomenon in the domestic realm. In sharp contrast to the obligation contained in the Economic, Social and Cultural Rights Covenant, the action required is expressed as being 'without delay'. In addition to the obligation of what the State needs to proscribe, comes the positive obligation to 'promote understanding among races'. These two iterations of the obligation are then substantiated in the more specific obligations articulated in sub-articles (a) through to (e).

One of the more crucial obligations that the Covenant specifies is the need to put in place affirmative action measures. These measures are identified as vital tools within human rights law, to combat some of the historical grievances that have resulted in deep-rooted discrimination against particular groups.[9] Although broad in scope, States are required to design "positive discrimination" measures that aim to provide groups that have faced long-standing systemic discrimination with a means towards equal access to the fruits of human rights. This could be conceptualised as an elevator mechanism designed to raise a particular segment of the population that is at a lower level (in terms of quantifiable indicators such as access to services, employment within the private and public sector, political participation, level of education and access to education, and other civil, political, economic, social and cultural rights) to the level that the rest of the population enjoys. The causes for this difference between the target group and the rest of the population i.e. "the gap", is often the result of invidious structural discrimination.[10] However rather than a revision of history which is impossible and undesirable,[11] an elevator mechanism accepts the need for the focussing of specific measures aimed at the alleviation of a particular disadvantage faced by specific groups.

In defining affirmative action more accurately Bossyut stated that it is:

> ...a coherent package of measures, of a temporary character, aimed specifically at correcting the position of members of a target group in one or more aspects of their social life, in order to obtain effective equality.[12]

The determination of when a group is entitled to special packages is an intensely political discussion. While the function of law, especially at international level, in determining the groups is limited, it nonetheless does imply some empirical standards. It could be argued that the test to examine the claim for affirmative action ought to be based on at least two factors:

(i) Existence of determinable and persistent status of inequality; and,
(ii) Effective articulation of the legal right to special measures by representatives.[13]

---

[9] For a general reading on affirmative action measures see Michael Banton, *International Action Against Racial Discrimination* (Oxford: Oxford University Press, 1996). Also see Gertrude Ezorsky, *Racism and Justice: the Case for Affirmative Action* (Ithaca, New York: Cornell University Press, 1991).

[10] For a discussion of 'affirmative action' in general see Robert Fullinwider, "Affirmative Action," in The Stanford Encyclopaedia of Philosophy, ed. Edward N. Zalta, Spring 2002 Edition, available at <http://plato.stanford.edu/archives/spr2002/entries/affirmative-action/>.

[11] Some argue that affirmative action could be seen as a price for previous discrimination see e.g. Howard McGary, "Justice and Reparations," *Philosophical Forum* 9 (1977–1978): 250–63.

[12] Marc Bossyut, *Special Rapporteur to Sub-Commission. Progress Report*, June 2001 (E/CN.4/Sub.2/2001.15).

[13] Ibid., 4

The purpose underlying point (ii) is to ensure that the measures have the consent of the group concerned, especially to allow persons to opt out.[14] Of course there are numerous other issues germane to the determination of affirmative action.[15] For instance, it is likely that affirmative action programmes will create new disadvantaged groups e.g. in India, in affirmative action by way of reservation of seats at University towards specific disadvantaged groups.[16] Since University entrance is competitive, this has often resulted in people from privileged backgrounds seeking certification of their categorization as minorities[17] in order to avail of the lower threshold of entry into University in the reserved quota. Another related issue is the belief that minorities express; that by availing of special measures, their own achievements are belittled by the majority, who see them as tokens and beneficiaries of policy rather than as meritorious of the benefit accrued to them.

The justification for special measures though, remains manifold. First, it is a key legal guarantee through which traditional power relationships within a system are challenged. While not always successful, the attempt to redress has to be acknowledged as reasonable within societies that have perpetrated historical injustices towards segments of the population. Second, measures of affirmative action attempt to remedy social and structural discrimination.[18] While not tackling the prejudice that might exist in societies towards specific groups, these measures aim to create mechanisms to break down existing structural and institutional imbalances. Third, it attempts the creation of diversity or proportional

[14] For a discussion of the right of a minority to "opt out" see UN. *Sandra Lovelace* v. *Canada*, Communication No. 24/1977, 31 July 1980 [CCPR/C/OP/1 at 37 (1984)].

[15] For a general reading on affirmative action see Francis J. Beckwith and Todd E. Jones, *Affirmative Action: Social Justice or Reverse Discrimination* (Amherst, New York: Prometheus Books, 1997).

[16] Via the Mandal Commission and as guarantees in the Indian Constitution. For a general reading on this issue in India see Chiranjivi J. Nirmal, *Human Rights in India: Historical, Social and Political Perspectives* (New Delhi: Oxford University Press, 2000). Also see Joshua Castellino and Elvira Domínguez Redondo, *Minority Rights in Asia: A Comparative Legal Analysis* (Oxford: Oxford University Press, 2006), Chapter IV.

[17] The reservations are in place for "Scheduled Castes", "Scheduled Tribes" and "Other Backward Classes". These three categories cannot strictly be considered minorities since the Indian constitution specifies these as being based on language and religion. This issue was discussed by Judge Khare in *T.M.A. Pai Foundation and Ors.* v. *State of Karnataka and Ors.* WP (Civil) No. 317/1993 (31 October 1992); (2002) 8 SCC 481. However it can be argued that in terms of the international definition the groups ought to be considered minorities – an argument made in Castellino and Redondo, *Minority Rights in Asia*, ibid., Chapter IV.

[18] For an empirical study on the effect of affirmative action policies in the United States see William G. Bowen and Derek Bok, *The Shape of the River: Long-Term Consequences of Considering Race in College and University Admissions* (Princeton: Princeton University Press, 1998).

group representation.[19] While this may be criticised as tokenism, it has the effect of creating new aspirations and expectations within minorities with a view towards fuller participation in all aspects of public life.[20] A fourth argument in favor of affirmative action is a social utilitarian one which stresses that society as a whole is better off with all its components participating in processes that affect them. This is likely to calm future social unrest as potentially antagonistic groups come into greater contact,[21] contributing to healthier 'nation-building';[22] with multi-dimensional vision of the State.[23]

It is clear however that affirmative action measures could be used to provide particular groups with privileges.[24] To avoid this, the following conditions could be considered as being implied in the transposition of this norm at domestic level:[25]

---

19 Diversity as a justification for racial preference in higher education was discussed in USA Case. *DeFunis* v. *Odegaard*, 416 US 312 (1974). Also see USA Case. *Regents of the University* v. *Bakke*, 483 US 265, 1978 and the commentary on this case in Robert Post, "Introduction: After Bakke," in *Race and Representation: Affirmative Action*, ed. Robert Post and Michael Rogin (New York: Zone Books, 1998), 13–27.

20 By contrast the argument of benefiting the "creamy later" (i.e. the elite among the target population) needs to be acknowledged. See "Conclusion" Castellino and Redondo, *Minority Rights in Asia.*

21 This is referred to in political science as the "Contact Hypothesis". A book that presents the arguments and counter arguments on the subject see Hugh Donald Forbes, *Ethnic Conflict, Commerce, Culture, and the Contact Hypothesis* (New Haven: Yale University Press, 1997).

22 For an enunciation of the notion of state building see Karl Deutsch and William Foltz, *Nation Building* (New York, N.Y.: Atherton Press, 1963).

23 USA case law is particularly developed on this issue. Since the famous judgment in USA Case. *Plessy* v. *Ferguson*, 163 US 537 (1896) which upheld racial segregation of public services, there has been a constant attempt to challenge various aspects of race connotations. See e.g. USA Case. *Brown* v. *Board of Education*, 347 US 483 (1954) which overturned the ruling in USA, *Plessy* v. *Fergusson*, op. cit. Also see USA Case. *Griggs* v. *Duke Power Co.*, 401 US 424 (1971), USA Case. *Washington* v. *Davis*, 426 US 299 (1976), USA Case *Regents of the University of California* v. *Bakke*, op. cit., USA Case. *United Steelworkers of America AFL-CIO-CLC* v. *Weber*, 443 US 193 (1979) and USA Case. *Fullilove* v. *Klutznick*, 448 US 448 (1980).

24 The apartheid argument in South Africa was for "separate" systems of development for each of the 'races of South Africa. While never mooted as affirmative action, it was nonetheless a policy ostensibly designed with the "capacities" of each "race" in mind. Controversially in Malaysia, the privileged status of the majority Malay population is guaranteed by Article 153 of the Federal Constitution. For more on this, including an analysis of whether this can be justified as a measure of affirmative action see Castellino and Redondo, *Minority Rights in Asia,* Chapter VI.

25 The discussion in USA case law on the cases concerning restriction of affirmative action measures is also significant. See USA Case. *Firefighters* v. *Stotts*, 467 US 561 (1984); USA Case. *Wygant* v. *Jackson Board of Education*, 476 US 267 (1986); USA Case. *Richmond* v. *J.A. Croson Co.*, 488 US 469 (1989) and USA Case. *Adarand Constructors Inc.* v. *Pena*, 515 US 200 (1995).

a. The target group should be demonstrably disadvantaged;[26]
b. The aspiration for equality should be justified;[27]
c. The measure should be designed to ensure closure of the gap;[28]
d. Empirical evidence should examine its success;[29]
e. The measures should not be unreasonably discriminating against the majority;[30]
f. The measures should cease on the achievement of equality;
g. The measures should cease should it be demonstrated that they are ineffective.

In putting in place affirmative action measures the Convention also requires that Article 2(2) quoted above be read in conjunction with Article 1(4), which states;

> [...] Special measures taken for the sole purpose of securing adequate advancement of certain racial or ethnic groups or individuals requiring such protection as may be necessary in order to ensure such groups or individuals equal enjoyment or exercise of human rights and fundamental freedoms shall not be deemed racial discrimination, provided, however, that such measures do not, as a consequence, lead to the maintenance of separate rights for different racial groups and that they shall not be continued after the objectives for which they were taken have been achieved.[31]

This is further supplemented by a General Recommendation XV from the Committee which reifies:

> [...] a differentiation of treatment will not constitute discrimination if the criteria for such differentiation, judged against the objectives and purposes of the Convention, are legitimate or fall within the scope of article 1, paragraph 4, of the Convention. In considering the criteria that may have been employed, the Com-

26 This can be effectively measured through socio-economic statistical indicators such as access to education, birth rates, employment, health care, access to public housing etc.

27 Important in the context where groups often construct themselves as desiring of special protection when their aims may not necessarily be in keeping with the threshold required in a democratic society. For instance a special measure directed at a group propagating racist ideology would not be considered as meritorious of special measures. For more on this issue see *Canadian (Human Rights Commission)* v. *Taylor* [1990] 3 SCR available at: <http://www.lexum.umontreal.ca/csc-scc/en/pub/1990/vol3/html/1990scr3_0892.html> (accessed 28 September 2008).

28 Measures that are badly defined often affect the majority badly and generate against the minority. See S. Rothman, "Racial Diversity Reconsidered," *Public Interest* 151 (2003): 25–38.

29 This can be measured by recourse to the statistics such as the level of education of the minority, per capita incomes, employment in the public and private sectors, degree of life expectancy and other such indicators.

30 If a measure proves generally discriminatory towards the majority it will fall foul of evolving human rights standards that seek quality as a basic guarantee of the legal system.

31 International Convention on the Elimination of All Forms of Racial Discrimination (ICERD), Article 1.

> mittee will acknowledge that particular actions have varied purposes. In seeking to determine whether an action has an effect contrary to the Convention, it will look to see whether that action has an unjustifiable disparate impact upon a group distinguished by race, colour, descent, or nationals or ethnic origin.[32]

Thus the Committee is required to be alert to all situations where rights and duties (as contained in Article 5 of the Convention) have been denied or impinged upon by discrimination. In addition such discrimination need not only occur on a single ground.[33]

One of the more controversial articles in international human rights law is the provision *vis-à-vis* State obligations expressed in Article 2 of the Convention for the Elimination of All Forms of Discrimination against Women, as follows:

> States Parties condemn discrimination against women in all its forms, agree to pursue by all appropriate means and without delay a policy of eliminating discrimination against women and, to this end, undertake:
>
> (a) To embody the principle of the equality of men and women in their national constitutions or other appropriate legislation if not yet incorporated therein and to ensure, through law and other appropriate means, the practical realization of this principle;
> (b) To adopt appropriate legislative and other measures, including sanctions where appropriate, prohibiting all discrimination against women;
> (c) To establish legal protection of the rights of women on an equal basis with men and to ensure through competent national tribunals and other public institutions the effective protection of women against any act of discrimination;
> (d) To refrain from engaging in any act or practice of discrimination against women and to ensure that public authorities and institutions shall act in conformity with this obligation;
> (e) To take all appropriate measures to eliminate discrimination against women by any person, organization or enterprise;
> (f) To take all appropriate measures, including legislation, to modify or abolish existing laws, regulations, customs and practices which constitute discrimination against women;
> (g) To repeal all national penal provisions which constitute discrimination against women.

While the tone of the article is similar in terms of its exhortation to put in place adequate measures at domestic level and to ensure that such measures

[32] Committee on the Elimination of Racial Discrimination (CERD). *General Recommendation XIV* on Article 1, para 1.

[33] For instance the Committee is also mindful of multiple discrimination in the implementation of human rights law at domestic level. See CERD. *General Recommendation XXV on Gender Related Dimensions of Racial Discrimination.* Fifty-sixth session, 2000, para 1.

are accessible without discrimination, this article goes the farthest in terms of seeking adequate domestic implementation.[34] A key notion here is the notion of seeking to proscribe discrimination 'in all its forms' and in taking 'appropriate actions'. While in many Conventions the language contained in the main Article 2 would suffice, in this particular Convention the drafters clearly spell out what is at stake. While the sub-articles (a) to (e) and (g) remain onerous enough for many States but strictly necessary in keeping with the ethos of the Convention, it is Article 2(f) that has been the subject of much controversy.[35] By insisting that the State 'modify or abolish existing laws, regulations, customs and practices which constitute discrimination against women' the Convention stays true to its object and purpose, but places a significant obligation upon State Parties. From a human rights perspective this obligation is clearly at the heart of tackling discrimination against women.[36] From the perspective of some States it directly attacks cultural norms. As a result many States entered reservations to this article, with a controversy raging as to the extent to which these reservations are valid, seeing as they defeat the object and purpose of the treaty and would therefore be considered inappropriate and possibly illegal under the Vienna Convention on the Law of Treaties (which sets down the basic norms governing treaty law).[37]

Irrespective of this discussion the reservations have been allowed to stand on the grounds that it is better to have the States within the fold of treaty protection, rather than outside; a position that does not reflect wide consensus. In effect it would seem that several States have taken on this obligation on the grounds that they accepted those enshrined in the Covenant on Economic, Social and Cultural Rights, i.e. as an obligation that ought to be progressively realized. One good example of this is the case of Malawi which has entered a reservation using precisely this language.[38]

---

[34] For general reading of the issues germane to the protection of the rights of women see Rebecca Cook, ed., *Human Rights of Women: National and International Perspectives* (Philadelphia: University of Pennsylvania Press, 1994).

[35] See Belinda Clark, "The Vienna Convention Reservations Regime and the Convention on Discrimination Against Women," *American Journal of International Law* 85, no. 2 (1991): 281–321.

[36] See Donna J. Sullivan, "Women's Human Rights and the 1993 World Conference on Human Rights," *American Journal of International Law* 88, no. 1 (1994): 152–67.

[37] Elizabeth Evatt, "Eliminating Discrimination Against Women: The Impact of the UN Convention," *Melbourne University Law Review* 18, nos. 1 & 2 (1991): 435–49.

[38] The original reservation entered by Malawi read as follows: "Owing to the deep-rooted nature of some traditional customs and practices of Malawians, the Government of the Republic of Malawi shall not, for the time being, consider itself bound by such of the provisions of the Convention as require immediate eradication of such traditional customs and practices. While the Government of the Republic of Malawi accepts the principles of article 29, paragraph 2 of

However in terms of the domestic implementation of Convention rights it is clear that the State bound by this Convention is required to take a host of measures, including challenging cultural norms where they discriminate against women. The justification for this is clear: in the context of guaranteeing the inherent dignity and worth of every woman, any norm that treats her in a differentiated manner from her male counterpart could be considered discriminatory. This does not mean that women cannot be treated in a differentiated manner, e.g. in the context of maternity and other issues that are particularly pertinent to women, a differentiated understanding of rights is crucial, however aside from these very specific circumstances, where a *lex specialis* is necessary, it is anticipated that the rights of women are on par with men: a fundamental requirement if the promise of human rights is to be fulfilled.

The issue of 'culture' and its application in human rights law has also risen, albeit less controversially, in the context of the Convention the Rights of the Child. The State obligation in this Convention is captured in Article 4:

> States Parties shall undertake all appropriate legislative, administrative, and other measures for the implementation of the rights recognized in the present Convention. With regard to economic, social and cultural rights, States Parties shall undertake such measures to the maximum extent of their available resources and, where needed, within the framework of international co-operation.

This article, like that of the Covenant on Economic, Social and Cultural Rights, emphasizes the 'progressive realization of rights', framing this in the context of requiring States to undertake measures to the 'maximum extent of available resources', a reflection on the importance expected in the creation of a regime that effectively protects the rights of the child.

The words of Article 2 of the Convention Against Torture and Other Cruel, Degrading treatment or Punishment, unlike the other universal treaties is framed very specifically:

> 1. Each State Party shall take effective legislative, administrative, judicial or other measures to prevent acts of torture in any territory under its jurisdiction.
> 2. No exceptional circumstances whatsoever, whether a state of war or a threat of war, internal political in stability or any other public emergency, may be invoked as a justification of torture.
> 3. An order from a superior officer or a public authority may not be invoked as a justification of torture.

---

the Convention this acceptance should nonetheless be read in conjunction with [its] declaration of 12th December 1966, concerning the recognition, by the Government of the Republic of Malawi, as compulsory the jurisdiction of the International Justice under article 36, paragraph 2 of the Statute of the Court.» This reservation was subsequently withdrawn on the 24th October 1991. Details available on http://www.bayefsky.com/./html/malawi_t2_cedaw.php (accessed 15 September 2008).

This Convention is particularly relevant in the context of events post September 11th, where some sought to question the norm on the prohibition of torture and colluded in practices such as extraordinary rendition where torture is likely to have occurred. The words of Article 2(2) make it clear that such actions are proscribed and that States need to ensure that exceptional circumstances are not used as justification for proscribed acts.

The identification of the domestic obligation in the International Convention on Migrant Workers and their Families is contained in Article 7:

> States Parties undertake, in accordance with the international instruments concerning human rights, to respect and to ensure to all migrant workers and members of their families within their territory or subject to their jurisdiction the rights provided for in the present Convention without distinction of any kind such as to sex, race, colour, language, religion or conviction, political or other opinion, national, ethnic or social origin, nationality, age, economic position, property, marital status, birth or other status.

One of the progressive features of this particular convention is that 'all migrant workers' also includes those who may be documented. While the tone of the Convention is progressive the relatively few States that are bound by this standard makes its domestic realization on a global scale a distant prospect.

4. *Conclusion*

When the Universal Declaration of Human Rights was passed in 1948 it was hard to imagine such a complex network of human rights treaties. Of the seven fundamental human rights treaties briefly discussed here, all (with the exception of the Migrant Workers Convention) merit wide, international coverage. In addition to these standards there are several soft law standards that exist by way of declarations, guidelines etc., In addition to soft law instruments, the work of the United Nations Special Procedures has also contributed in highlighting human rights violations and the measures taken to address them. The key difference between the soft-law standards and the other human rights work of the United Nations is that these do not create direct state obligations at domestic level. It is in this particular realm that the existing fundamental human rights treaties are particularly important.

With the exception of norms considered part of customary international law or norms of *jus cogens*, States can only be bound in international law to the extent of their consent. The treaties discussed above show the extent to which States have accepted the need for human rights protection, and have agreed legally binding standards which seek to regulate them. However as discussed in the introduction, the agreement of international norms of these kinds, while a complex process, is nonetheless only part of the process through which human rights may be realized. The crucial element to make rights realizable remains the extent to which they have been implemented in domestic law. It is only when these rights are enshrined with their full import in domestic law, and when individuals and groups can challenge the State and access them, that the process of rights realization could be said to have begun in earnest. In the systems envisaged in international human rights law, there are thus three discernible steps: a) the agreeing of international norms as reflected in legally binding standards; b) the implementation of these norms at domestic level; and c) the monitoring of the extent to which the agreed norms are being implemented/realized within States. It could be argued that a significant portion of the time between 1948 until 2008 has been engaged in gaining consensus for the international norms, and in agreeing the tone and spirit of the legal obligation to be created around these norms. A pie-chart into human rights activities would also probably reveal a significant proportion of time spent on monitoring States Parties compliance, whether through the quasi-legal monitoring bodies of the respective conventions, the erstwhile Human Rights Commission, the Special Procedures of the United Nations, or even through the work of international NGOs. This notional pie-chart would probably reveal the relatively small amount of time spent on the domestic implementation of international norms. Yet it is this crucial aspect of the human rights regime which arguably can move us towards realizing the human rights dream: i.e. the creation of a system of law, accessible to everyone, especially vulnerable groups, at local and domestic level, that ultimately upholds the dignity and worth of every human being, and enshrines robust protection mechanisms for these.

Select Bibliography

Alston, Phillip and Crawford James. *The Future of UN Treaty Monitoring*. Cambridge: Cambridge University Press, 2000.

Askin, Kelly D., and Dorean M., Koenig. *Women and International Human Rights Law*. New York: Transnational Publishers, 2000.

Banton, Michael. *International Action Against Racial Discrimination*. Oxford: Oxford University Press, 1996.

Beckwith, Francis J., and Todd E. Jones. *Affirmative Action: Social Justice or Reverse Discrimination*. Amherst, New York: Prometheus Books, 1997.

Bowen, William G., and Derek Bok. *The Shape of the River: Long-Term Consequences of Considering Race in College and University Admissions*. Princeton: Princeton University Press, 1998.

Byrnes, Andrew, Janes Connors, and Lum Bik. *Advancing the Human Rights of Women: Using International Human Rights Standards in Domestic Litigation*. London: Commonwealth Secretariat, 1997.

Brems, Eva. *Human Rights: Universality and Diversity*. The Hague: Martinus Nijhoff, 2001.

Castellino, Joshua, and Elvira Domínguez Redondo. *Minority Rights in Asia: A Comparative Legal Analysis*. Oxford: Oxford University Press, 2006.

Castellino, Joshua and Keane, David. *Indigenous & Minority Rights in the Pacific: A Comparative Legal Analysis*. Oxford: Oxford University Press, 2009.

Clark, Belinda. "The Vienna Convention Reservations Regime and the Convention on Discrimination Against Women." *American Journal of International Law* 85, no. 2 (1991): 281–321.
Cook, Rebecca, ed. *Human Rights of Women: National and International Perspectives*. Philadelphia: University of Pennsylvania Press, 1994.
Deutsch, Karl, and William Foltz. *Nation Building*. New York, N.Y.: Atherton Press, 1963.
Evatt, Elizabeth. "Eliminating Discrimination Against Women: The Impact of the UN Convention." *Melbourne University Law Review* 18, nos. 1 & 2 (1991): 435–49.
Forbes, Hugh Donald. *Ethnic Conflict, Commerce, Culture, and the Contact Hypothesis*. New Haven: Yale University Press, 1997.
Gudmundur, Alfredsson, and Eide Asbjörn, eds. *The Universal Declaration of Human Rights; A Common Standard of Achievement*. The Hague: Martinus Nijhoff Publishers, 1999.
Jayawickrama, Nihal. *Judicial Application of Human Rights Law: National, Regional and International Jurisprudence*. Cambridge, Cambridge University Press, 2002.
Leckie, Scott, and Anne Gallagher, eds. *Economic, Social and Cultural Rights: A Legal Resource Guide*. Philadelphia: University of Pennsylvania Press, 2006.
Merali, Isfahan, and Valerie Ossterveld, eds. *Giving Meaning to Economic, Social and Cultural Rights*. Philadelphia: University of Pennsylvania Press, 2001.
Morsink, Johannes. *The Universal Declaration of Human Rights: Origins, Drafting and Intent*. Philadelphia: University of Pennsylvania Press, 1999.
Nirmal, Chiranjivi J. *Human Rights in India: Historical, Social and Political Perspectives*. New Delhi: Oxford University Press, 2000.
Post, Robert. "Introduction: After Bakke." In *Race and Representation: Affirmative Action*, edited by Robert Post and Michael Rogin, 13–27. New York: Zone Books, 1998.
Rothman, S. "Racial Diversity Reconsidered." *Public Interest* 151 (2003): 25–38.
Schwelb, Egon. *Human Rights and the International Community: The Roots and Growth of the Universal Declaration of Human Rights, 1948–1963*. Michigan: Michigan University Press, 1964.
Sullivan, Donna J. "Women's Human Rights and the 1993 World Conference on Human Rights."' *American Journal of International Law* 88, no. 1 (1994): 152–67.

International Legal Documents

International Convention for the Protection of All Persons from Enforced Disappearance
International Convention on the Elimination of All Forms of Racial Discrimination (ICERD), 1966
United Nations Declaration on the Rights of Indigenous Peoples, 2007
UN Doc. A/RES/61/295 2nd October 2007.
Committee on the Elimination of Racial Discrimination (CERD).

Cases

Adarand Constructors Inc. v. *Pena*, 515 US 200 (1995)
Brown v. *Board of Education*, 347 US 483 (1954)
Canadian (Human Rights Commission) v. *Taylor* [1990] 3 SCR available at: <http://www.lexum.umontreal.ca/csc-scc/en/pub/1990/vol3/html/1990scr3_0892.html>
Firefighters v. *Stotts*, 467 US 561 (1984)
Fullilove v. *Klutznick*, 448 US 448 (1980)
Griggs v. *Duke Power Co.*, 401 US 424 (1971)
Plessy v. *Ferguson*, 163 US 537 (1896)
Regents of the University v. *Bakke*, 483 US 265, 1978
Richmond v. *J.A. Croson Co.*, 488 US 469 (1989)
T.M.A. Pai Foundation and Ors. v. *State of Karnataka and Ors.* WP (Civil) No. 317/1993 (31 October 1992); (2002) 8 SCC 481
United Steelworkers of America AFL-CIO-CLC v. *Weber*, 443 US 193 (1979)
Washington v. *Davis*, 426 US 299 (1976)
Wygant v. *Jackson Board of Education*, 476 US 267 (1986)
General Recommendation XXV on Gender Related Dimensions of Racial Discrimination. Fifty-sixth session, 2000.

Chapter Ten

Role of Regional Human Rights Instruments in the Protection and Promotion of Human Rights

Azizur Rahman Chowdhury, V. Seshaiah Shasthri**, Md. Jahid Hossain Bhuiyan****

1. *Introduction*

This work looks into three regional human rights instruments, namely the European Convention on Human Rights and Fundamental Freedoms, 1950; the Inter American Convention on Human Rights, 1969 and the African Charter on Human and People's Rights, 1981 and examines (a) the circumstances leading to the establishment of the regional human rights enforcement mechanisms; (b) the nature and scope of rights & guarantees and (c) safeguarding procedures under these instruments. This work, in fact, examines whether the enforcement mechanisms are, consistent with State sovereignty, and whether they are gradually enhancing the promotion of fundamental human rights and freedoms.

2. *European Human Rights Treaties and Their Implementation*

2.1. *Introduction*

The Council of Europe adopted the European Convention on Human Rights in 1950 (European Convention), and it entered into force on 3 September 1953. Taking as their starting point the 1948 Universal Declaration of Human Rights, the framers of the European Convention sought to pursue the aims of the Council of Europe through the maintenance and further realization of

* Azizur Rahman Chowdhury, Professor, Department of Law, University of Dhaka, Bangladesh.

** V. Seshaiah Shasthri, Associate Professor and Assistant Dean (Academic Affairs), Faculty of Law, National Law University, Jodhpur, India.

*** Md. Jahid Hossain Bhuiyan teaches law in the Department of Law, ASA University Bangladesh, Bangladesh.

human rights and fundamental freedoms. In this sense, the European Convention represents the first steps for the collective enforcement of certain rights set out in the Universal Declaration of Human Rights. Under the European Convention, three institutions were entrusted with this responsibility, namely (i) The European Commission of Human Rights set up in 1954; (ii) The European Court of Human Rights set up in 1959; and, (iii) The Committee of Ministers of the Council of Europe, which in turn consists of (a) the Ministers of Foreign Affairs of the member States; or (b) their representatives. Complaints could be brought against Contracting States either by other Contracting States, or by individual applicants, which include (i) individuals; (ii) groups of individuals; and (iii) non-governmental organizations. Recognition of the right of individual applications was, however, optional and can, therefore, only be exercised against those States which have accepted it.

2.2. *Complaint making procedure*

The complaints are first the subject of a preliminary examination by the Commission, which determines their admissibility. Where an application is declared admissible, the Commission places itself at the parties' disposal with a view to brokering a friendly settlement. If no settlement is forthcoming, it draws up a report establishing the facts and expressing an opinion on the merits of the case. Thereafter, it transmits the report to the Committee of Ministers.

Where the respondent State has accepted the compulsory jurisdiction of the Court, the Commission and/or any Contracting State concerned has a period of three months following the transmission of the report to the Committee of Ministers within which to bring the case before the Court for a final and binding adjudication. Individuals are not entitled to bring their cases before the Court. If a case was not referred to the Court, the Committee of Ministers decided whether there had been a violation of the Convention and, if appropriate, awarded "just satisfaction" to the victim. The Committee of Ministers also had responsibility for supervising the execution of the Court's judgments. Through the adoption of Protocol No. 11 to the Convention, which entered into force on 1 November 1998, the control machinery was restructured so that all allegations are now directly referred to the European Court of Human Rights in Strasbourg, France. This Court is the first permanent human rights court sitting on a full-time basis. The Additional Protocols Nos. 1, 4, 6 and 7 have gradually, over the years, expanded the scope of the rights guaranteed under the Convention.[1]

[1] Protocol No. 12 which concerns with the prohibition of discrimination was opened for signature on 4 November 2000 in Rome. Protocol No. 13 opened for signature in Vilnius on 3 May 2002 and concerns the abolition of the death penalty *in all circumstances*.

2.3. *The undertakings of the High Contracting Parties:*

As envisaged under Art. 1, the High Contracting Parties "shall secure to everyone within their jurisdiction the rights and freedoms defined in Section I of the Convention." This, in other words, means that they shall provide everyone whose rights and freedoms, guaranteed by the European Convention, have been violated, with "an effective remedy before a national authority notwithstanding that the violation has been committed by persons acting in an official capacity."

2.4. *Scope of the rights guaranteed*

The European Convention guarantees the following civil and political rights, namely (i) the right to life (Art. 2); (ii) the prohibition of torture, inhuman or degrading treatment or punishment (Art. 3); (iii) the prohibition of slavery, servitude, and forced or compulsory labor (Art. 4); (iv) the right to liberty and security (Art. 5); (v) the right to a fair trial (Art. 6); (vi) prohibition of *ex post facto* laws (Art. 7); (vii) the right to privacy and family life (Art. 8); (viii) the right to freedom of thought, conscience and religion (Art. 9); (ix) the right to freedom of expression (Art.10); (x) the right to freedom of assembly and association (Art. 11); (xi) the right to marry and to found a family (Art. 12); (xii) the right to an effective remedy in case of violation of any right under this Convention (Art. 13); and, (xiii) prohibition of discrimination (Art. 14).

2.5. *Protocol to the European Convention and their application*

There are currently fourteen protocols to the European Convention. Protocol No. 1 was adopted on 20th March 1952, and entered into force on 18 May 1954. It provides for the enforcement of certain rights and freedoms not included under the Convention. Noteworthy amongst them are the important rights and undertakings between the States Parties, namely, (i) the right to peaceful enjoyment of one's possessions – Art. 1; (ii) the right to education and the right of parents to ensure such education and teaching in conformity with their own religious and philosophical convictions (Art. 2); and, (iii) the holding of free elections at reasonable intervals by secret ballot (Art. 3). Protocol No. 2 adopted on 6th May 1963 refers to Conferment of Competence on the European Court to render Advisory Opinion. It provides importantly for the scope of the Court to render advisory opinions on legal questions concerning the interpretation of the Convention and the Protocols without going into the content or scope of the rights or freedoms defined in Section I of the Convention and in the Protocols. Protocol No. 3 adopted on 6th May 1963, is procedural i.e. it provides for the powers of the Commission either to reject a petition by reason of the non-existence of the grounds for non-acceptance as provided under Art. 27. Protocol No. 4, adopted on 16th September 1963 and entered into force on 2 May 1968 added the following rights namely (i) the right not to be deprived of one's liberty merely on the ground of inability to fulfill a contractual obligation (Art. 1); (ii) the right to freedom of movement and of residence; the right to leave any country, including one's own (Art. 2); (iii) the right not to be expelled from the country of which one is a national and the right not to be refused entry into the State of which one is a national, (Art. 3); and, (iv) prohibition of the collective expulsion of aliens (Art. 4). Protocol No. 6, adopted in 28th April 1983 and entered into force on 1st November 1998, is concerned with the abolition of the death penalty (Art. 1). However, as the Protocol recognized, a State Party may nonetheless "make provision in its law for the death penalty in respect of acts committed in time of war or of imminent threat of war" (Art. 2). The important issue under this Protocol is that no derogations can be made from the provisions of these articles under Article 15 of the Convention, nor can any reservations be made to this Protocol (Arts. 3–4). Protocol No. 7, adopted in 1984, entered into force on 1 November 1988 extended the scope of the Convention by providing for the following additional protection, namely (i) certain protections against arbitrary expulsion of aliens lawfully resident in the territory of the High Contracting Parties (Art. 1); (ii) the right to appeal against a criminal conviction (Art. 2); (iii) the right to compensation in case of a miscarriage of justice (Art. 3); (iv) the right not to be tried again for the same offence within the jurisdiction of the same State – a provision which cannot be derogated from under Article 15 of the Convention (Art. 4); and (v) equality of rights and responsibilities between spouses as to marriage, during marriage, and in the event of its dissolution (Art. 5). Protocol No. 11, adopted on 5th November 1994 and entered into force on 1st November 1998, introduced important structural and institutional changes in the context of the System namely (i) abolition of the European Commission on Human Rights; (ii) enlargement of the scope of the Court; and importantly, (iii) allowance to the individuals to take the cases directly to the Court. Protocol No. 12 adopted in 2000, provides a general prohibition of discrimination, which is independent of the other rights and freedoms guaranteed by the Convention. According to Article 1(1) of the Protocol, "the enjoyment of any right set forth by law shall be secured without discrimination on any ground such as sex, race, color, language, religion, political or other opinion, national or social origin, association with a national minority, property, birth or other status". Article 1(2) of the Protocol specifies that "no one shall be discriminated against by any public authority on any ground such as those mentioned in paragraph 1". Interestingly, this Protocol has not entered into force, having received only one out of the necessary ten ratifications. Protocol No. 13 adopted on 3rd May 2002 demonstrates the emerging trend within the framework of the Council of Europe towards the abolition of the death penalty. Hence, taking the development of law from Protocol 6 a step forward; it seeks complete abolition of the death penalty under all circumstances. However, this Protocol, which requires ratification by a minimum of ten States, has not yet entered into force. The latest addition to the European Convention, in terms of its continuing growth and development, is Protocol 14 which amends the control system of the Convention. This Protocol was adopted on 13th May 2004. Prominently. the Protocol outlines new proposals for the election of judges and their tenure. Besides reiterating the role of the Court as an important custodian of protection and safeguarding of human rights and fundamental freedoms envisaged under the Convention, it seeks for the High Contracting Parties to abide by the final judgment of the Court and also provides for the accession of European Union to the Convention.

Broadly speaking, these Protocols fall into two main groups i.e. those changing the machinery of the Convention, and those adding additional rights to those protected by the Convention. While the Convention has been amended several times by means of Protocols, these amendments affect only the Convention machinery and not the substantive content of the rights. One characteristic of the European Convention is that the Protocols required universal ratification to enter into force in order to maintain the institutional unity of the Convention machinery.

2.6. *Permissible limitations on the exercise of rights*

The European Convention empowers States Parties to impose restrictions on the exercise of the rights envisaged in particular and defined circumstances.[2] However, such restrictions must, (i) be imposed "in accordance with the law", or, (ii) be "provided for by law" or, (iii) be "prescribed by law"; (iv) with the exception of Article 1 of Protocol No. 1, they must also be "necessary in a democratic society" for the particular purposes specified in the various articles, such as, for instance, in the interests of public safety, for the protection of public order, health or morals, the prevention of disorder or crime or the protection of the rights and freedoms of others (the legitimate reasons vary depending on the right protected).

While the notion of a democratic society is not referred to in connection with restrictions that might be imposed on the right to peaceful enjoyment of one's possessions, the notion of democracy and a democratic constitutional order is

---

[2] This is the case with the right to respect for one's private and family life (Article 8); the right to freedom of thought, conscience and religion (Article 9); the right to freedom of expression (Article 10); and, the right to peaceful assembly and freedom of association (Article 11) of the Convention. The same holds true with regard to the right to peaceful enjoyment of one's possessions (Article 1, Protocol No. 1) & the right to freedom of movement and residence (Article 2, Protocol No. 4).

ever-present in the Convention and is a precondition for States that wish to join the Council of Europe. Therefore, restrictive measures alien to a democratic society respectful of human rights standards, would not be considered to be in "the public interest" within the meaning of Article 1 of Protocol No. 1.

The pronouncements of the European Convention on Human Rights (ECHR) contain rich and numerous interpretations of the term "*necessity*" in the various limitations provisions. Although "it is for the national authorities to make the *initial* assessment of the reality of the *pressing social need* implied by the notion of 'necessity'" in the context of freedom of expression, for instance, it is for the Court to give the final ruling on the conformity of any measure with the terms of the Convention, a competence that "covers not only the basic legislation but also the decision applying it, even one given by an independent court". The supervision, thus, comprises the "aim" and "necessity" of the measure challenged. In exercising its supervisory functions, with respect to the right to freedom of expression, for instance, the Court has, time and again, reiterated that it is obliged "to pay the utmost attention to the principles characterizing a 'democratic society'". The Court must consequently decide whether the reasons provided by the national authorities to justify the necessity of the interference in the exercise of the right concerned "are relevant and sufficient". In other cases, it has emphasized that the exceptions to the right to privacy in Article 8(2) must be "interpreted narrowly" and the necessity thereof must be "convincingly established". It is not sufficient that the interference concerned might be useful, or that it is simply so harmless that it does not disturb the functioning of a democratic society. On the contrary, the High Contracting Parties are under a legal obligation to provide sufficient reasons to prove the necessity in a democratic society both of the law on which the measure is based and of the measure itself.[3]

2.7. *European Court of Human Rights*

With the entry of the restructured control machinery after 1 Nov. 1998, all alleged violations of the rights and freedoms guaranteed by the Convention and its Protocols are referred directly to the European Court of Human Rights, which shall "ensure the observance of the engagements undertaken by the High

[3] The European Convention on Human Rights and its Protocols 1, 4, 6 and 7 provide extensive protection of the rights and freedoms of the human person at the European level. Limitations on the exercise of certain rights protected by the Convention may be permissible, provided that they comply with the principles of (i) legality; (ii) the legitimate needs of a democratic society; and (iii) necessity/proportionality, in that the measures must be necessary in a democratic society for one or more of the specified purposes.

Contracting Parties" (Art. 19). The Court is permanent, and consists of a number of judges equal to the number of Contracting Parties (Art. 20). The Court can sit in committees of three judges, in Chambers of seven judges or in a Grand Chamber of seventeen judges (Art. 27). Apart from being competent to receive and examine *inter-State* complaints, (Art. 33), the Court "may receive applications from any person, non-governmental organization or group of individuals claiming to be the victim of a violation by one of the High Contracting Parties of the rights set forth in the Convention or the protocols thereto" (Art. 34).

The "High Contracting Parties undertake not to hinder in any way the effective exercise of this right." The right to bring inter-State and individual complaints to the Court does not depend on any specific act of acceptance. The Court may not, however, deal with an application of any kind unless domestic remedies have been exhausted and the application has been submitted within six months from the date on which the final decision was taken (Art. 35). Further criteria of admissibility exist with regard to individual applications, which must not, for instance, be anonymous or "substantially the same as a matter that has already been examined by the Court or has already been submitted to another procedure of international investigation or settlement and contains no relevant new information." The Court decides on the admissibility and merits of the case and, if necessary, undertakes an investigation.

After having declared a case admissible, it also places itself "at the disposal of the parties concerned with a view to securing a friendly settlement of the matter on the basis of respect for human rights as defined in the Convention and the protocols thereto." (Art. 38). Hearings before the Court are public, unless it decides otherwise in "exceptional circumstances." (Art. 40). Within a period of three months from the date of the judgment, any party to the case may, in exceptional circumstances, request that the case be referred to a Grand Chamber. If the request is accepted, the Grand Chamber shall decide the case by means of a judgment that shall be final. (Art. 43). Otherwise, the judgment of the Chamber will be final when the parties declare that they have no intention of requesting referral to the Grand Chamber; or three months after the judgment in the absence of such a request; or, finally, when the request for referral has been rejected. (Art. 44). The High Contracting Parties "undertake to abide by the final judgment of the Court in any case to which they are parties"; the execution of the final judgment is supervised by the Committee of Ministers of the Council of Europe. (Art. 46).

3. *The Inter-American Convention on Human Rights, 1969*

3.1. *Scope of the rights*

The Inter-American Convention on Human Rights, 1969 (to be referred to as the 'American Convention') guarantees a variety of civil and political rights.[4] Besides, the 'American Convention' also requires the States Parties in general terms "undertake to adopt measures, both internally and through international co-operation, with a view to achieving progressively, by legislation or other appropriate means, the full realization of the rights implicit in the economic, social, educational, scientific, and cultural standards set forth in the Charter of the Organization of American States as amended by the Protocol of Buenos Aires." (Art. 11). As the title of the article indicates, it is more concerned with the "Progressive development" of these rights than with their immediate enforcement through judicial means. However, with the entry into force of the Additional Protocol to the Convention in relation to the Economic, Social and Cultural Rights, these rights have been given a more detailed legal definition, although the "full observance" thereof is still to be achieved "progressively." The Additional Protocol recognizes a number of important economic, social and cultural rights.[5]

---

[4] They include for example, (i) the right to juridical personality – Art. 3; (ii) the right to life, including careful regulation of the death penalty from an abolitionist perspective – Art. 4; (iii) the right to humane treatment, including freedom from torture and cruel, inhuman or degrading treatment or punishment – Art. 5; (iv) freedom from slavery, servitude, forced and compulsory labor – Art. 6; (v) the right to personal liberty and security, including freedom from arbitrary arrest or detention – Art. 7; (vi) the right to a fair trial – Art. 8; (vii) the right to freedom from *ex post facto* laws – Art. 9; (viii) the right to compensation in the event of a miscarriage of justice – Art. 10; (ix) the right to privacy – Art. 11; (x) the right to freedom of conscience and religion – Art. 12; (xi) the right to freedom of thought and expression – Art. 13; (xii) the right of reply in case of dissemination of inaccurate and offensive statements – Art. 14; (xiii) the right to peaceful assembly – Art. 15; (xiv) the right to freedom of association – Art. 16; (xv) the right to marry freely and to found a family – Art. 17; (xvi) the right to a name – Art. 18; (xvii) the rights of the child – Art. 19; (xviii) the right to a nationality – Art. 20; (xix) the right to property – Art. 21; (xx) the right to freedom of movement and residence – Art. 22; (xxi) the right to participate in government – Art. 23; (xxii) the right to equality before the law and equal protection of the law – Art. 24; and, (xxiii) the right to judicial protection – Art. 25.

[5] These rights include (i) the principle of non-discrimination in the exercise of the rights set forth in the Protocol – Art. 3; (ii) the right to work – Art. 6; (iii) the right to just, equitable and satisfactory conditions of work – Art. 7; (iv) trade union rights – Art. 8; (v) the right to social security – Art. 9; (vi) the right to health – Art. 10; (vii) the right to a healthy environment – Art. 11; (viii) the right to food – Art. 12; (ix) the right to education – Art. 13; (x) the right to the benefits of culture – Art. 14; (xi) the right to the formation and protection of

3.2. *Undertakings of the States Parties*

The States Parties to the 'American Convention' undertake to respect the rights and freedoms recognized therein and to ensure to all persons subject to their jurisdiction the free and full exercise of those rights and freedoms, without any discrimination on certain cited grounds. (Art. 1, Protocol I). Therefore, the legal duty of the States Parties to the American Convention to "respect" and to "ensure" is multi-faceted and goes to the very heart of the entire State structure, including the particular conduct of the Governments themselves. Thus, the legal obligation to "ensure" the rights and freedoms contained in the American Convention on Human Rights means that the States Parties must prevent, investigate and punish human rights violations and that they must, if possible, restore the rights violated, and provide compensation as warranted for damages.

3.3. *Permissible limitations on the exercise of rights*

The exercise of the right to manifest one's religion and beliefs (Art. 12); the right to freedom of thought and expression (Art. 13); the right to the freedoms of assembly and of association (Arts. 15 and 16) and; the right to freedom of movement and residence, including the right to leave any country, including one's own (Art. 22) may be subject to limitations, if necessary, on the grounds of the protection of public safety, health, morals, (public) order, national security or the rights and freedoms of others (the legitimate reasons vary depending on the right protected). In addition, the law may, on certain specified grounds, "regulate the exercise of the rights and opportunities" linked to the right to participate in government. (Art. 23)

While all limitation provisions stipulate that the limitations imposed must be prescribed by law, established by law, imposed in conformity with the law, or pursuant to law, Article 30 contains a general provision whereby restrictions on the exercise of rights foreseen in the American Convention "may not be applied except in accordance with the laws enacted for reasons of general interest and in accordance with the purpose for which such restrictions have been established". Therefore it is "essential that State actions affecting basic rights not be left to the discretion of the government but, rather, that they be surrounded by a set of guarantees designed to ensure that the inviolable attributes of the individual not be impaired". Hence, the most important of these guarantees is that restrictions to basic rights only be established by a law passed by the Legislature in accordance with the Constitution. The term "laws" in Article 30 means "formal

families – Art. 15; (xii) the rights of children – Art. 16; (xiii) the right of the elderly to protection – Art. 17; and, (xiv) the right of the handicapped to protection – Art. 18.

law", namely, "a legal norm passed by the legislature and promulgated by the Executive Branch, pursuant to the procedure set out in the domestic law of each State". Article 30 also links the term "laws" to the "general interest", which means that "they must have been adopted for the 'general welfare'" as referred to in Article 32(2) of the Convention. Hence, this would require a harmonious interpretation and understanding that it is an integral element of public order in democratic States, the main purpose of which is "the protection of the essential rights of man and the creation of circumstances that will permit him to achieve spiritual and material progress and attain happiness". These articles, in particular, define "the context within which the restrictions permitted under Article 13(2) must be interpreted".

3.4. *The competence of the implementation mechanisms*

As already stated, the inter-American system for the protection of human rights is two-fold i.e. it comprises of the Inter-American Commission on Human Rights and, the Inter-American Court of Human Rights for those States Parties having accepted its jurisdiction.

3.4.1. *The Inter-American Commission on Human Rights*

The American Convention on Human Rights, 1969, also commonly called the Pact of San José, Costa Rica, entered into force on 18 July 1978. The Convention reinforced the Inter-American Commission on Human Rights (IACHR), which since 1960 existed as "an autonomous entity of the Organization of American States".[6] It became a competent treaty body, together with the Inter-American Court of Human Rights, in addressing the matters relating to the fulfillment of the commitments made by the States Parties to the Convention. (Art. 13). The Commission has its headquarters in Washington, D.C., and its mandate is found in the Organization of American States (OAS) Charter and the American Convention on Human Rights. The Commission represents all of the Member States of the OAS. It has seven members who act independently, without representing any particular country. (Art. 34).

The members of the Commission are elected by the General Assembly of the OAS. The Commission is a permanent body which meets in ordinary and special sessions several times a year. The Executive Secretariat carries out the tasks delegated to it and provides legal and administrative support to the Commission in its work. The birth of the Inter-American human rights system dates back to the adoption of the American Declaration of the Rights and Duties of Man in Bogotá, Colombia in April, 1948. The Commission was created in

6 See *Annual Report of the Inter-American Commission on Human Rights, 1992–1993*, 5.

1959 and held its first session in 1960. By 1961, the Commission had begun to carry out on-site visits to observe the general human rights situation in a country or to investigate specific situations. In relation to its visits for the observation of the general human rights situation of a country, the Commission enjoys the power to publish special country reports.

In 1965, the Commission was expressly authorized to examine complaints or petitions regarding specific cases of human rights violations. The Commission also possesses additional faculties which pre-date and are not derived directly from the Convention, such as the processing of cases involving countries which are still not parties to the Convention.

3.4.1.1. Composition

The Commission's ranking officers are its seven commissioners. The commissioners are elected by the OAS General Assembly for four-year terms, with the possibility of re-election on one occasion, for a maximum period of eight years. They serve in their personal capacity and are not considered to represent their countries of origin, but rather "all the member countries of the Organization" (Art. 43) and must be "persons of high moral character and recognized competence in the field of human rights". (Art. 42). While no two nationals of the same Member State may be commissioners simultaneously, the commissioners shall refrain from participating in the discussion of cases involving their home countries.

3.4.1.2. Functions and Powers

Promoting the observance and the defence of human rights are the principal functions of the Commission. To this effect, the Commission:

a) Receives, analyzes and investigates individual petitions which allege human rights violations.
b) Observes the general human rights situation in the member States and publishes special reports regarding the situation in a specific State, when it considers it appropriate.
c) Carries out on-site visits to countries to engage in more in-depth analysis of the general situation and/or to investigate a specific situation, usually resulting in the preparation of a report regarding the human rights situation observed, and publication which is sent to the General Assembly.
d) Stimulates public consciousness regarding human rights in the Americas. To that end, carries out and publishes studies on specific subjects, such as: measures to be taken to ensure greater independence of the judiciary; the activities of irregular armed groups; the human rights situation of minors and women, and; the human rights of indigenous peoples.
e) Organizes and carries out conferences, seminars and meetings with representatives of Governments, academic institutions, non-governmental groups, etc. in order to disseminate information and to increase knowledge regarding issues relating to the inter-American human rights system.

f) Recommends to the Member States of the OAS the adoption of measures which would contribute to human rights protection.
g) Requests States to adopt specific "precautionary measures" and avoid serious & irreparable harm to human rights in urgent cases. The Commission may also request that the Court order "provisional measures" in urgent cases which involve danger to persons, even where a case has not yet been submitted to the Court.
h) Submits cases to the Inter-American Court and appears before the Court in the litigation of cases. Importantly, the Commission also
i) Requests advisory opinions from the Inter-American Court regarding questions of interpretation of the American Convention.

3.4.1.3. Processing of Individual Cases

Any person, group of persons or non-governmental organization may present a petition to the Commission alleging violations of the rights protected in the American Convention and/or the American Declaration. The petition may be presented in any of the four official languages of the OAS and on behalf of the person filing the petition or a third person. (Art. 44). On the other hand, inter-State complaints require a specific declaration whereby the State concerned recognizes the competence of the Commission to examine communications brought against another State Party having made the same declaration. (Art. 45).

The Commission may process individual cases where it is alleged that one of the member States of the OAS is responsible for the human rights violation at issue. While the Commission applies the Convention to process cases brought against those States which are parties to that instrument, for those States which are not parties, it applies the American Declaration. The Commission may, of course, study those petitions alleging that human rights violations were committed by State agents. However, the Commission may also process cases where it is asserted that a State failed to act to prevent a violation of human rights or failed to carry out proper follow-up after a violation, including the investigation and sanction of those responsible, as well as the payment of compensation to the victim. The petitions presented to the Commission must show that the victim has exhausted all means of remedying the situation domestically.

If domestic remedies have not been exhausted, it must be shown that the victim tried to exhaust domestic remedies but failed because: 1) those remedies do not provide for adequate due process; 2) effective access to those remedies was denied, or; 3) there has been undue delay in the decision on those remedies. If domestic remedies were exhausted, the petition must be presented within six months after the final decision in the domestic proceedings. If domestic remedies have not been exhausted, the petition must be presented within a reasonable time after the occurrence of the events complained of. The petition must also fulfill other minimal formal requirements which are found in the Convention and the Rules of Procedure of the Commission. (Art. 46). When the Commission receives a petition which meets, in principle, the requirements established in the Convention, the Commission assigns a number to that petition and begins to process it as a case. This decision to open a case does not prejudge the Commission's eventual decision on the admissibility or the merits of the case.

This means that the Commission may still declare the petition inadmissible and terminate the process without reaching the merits, or may find that no violation has occurred. (Art. 47). If the Commission decides that a case is inadmissible, it must issue an express decision to that effect, which is usually published. On the other hand, the Commission need not formally declare a case admissible before addressing the merits. (Art. 48). In some, but not all, cases, the Commission will declare a petition admissible before reaching a decision on the merits. In other cases, the Commission will include its discussion regarding the admissibility of a petition with its final decision on the merits.

When a case is opened and a number is assigned, the pertinent parts of the petition are sent to the Government with a request for relevant information. During the processing of the case, each party is asked to comment on the responses of the other party. The Commission also may carry out its own investigations, conduct on-site visits, and request specific information from the parties. The Commission may also hold a hearing during the processing of the case, in which both parties are present and are asked to set forth their legal and factual arguments. In almost every case, the Commission will also offer to assist the parties in negotiating a friendly settlement, if they so desire. When the parties have completed the basic back-and-forth of briefs, and when the Commission decides that it has sufficient information, the processing of a case is completed.

The Commission then prepares a report which includes its conclusions and also generally provides recommendations to the State concerned. This report is not a public document. The Commission gives the State a period of time to resolve the situation and to comply with the recommendations of the Commission. Upon the expiration of this period of time granted to the State, the Commission has two options. The Commission may prepare a second report, which is generally similar to the initial report, and which also generally contains conclusions and recommendations. In this case, the State is again given a period of time to resolve the situation and to comply with the recommendations of the Commission, if such recommendations are made. At the end of this second period granted to the State, the Commission will usually publish its report, although the Convention allows the Commission to decide otherwise. Alternatively, the Commission may decide to take the case to the Inter-American Court. If it wishes to take the case to the Court, it must do so within three months from the date in which it transmits its initial report to the State concerned. The initial report of the Commission will be attached to the application to the Court. The Commission will appear in all proceedings before the Court. The decision as to whether a case should be submitted to the Court or published should be made on the basis of the best interests of human rights in the Commission's judgment.

If a settlement is not reached, the Commission will "draw up a report setting forth the facts and stating its conclusions", a report that will be submitted to the States Parties, "which shall not be at liberty to publish it." (Art. 50). If, after a prescribed period, the matter has not been settled or submitted to the Court, the Commission may "set forth its opinion and conclusions concerning the question submitted for its consideration" and may in cases where the State concerned fails to take "adequate measures", ultimately decide to publish its report. (Art. 61). With regard to those OAS Member States which have not yet ratified the American Convention on Human Rights, the Commission is competent to receive petitions alleging violations of the American Declaration on the Rights and Duties of Man. Another interesting aspect of the Commission's powers is its competence to request advisory opinions from the Inter-American Court of Human Rights. (Art. 64).

3.4.1.4. Special Rapporteurs
Monitoring of OAS States' compliance with inter-American human rights treaties

3.4.1.4.i. OAS Special Rapporteur for Freedom of Expression
The Commission established the Special Rapporteur on Freedom of Expression of the Organization of American States (OAS) in 1997 to monitor OAS Member States' compliance with the American Convention on Human Rights in the area of freedom of expression. Accordingly, the Special Rapporteur analyzes the complaints of free expression violations received by the Commission and on cases, including requests for "precautionary measures" from OAS Member States to protect journalists and others who face threats or the risk of irreparable harm. In cases involving a serious violation of freedom of expression, the Special Rapporteur issues press releases about the information it has received, expresses its concern to the authorities, and makes recommendations for reinstating this right. In other cases, the Special Rapporteur directly contacts government authorities to obtain further information, and/or to request that the government take measures to rectify the harm that has been inflicted. The Special Rapporteur also makes recommendations to OAS Member States to reform laws and regulations that violate free expression rights guaranteed under the Convention. The Special Rapporteur participates in education, training and other activities to promote the right to freedom of expression and support local journalists and human rights defenders, and conducts fact-finding missions to investigate reports of abuses in OAS Member States. Each year, the Rapporteur

issues an annual report detailing the state of freedom of press and freedom of expression in each country in the Americas. The OAS Rapporteur is one of the three International Mechanisms for Promoting Freedom of Expression, the others being the UN Special Rapporteur on Freedom of Opinion and Expression, and the OSCE Representative on Freedom of the Media. Each year, they issue a joint declaration calling attention to worldwide free expression concerns.

3.4.1.4.ii. Special Rapporteur on Migrant Workers and their Families

In 1997, responding to a specific request on the part of the Organization of American States' (OAS) General Assembly,[7] the Commission established the Special Rapporteurship on Migrant Workers and their Families. The creation of the Special Rapporteurship illustrates the interest that OAS Member States have on the condition of a group that is characterized by special vulnerabilities and thus is particularly prone to human rights violations. The Commission restricted the scope of action of the Special Rapporteurship exclusively to migrant workers and their families who live in countries of which they are not nationals. The Commission appointed one of its seven Commissioners as *Special Rapporteur on Migrant Workers and Their Families*.[8] In 2008, the IACHR appointed the current Rapporteur, Commissioner Felipe González, to a four year term. Main activities of the Special Rapporteurship on Migrant Workers and their Families include:

(a) Monitoring

The Rapporteur monitors developments in relation to migration in the region and how the latter affect the condition of migrant workers and their families. The Rapporteur closely follows the effects that political and economic crises have on migratory flows in the region; examines changes in – and debates

[7] See (AG/RES. 1404 XXVI-O/96 and AG/RES 1480 XXVII-O/97).

[8] During its first period (1997–2000) Colombian historian Álvaro Tirado was in charge of the Special Rapporteurship. Subsequently, in 2000 the IACHR designated in the position Argentine jurist Professor Juan E. Méndez. In February 2004, the IACHR appointed Freddy Gutiérrez Trejo, a Venezuelan attorney and professor, as Special Rapporteur. It was determined that the Special Rapporteur would undertake his/her functions for a four-year period. The Special Rapporteurship on Migrant Workers undertakes promotional work regarding human rights issues pertaining to this population. The principal objectives of the Rapporteurship include: (a) To generate awareness of the States' duty to respect the human rights of migrant workers and their families; (b) To make specific recommendations to the Member States on areas related to the protection and promotion of the rights of migrant workers and their families, so that they adopt measures in their favor; (c) To prepare reports and special studies on the situation of migrant workers and, more broadly, studies on issues pertaining to migration; and, (d) To act promptly on petitions or communications in which it is noted that the human rights of migrant workers and their families are violated in any Member State of the OAS.

on – legislation and policies regarding migration, and investigates state practice in this realm.

(b) Promotional Work and Training

The Rapporteur undertakes workshops for non-governmental organizations working in the area of migration in the Americas. As part of these activities, the Rapporteur promotes the Inter American human rights system underscoring and explaining concretely how the latter may be used to guarantee and enhance the rights of migrant workers and their families. These activities have been carrying out in several OAS Member States.

(c) Participation in Conferences and Intergovernmental Fora

The Rapporteur regularly attends intergovernmental meetings where governments debate migration affairs in the region. Attending these events allows the Rapporteur to gather information concerning migration issues, survey discussions regarding migratory policy in the region, and develop working relationships with officials in charge of implementing migratory policies in their countries. The Rapporteur participates as an observer in the Regional Conference on Migration (RCM) and has monitored the activities of the South American Conference on Migration.

(d) Institutional Links

The Rapporteur maintains contact with several international organizations and research centers working on migration issues in the Americas.

(e) Inter-American Program for the Protection and Promotion of the Human Rights of Migrants

Following a specific mandate advanced by the Heads of States and Government during the Third Summit of the Americas and a Specific Resolution by the OAS General Assembly,[9] the Special Rapporteur actively participates in the discussion and preparation of an Inter-American Program for the Protection and Promotion of the Human Rights of Migrants.

(f) Advisory Opinion

The Rapporteur participates in the procedure of the Advisory Opinion before the Inter-American Court of Human Rights. As part of this process, in conjunction with the Executive Secretariat of the IACHR, the Rapporteur elaborates and submits a brief to the Court where after the Court issued its advisory Opinion. For example, when Mexico sought the advisory opinion to clarify

[9] See AG/RES. 1928 (XXXIII-O/03).

the scope of the right to equality and the principle of non-discrimination, and their application to the labor rights of workers whose immigration status in the State in which they live and work is irregular based on the elaborate report submitted by the Rapporteur the Court rendered its advisory opinion on 17 September 2003.

3.4.1.4.iii. Special Rapporteur on the Rights of Women

The Commission established its Rapporteurship on the Rights of Women in 1994 to renew its commitment to ensuring that the rights of women are fully respected and ensured in each Member State. While the constitutions of each Member State formally guarantee equality, the Commission's examination of national legal systems and practices had increasingly revealed the persistence of discrimination based on gender. Accordingly, the Rapporteurship was established with an initial mandate to analyze the extent to which Member State law and practices that affect the rights of women comply with the broad obligations of equality and non-discrimination set forth in the American Declaration of the Rights and Duties of Man and the American Convention on Human Rights. Following the intensive study carried out by the Rapporteurship, the IACHR published its *Report on the Status of Women in the Americas* to: provide an overview of the situation; issue recommendations designed to assist the Member States in eradicating discrimination in law and practice; and establish priorities for further action by the Rapporteurship and the Commission.

The obligations of equality and non-discrimination continue to serve as the points of orientation for the selection of issues being addressed by the Rapporteurship. Further, the Commission and its Rapporteurship place special emphasis on the problem of violence against women, itself a manifestation of gender-based discrimination, as recognized in the Inter-American Convention on the Prevention, Punishment and Eradication of Violence Against Women. The Rapporteurship has played a vital role in the Commission's work to protect the rights of women through the publication of thematic studies; assisting in the development of new jurisprudence in this area within the individual case system; and supporting the investigation of broader issues affecting the rights of women in specific countries of the region through on site visits and country reports.

More specifically, the Rapporteurship on the Rights of Women served to (a) raise awareness of the need for further action to ensure that women are able to fully exercise their basic rights; (b) provide specific recommendations aimed at enhancing Member State compliance with their priority obligations of equality and nondiscrimination; (c) promote the mechanisms – for example, the filing of individual complaints of violations – that the inter-American human rights system emphasizes to protect the rights of women; (d) conduct specialized studies and prepare reports in this area; and, importantly (e) assist the Commission in responding to petitions and other reports of violations of these rights in the region. The priority given by the Commission and its Rapporteurship to the protection of the rights of women reflects the importance given to this area by the Member States themselves.

In particular, the Plan of Action adopted by the Heads of State and Government during the Third Summit of the Americas recognizes the importance of women's empowerment, and their full and equal participation in development, in the political life of their countries, and in decision-making at all levels. To this end, the Plan of Action endorses the Inter-American Program on the Promotion of Women's Human Rights and Gender Equality and other regional initiatives aimed at implementing the commitments set forth in the Beijing Declaration and its Platform for Action. The Rapporteurship work under the direction of a member named by the plenary of the Commission.

3.4.2. *Inter American Court on Human Rights*

3.4.2.1. Composition and Election

According to the American Convention on Human Rights, the Court shall be composed of seven members, who shall be persons of high moral character and recognized competence in the field of human rights, elected in a personal capacity by the General Assembly of the Organization from a list of candidates proposed by the governments of the Member States. Each of those governments may propose up to three candidates, who may be nationals of the States proposing them or of any other Member State of the Organization of American States. When a slate of three is proposed, at least one of the candidates shall be a national of a State other than the one proposing the candidate. The members of the Court are elected for a term of four years and may be re-elected only once. The Court consists of seven judges elected in their individual capacity (Art. 52). The Secretariat is in San José, Costa Rica. Before the Court can hear a case, the procedure before the Commission must be completed.[10] "In cases of extreme gravity and urgency", the Court "shall adopt such provisional measures as it deems pertinent", and, at the request of the Commission, it may in fact also do this with respect to cases not yet submitted to it. (Art. 63(2)). The Court's judgments are final, and the States Parties undertake to comply with the terms thereof "in any case to which they are parties" (Art. 67). The enforcement mechanism under the Additional Protocol in the area of Economic, Social and Cultural Rights differs from the procedures under the Convention in that the States Parties only undertake "to submit periodic reports on the progressive

[10] Therefore, in order for the Court to hear a case, it is necessary that the procedures set forth in Articles 48 to 50 shall have been completed.

measures they have taken to ensure due respect for the rights set forth" therein (Art. 19 (1)). Only with regard to the right to organize and join trade unions and the right to education (Art. 8(a)) the Protocol provides for application of the complaints procedure before the Commission and Court, and then only in cases where the alleged violation is "directly attributable" to a State Party (Art. 19 (6)). Both the Commission and the Court have dealt with a considerable number of cases, which can be found in their respective annual reports. The annual report of the Inter-American Commission on Human Rights also provides important information about the Commission's activities in general, which reaches far beyond the framework of the American Convention on Human Rights.

3.4.2.2. Contribution of the Court

Over a period of time the Inter American Court on Human Rights has elaborated on the protection of the rights and this includes (i) Right to Life, Liberty, Personal Security, to Equality and to a Fair Trial;[11] (ii) Right to Life, Personal Integrity, Circulation, Residence, and to Special Protection of Children in the Family;[12] (ii) Right to life, to a Fair Trial, and to Information about Consular Protection;[13] (iii) Right to a Fair Trial and to Judicial Protection;[14] (iv) Right to a Fair Trial and of Asylum;[15] (v) Right to a Fair Trial and to the Protection

[11] Inter-American Commission on Human Rights, Admissibility Report N° 28/93, Case 10.675, Haitian Boat People (United States of America), 13 October 1993; Inter-American Commission on Human Rights, Merits Report No. 51/96, Case 10.675, Haitian Boat People (United States of America), 13 March 1997.

[12] Inter-American Court of Human Rights, Provisional Measures, Haitians and Haitian Origin Dominicans in the Dominican Republic, Orders of 14 September 2000; 12 November 2000; and 26 May 2001.

[13] Inter-American Commission on Human Rights, Admissibility Report N° 61/03, Petition P4446/02, Roberto Moreno Ramos (United States of America), 10 October 2003; Inter-American Commission on Human Rights, Admissibility Report N° 108/00, Petition 11.753, Ramón Martínez Villareal (United States of America), 4 December 2000; Inter-American Commission on Human Rights, Merits Report N° 52/02, Petition 11.753, Ramón Martínez Villareal (United States of America), 10 October 2002.

[14] Inter-American Commission on Human Rights, Admissibility Report N° 37/01, Case 11.529, José Sánchez Guner Espinales et al. (Costa Rica), 22 February 2001; Inter-American Commission on Human Rights, Admissibility Report N° 89/00, Case 11.495, Juan Ramón Chamorro Quiroz (Costa Rica), 5 October 2000; Inter-American Commission on Human Rights, Report N° 38/99, Víctor Saldaño (Argentina), 11 March 1999.

[15] Inter-American Commission on Human Rights, Admissibility Report N° 6/02, Petition 12.071, 120 Cuban Nationals and 8 Haitian Nationals detained in the Bahamas (Bahamas), 27 February 2002.

of the Family;[16] (vi) Right to Personal Integrity, to a Fair Trial, to Privacy, to Property, to Judicial Protection, Freedom of Conscience and Religion and of Association;[17] (vii) Right to Personal Liberty and to Information on Consular Protection;[18] (viii) Right to Personal Liberty, to a Fair Trial, and to Information on Consular Protection;[19] (ix) Right to Personal Liberty, to a Fair Trial, to Movement and Residence and to Judicial Protection;[20] (x) Right to Liberty and Protection from Arbitrary Arrest;[21] (xi) Right to Equality and to Non-Discrimination;[22] (xi) Right to Residence and Movement;[23] (xii) Right to Residence and Movement and to Due Process of Law;[24] (xiii) Right to a Nationality;[25] (xiv) Right to Nationality and to Education;[26] and, (xv) Right to

[16] Inter-American Commission on Human Rights, Report 27/93, Petition 11.092 Cheryl Monica Joseph (Canada), 6 October 1993; Inter-American Commission on Human Rights, Report N° 19/02, Petition 12.379 Mario Alfredo Lares-Reyes, Vera Allen Frost and Samuel Segura (United States of America), 27 February 2002.

[17] Inter-American Commission on Human Rights, Admissibility Report N° 34/98, Case 11.610, Loren Laroye Riebe Star, Jorge Barón Guttlein and Rodolfo Izal Elorz (Mexico), 5 May 1998; Inter-American Commission on Human Rights, Merits Report N° 49/99, Case 11.610, Loren Laroye Riebe Star, Jorge Barón Guttlein and Rodolfo Izal Elorz (Mexico), 13 April 1999.

[18] Inter-American Commission on Human Rights, Admissibility Report N° 12/02, Petition 12.090, Jesús Enrique Valderrama Perea (Ecuador), 27 February 2002.

[19] Inter-American Commission on Human Rights, Admissibility Report N° 77/03, Petitions 12.091 and 172/99, Juan Carlos Chaparro Álvarez (Ecuador); Inter-American Court of Human Rights, Advisory Opinion OC-16/99, the Right to Information on Consular Assistance in the Framework of Due Process Guarantees, 1 October 1999.

[20] Inter-American Commission on Human Rights, Merits Report, Resolution No. 30/81, Case 7378, Carlos Stetter (Guatemala), 25 June 1981.

[21] Inter-American Commission on Human Rights, Admissibility and Merits Report N°51/01, Case 9903, Rafael Ferrer-Mazorra et al. (United States of America), 14 April 2001; Inter-American Commission on Human Rights, Admissibility Report N°7/02, Petition 11.661, Manickavasagam Suresh (Canada), 27 February 2002; Inter-American Commission on Human Rights, Report to Close Case, Case 1170, Héctor Pérez Gómez (Mexico), 17 December 1974.

[22] Inter-American Commission on Human Rights, Admissibility Report N° 59/04, Petition 292/03 Margarita Cecilia Barbería Miranda (Chile), 13 October, 2004; Inter-American Court of Human Rights, Advisory Opinion OC-18), Legal Status and Rights of Undocumented Workers, 17 September 2003.

[23] Inter-American Commission on Human Rights, Merits Report, Resolution N° 56/81, Case 5713, Alberto Texier (Chile), 16 October 1981.

[24] Inter-American Commission on Human Rights, Merits Report, Resolution N° 40/79, Case 2777, Thelma King et al. (Panama), 7 March 1979.

[25] Inter-American Commission on Human Rights, Admissibility Report No. 20/98, Case 11.762, Baruch Ivcher Bronstein (Peru), 3 March 1998. Inter-American Court of Human Rights, Case Baruch Ivcher Bronstein (Peru), Judgment, 6 February 2001.

[26] Inter-American Commission on Human Rights, Admissibility Report No. 28/01, Case 12.819, Dilcia Yean and Violeta Bosica (Dominican Republic), 22 February 2001.

Equality and to Non-Discrimination.[27] In 1988, the General Assembly of the OAS adopted the Additional Protocol to the American Convention on Human Rights in relation to Economic, Social and Cultural Rights, also known as the Protocol of San Salvador. Under the terms of this Protocol, States Parties agree to adopt measures, both internally and through international co-operation, with a view to achieving progressively, by legislation or other appropriate means, the full realization of the rights implicit in the economic, social, educational, scientific and cultural standards set forth in the Charter of the OAS as amended by the Protocol of Buenos Aires. This Protocol entered into force on 16 November 1999.

4. *The African Charter on Human and Peoples' Rights, 1981*[28]

4.1. *Introduction*

The adoption of the African Charter on Human and Peoples' Rights ('African Charter') in 1981, which entered into force on 21st October 1986, is the beginning of a new era in the field of human rights in Africa. Despite the influence of the Universal Declaration of Human Rights, 1948 and the two International Covenants on human rights namely on Civil and Political Rights, 1966 and Social, Economic and Cultural Rights, 1966 and the then existing regional human rights conventions, i.e. European Convention on Human Rights and Fundamental Freedoms, 1950 and the Inter American Convention on Human Rights 1969, the 'African Charter' reflects a high degree of specificity due in particular to the African conception of the term "right" and the place it accords to the responsibilities of human beings. The 'African Charter' contains a long list of rights, covering a wide spectrum not only of civil and political rights, but also of economic, social and cultural rights. The 'African Charter', as a matter of monitoring mechanism contemplated the establishment of the African Commission on Human and Peoples' Rights, so as "to promote human and peoples' rights and ensure their protection in Africa" (Art. 30). 57 years after the adoption of the Universal Declaration on Human Rights, 1948 and 24 years after the adoption of the Charter of the Organization of African Unity (OAU) the African Union adopted its own African Charter on Human and Peoples'

[27] Inter-American Court of Human Rights, Case of Daniel Tibi (Ecuador), Setence of 7 September 2004.

[28] See African Charter at http://www.achpr.org/english/_info/charter_en.html. Also being referred to as the "Banjul Charter, this agreement was adopted in 1981, but did not enter into force until 21 October 1986.

Rights, 1989.[29] In the second half of the 1990s, advancements of democracy in several African states (e.g. Namibia, Malawi, Benin, South Africa, Tanzania, Mali, and Nigeria) and the weak record of the African Commission heightened the need for stronger domestic and regional guarantees for the protection of human rights, making the establishment of the ACHPR possible. While in 1998, the Protocol to the 'African Charter' on the establishment of an African Court of Human Rights was adopted, work on an additional protocol concerning the rights of women in Africa is still in progress. This work is being undertaken by African Commission on Human and Peoples' Rights, ('African Commission') with assistance from the Office of the United Nations High Commissioner for Human Rights (UNHCHR).

4.1.1. *The undertakings of the States Parties*

The States Parties to the 'African Charter' "shall recognize the rights, duties and freedoms enshrined therein and shall undertake to adopt legislative or other measures to give effect to them". In addition, the African Charter also contemplates on the part of the States Parties that they owe the duty to promote and ensure through teaching, education and publication, the respect of the rights and freedoms contained in the present African Charter, and to see to it that these freedoms and rights as well as corresponding obligations and duties are understood (Art. 25) and the States Parties shall have the duty to guarantee the independence of the Courts and shall allow the establishment and improvement of appropriate national institutions entrusted with the promotion and protection of the rights and freedoms guaranteed by the Charter. (Art. 26). Thus, these two obligations collectively emphasize the extent of responsibility on the States Parties as well as the felt need for education, information and an independent administration of justice in order to ensure the effective protection of human rights. Lastly, several provisions of the African Charter are couched in the form of duties of the States Parties to ensure certain rights.[30]

4.1.2. *Recognition of individual and collective rights and duties*

Unlike the other regional human rights conventions considered above, the African Charter recognizes both civil and political rights and economic, social and

---

[29] To understand the criticisms leveled against the African human rights system for its failure to establish a court that would safeguard and enforce the rights guaranteed in the Charter, See Mirna E. Adjami "African Courts and Human Rights," abstracted from: Mirna E. Adjami, "African Courts, International Law, and Comparative Case Law: Chimera or Emerging Human Rights Jurisprudence?" *Michigan Journal of International Law* 24 (2002): 103–08.

[30] Examples in this regard are the "promotion and protection of morals and traditional values recognized by the community" (Art. 17(3)) and the right to development (Art. 22(2)).

cultural rights in the one instrument.[31] Furthermore, it also recognizes the collective or community rights of all peoples.[32]

4.1.3. *The individual duties*

In the context of individual duties, it is significant to note that the African Charter demonstrates a great degree of advance under Articles 27, 28 and 29 collectively.[33]

---

[31] For example, (i) Right to freedom from discrimination on any grounds in the enjoyment of the rights and freedoms guaranteed in the Charter – Art. 2; (ii) Right to equality before the law and to equal protection of the law – Art. 3; (iii) Right to respect for one's life and personal integrity – Art. 4; (iv) Right to respect for one's inherent dignity as a human being, including freedom from slavery, the slave trade, torture, cruel, inhuman or degrading punishment and treatment – Art. 5; (v) Right to liberty and to the security of one's person; freedom from arbitrary arrest or detention – Art. 6; (vi) Right to have one's cause heard, and "the right to an appeal to competent national organs against acts of violating" one's human rights; the right to be presumed innocent until proven guilty by a competent court or tribunal; the right to defence; and the right to be tried within a reasonable time by an impartial tribunal; freedom from *ex post facto* laws – Art. 7; (vii) Freedom of conscience, the profession and free practice of religion – Art. 8; (viii) Right to receive information and the right to express and disseminate one's opinions "within the law" – Art. 9; (ix) Right to freedom of association (Art. 10) and the right to assemble freely with others – Art. 11; (x) Right to freedom of movement and residence within the borders of a State; the right to leave any country including one's own and to return to one's country; the right to asylum in case of persecution; prohibition of mass expulsions – Art. 12; (xi) Right to participate freely in the government of one's country, either directly or through freely chosen representatives; the right to equal access to the public service of one's country and to access to public property and services – Art. 13; (xii) Right to property – Art. 14; (xiii) Right to work and the right to equal pay for equal work – Art. 15; (xiv) Right to enjoy the best attainable state of physical and mental health – Art. 16; (xv) Right to education, and freely to take part in the cultural life of one's country – Art. 17; (xvi) Right of the family, the aged and the disabled to special measures of protection – Art. 18 etc.

[32] These rights include for example, (i) Right of peoples to equality – Art. 19; (ii) Right to existence of all peoples, including the right to self-determination; (iii) Right of all peoples to assistance in their liberation struggle against foreign domination, "be it political, economic or cultural" – Art. 20; (iv) Right of all peoples freely to dispose of their wealth and natural resources – Art. 21; (v) Right of all peoples to their economic, social and cultural development – Art. 22; (vi) Right of all peoples to national and international peace and security – Art. 23; (vii) Right of all peoples "to a general satisfactory environment favourable to their development" – Art. 24.

[33] Article 27 (1) which deals with individual duties recognizes the scope of the same towards certain specifically enumerated *groups namely family, society, State and other legally recognized communities and international community.* Article 28 speaks of the individual's duties towards *other individuals*, providing that "every individual shall have the duty to respect and consider his fellow beings without discrimination, and to maintain relations aimed at promoting, safeguarding and reinforcing mutual respect and tolerance". Article 29 enumerates several other specific individual duties, such as the duties (a) to preserve the harmonious development of the family – Art. 29(1); (b) to serve one's national community – Art. 29(2); (c) not to compromise

4.1.4. *Permissible limitations on the exercise of rights*

The exercise of a substantial number of these rights and freedoms is conditioned by limitation provisions, either in the form of specific aims for which limitations might be imposed, or by referring to the conditions laid down in national law.[34]

4.1.5. *Derogations from legal obligations*

The 'African Charter' does not provide for any right of derogation for the States Parties in public emergencies. This absence has been interpreted by the 'African Commission' to mean that derogations are not permissible under the African Charter.[35] The 'African Charter' is further specific in that it protects not only rights of individual human beings but also rights of peoples. The 'African Charter' also emphasizes the individual's duties towards certain groups and other individuals. While some provisions of the 'African Charter' allow for limitations to be imposed on the exercise of the rights guaranteed, no derogations are ever allowed from the obligations incurred under this treaty.

4.1.6. *The implementation mechanisms*

The African Charter has its own thoughts to reach the goal. To do that the Charter devotes to mechanisms destined for implementation.

4.1.6.1. The African Commission

4.1.6.1.i. Introduction

The 'African Commission' consists of eleven members serving in their individual capacity (Art. 31). It has twofold functions namely (i) promoting human and peoples' rights; and, (ii) protecting these rights (Art. 30), including the right to receive communications both from States and from other sources. As

---

the security of the State – Art. 29(3); (d) to preserve and strengthen the social and national solidarity – Art. 29(4); (e) to preserve and strengthen the national independence and territorial integrity of one's country – Art. 29(5); (f) to work to the best of one's abilities and competence, and to pay taxes – Art. 29(6); (g) to preserve and strengthen positive African cultural values – Art. 29(7); and, finally, (h) the duty to contribute to the best of one's abilities to the promotion and achievement of African unity – Art. 29(8).

[34] For example, Article 12(2) of the Charter provides that the right to leave any country including one's own, and to return to one's own country, "may only be subject to restrictions provided for by law for the protection of national security, law and order, public health or morality". However, everyone has the right to free association "provided that he abides by the law" (Art. 10), without there being any indication as to the grounds the national law can legitimately invoke to limit that freedom of association.

[35] *ACHPR, Commission Nationale des Droits de l'Homme et des Libertés* v. *Chad, No, 74/92, decision taken at the 18th ordinary session, October,1995*, para. 21; for the text see the following web site: http://www1.umn.edu/humanrts/africa/comcases/74–92.html.

to the function of promoting human and peoples' rights, it is incumbent on the part of the 'African Commission', in the first place, in particular to (a) collect documents; (b) undertake studies and researches on issues and problems specifically relating to the African continent; (c) organize conferences; (d) encourage domestic human rights institutions; and importantly (e) "should the case arise, give its views or make recommendations to Governments". On the other hand, it shall also involve and demonstrate its contribution to the "formulation and laying down of principles and rules that are aimed at solving legal problems relating to human and peoples' rights". The last, and the most important, function of the 'African Commission' is to cooperate with other African and international institutions concerned with the promotion and protection of these rights. Interestingly, in relation to the function of ensuring "the protection of human and peoples' rights under conditions laid down by the Charter", the Commission is not only competent to receive communications from States and other sources, but is also expressly authorized to "interpret all the provisions of the Charter at the request of a State Party, an institution of the OAU or an African Organization recognized by the OAU." (Art. 45).

4.1.6.1.ii. Inter-State communications

On the ground that a State Party has good reasons to believe that a State Party to the African Charter has violated the provisions thereof, it may draw, by written communication, the attention of that State to the matter (Art.47). The State to which the communication is addressed, within three months from the receipt of the communication, must submit a written explanation. If the matter has not been settled, to the satisfaction of the two State Parties involved, through bilateral negotiation or by any other peaceful procedure, either State may bring the same to the attention of the 'African Commission' (Art. 48). Notwithstanding these provisions, a State Party can refer the matter directly to the 'African Commission' (Art. 49). However, the 'African Commission' may deals with the matters after all domestic remedies are exhausted in the given case, "unless the procedure of achieving these remedies would be unduly prolonged" (Art. 50). The States concerned may be represented before the 'African Commission' and submit written and oral statements. When in possession of all necessary information and "after having tried all appropriate means to reach an amicable solution based on the respect of Human and Peoples' Rights", the 'African Commission' shall prepare a report "stating the facts and its findings", which shall be sent to the States concerned and to the Assembly of Heads of State and Government ('Assembly') (Art. 52). In transmitting its report, the 'African Commission' may make to the aforesaid 'Assembly' "such recommendations as it deems useful" (Art. 53).

4.1.6.1.iii. Communications from sources other than those of States Parties

While the 'African Charter' does not specify whether the 'African Commission' is competent to deal with *individual* complaints, as such, but merely provides that, before each session of the 'African Commission', it is obligatory for its Secretary to make a list of the communications other than those of States Parties and transmit them to the members of the Commission, who shall indicate which communication should be considered by the Commission. (Art. 55 (1)).

As Art. 56 envisaged, following criteria shall be fulfilled before the Commission can consider the case namely (1) the communication must indicate the author; (2) it must be compatible both with the Charter of the OAU and with the African Charter on Human and Peoples' Rights; (3) it must not be written "in disparaging or insulting language"; (4) it must not be "based exclusively on news disseminated through the mass media"; (5) it must be submitted only after all domestic remedies have been exhausted, "unless it is obvious that this procedure is unduly prolonged"; (6) it must be submitted "within a reasonable period from the time local remedies are exhausted"; and, finally (7) the communications must not "deal with cases which have been settled by these States involved in accordance with the principles of the Charter of the United Nations", the Charter of the OAU or the African Charter on Human and Peoples' Rights. The Charter does not allow individuals or groups of individuals to appear in person before the Commission. Before a substantive consideration is made of a communication, it must be brought to the attention of the State concerned. (Art. 57). Subsequently, "when it appears after deliberations of the Commission that one or more communications apparently relate to special cases which reveal the existence of a series of serious or massive violations of human and peoples' rights, the Commission shall draw the attention of the Assembly of Heads of State and Government to these special cases"; the latter may then request the Commission "to undertake an in-depth study of these cases and make a factual report, accompanied by its findings and recommendations." (Art. 58). Lastly, the Charter provides a procedure for emergency cases which shall be submitted by the Commission to the Chairman of the Assembly, "who may request an in-depth study."

4.1.6.1.iv. Periodic reports

State Parties to the Charter also undertake to submit, every two years, "a report on the legislative or other measures taken with a view to giving effect to" the terms of the Charter (Art. 62). Although the Charter provides no explicit procedure for the examination of these periodic reports, the African Commission on Human and Peoples' Rights has proceeded to examine these reports in public sessions.[36] Thus, the African Commission on Human and Peoples' Rights is, in particular,

[36] See report of Ghana, *The African Commission on Human and Peoples' Rights Examination of State Reports, 14th Session, December 1993: Ghana,* http://www1.umn.edu/humanrts/achpr/sess14–complete.htm.6OAU doc. CAB/LEG/24.9/49 (1990).

competent to: (i) promote human rights by collecting documents, undertaking studies, disseminating information, making recommendations, formulating rules and principles and cooperating with other institutions; (ii) ensure the protection of human and peoples' rights by receiving (a) inter-State communications; (b) communications other than those of the States Parties; and (c) periodic reports from the States Parties.

The African Charter created the African Commission as the only mechanism for supervising State Parties' compliance with obligations arising under it. The Commission had four areas of mandate, namely promotional activities; protective activities, including complaints; the examination of State Party reports; and the interpretation of the Charter. While the Commission has an elaborate promotional mandate under the Charter, it does not possess sufficient protective powers. In reality, neither the Charter nor the Commission provides for enforceable remedies. This is hardly surprising because virtually no African State, with the exceptions of the Gambia, Senegal, and Botswana could even boast of a nominal democracy in 1981, the year that the OAU adopted the African Charter, or a mechanism for encouraging and tracking state compliance with the decisions of the Commission. Despite some positive developments in the Commission's individual compliant mechanism, its decisions are non-binding, and attract little, if any, attention from governments of Member States.

4.1.6.2. African Court of Human and People's Rights

4.1.6.2.i. Introduction

The idea of an African Court on Human and People's Rights was mooted in 1961 at the meeting of African jurists in Lagos, Nigeria, which agreed that a human rights charter with a court was necessary. It was at this meeting that the proposal for continental human rights institutions was first set forth.[37] However, when the Assembly of Heads of States adopted the African Charter on Human and people's Rights in 1981, the issue of a court was replaced with a Commission whose responsibility it was to promote and ensure protection of human rights. During its functional process, the Commission is however constrained by the mere advisory powers under the charter and therefore, the

[37] See the preamble, the Law of Lagos: "In order to give full effect to the Universal Declaration of Human Rights of 1948, this conference invites the African Governments to study the possibility of adopting an African Convention of Human Rights in such manner that the conclusions of this conference will be safeguarded by the creation of a court of appropriate jurisdiction and that recourse thereto be made available for all persons under the jurisdiction of the signatory states." International Commission of Jurists, African Conference on the Rule of Law: A Report on the Proceedings of the Convention 11 (1961).

African Court on Human and Peoples' Rights was contemplated to overcome the limitations of the Commission as an advisory body.

Against this background, human rights NGOs and academics spearheaded aggressive campaigns for an African Court on Human and Peoples' Rights. In 1994, the OAU Assembly of Heads of State and Governments asked its Secretary General to call a meeting of government experts to "ponder in conjunction with the African Commission on Human and Peoples' Rights over the means to enhance the efficiency of the Commission in considering particularly the establishment of an African Court on Human and Peoples' Rights."[38] In September 1995, OAU Secretariat's meeting of experts organized in Cape Town, South Africa in collaboration with the African Commission and the International Commission of Jurists, produced a document regarding the establishment of an African Human Rights Court. In December 1997, after a series of meetings, the conference of OAU Ministers of Justice/Attorneys General, adopted a draft protocol. On 10 June 1998, this was adopted by the Assembly of Heads of State and Governments of the Organization of African Unity establishing the African Court in Ouagadougou, Burkina Faso. The key purpose for the establishment of an African Human Rights Court was to compliment and strengthen the protective mandate of the African Commission on Human and Peoples' Rights. The protocol establishing the African Court came into force on 25 January 2005 after receipt of the 15th instrument of ratification of the Comoros on 25 December 2004.

The African Court on Human and Peoples' Rights (to be referred to as 'African Court') is the most recent of the three regional human rights judicial bodies. Envisioned by the African Charter on Human and Peoples' Rights concluded, in 1981, its structure was not planned until the Organization of African Unity (OAU) promulgated a protocol for its creation in 1998. Unlike the European and Inter-American systems for the protection of human rights, where the ECHR and the IACHPR are integral parts of the cardinal instrument of the system *ab initio*, in the case of Africa, the establishment of a regional judicial body to ensure the implementation of the fundamental agreement is rather an afterthought. The reason for the ability to reach agreement was stated in the preamble of the Protocol for establishment of an African Court, which stated that the Member States were firmly convinced that the attainment of the objectives of the African Charter on Human and People's Rights requires the

[38] See Report of Government Experts Meeting, AHG/Res 230 (xxx), 30th Ordinary Session of the Assembly of Heads of State and Government, Tunis, Tunisia, June 1994, cited in Ibrahim Ali Badawi El-Sheikh, "Draft Protocol of the African Charter on Human and Peoples' Rights: Introductory Note," *African Journal of International and Comparative Law* 9 (1997), 943, 944.

establishment of an African Court on Human and People's Rights to complement and reinforce the functions of the African Commission on Human and People's Rights.

Such a renewed impetus towards more effective protection of human rights accounts also for certain features of the African Court which set it apart, not only from its American and European congeners, but from all other judicial bodies.[39] In particular, the Protocol provides that actions may be brought before the Court on the basis of any instrument, including international human rights treaties, which have been ratified by the State Party in question. (Art. 3). The Protocol provides for an optional jurisdiction for cases submitted by individuals or non-governmental organizations with observer status. For the African Court to be able to hear cases from these individual entities, the State that is the subject of the complaint must have first recognized such competence at the time of ratification or any time thereafter. The African Court cannot hear petitions against States that have not opted to allow that type of competence by the Court.

However, the Court can apply, as sources of law, any relevant human rights instrument ratified by the State in question, in addition to the African Charter (Art. 7). In other words, the African Court could become the judicial arm of a panoply of human rights agreements concluded under the aegis of the United Nations (e.g. the International Covenant on Civil and Political Rights, the Convention on the Elimination of all Forms of Discrimination against Women, and the Convention on the Rights of the Child) or of any other relevant legal instrument codifying human rights (e.g. the various conventions of humanitarian law, those adopted by the International Labor Organization, and even environmental treaties). Very few of those agreements contain judicial mechanisms of ensuring their implementation, and therefore, at least potentially, several African States could end up with a dispute settlement and implementation control system stronger and with more bite than the one ordinarily provided for by those treaties for the rest of the world.

The African Court demonstrates a clear and positive concern towards the standing of individuals and NGOs. Advisory opinions can be asked for, by not only Member States and OAU organs, but by any African NGO that has been recognized by the OAU, provided that at the time of ratifying of the Protocol or thereafter, the State at issue has made a declaration accepting the jurisdiction of the Court to hear such cases. Again, this is another provision

---

[39] Protocol to the African Charter on Human and Peoples' Rights on the Establishment of an African Court on Human and Peoples' Rights, CAB/LEG/665, Adopted 9 June 1998 and entered into force 1 January 2004, at http://www.achpr.org/english/_info/court_en.html. (accessed 13 December 2008).

that might eventually strengthen the African Court's promotional function. In the area of contentious jurisdiction, individuals also can bring cases if the above declaration has been made by the State at issue. This is a step forward from the Inter-American Court, where individuals have no standing at all, but it is still far from the progressive attitude of the European Court of Human Rights.[40]

Thus, the formation of the African Court on Human and People's Rights is possibly a watershed moment in human rights enforcement in Africa. In reality the last several decades to the occurrences of large scale instances of mass atrocities like genocide give rise to establishment of an International Criminal Tribunal to address the most brutal non-international armed conflict. But between two traditional groups of Africa the matter took decades to create the African Court, although human rights advocates in Africa look at it as the beginning of true human rights enforcement in Africa.

5. *Concluding Remarks*

The role of regional international human rights instruments in the protection and promotion of human rights is remarkable in the sense that the treaties have significantly and immensely contributed to important changes in the laws of many countries. In view of the large number of States that have ratified, acceded or adhered to them, they are also becoming particularly important for the work of judges, prosecutors and lawyers, who may have to apply them in the exercise of their professional duties. Many of the provisions of the regional treaties (including the protocols) have been extensively interpreted, *inter alia* with regard to the administration of justice and treatment of persons deprived of their liberty; and this case-law constitutes an important source of information and guidance for judges and lawyers.

Bibliography

Books and Articles

Adjami, Mirna E. "African Courts, International Law, and Comparative Case Law: Chimera or Emerging Human Rights Jurisprudence?" *Michigan Journal of International Law* 24 (2002): 103–167, 103–108.

Ahmed, Tawhida, and Israel de Jesús Butler. "The European Union and Human Rights: An International Law Perspective," *European Journal of International Law* 17, no.4 (2006): 771–801.

[40] Examples are: Algeria, Burkina Faso, Burundi, Côte D'Ivoire, Comoros, Gabon, Gambia, Ghana, Kenya, Libya, Lesotho, Mali, Mozambique, Mauritania, Mauritius, Nigeria, Niger, Rwanda, South Africa, Senegal, Tanzania, Togo, Uganda.

Boyle, Elizabeth Heger, and Melissa Thompson. "National Politics and Resort to the European Commission on Human Rights." *Law & Society Review* 35, no. 2 (2001): 321–44.
Bowett, D. W. Reviewed work(s): *Yearbook of the European Convention on Human Rights 1958–1959* by *Directorate of Human Rights of the Council of Europe, The International and Comparative Law Quarterly*, 10, no. 3 (1961): 651.
Grob, Gerald N. "Public Policy and Mental Illnesses: Jimmy Carter's Presidential Commission on Mental Health." *The Milbank Quarterly* 83, no. 3 (2005): 425–56.
MacCormick, Neil. "Democracy, Subsidiarity, and Citizenship in the 'European Commonwealth'." *Law and Philosophy* 16, no. 4 (1997), Constructing Legal Systems: "European Union" in Legal Theory: 331–56.
Odinkalu, Chidi Anselm. "Back to the Future: The Imperative of Prioritizing for the Protection of Human Rights in Africa." *Journal of African Law* 47, no. 1 (2003): 1–37.
Roermund, Bert Van. "Jurisprudential Dilemmas of European Law." *Law and Philosophy* 16, no. 4 (1997), Constructing Legal Systems: "European Union" in Legal Theory: 357–76.
Suárez, David. "Education Professionals and the Construction of Human Rights Education. *Comparative Education Review* 51, no. 1 (2007): 48–70.

Websites

http://www1.umn.edu/humanrts/africa/comcases/74–92.html
http://www.achpr.org/english/_info/charter_en.html
http://www1.umn.edu/humanrts/achpr/sess14–complete.htm.6OAU doc. CAB/LEG/24.9/49 (1990).
http://www.achpr.org/english/_info/court_en.html
http://www.britannica.com/EBchecked/topic/1000427/European-Commission-of-Human-Rights
http://ue.eu.int/uedocs/cmsUpload/GuidelinesDefenders.pdf

Annual Reports

Report of Ghana, *The African Commission on Human and Peoples' Rights Examination of State Reports, 14th Session, December 1993: Ghana,* http://www1.umn.edu/humanrts/achpr/sess14–complete.htm.6OAU doc. CAB/LEG/24.9/49 (1990)
Report of Government Experts Meeting, AHG/Res 230 (xxx), 30th Ordinary Session of the Assembly of Heads of State and Government, Tunis, Tunisia, June 1994
Annual Report of the Inter-American Commission on Human Rights, 1992–1993, p. 5

International Legal Instruments

African Charter on Human and People's Rights, 1981
American Declaration of the Rights and Duties of Man, 1948
Charter of the United Nations, 1945
Convention on the Elimination of all Forms of Discrimination against Women, 1979
Convention on the Rights of the Child, 1989
European Convention on Human Rights and Fundamental Freedoms, 1950
Inter American Convention on Human Rights, 1969
International Covenant on Civil and Political Rights, 1966
International Covenant on Social, Economic and Cultural Rights, 1966
The European Convention on Human Rights and its Protocols 1, 4, 6, 7, 11, 12, 13, 14
Universal Declaration of Human Rights, 1948

Resolution

AG/RES. 1404 XXVI-O/96 and AG/RES 1480 XXVII-O/97
AG/RES. 1928 (XXXIII-O/03)

Commission and Court

ACHPR, Commission Nationale des Droits de l'Homme et des Libertés v. *Chad, No, 74/92, decision taken at the 18th ordinary session, October, 1995*

Inter-American Commission on Human Rights, Report to Close Case, Case 1170, Héctor Pérez Gómez (Mexico), 17 December 1974

Inter-American Commission on Human Rights, Merits Report, Resolution N° 40/79, Case 2777, Thelma King et al. (Panama), 7 March 1979

Inter-American Commission on Human Rights, Merits Report, Resolution No. 30/81, Case 7378, Carlos Stetter (Guatemala), 25 June 1981

Inter-American Commission on Human Rights, Merits Report, Resolution N° 56/81, Case 5713, Alberto Texier (Chile), 16 October 1981

Inter-American Commission on Human Rights, Report 27/93, Petition 11.092 Cheryl Monica Joseph (Canada), 6 October 1993

Inter-American Commission on Human Rights, Admissibility Report N° 28/93, Case 10.675, Haitian Boat People (United States of America), 13 October 1993

Inter-American Commission on Human Rights, Merits Report No. 51/96, Case 10.675, Haitian Boat People (United States of America), 13 March 1997·

Inter-American Commission on Human Rights, Admissibility Report No. 20/98, Case 11.762, Baruch Ivcher Bronstein (Peru), 3 March 1998

Inter-American Commission on Human Rights, Admissibility Report N° 34/98, Case 11.610, Loren Laroye Riebe Star, Jorge Barón Guttlein and Rodolfo Izal Elorz (Mexico), 5 May 1998

Inter-American Commission on Human Rights, Admissibility Report N° 89/00, Case 11.495, Juan Ramón Chamorro Quiroz (Costa Rica), 5 October 2000; Inter-American Commission on Human Rights, Report N° 38/99, Víctor Saldaño (Argentina), 11 March 1999

Inter-American Commission on Human Rights, Merits Report N° 49/99, Case 11.610, Loren Laroye Riebe Star, Jorge Barón Guttlein and Rodolfo Izal Elorz (Mexico), 13 April 1999

Inter-American Court of Human Rights, Advisory Opinion OC-16/99, the Right to Information on Consular Assistance in the Framework of Due Process Guarantees, 1 October 1999

Inter-American Commission on Human Rights, Admissibility Report N° 108/00, Petition 11.753, Ramón Martínez Villareal (United States of America), 4 December 2000

Inter-American Court of Human Rights, Case Baruch Ivcher Bronstein (Peru), Judgment, 6 February 2001

Inter-American Commission on Human Rights, Admissibility Report No. 28/01, Case 12.819, Dilcia Yean and Violeta Bosica (Dominican Republic), 22 February 2001

Inter-American Commission on Human Rights, Admissibility Report N° 37/01, Case 11.529, José Sánchez Guner Espinales et al. (Costa Rica), 22 February 2001

Inter-American Commission on Human Rights, Admissibility and Merits Report N°51/01, Case 9903, Rafael Ferrer-Mazorra et al. (United States of America), 14 April 2001

Inter-American Court of Human Rights, Provisional Measures, Haitians and Haitian Origin Dominicans in the Dominican Republic, Orders of 14 September 2000; 12 November 2000; and 26 May 2001

Inter-American Commission on Human Rights, Admissibility Report N° 6/02, Petition 12.071, 120 Cuban Nationals and 8 Haitian Nationals detained in the Bahamas (Bahamas), 27 February 2002

Inter-American Commission on Human Rights, Report N° 19/02, Petition 12.379 Mario Alfredo Lares-Reyes, Vera Allen Frost and Samuel Segura (United States of America), 27 February 2002

Inter-American Commission on Human Rights, Admissibility Report N° 12/02, Petition 12.090, Jesús Enrique Valderrama Perea (Ecuador), 27 February 2002

Inter-American Commission on Human Rights, Admissibility Report N°7/02, Petition 11.661, Manickavasagam Suresh (Canada), 27 February 2002

Inter-American Commission on Human Rights, Merits Report N° 52/02, Petition 11.753, Ramón Martínez Villareal (United States of America), 10 October 2002

Inter-American Court of Human Rights, Advisory Opinion OC-18), Legal Status and Rights of Undocumented Workers, 17 September 2003

Inter-American Commission on Human Rights, Admissibility Report N° 61/03, Petition P4446/02, Roberto Moreno Ramos (United States of America), 10 October 2003

Inter-American Court of Human Rights, Case of Daniel Tibi (Ecuador), Setence of 7 September 2004

Inter-American Commission on Human Rights, Admissibility Report N° 59/04, Petition 292/03 Margarita Cecilia Barbería Miranda (Chile), 13 October, 2004

Index

www.ingramcontent.com/pod-product-compliance
Lightning Source LLC
LaVergne TN
LVHW080644011026
849160LV00014B/1319